Libraries in the Information Age

LIBRARIES IN THE INFORMATION AGE

An Introduction and Career Exploration

Second Edition

Denise K. Fourie and David R. Dowell

Library and Information Science Text Series

LIBRARIES UNLIMITED
An Imprint of ABC-CLIO, LLC

A B C ⬥ C L I O

Santa Barbara, California • Denver, Colorado • Oxford, England

Library of Congress Cataloging-in-Publication Data

Fourie, Denise K.

   Libraries in the information age : an introduction and career exploration / Denise K. Fourie and David R. Dowell. — 2nd ed.

     p. cm. — (Library and information science text series)

   Includes bibliographical references and index.

   ISBN 978-1-59158-434-6 (acid-free paper)

1. Library science. 2. Library science—Vocational guidance. I. Dowell, David R. II. Title.

  Z665.F74 2009

  020—dc22   2009030329

13 12 11 10 9   1 2 3 4 5

This book is also available on the World Wide Web as an eBook. Visit www.abc-clio.com for details.

ABC-CLIO, LLC
130 Cremona Drive, P.O. Box 1911
Santa Barbara, California 93116–1911

This book is printed on acid-free paper ∞
Manufactured in the United States of America

Copyright Acknowledgments

The authors and publisher gratefully acknowledge permission for use of the following material:

Figure 2.1 reprinted by permission of Dover Pictorial Archives, Mineola, New York. From *Ready-to-Use Old-Fashioned illustrations of Books, Reading & Writing*. Selected by Carol Belanger Grafton. © 1992 Dover Publications.

Figures 2.4, 2.5, 2.6, 2.7 reprinted by permission of Jane Kimball.

Figure 2.8 reprinted by permission of Kennedy Library, Cal Poly State University, San Luis Obispo.

Figure 3.1 reprinted by permission of Paula Zima.

Figure 3.2 reprinted by permission, private collection.

Figure 5.1 reprinted by permission of Pasadena City College Library.

Figure 5.2 reprinted by permission of Kennedy Library, Cal Poly State University, San Luis Obispo.

Figure 6.1 reprinted by permission of 3M Library Systems.

Figure 6.2 reprinted by permission of Cuesta College Library.

Figure 6.3 reprinted with permission of Paul V. Galvin Library, Illinois Institute of Technology.

In memory of Joan Foster (1931–2007), friend, colleague, librarian and an inspiration to all who knew her

Contents

List of Figures

ix

Preface

Ongoing change is the constant for today's library or information center. And for staff at all levels, welcoming and embracing the ongoing excitement and introduction of new services, products, and the ever-expanding boundaries of information access presents both an inspiration and a challenge. The electronic information era has directly impacted libraries, archives, information centers and media centers, making what was once the promise of instant information a frequent reality and has revitalized the library industry in many different ways.

The revised second edition of this textbook is designed for students and others interested in an overview of the world of modern libraries and information centers with major emphasis on the United States. This book is intended to provide an overview of the current working environment in libraries. As such, the first edition was widely adopted as a text in programs for Library Technical Assistants. It was also used to give needed background to graduate library school students who did not have extensive work experience in library settings. Major additions to this edition include discussions of the use of social networking by libraries and an expansion of the discussion of the ethical obligation of library workers to provide users with the information they need to exercise their rights as citizens.

The book is also versatile enough to accompany continuing education courses for staff, or to be used for on-the-job reference. In compiling this new edition, we have used input from students and instructors using the text at both academic levels of coursework, as well as from reviewers and general readers. Each chapter has been updated to reflect new trends, events, products, and services found in the ever-evolving library and information industries. The resource sections at the end of each chapter have also been revised. The authors have woven in more details on library history beyond the West and expanded discussions of current trends as they relate to the industry globally as well as nationally.

Libraries in the Information Age: An Introduction and Career Exploration begins by examining the redefined and revitalized role of libraries in the era of electronic information, then provides historical background on the evolution of libraries. Job opportunities in a variety of library and information center settings are discussed, followed by a detailed look at the typical major library activities of collections, processing, circulation, and reference. The critical role of resource sharing networks is examined, along with the ethical issues surrounding information access, and an overview of basic job-hunting skills. The text concludes with a look at the continuing impact of the Internet on library services.

Overall, the book introduces the novice to trends and issues that affect the current library agency. Hopefully, too, the text can help readers and those attracted to the field to identify key aptitudes and skills needed for success and to alert them to job niches within the industry that may appeal to their individual interests. At the end of each chapter, references to print and electronic resources are provided to further help the reader in learning and information gathering. A good textbook represents the first step in assimilating knowledge about a course of study or, in this case, a potential career path. But going beyond the text is an enriching second step. Especially helpful to students is the opportunity to communicate electronically with practitioners via e-mail, listservs, blogs, social networks, and Web sites.

Acknowledgments

The authors wish to give a special acknowledgment to the late Barbara E. Chernik, whose *Introduction to Library Services* (Libraries Unlimited 1992) was the trailblazer that inspired us to write the original edition of *Libraries in the Information Age.* As Ms. Chernik's book had gone out of print, we wanted to continue on her path with a new textbook. Chernik's work forms the foundation for chapter 3, "Types of Library Job Opportunities."

The authors further wish to acknowledge the following persons and entities for their valuable support toward the publication of this revised edition.

The ALA Reference Desk
Kevin Bontenbal
Johanna Brown
Richard Brumley
Del Chausse
Oscar Chavez
Cuesta College
Jennifer Cooper
Jennifer Correa
Hiram Davis
Kathy DeCou
Denise Dowell
Sue Easun
Sohair F. Wastawy
Martha Greene

Kathy Headtke
Ruth Jordan
Tina Lau
Mary Ann Laun
Nancy Loe
Carina Love
Ron Maas
Nancy Meddings
Leslie Mosson
Dominik Muggli
Mike Multari
Nancy P. O'Neill
Marisa Ramirez
Rebecca True
Beth Wimer

1

Redefining the Role of Libraries

The 1990s ushered in a new era for libraries and information centers because of the incredible growth seen in the electronic dissemination of information. This trend was most clearly seen in the explosion in use of the World Wide Web. Although considered by many to be synonymous with the Internet, the global network of networks, the Web, is the multimedia portion of the Internet that, because of its ease of use and graphics, has made earlier Internet protocols, such as Gopher and Telnet, obsolete.

In addition to the impact of the Internet, the maturity and widespread use of electronic periodical indexes and full-text databases and of automated holdings catalogs have penetrated to the far corners of the globe and greatly impacted library agencies, whether rural or urban, small or large. No longer are libraries defined by the size of their physical collections, but rather by the amount of information to which they can provide access.

Along with this new standard of electronically disseminating and accessing information, libraries of all sizes have found themselves redefining their roles. Will the printed book become obsolete? Will physical library buildings become unneeded? Will salaries rise with the increased need for technological know-how? And, ultimately, what does all of this mean for people employed in the library industry in the 21st century?

Although there is no crystal ball to give us definite answers, we can discern some trends in the library industry. As we continue into the new century, information services personnel have higher profiles and increased status among both the general public and their coworkers because they are often the Internet trainers in school, academic, special, and public library settings. They are expected to be knowledgeable and to help lead their organizations in planning for new technologies. Patrons view both the availability of technology and libraries as vital. In a 2006 survey conducted for the American Library Association, 92 percent of the respondents indicated that they think libraries will still be needed "in the future" despite all of the information available on the Internet.[1] "Two-thirds—or more than 135 million adult Americans—report using their public library in-person last year [2005]."[2]

Whether one is working in an elementary school media center or a university research library, the job environment is faster paced than in the past. Continual retraining is needed as the newest information storage methods and communications media become mainstream. Few libraries or information centers are tied to any single medium of information storage anymore. Rather, multiple formats are in use simultaneously: microforms, paper, optical discs, and digital data. There is a continuous learning curve for staff and, correspondingly, for patrons and researchers. Increasingly, the role of librarians and technicians is that of trainer and navigator—instructing customers on the use of tools and recommending relevant resources among the welter of available information.

LIBRARIES IN THE AGE OF "I"

When the first edition of this text was written, the authors embraced the term "Information Age" to describe the period through which libraries were transitioning. Library school faculties have debated whether they were in "l-schools" (library schools) or "i-schools" (information studies). In some discussions this discourse has used the terms "l-word" or the "i-word"—sometimes as terms of derision. In some ways our profession has been ahead of the popular culture that has come to embrace anything "i-" (e.g., i-tunes, i-pods, i-phones).

Many in the profession find the term "information science" to be a liberating one for understanding the activity that goes on in libraries. This emphasizes that the activities in which we are involved deal with the content of books and other media and not just with the physical objects themselves. One of the authors of this text has had the vanity plate "InfoDoc" for two decades.

Many in the profession still resist this terminology—some because of resistance to change. However, others resist because something seems to be missing in this new paradigm. While the character > data > information > knowledge > wisdom hierarchy model is useful, it is also limiting.

While we need to embrace all aspects of providing information to our communities, it is time to move beyond the somewhat limiting conception of libraries being about a single "i." We need to start recognizing that there are at least two other products provided by libraries: imagination and inspiration. Much of the great literature, art, music, and other products of humane studies now contained in libraries really is not designed to be informational. These things were created to help readers imagine and envision, and perhaps even escape from the world of facts as we currently know them. In addition, some of the items in our collections were designed to inspire readers to action by being motivational instead of strictly informative.

This book is not intended to be theoretical. It is intended to describe libraries as they now exist. In that sense, it is designed primarily to be informational. However, it is hoped that readers will also use their imaginations and be inspired to become the next generation of library workers and thinkers who will be able to move our profession further along its evolutionary path. Libraries can become not just repositories that inform our patrons about the past and the present, but also institutions that can help patrons imagine what can be and inspire them to chart bold courses into the future.

COMPUTER SKILLS ESSENTIAL

For library and information center personnel, the emphasis on computer skills cannot be stressed enough. Although a knowledge of and reverence for books is still valued, these alone are insufficient for entering a field that increasingly depends on digital resources and applications.

This does not mean that hardcore programming skills and in-depth knowledge of mainframe computer operations are necessary. Although some understanding of these subjects is often useful, the emphasis must be on using the computer as a tool to unlock the world of digital resources and to transmit appropriate information to patrons regardless of whether they are physically present in the library. Skillful use of productivity tools (e.g., word processing programs, spreadsheets, databases, e-mail) that enable the internal operations of libraries to function quickly and effectively are also required. Increasingly, some knowledge of Web page design is becoming useful in the toolbox of library workers. In addition to applying these skills behind the scenes, library staff members are being called upon to provide basic computer instruction to library users.

The World Wide Web is but the most recent manifestation of the impact of computers on the working conditions in libraries. For the past four decades, automation of behind-the-scenes processes in libraries has been gaining speed. Repetitive (translate that as "boring") routines have gradually been reduced to a set of programmable instructions that a computer can execute. These tasks include card filing, the physical formatting of catalog cards, generation of overdue notices, and so on. More recently, these advances have allowed library catalogs to be searched from remote locations—either within the same organization or from far greater distances. With each step of this automation process, the tasks of library staff members have become less routine and more reliant on the ability to manipulate computers.

In addition to changing the day-to-day activities of library staff, automation increasingly has added value for library users. For example, after libraries automate both their catalog and circulation records, the two records for an item can be linked together. As a result, library catalog users can determine not only whether the library owned a particular item, but also whether it was checked out. If it was checked out, then they could see when it was due. Other internal library records once reserved for staff, such as on-order files, in-process files, and periodicals check-in files, can also be made available to the public.

Although at each step along the way library staff have feared that automation would reduce jobs, these fears have not been justified. No libraries, to the authors' knowledge, have reduced staff because of increased automation. In a few isolated cases, automation has been used as a justification for staff reductions, but in each of these cases the real motivation was to reduce the budget—automation was just a convenient excuse. In fact, automation often allows staff to process a greater volume of transactions. And the list of benefits to patrons continues to grow. Increasingly, it is the content of whole documents, rather than just brief summaries, that is available. With this shift, the role of library staff in assisting library users is changing with accelerating speed. The increasing pervasiveness of the World Wide Web, begun in the 1990s, has accelerated the trend toward digital resources that gained momentum in libraries throughout the last one-third of the 20th century.

Social networking technology offers a new vehicle for promoting the benefits of and also distributing the services of libraries to a wider range of individuals in the communities we serve. Efforts are currently being made to enact legislation to protect children from misuse of some of this technology, such as *YouTube* and *MySpace* and similar sites that catch the fancy of young people. As with all means of communication, social networking has the power to bring about tremendous good, as well as the potential for abuse. At this writing some innovative police forces and libraries are discovering the possibilities of accomplishing their core missions by using these new social networking venues.

It has been said that the vast majority of librarians are text-based learners, while the vast majority of those we serve have other primary learning styles. If we are going to keep library services relevant to all those who could benefit from them, we must design our offerings with the learning styles of all our potential customers in mind.

New Paradigm for Evaluating Information

The rising challenge is to help library users become skillful in evaluating the usefulness and reliability of the wide array of information that is now available. Until the advent of the World Wide Web, information available through libraries went through two separate refinement processes before reaching readers.

The first process was the publishing process. As uneven as this process was, at the very least it ensured that a second set of eyes, and sometimes multiple sets of eyes, passed over information before it found its way into print. The process of writing and publishing a book often requires two years or more. The author carefully crafts the text so that the editor and the publisher will accept it. The editor often makes suggestions about content and accuracy. The publisher has to be concerned about potential litigation. This process does not ensure the accuracy or the relevance of the information, but it does improve the likelihood of a credible product. In addition, readers had the opportunity to consider the reputation of the publishers who were willing to market the author's product.

The second refinement process was the decision to add a title to a library's collection. This decision was based on selecting resources—from all of the many resources competing for the library's scarce acquisitions dollars—that appeared to best meet the customers' unique information needs for that specific library.

Web-based information is not required to meet such scrutiny. The electronic page shares at least one characteristic with the paper page. A favorite history professor used to remark, "Paper is a very neutral medium. It will record any nonsense any fool writes down." Within the professor's context, today any "fool" can write any nonsense that pops into his or her head and, using the power of computer word processing and automatic Web page creation, publish it on the Internet in a couple of hours without the review of another human.

The same tool that allows brilliant insight to be communicated worldwide at near the speed of light also allows any fool to broadcast lesser thoughts just as efficiently.

The greatest opportunity for information professionals in the 21st century is to take a leadership role in the *evaluation* of online information. Many patrons require assistance and training in how to gain access to electronic data, but this task pales in comparison to the daunting task of training patrons to evaluate the information they find. Critical thinking skills are not easily transmitted. In school and academic libraries, this responsibility is shared with classroom teachers. Staff members in special libraries have a responsibility to sift through and evaluate data for other professional colleagues within their organizations. The role of the public library is less clear and more of a double-edged sword. The general public these libraries serve deserves as much assistance as the patrons of other types of libraries, but balancing access to information with the frequent demand to mediate offensive materials often leaves public library staff walking a tightrope.

CHARACTERISTICS OF LIBRARY PERSONNEL

A wide variety of job knowledge and skills are required for any library to operate smoothly. In a small, one-person location, the solo staff member must possess a wide array of these skills. In a large library, these attributes may be spread among literally hundreds of different individuals.

In one-person libraries, a single staff member must do everything. At certain times, they may perform tasks that would generally be considered professional. At other times, the tasks may often be purely clerical or, in emergency situations, even janitorial. Whatever needs to be done *is* done by that single person. Such staff members must be Jacks (or Jills) of all trades and perhaps masters of none.

Solo Library Worker or Part of a Larger Team

If a person likes a wide variety of very different tasks during the workday, the small library offers such an opportunity. Such a person must be a self-starter who can see what needs to be done, can organize and prioritize the tasks at hand, and can work through them until they are completed. No supervisor is physically close at hand to advise when difficult situations arise. In fact, no colleague is nearby to assist with any technical matter. Flexibility is an important attribute of a solo library worker because the arrival of a single customer can cause the reordering of the work plan. The main priority is helping the customer, whether that customer is a student or teacher using a school library, a professional in a firm using a special library, or a member of the general public using a small public library.

Even if the location is part of a larger library agency, a certain amount of physical processing of materials and of database maintenance is required. Other staff members at that location may provide assistance with peripheral tasks such as janitorial, computer, and bookkeeping support. They may also be available to assist with difficult-to-please patrons and to provide general moral support and camaraderie. However, they cannot be relied upon to assist with library technical matters. If the small library is a branch of a larger system, advice may be readily available by telephone, e-mail, or a visit. If the site is not part of a larger organization, there is danger of a sense of isolation becoming a morale issue. The solo library worker, in this case, must become a skilled advocate and protector of the library turf as well as a highly skilled technician. This kind of assignment makes good use of general skills, but does not allow the luxury of specialization.

A large library, on the other hand, requires a certain amount of specialization. The larger the library, the more compartmentalized each position becomes. In the largest libraries with hundreds of staff members, tasks are carefully defined and everyone is a specialist of sorts. In such libraries, it is often hard to keep track of the big picture of what the entire organization is trying to achieve. Each person is important to achieving the desired outcome, but sometimes that fact is forgotten in the stress of everyday life in the workplace. In such larger libraries, many levels of staff with different sets of specialized knowledge and skills are employed throughout the organization.

Each person in a large library performs a part of the entire process and must depend on other staff members to do their parts of the work. Working as part of a team is critical in providing good service to the customer. One staff member may decide which items to purchase for a subject area of the collection, another may verify the bibliographic information needed to complete the order, another may select the vendor and place the order, another may receive the order, and yet another may pay the invoice. Then the creation of the bibliographic record begins.

In some libraries, the physical description of an item (i.e., descriptive cataloging) may be performed by one person and the subject analysis (i.e., subject cataloging) by another. In very large libraries, the descriptive work may be divided among foreign language specialists, and the subject headings and classification work may be performed by subject specialists. Physical processing, such as bar or RFID coding, "tattle taping," and ownership marking, is likely performed by yet another person. Serials and government documents, manuscripts, and other special collections are likely to have separate but parallel assembly lines in which information necessary to establish and maintain bibliographic control over the item is accumulated. All of these staff members are involved before an item is ready to be offered to the public.

No attempt is made here to list all the possible specialties within libraries. Rather, the point is that the size of the library determines whether staff members are primarily specialists or generalists.

Public Service Versus Behind the Scenes

The tasks described in the previous paragraphs have something in common. They are performed behind the scenes. These tasks require attention to detail, extreme accuracy, and the ability to follow through on long complex procedures, and they are often best performed away from the distracting interruptions of customers arriving and telephones ringing. People who thrive in this environment are similar to those who do well in jobs such as computer programming and accounting or bookkeeping.

Other types of individuals are also needed in libraries. Public service staff members require the same attributes that lead to success in other jobs that either flourish or fail depending on how well the needs of individual customers are satisfied—one customer at a time. Great oral communication skills—especially intuitive listening ability—tops the list of required characteristics. Ability to function without getting frustrated when three customers are competing for attention and two phones are ringing is also important. Juggling multiple priorities, which change from minute to minute, often becomes the order of the day at a busy library public service desk. Variety can be great, but many of the service requests can be repetitive and seemingly mundane. However, all customers believe that their requests are very important, and the customers must be treated with courtesy, speed, and skill. Successful experience as a sales or waitperson may be excellent preparation for this kind of library assignment. No single background, aptitude, or personality is best for all library work. A variety of individual attributes is needed to staff today's libraries.

Staff Categories

To the general public, anyone who sits at a desk in a room where a substantial number of books are shelved is a librarian. Even supposedly sophisticated university faculty have often approached a library administrator with some emotion and stated, "Your librarian told me...!" In reality, the staff member with whom the professor had just had an unfortunate encounter was a new part-time student assistant with less than two weeks of experience. Such a casual use of the term *librarian* is akin to calling anyone who works in a medical clinic a doctor. To more knowledgeable individuals, the term librarian has a much more precise definition.

Within the knowledge and skill sets required for efficient delivery of quality services, there are at least two different career ladders, each with multiple rungs. In the small library discussed previously, as many of these as possible need to be packaged into one person. As the size of the library increases, a narrowing of focus and a corresponding depth of specialization of knowledge and skills becomes increasingly necessary.

LIBRARY AND INFORMATION STUDIES AND HUMAN RESOURCE UTILIZATION STAFFING RECOMMENDATIONS

The following discussion of staff roles in libraries is based on *Library and Information Studies and Human Resource Utilization* (LISHRU), a policy statement of the American Library Association. This statement has survived the test of time and remains an excellent framework for understanding the division of labor in libraries. The full document is included in this book as Appendix A.

A word of caution is in order. Libraries are not compelled to follow ALA policy. Library staff are not certified and regulated to the extent that medical staff are. For example, most states regulate and mandate the exact education and experience required for physicians, physician associates, registered nurses, licensed practical nurses, pharmacists, pharmacist assistants, and so on. Although most states prescribe the minimum requirements for certification as a school librarian, other categories and types of libraries are generally ignored. As a result, each employer generally is free to deviate from the concepts espoused by the national professional association. Therefore, for any concept expressed herein, it will not be difficult to discover libraries that are organized in ways that diverge from this model. This model, however, has shown that it does generally balance the needs of the organization to operate in a cost-effective manner with the needs of employees to be treated realistically and fairly and the interests of the profession to provide good library services to all.

Basic to the understanding of LISHRU is the appreciation of various groups of tasks within libraries. These levels are summarized here into three categories: (1) clerical, (2) paraprofessional, and (3) professional. Another term in common usage is "library support staff." The term *support staff* refers to all non-librarians, whether they are clerical or paraprofessional, full-time or part-time.

Clerical Staff

Libraries are not only places where books are stored and made available, but are also organizations that must maintain themselves in the same manner as do other types of bureaucratic organizations. In this aspect of their activities, libraries have many tasks that are similar to all such organizations. Some of these maintenance tasks are primarily clerical in nature. Clerical tasks are the same as those performed by office workers in most any kind of organization. Keyboarding, filing, greeting customers, and paying bills are a few examples of clerical tasks performed in libraries. In large libraries, some positions will be almost exclusively for such tasks. This does not mean that the positions are all entry level. Within larger libraries, there can be several levels of clerical positions, depending on the responsibility level of the position (e.g., Secretary I, Secretary II, Secretary III, or Account Clerk I, Account Clerk II).

Entry into such positions generally will be through clerical training, clerical experience, or both. Knowledge of basic library terminology and concepts that may be required can be learned on the job. For such positions, it is almost incidental that they are located in a library.

Paraprofessional Staff

Paraprofessional positions in libraries are generally called Library Technical Assistants (LTAs), Library Assistants, or Library Technicians. The LISHRU statement also envisions another category: Library Associates. Only the very largest of libraries would have both categories in use; however, it is not unusual for even medium-sized libraries to have three or four levels of library assistants or library technicians. These positions are differentiated from the clerical positions in that they require library education, training, or experience, or all three, before incumbents can fulfill the requirements of their positions.

In actual practice, the demarcation between all of these titles is blurred. The title Library Associate, as used in LISHRU, describes a position for which a bachelor's degree is required and general education is more important than library knowledge. Sometimes foreign language capability or knowledge of a specific subject discipline may be required. On the other hand, the LTA classifications as used in LISHRU "assume certain kinds of specific 'technical' skills, [but] they are not meant simply to accommodate advanced clerks."[3] Although clerical duties may be required, the emphasis is on special technical skills specifically associated with library work, such as handling multimedia equipment or bibliographic searching. Small to medium libraries tend to combine these categories into one hierarchical series of position classifications (e.g., LTA I, LTA II, LTA III or Library Assistant I, Library Assistant II).

The ideal preparation for an LTA is an associate's degree or a certificate in library technology from a community college program. However, there are currently not enough such programs in the United States to train the number of paraprofessionals needed by libraries. As a result, many libraries are forced to hire candidates with general education and provide them with on-the-job training so they can gain the knowledge and skills needed to perform their duties. At this writing the Allied Professional Association affiliated with ALA and known by the initialism ALA-APA is poised to begin offering the first national voluntary certification program for library support staff in January, 2010.

LISHRU differentiates between the kind of training appropriate for LTAs and that needed for those who want to become professionals in libraries: "Emphasis in the two-year Technical Assistant programs should be more on skills training than on general library concepts and procedures."[4] This is a conceptual starting point.

However, astute students of career development are learning that there is not one correct path of career progression. Now, instead of employers defining how careers should develop, employees increasingly are fitting their careers around other priorities in their lives.[5] Likewise, one cookie cutter approach does not provide the single, correct way to enter a career in librarianship. Library work is a career choice often made by individuals in their late twenties and those in their thirties, forties, and even older. For such persons, it is often an easier transition for them to explore a career by investing in an LTA degree or certificate. The career lattice included in the LISHRU statement in Appendix A illustrates many entry points into library employment and internal career pathways once an individual is employed. This provides options for individuals who already have a college degree and perhaps considerable work experience in another occupation before entering the library field. An LTA program may be attractive to a student who already holds an associate's degree, a bachelor's degree, or even a graduate degree. In this case, the student is seeking a credential just to have vocational credibility. For many such individuals, the paraprofessional level is their desired final goal. For others it is a careful first step that may lead to experience as a paraprofessional and, subsequently, to a Master of Library Science (M.L.S.) and a position as a librarian. Others may decide to go directly to a graduate school to enter the library industry as librarians.

Librarians

Librarians are responsible for looking at the information needs of the primary customers of a particular library. Then they look at the information and library resources that are available to meet those needs. Finally, they plan strategies to make the most relevant information sources available to their primary clientele in ways that will be most useful to those individuals.

> "The title '*librarian*' carries with it the connotation of '*professional*' in the sense that professional tasks are those which require a special background and education on the basis of which library needs are identified, problems are analyzed, goals are set, and original and creative solutions are formulated for them, integrating theory into the practice, and planning, organizing, communicating, and administering successful programs of service to users of the library's materials and services. In defining services to users, the professional person recognizes potential users as well as current ones, and designs services which will reach all who could benefit from them."[6]

Normally, to qualify for the title *librarian*, one must have a master's degree in library and information science. Often this degree must be from a graduate program accredited by the American Library Association. Some states stipulate this requirement for such a designation in school and public libraries. A teaching credential with a specialization in school library and media services may suffice for entry-level school library assignments in other states. However, individuals who want the flexibility to move from one type of library to another as their careers unfold would do well to secure a master's of library science and to attain their degree from an ALA accredited institution.

"Positions which are primarily devoted solely to the routine application of established rules and techniques, however useful and essential to the effective operation of a library's ongoing services, should not carry the word '*Librarian*' in the job title."[7]

Both librarians and LTAs carry out duties that are fairly routine applications of established rules and techniques. The librarian, though, also has a fundamental responsibility to constantly review those established rules and techniques and replace them when they no longer provide the most effective means of delivering services for the unique clientele served by that library. At the Cuesta College Library, a librarian was the project manager responsible for implementing the current automation system. After the system stabilized, day-to-day administration of it was turned over to an LTA. However, the librarian still takes the lead in implementing upgrades and new modules. Expanding on this example, the primary responsibilities of support staff members are to keep library services operating on a day-to-day basis. This frees librarians to devote at least a portion of their time to working with others outside the library to determine what future services will be needed, planning those services, and working to secure external support for implementing them. However, anyone who has observed the operation of libraries knows that distinctions between professional and paraprofessional responsibilities are not always as clear in practice as in theory. The degree alone does not a good librarian make.

Background Research

Nevertheless, research has provided support for the value of the M.L.S. Four little-known dissertations completed in the 1960s relate to this issue. John McCrossan found that M.L.S. holders were likely to perform better in collection development than others.[8] Charles Bunge showed that although the end result might not differ, library school graduates were more efficient in performing reference searches than those with similar library experience.[9] Lucille Wert's study showed that school librarians who held an M.L.S. offered more services and spent less time in housekeeping tasks than did those with similar experience and responsibilities who had an undergraduate minor in library science.[10] In a slightly different exploration, Gordon Baillie found a positive correlation between library school grade point average and successful performance on the job.[11] Since this research, library education has changed, libraries have changed, and the tasks performed by librarians have changed. Similar research needs to be conducted today to see if these results still hold.

Specialists

One other category in LISHRU that deserves brief mention is that of *specialist.* Specialists in LISHRU are a professional parallel to librarians in education and in function. Their education, however, is not librarianship. They work primarily in larger libraries as systems analysts, personnel experts, accountants, or other types of specialists. Such specialists may even hold an M.L.S. degree.

One of the authors had a running discourse of several years with a top administrator of the Library of Congress that went something like the following:

> *Library of Congress administrator* (upon sighting the author at a library conference): I'm surprised to see you. I thought you would be in jail. I saw your name in *American Libraries* in an advertisement requiring an ALA-accredited M.L.S. for a librarian position. You know that we have proved at the Library of Congress that an M.L.S. is not required to be a librarian. Therefore, it is illegal to require an ALA-accredited M.L.S.
>
> *Author:* You don't operate a library. You operate a factory. You don't hire librarians at Library of Congress. You hire specialists—language specialists and content specialists. If any of them tried to act as a librarian in the manner in which I expect librarians to operate, you would fire them or severely discipline them for not following established routines. You don't want them to be looking at ultimate users and making judgments about how best to serve them. You just want them to keep production up.

Specialists meet a valid need, particularly in very large libraries. Some libraries try to find individuals who have both an M.L.S. and a relevant specialty degree. Others just seek the specialty. Whatever other strengths may be brought to an organization by a specialist, the expectations for them should not be the same as those for librarians, unless the person is also educated as a librarian.

Librarians alone have responsibility for moving library services forward. As the LISHRU states:

> The objective of the Masters programs in librarianship should be to prepare librarians capable of anticipating and engineering the change and improvement required to move the profession constantly forward. The curriculum and teaching methods should be designed to serve this kind of education for the future rather than to train for the practice of the present.[12]

There is a myth about a great medical controversy that allegedly took place a couple of centuries ago. The principle under discussion was whether anyone other than a physician should be allowed to touch a patient. The specific question was who should be allowed to empty bedpans. Speculate for a moment what our medical care today would be like if this argument had been resolved in a different way.

Today libraries must resolve many similar issues. For both the profession and library services to move forward, more of today's routine practice needs to be delegated to supporting staff. A couple of decades ago, copy cataloging was an issue.[13] Today, it is original cataloging and reference work. We can only speculate what the bedpan issues of this century will be.

As we move into that great future, librarians will need some of the same characteristics that lead to success in other professions—analytical ability, communication skills, intellectual curiosity, and service orientation. In addition, librarians must be committed to continuous improvement of services to the patrons of their libraries.

Colleague Brian Nielson described it slightly differently:

> I think it would be nice to be able to hire a fresh M.L.S. grad who knew how to build a hypercard stack, or a Gopher server, or a series of scripts to make using an online catalog easier. Better yet, to hire a student who knew how to teach herself how to pick up the next new information tool which will come along next year.

AVAILABLE RESOURCES

The following two online glossaries of library-related terms are recommended to students for immediate use as they read this textbook, and also for later reference as they seek employment or work in the field:

Pepperdine University Libraries maintains "Library Vocabulary: Common Terms Defined," a brief listing of the most common vocabulary terms that library users may encounter. See http://library.pepperdine.edu/services/instruction/terms.html

A more comprehensive and much larger listing (and it may load slowly) was developed by Joan M. Reitz, a librarian at Western Connecticut State University. ODLIS: Online Dictionary of Library and Information Science is a glossary containing words and concepts dealing with instruction, computer usage and programming, library and print history, and more. See: http://lu.com/odlis/

Information on the new national, voluntary certification program for library support staff who work in public and academic libraries by the ALA-APA is available: http://www.ala-apa.org/lsscp/index.html (accessed July 2, 2009)

NOTES

1. American Library Association, "@ your library: Attitudes Toward Public Libraries Survey 2006," http://www.ala.org/ala/ors/reports/2006KRCReport.pdf (accessed August 22, 2007).

2. Ibid.

3. American Library Association, "Library and Information Studies and Human Resource Utilization: A Statement of Policy," paragraph 15, adopted January 23, 2002, http://www.ala.org/ala/hrdr/educprodev/lepu.pdf (accessed January 15, 2007).

4. Ibid., Paragraph 25.

5. Douglas T. Hall and Associates, *The Career is Dead—Long Live the Career: A Relational Approach to Careers,* (San Francisco, CA: Jossey-Bass, 1996).

6. American Library Association, "Library and Information Studies and Human Resource Utilization: A Statement of Policy," paragraph 8.

7. Ibid., Paragraph 9.

8. John Anthony McCrossan, "Library Service Education and Its Relationship to Competence in Adult Book Selection in Public Libraries" (PhD diss., University of Illinois, 1966).

9. Charles Albert Bunge, "Professional Education and Reference Efficiency" (PhD diss., University of Illinois, 1967).

10. Lucille Mathena Wert, "Library Education and High School Library Services" (PhD diss., University of Illinois, 1970).

11. Gordon Stuart Baillie, "An Investigation of Objective Admission Variables As They Relate to Academic and Job Success in One Graduate Library Education Program" (PhD diss., Washington University of Illinois, 1961).

12. American Library Association, "Library and Information Studies and Human Resource Utilization: A Statement of Policy," paragraph 29.

13. David R. Dowell, "From Cataloger to Catalog Librarian," in "Catalogs and Catalogers: Evolution Through Revolution," ed. Tillie Krieger. *Journal of Academic Librarianship,* 2: 173–74 (1976).

Chapter 2

A Brief History of Libraries

The story of libraries begins with the history of the written record. The oral tradition, which relied on the memorization of history, legends, and folklore, was the earliest form of preserving and transmitting data among people. As humans developed methods of recording data on cave walls, stones, tree bark, and in other formats, the era of written communication began. Whether using pictures, symbols, letters, or language to express themselves, humans made the transition from human memory as the predominant storage device to the written record some 5,000 years ago. With the 21st century has come an era in which most data are increasingly recorded in sophisticated electronic formats. In addition to storing data, the computer also gives us amazing means for composing, transmitting, publishing, and manipulating information.

With the accumulation of written records—whether clay tablets, papyrus rolls, parchment leaves, paper, and now digital format—arose the need to store, preserve, and access them.

THE ANCIENT WORLD

By surveying some of the major inventions, institutions, and technologies of ancient civilizations, one can glimpse the issues that surrounded the development of early libraries. In addition, it is insightful to think about certain common information needs that historians have identified that helped drive the collecting of written materials, then and now. These information needs fall into the following broad categories: government records, religious records, business records, and household records. Tax receipts, property ownership, laws of the land, military intelligence and campaigns, and population censuses are typical examples of government data. Sacred laws, songs and rituals, creation stories, and legends of gods and goddesses typify vital religious records. Successful commerce depends on sales records, accounts, inventories of goods, employee records and salaries, trade routes and explorations, inventions, formulas, and trade secrets. Individual families collect and pass on their genealogical and marriage information, land and property records, personal correspondence, culinary information and recipes, family legends, history, and literature.

The Middle East

The oldest form of writing that survives today is known as cuneiform. This significant contribution to civilization was developed in the Middle East by the ancient Sumerians. They occupied an area once called the Fertile Crescent, a valley bounded by the Tigris and Euphrates rivers, now within the present-day country of Iraq. Very little stone or wood was available for building in the arid environment, so the Sumerians fashioned houses and structures out of native clay and sticks. Around 3300 B.C., the Sumerians began using a sharpened reed called a stylus to make wedge-shaped marks in damp clay to keep track of grain supplies and other agricultural products. The clay tablets were then dried and baked, leaving a permanent and durable written record.

Contemporary scientists continue to uncover buried collections of these cuneiform tablets.[1] In 1987, archaeologists unearthed a cache of more than 1,000 clay tablets, dating back to about 1740 B.C., that inventoried the royal wine supply, tracked the deployment of spies in warfare, calculated taxes, and contained correspondence between regional kings.[2] Not surprisingly, all of these topics are still vital to humans today.

Throughout the Middle East, libraries arose by about 2700 B.C. to house the tablets of the Sumerians, as well as those of later civilizations, such as the Babylonians and Assyrians. Historians have evidence of significant official libraries at Telloh (southern Iraq) and Nineveh (northern Iraq), each with thousands of clay tablets.

The Ancient Egyptians

At about the same time the Sumerians and others were creating records on clay tablets, in a different part of the ancient world, the Egyptians were making use of the native papyrus plant to develop their writing medium. Sheets of the beaten and pressed central pith of the plant were joined to make long and fragile scrolls. Although easily damaged by dampness or torn because of its brittleness when dry, papyrus paper was economical to produce and easily transported. With a brush-like reed pen, Egyptians recorded information in a hieroglyphic-style of writing. For more than 4,000 years, papyrus remained the standard writing medium in Egypt and along the Mediterranean shore. Use of papyrus continued until about 300 A.D. in parts of Europe and as late as 1022 A.D. in Egypt.[3]

A few papyrus scroll fragments are held at La Bibliothèque Nationale de France in Paris, the Beinecke Rare Book and Manuscript Library at Yale University, and other major museums. Unlike collections of clay tablets, libraries of papyrus scrolls have long disappeared, and the descriptions of their existence are based on second-hand accounts.

Thus, historians know that by about 2500 B.C., large governmental libraries of papyrus scrolls existed, including one at Gizeh near the great pyramids.

By 1250 B.C., ruler Ramses II had developed an extensive library at Thebes, an ancient Egyptian capital, that stored rolls of papyrus in clay jars with keywords visible on the end of each scroll to denote the content.

The Greeks

As with many aspects of European civilization, libraries and knowledge reached a pinnacle during the time of the ancient Greeks. Socrates, Sophocles, and Herodotus, great writers and thinkers, were just a few of the scholars active during the period known as the Golden Age (fifth century B.C.).

The noted playwright and scholar Aristotle had one of the great private libraries of the ancient world housed at his school, The Lyceum. His collection was coveted and changed hands many times after his death. Governmental and royal libraries were commonplace throughout the Greek world.

Among the great cultural accomplishments of the Greeks was the founding of the ancient library in Alexandria, Egypt, by Ptolemy I, circa 300 B.C. Part of a large scholarly facility, the library's purpose was to collect every book in the world and translate them into Greek to help the expanding empire better understand the cultures they ruled. The Alexandrian library flourished for approximately 600 years, and was by all accounts the greatest, richest library of the ancient world, with an estimated 700,000 papyrus scrolls.

This academic community functioned like a university, with noted scholars, librarians, and historians being responsible for inventions such as the first encyclopedia and dictionary and the use of alphabetization as an ordering system.[4]

Scribes went to great lengths to copy everything in order to enlarge the Greeks' knowledge and power base. No trace of the fabled library remains today. There are differing opinions among historians as to the degree of destruction sustained by the facility at the time of the Roman conquest in the fourth century A.D.

Today, Egyptian officials and the United Nations Educational, Scientific, and Cultural Organization (UNESCO) have partnered in an ambitious new learning center at the old library site. The new Library of Alexandria emulates its famous ancient namesake by embodying its core concepts and by "reinventing the library and restoring its role as an institute of learning, culture and intellectual interaction," according to Dr. Sohair F. Wastawy, the Chief Librarian. The new Alexandrian library facility will include multiple specialized libraries, three museums, a planetarium, a children's exploratorium, art galleries, a conference center, and eight research institutes—in addition to being a book repository of over a million volumes.

The Bibliotheca Alexandrina also strives to be a place of dialogue, learning, and understanding between cultures and peoples, thus recapturing the spirit of the ancient library.[5]

In use by both the Greeks and the Romans by the second century A.D was the codex, a forerunner of the book as we know it today. This storage format used parchment (i.e., sheep's skin) or vellum (i.e., calf's skin) rather than papyrus. Both sides of the parchment could be written upon, and the individual parchment leaves bound or fastened together, forming pages that could be opened flat and read in sequence. The codex represented a more convenient format for both writing and reading.

Although both papyrus and parchment were used in various places throughout the ancient world for centuries, the eventual displacement of papyrus as the standard writing medium was fueled by a rivalry. As Alexandria was accumulating volumes and copies of documents, so was the library in Pergamum. Another important center of scholarship, the Greek kingdom of Pergamum was located in present-day Turkey and was founded in the second century B.C. Not to be outdone by a competitor, Egypt placed an embargo on the export of the native papyrus, thus preventing Pergamum from obtaining the needed writing medium. Cutting off the supply of papyrus only led the scholars in Pergamum to improve parchment and to rely on it as their main writing material. By the waning of the western Roman Empire in 476 A.D., the parchment codex had become the predominant form of the book, replacing the papyrus roll.

The Romans

As the Roman civilization flourished from 650 B.C. to 476 A.D., it was greatly influenced by the Greeks and continued that society's emphasis on learning and literature, science, mathematics, and technology. Throughout the expansion of the Roman Empire, libraries were considered important spoils of war, and Roman army leaders routinely pillaged the contents from collections in fallen cities.

The library as an institution for the general public was a new concept that emerged from the golden days of the Roman Empire. Enumerated on a census of noteworthy buildings in Rome circa 40 B.C. was the first public library, which was based on the private collection of a wealthy donor.[6] Almost 400 years later, the number of libraries increased to 28. Library facilities were part of the Romans' extensive municipal building program, with reading rooms in the lavish public baths.[7] As such, libraries were available to all literate people, whether slaves or free, not exclusively a resource for the wealthy and privileged.

Asia

Although histories of libraries often focus on the evolution of technologies in Europe, many innovations took place even earlier in Asian civilizations. During the time of the creative Han dynasty, paper was invented (105 A.D.), some 1,000 years before its introduction to European countries.

Wooden block printing was in use throughout Eastern Asia about 700 years before the German Gutenberg was credited with the invention of movable type printing in 1456. First used in China, block printing then spread to neighboring Korea and Japan and became a standard for several hundred years. Baked clay blocks were used from 1045 A.D. in China, and in 1403 A.D. printing with movable metal type was invented in Korea.

The appearance of pictographic writing on bone and other natural materials dates from the Shang period, 1766–1122 B.C., sometime after the advent of the Sumerian cuneiform. This early Chinese script persisted and formed the basis for modern written Chinese.

Mexico

Although little information survives about whether written works were gathered and organized in libraries in what is now Mexico, a vast array of literature existed in the New World before the arrival of the Spanish. Unfortunately, most of the evidence of these writings soon disappeared "owing to the diligence of church and government officials who rooted out any manifestations of this visible symbol of 'paganism.'"[8] The Franciscan Bishop Diego de Landa—known for both his detailed accounts of Mayan life in the 1500s and his destruction of their writings—described some of that destruction and the Indian reaction: "We found a large number of books in these characters and, as they contained nothing in which there were not to be seen superstition and lies of the devil, we burned them all, which they regretted to an amazing degree, and which caused them much affliction."[9] Among the few surviving specimens shipped to Europe by early colonists, three survive today. The information in these books was recorded by painting glyphs (pictographs) on paper made from the bark of fig trees.

Fragments of a variety of forms of recorded information have survived and their content indicates that many of the pre-Colombian Indians had a high degree of culture. These include myths, hymns, poetry, drama, history, and other forms of expression. Carbon-dating tests have established that by 600 B.C., sophisticated writing and calendar systems existed. In fact, the Mayan calendar of that era was so accurate that it appeared to have evolved over a long period of time.

LIBRARIES IN THE WESTERN WORLD

Middle Ages

With the decline and subsequent collapse of the western Roman Empire in 476 A.D., that portion of Europe entered a dark period between 500 A.D. and 1000 A.D., when libraries, learning, and scholarship slumbered. Although many Roman libraries were sacked in the fall of the Empire, some collections had earlier been moved east to Byzantium (present-day Turkey) when Emperor Constantine relocated the capital of the empire there and continued the library tradition of the Greeks and Romans. Thus, it is believed that part of Aristotle's renowned private collection survived the fall.

Meanwhile, a continuous stream of barbarians seeking land and resources invaded Western Europe. During the upheaval of the early Middle Ages, Christian monasteries were the main protectors of books, culture, and education in the region. In addition, with the spread of the Muslim empire into Europe, Islamic libraries in Spain, Sicily, and North Africa arose where Christian works were copied and translated into Arabic. In the Middle East, grand Islamic libraries were founded by the caliph al-Ma'mun in Baghdad in the ninth century and by the caliph al-Mustansir in 11th-century Cairo.

In the Christian monasteries of continental Europe, Ireland, England, parts of Asia, and Northern Africa, scribes toiled in their copy rooms or scriptoriums, laboriously hand copying any written document made available to them, whether secular or religious in nature. Because of the labor-intensive effort in producing additional copies of each text, books were very valuable and were literally chained to the shelves. Libraries in the monasteries contained literature on parchment scrolls and codexes. The great works of antiquity—the Bible, Homer's writings, Greek plays, and Roman law—were preserved for humanity through the dedicated copying efforts of the monastic centers.

Additionally, in the late eighth century during what became known as the Carolingian Renaissance, a culture of learning flourished under Charlemagne, king of the Franks. At his palace in Aachen (present-day Germany), the ruler established a court library and allowed these books to be copied in order to share their contents with other fledgling libraries, thus helping to keep learning alive during this era.

An especially beautiful art form that flourished primarily in Western Europe from the Middle Ages and into the early Renaissance (about 500–1500 A.D.) was the illuminated manuscript. It combined the hand copying of text (usually religious) with colorful miniature painting. Manuscripts were artfully decorated within the text as well as along the borders and margins with gold and silver paint and vividly colored inks made from lapis, cinnabar, and other sources.

There are many surviving examples available on display for public viewing, including the renowned Book of Kells (ca. 800 A.D) at the Trinity College Library, Dublin, and the large collection of illuminated manuscripts at the Getty Museum in Los Angeles. (See resources section below.)

Figure 2.1. During Europe's dark ages, the task of preserving written works fell to the scribes in monasteries.

Early Renaissance

Monasteries remained the primary centers of learning and study until the rise of the modern universities, which began during the 12th century. The Crusades had brought the West in touch with ideas and literature from Asia, and increasing economic stability led to a revival of interest in education.

Among the early universities were those in Bologna, Oxford, Cambridge, and Paris—still major institutions of learning today. Book dealers and professional scribes arose to provide an important service to the urban university community; no longer was the lone monk in his monastic setting the primary copyist of knowledge. In addition to the scribes, lay craftsmen included parchment makers, illuminators, and binders.

To meet the demand for textbooks, authorized texts were copied and then rented to the students. Eventually, the number of students increased, and libraries were formed, with each college of the university maintaining a separate collection to support its scholars.

By the 14th century, the Renaissance, or the rebirth of learning and the classical influences, was stirring in Italy. This marked the emergence of Western Europe from the Middle Ages into a period of incredible discovery, artistic brilliance, technological inventions, and cultural development. With the renewed emphasis on learning, art, and study, the demand for books—books written not only in the scripts of the clergy (which was mostly in Latin) but also in the vernacular languages of the people, such as Italian, French, and German—was great.

Ownership of books was a mark of status, and the ownership of personal libraries among wealthy individuals expanded during this period. But the multiplication of manuscripts by hand copying was too inefficient and unable to keep up with the burgeoning demand. With the fertile climate of the Renaissance as a backdrop, the introduction of a new technology for more easily producing books was imminent and would revolutionize the world.

The Invention of Movable Type

As with many major inventions, several parties were hard at work perfecting the movable type printing press, but Johann Gutenberg of Mainz, Germany, is credited as the first European printer to use the new technology. This was not the birth of the art of printing—wooden blocks and other molds had been used in China since the ninth century. Paper was discovered by the Chinese by 105 A.D. or earlier, eventually making its way to Europe, where it was readily available by the mid-15th century. The convergence of cheap paper and the invention of the printing press combined to make Gutenberg's technology revolutionary.

The Gutenberg Bible, also known as the 42-line Bible or Mazarin Bible, was the first Western full-length book produced using movable metal typeface. Historical evidence suggests that 180 copies of the work were produced around the year 1455. Large, handsomely illustrated, and written in Latin, the Bibles were hand-finished with colorful illumination and underlining. Extant copies of the rare Bibles are held today by the Library of Congress, La

Bibliothèque Nationale, the National Library of Scotland, The Huntington Library, and other major research facilities, as well as in private collections.

The significance of Gutenberg's invention was that the mass printing of documents, broadsides, and books became much faster, cheaper, and more accurate. Compared to the previous method for the multiplication of books—laborious and error-prone hand copying—the printing press was an incredible advancement. With this new technique, printers were able to produce a wider variety of reading material, including texts, romances, poetry, travel books, histories, and religious works, for a general audience.

Early examples of books printed after the seminal Gutenberg Bible until 1501 are referred to as *incunabula*. Today, a leading project to publish on the Internet freely accessible, full text of classic works found in the public domain is appropriately titled Project Gutenberg. (See resources section at end of this chapter for the Web site address.)

Post-Renaissance Europe

During the 1600s and 1700s, libraries and literacy thrived, with a diverse array of facilities being established or expanded. Great university libraries continued to grow throughout Europe, as did the leading national libraries, such as France's La Bibliothèque Nationale, the British Library, Germany's state library in Berlin, and Catherine the Great's state library in Leningrad. Earlier collections, such as the incredible Vatican Library of the Roman Catholic Church, developed during the 15th century, were joined by flourishing Italian state and private libraries. Periodicals and newspapers appeared during this time.

City and town libraries were popular throughout Germany during the 18th and 19th centuries. In the United Kingdom, circulating libraries began to show up in the 1740s, and by the 1780s were important institutions that provided the middle class access to popular reading materials, particularly novels. Another variation on an early type of library, a circulating library was also known as a rental library or lending library. The *Bookman's Glossary* defines such a library as a "collection of books, usually current fiction, for lending at a rental fee for a stated period."[10] Unlike a subscription library—which demanded the outlay of a more substantial membership fee—circulating libraries were more affordable since one could pay a small fee for the loan of just a single item.

In addition, the concept of locally supported libraries had also been evolving in Britain; a much cited early example is the town library in Manchester. Merchant Humphrey Chetham left money in his will to establish this facility in 1653. Both the "pay-to-use" circulating library and the Manchester town model bolstered the cultural foundation for free, public libraries and led to England's instituting the Public Libraries Act in 1850.

NORTH AMERICAN LIBRARIES

Books were highly cherished possessions brought by the first settlers from their homelands to the New World. During the early decades of the colonies, these private book collections were a mark of intelligence and property. Because few printers existed in America, anyone desiring to obtain a book had to purchase it from England. Today, genealogists and other researchers perusing historical insurance policies and estate inventories often note the estimated worth of book collections listed alongside the house, livestock, silverware, china, piano, and other valuables.

The largest private holdings in the colonies formed the nuclei for what would become the fledgling academic libraries at Harvard, Yale, and Princeton. In addition, lending libraries were common among church ministers during the 1600s and 1700s. The Rev. Thomas Bray, an Anglican clergyman, was instrumental in establishing early parochial libraries as he recruited ministers to promote the Church of England in the New World. In 1696, he began his work in the Colony of Maryland, requiring his new clergy to establish libraries for their own education and use; these, in fact, grew to some 30 small libraries throughout the American colonies.[11] Although Bray only visited the Colonies for a few months, his efforts on behalf of parish libraries there were sustained.

Early College Libraries

Today, academic libraries pride themselves on their student-centered policies and learning resources, with extended operating hours, computer labs, special collections, and 24/7 remote access to electronic holdings—all considered basic library services. Such offerings are in stark contrast to the limited services found in early American colonial colleges.

Harvard was the site of the earliest college library. It was established in 1638 when clergyman John Harvard donated his theological book collection of about 400 volumes to the young school.[12]

This was typical of most colonial college libraries, which were established with the donation a private collection of books by the libraries' founders or supporters. However, these cherished volumes were hardly available to the toiling students, because college libraries were open only an hour or two a day at best and the books were chained to tables and shelves in poorly lit, cold buildings. Preservation, accumulation, and storage of books, not service to students, were the primary tasks of the academic library. That philosophy did not change much until 1877, when Boston Public Library administrator Justin Winsor became head of Harvard University Library. He brought with him a new philosophy that caused academic libraries to shift to a more customer-service orientation, offering expanded hours, reserve collections, open stacks, and early interlibrary loaning.

Subscription Libraries

Benjamin Franklin—printer, scholar, diplomat, and inventor—at 25 years of age, was responsible for starting up one of the first American subscription libraries. Precursors to the concept of the community-funded public library, subscription or social libraries were similar to clubs. In the case of the Library

Company of Philadelphia, Franklin gathered together 50 men who shared with him an interest in obtaining significant books on history, political science, agriculture, and other topics of interest. With an initial contribution of 40 shillings each, to be followed by 10 shillings annually, the association was formed in 1731 as an effort to provide a resource for the self-education of its members.

Books were purchased with the collected dues, and members then borrowed the titles at no charge; the association retained ownership of the books. The concept of forming subscription libraries was a popular one until the mid-1800s. Many different types of readers founded such library associations. Women's groups often formed general reading libraries. Merchants and clerks formed mercantile libraries, and tradesmen and apprentices formed mechanics' institute libraries.

Today, serious researchers can study the fine collection of 17th-, 18th-, and 19th-century volumes that are housed in the Library Company of Philadelphia's special collection. The Mechanics' Institute of San Francisco, formed in 1854 as an early subscription library in the gold rush days, and the Charleston Library Society (South Carolina), begun about 1748, are also both examples of extant membership libraries.

National Libraries Established

By 1800, leaders of the new nation realized the need for a designated library collection in the capital to serve their information needs. Thus, the Library of Congress—now the largest library in the world with more than 130 million items—came into being with a start-up budget of $5,000.[13] During the War of 1812, the British burned Washington, DC, and the fledgling legislative collection of 3,000 tomes was destroyed. In 1815, former president Thomas Jefferson sold his private collection—then one of the largest personal collections in the nation—of 6,487 books to Congress for $23,950 as a nucleus from which to rebuild the collection.[14] Housed for many years inside the Capitol building, the Library of Congress moved into its first permanent building, The Thomas Jefferson Building, in 1897.

Figure 2.2 shows the Library of Congress, Jefferson Building. In rebuilding the library around Jefferson's volumes, the Library of Congress also adopted his classification system for the collection, which formed the basis for the first Library of Congress (LC) classification scheme. Figure 2.3 shows the modern-day Library of Congress Web page.

At the bequest of British scientist James Smithson, the Smithsonian Institution was founded in 1846 to serve the United States as a scholarly institution. Soon to be included in the research facility were art galleries, lecture halls, and a library. Charles Coffin Jewett, then librarian at Brown University, was hired as librarian of the Smithsonian Institution. As part of his start-up efforts, he advocated the concept of centralized cataloging and conducted a census of libraries. His census count, though probably conservative, indicated that there were 10,015 libraries in the United States in 1850.[15]

Figure 2.2. Library of Congress, Jefferson Building.

Earliest Public Libraries

While New England is credited as the birthplace of public libraries within the new American nation, Charles Town (now Charleston), South Carolina, was the site of one of the earliest public libraries in the American colonies. As a wealthy and cultured regional center surrounded by successful cotton, rice, and indigo plantations, this 4th largest city in the colonies organized a free public library in 1698 by a legislative act.[16]

As the young nation grew, two important events that occurred in New England during the early decades of the 19th century provide evidence of the grassroots momentum that was building in support of public education and for free public libraries. In 1803, educator and bookseller Caleb Bingham established a free library for local youths in his hometown of Salisbury, Connecticut, in an attempt to provide enrichment opportunities and improve the use of the youths' leisure time. After his initial donation of books, the municipality voted to provide some ongoing funds for the purchase of more titles. Then, 30 years later in Peterborough, New Hampshire, the first free, tax-supported public library was established by a vote of the citizens.

Figure 2.3. The Library of Congress provides access to a wealth of information through its sophisticated Web site.

Eventually, with Massachusetts leading the way, each state passed its own version of legislation giving cities and other jurisdictions legal authority to collect taxes for library support.

Melvil Dewey

The single most significant contributor to the development of library science in the 19th century, arguably, was Melvil Dewey. A leader and innovator in the emerging profession, Dewey initiated many tools that are still viable today. Most famous for devising his library organizational scheme known as the Dewey Decimal Classification, he also co-founded—along with publishers Frederick Leypoldt and R.R. Bowker—the first periodical devoted to the library field, *Library Journal.* He also helped establish the American Library

Association (ALA) in 1876 and started the Library Bureau, a specialized library supply and furnishings company still in existence today.

Dewey's decimal system, which divided human knowledge into 10 main groupings, tackled the major problem of organizing the works that libraries had been accumulating over the centuries, and it remains the standard in K–12 schools and public libraries. Realizing the importance of education for the field, Dewey established the School of Library Economy while serving as librarian at Columbia University in 1887. This program was the first organized training curriculum for library workers in the United States.

Dewey encouraged women to enter the fledgling profession at a time when many of his colleagues opposed women's entry into the field. Efficiency, organization, and time management were his mantras. As a child, he allegedly found delight in arranging the contents of his mother's pantry.[17] Along with Teddy Roosevelt and Andrew Carnegie, he was a proponent of the failed phonetic, reformed spelling movement.

Dewey's life was not without controversy. He was accused of sexual improprieties against young women at an ALA outing and of financial irregularities involving several business ventures. His fervor for new ideas coupled with his sometimes questionable personal behavior resulted in his resignations from library positions during his career.

Despite his faults, Dewey had a major impact on American librarianship with his standardization of library systems and staff education. In addition, he showed great foresight in advocating active library promotion, the consideration of user needs, and the development of new outreach services. The previous passive role of libraries merely warehousing books was insufficient.

John Cotton Dana

Another leader in these formative years of the library profession was a man of many talents, John Cotton Dana. Dana's 44-year career bridged the end of the 19th century and the beginning of the 20th century. Today, he is best known for his advocacy of library promotion. His name graces the annual public relations award co-sponsored by the H.W. Wilson Company and the American Library Association. During his nearly half century in the field, Dana pioneered many other new ideas, including separate children's departments, open stacks (where patrons could help themselves to books), and the use of displays.[18] He also founded the Special Libraries Association in 1909 and established a separate business collection at the Newark Public Library during his tenure as its director, and he collected foreign language materials for the large local immigrant population. Though these seem like standard services today, at the time they were very innovative ideas. A prolific writer, Dana wrote many essays that have been reprinted and still make for thoughtful reading today.[19]

Era of Philanthropy

By the last quarter of the 19th century, American libraries and librarianship were gaining momentum and acceptance. The Boston Public Library, often considered the institution that launched the modern library movement in the United States, opened in 1854. During the 1860s and 1870s, many major cities, including San Francisco, Detroit, Cleveland, and Chicago followed Boston's lead in opening their own public libraries. Dewey's many ideas were taking root, and tangible support for the institutions came in the form of contributions from wealthy philanthropists.

In 1882, Baltimore merchant Enoch Pratt provided land, a new library building, and $833,000 for library development. A condition of the bequest was that the city set up a $50,000 endowment fund to generate income for annual operating costs and to build four branch facilities. In gratitude, the city named their system the Enoch Pratt Free Library of Baltimore.

Phoebe Apperson Hearst, widow of the senator and mining magnate George Hearst and mother of publisher William Randolph Hearst, selected a variety of educational causes to support, among them early kindergartens, the Parent-Teacher Association (PTA), the University of California, and libraries. At the turn of the century, she outfitted free public libraries to serve miners and their families in the mining communities of her late husband's big strikes in Lead, South Dakota and Anaconda, Montana. The Hearst Free Library in Lead was unveiled to the residents as a Christmas gift in 1894, and came fully stocked with materials in English and in foreign languages to serve the many immigrant workers.[20] In addition, Hearst supported the founding of various local subscription libraries in areas where she lived.[21]

Andrew Carnegie

To date, the greatest philanthropist to libraries has been Scottish-born steel millionaire Andrew Carnegie. Born in 1835, Carnegie was the son of a handloom weaver. As the weaving trade became mechanized, his family followed relatives and emigrated to the United States in 1848, searching for improved economic opportunity. They settled in Allegheny, Pennsylvania, near Pittsburgh, where 13-year-old Andrew went to work as a bobbin boy and studied at night. Andrew worked a string of increasingly more responsible jobs, with the young man eventually working for the Pennsylvania Railroad. Shrewd investments in the Pullman sleeping car made him wealthy and were followed by further investments in railroad bridges, iron mills, and oil fields. By the 1870s, the demand for steel to expand the country's infrastructure was high, so Carnegie formed the Carnegie Steel Company. Immensely successful by 1901—when he sold his steel firm for a profit of $40 million—Carnegie was dubbed the richest man in the world. Known as a hard, aggressive businessman among his former partners, he was a controversial figure and very unpopular among labor and trade unions due to his labor policies.

From his own rags-to-riches success story, Carnegie valued the notion of self-improvement and lifelong learning. He also had a theory of philanthropy, which he detailed in essays published in 1889. In Carnegie's "Gospel of Wealth," he speaks of the moral obligation of the rich to distribute their wealth for benevolent purposes.[22] Among his many philanthropic projects were providing funding for public gardens in Scotland and pipe organs for churches, erecting Carnegie Hall and several museums, and creating educational endowments. But Carnegie's richest legacy is his library construction program.

Beginning in 1881, through the Carnegie Corporation, Andrew Carnegie gave more than $56 million for the construction of over 2,500 public library buildings in the English-speaking world.[23] Starting with his birthplace, Dunfermline, Scotland, Carnegie launched a unique effort to help communities construct public libraries. The first city in the United States to benefit from his philanthropy was his adopted hometown, Allegheny, Pennsylvania. In 1886, the town accepted his offer of $250,000 to build a new facility on the condition that it would be municipally supported. The Carnegie Free Library became the model for the many publicly funded libraries to follow from his construction program.

More than $41 million was distributed to American libraries, both urban and rural, over a 32-year period. By the conclusion of the Carnegie grant program in 1917, communities in nearly every state had received grants for a grand total of 1,679 individual library buildings.[24] Figures 2.4, 2.5, 2.6, and 2.7 are photographs of four Carnegie libraries built in California. Note the ornate architectural styles that are commonly seen in the Carnegie libraries.

Impact of Carnegie's Program

Carnegie's unique program had a lasting impact on American communities. Until this time, early free public libraries were limited primarily to larger, urban areas. Many communities had subscription libraries but not tax-supported resources. Because of Carnegie's largess, within a couple of decades public libraries for smaller communities became commonplace in the United States.

Photograph by Jane A. Kimball

Figure 2.4. Carnegie Library in Willets, California.

Figure 2.5. Carnegie Library in Gilroy, California.

Figure 2.6. Carnegie Library in Monterey, California.

Photograph by Jane A. Kimball

Figure 2.7. Carnegie Library in Petaluma, California.

In addition to the educational resources the libraries provided to residents, the surviving edifices themselves are often extraordinary examples of American architecture at the beginning of the 20th century.

In supporting individual communities, Carnegie was attempting to stimulate the movement for more free, public libraries. Carnegie's donation to a town was the building only, and formed a cooperative venture with the city that would then need to stock the building with books, staff it, and provide ongoing fiscal support. Carnegie's grants ranged from $5.2 million for the city of New York to $3,000 for smaller, rural towns.

An application process was required for candidate towns requesting a Carnegie library grant. Requirements were that the city not already have a permanent library building, that they had to provide the site on which to build the new library, and that they had to pledge to annually pay an amount equal to 10 percent of Carnegie's gift for upkeep of the facility.

A grand total of 1,412 American cities received Carnegie library building funds.

Today, many areas have outgrown their small, historic Carnegie buildings. As new library facilities are constructed, some communities such as Newberg Public Library, south of Portland, Oregon, cleverly find ways to incorporate the original facade into an otherwise modern-day building. Another trend is for the turn-of-the century Carnegie buildings to be converted to new community buildings, such as local history museums, art galleries, city halls, or chamber of commerce offices. Figure 2.8 shows how a community proudly announced its Carnegie library grant.

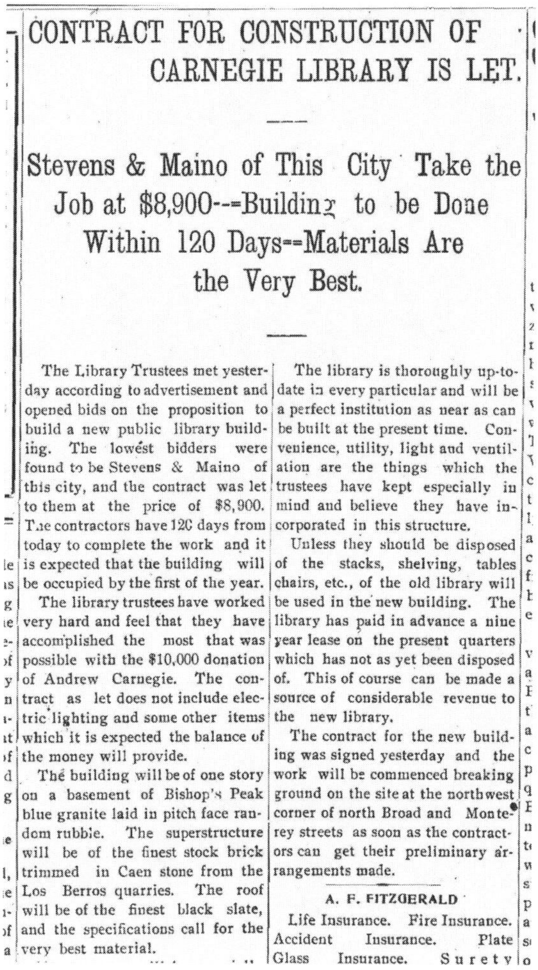

CONTRACT FOR CONSTRUCTION OF CARNEGIE LIBRARY IS LET.

Stevens & Maino of This City Take the Job at $8,900--=Buildin to be Done Within 120 Days==Materials Are the Very Best.

The Library Trustees met yesterday according to advertisement and opened bids on the proposition to build a new public library building. The lowest bidders were found to be Stevens & Maino of this city, and the contract was let to them at the price of $8,900. The contractors have 120 days from today to complete the work and it is expected that the building will be occupied by the first of the year.

The library trustees have worked very hard and feel that they have accomplished the most that was possible with the $10,000 donation of Andrew Carnegie. The contract as let does not include electric lighting and some other items which it is expected the balance of the money will provide.

The building will be of one story on a basement of Bishop's Peak blue granite laid in pitch face random rubble. The superstructure will be of the finest stock brick trimmed in Caen stone from the Los Berros quarries. The roof will be of the finest black slate, and the specifications call for the very best material.

The library is thoroughly up-to-date in every particular and will be a perfect institution as near as can be built at the present time. Convenience, utility, light and ventilation are the things which the trustees have kept especially in mind and believe they have incorporated in this structure.

Unless they should be disposed of the stacks, shelving, tables chairs, etc., of the old library will be used in the new building. The library has paid in advance a nine year lease on the present quarters which has not as yet been disposed of. This of course can be made a source of considerable revenue to the new library.

The contract for the new building was signed yesterday and the work will be commenced breaking ground on the site at the northwest corner of north Broad and Monterey streets as soon as the contractors can get their preliminary arrangements made.

A. F. FITZGERALD

Life Insurance. Fire Insurance. Accident Insurance. Plate Glass Insurance. Surety

Figure 2.8. The construction of a Carnegie library was often headline news in communities that were awarded a grant. From the San Luis Obispo, California, *Morning Tribune,* July 7, 1904.

The 20th Century

Special Populations

Library services for special populations, including children, the visually impaired, rural citizens, and new immigrants, began to develop in the 20th century. Children's departments first appeared in urban public libraries in the 1890s and became a mainstay in the 20th century. The Library of Congress's National Library Services for the Blind and Physically Handicapped (1931) and Braille Institute collections (1934) were originally developed to provide reading materials solely for the blind and visually disabled population; they have since expanded their scope to include people with other disabilities.

Washington County Free Library in Maryland operated the first traveling library service to rural citizens with the advent of its bookmobile wagon in 1905; similar services developed in rural areas throughout the United States.[25] City libraries responded to the wave of immigrants in the early decades of the 20th century by providing magazines and book collections in foreign languages.

Nonstop New Technologies

Movable-type printing was the dominant method of printing for 400 years. A major improvement came with the invention of linotype, or machine movable printing, in 1884. Today, the revolution of digital publishing is continually transforming the authoring, dissemination, and access to information as we have known it. The venerable printed book is facing serious competition as the dominant format in distributing the written word. However, for many purposes it remains the most cost-effective method for distributing information content.

Microform technology became commonly used in libraries just before World War II. Prior to the advent of electronic information storage, microforms were hailed as the solution to the never-ending library space dilemma. Today, microfiche and microfilm are still viable media for the archival preservation of large periodical back files and other historical materials, especially those with low usage levels. See Chapter 5, Preparing Materials for Use, for a more detailed discussion of current developments in the area of microform use and digitization.

The Library of Congress developed the MARC (MAchine Readable Cataloging) record in 1966, which became the world's standard format for the communication of bibliographic information between libraries via computer. With the establishment of the MARC standard, computer use and cooperation among libraries has grown tremendously. Most early computer use in libraries was for circulation systems or inventories, in-house functions such as database building and word processing, and union catalogs or cooperative bibliographic databases of library holdings.

OCLC (Online Computer Library Center) has been and remains one of the largest databases of library cataloging and holdings data, with more than 60,000 user libraries from around the globe as of 2007.[26] Total bibliographic records in its WorldCat database—the OCLC Online Union Catalog—number more than 70,000,000, with a new record added every 10 seconds.[27] Originally, OCLC was the acronym for the Ohio College Library Center, but it now stands for Online Computer Library Center.

Computers and libraries make for a natural match, as libraries have large amounts of data that need to be stored, sorted, retrieved, viewed, and printed. The first generation of automated library catalogs showed up in academic facilities in the 1970s. As we continue into the 21st century, the majority of American libraries have automated Online Public Access Catalogs (OPACs). Although no one source comprehensively tracks automation for all types of libraries, the following statistics provide a representative picture. An estimated 99.6 percent of all U.S. public libraries had OPACs in 2004, according to an ALA survey.[28] School libraries (both public and private) and small special libraries seem to be the areas most behind in adopting some kind of automated catalog, specifically because of funding and other issues.

Thus, the use of computers is now pervasive in all library tasks, with the online ordering of materials, full-text retrieval of periodicals, and Web-based OPACs (Online Public Access Catalogs) and job postings just a sampling of the automated functions in widespread use, in addition to familiar cataloging and circulation tasks.

In the early 1990s, another significant technical advance was realized. Although Hypertext Markup Language (HTML) was first invented by British scientist Tim Berners Lee in 1989, it wasn't until 1993 that the phenomenon known as the Web fully impacted academic and technical users. By 1995, the World Wide Web (WWW) revolution exploded, with commercial and consumer use swelling. Wider acceptance and myriad applications continued to emerge through the end of the decade; in the 21st century, increasingly sophisticated innovations that impact libraries have included Amazon's "Look Inside the Book" feature, Google Scholar, and social networking sites such as *Facebook*, *MySpace*, and *Flickr*. With its cross-platform environment, speed, ease of use, and round-the-clock global access (often free or nearly free), the Web presented advantages for turn-of-the-20th-century users that paralleled those of the movable-type printing press in 15th-century Europe. According to Internet World Stats, as of November 2007, about 1.2 billion users worldwide were connected to the Internet, with the number of users having more than doubled in the past five years.[29]

For libraries, Web technology has had a significant impact on customers' expectations for overall service and for libraries to provide access to current technology. This has resulted in a need for patron instruction and has greatly transformed many internal operations, such as materials ordering, interlibrary loan, and document delivery. In addition, the rapid pace of changes brought about by Web publishing of information has necessitated a re-evaluation of print collections and the ongoing retraining of staff.

Still, the costs involved in constantly upgrading technology prevent many libraries from keeping pace. Acknowledging this problem, billionaire Microsoft founder Bill Gates—through the Bill and Melinda Gates Foundation—has committed ongoing support to fund technology in public libraries in the United States as well as abroad. Gates grant awards have brought computers, Internet access, and staff training to needy public libraries in low-income and other qualifying communities across the United States since 1997.

Resource Sharing

Since the 1960s, formal resource sharing among libraries and information centers has burgeoned as facilities of all types and sizes realize that in numbers there is strength and increased benefits to customers. Consortia have taken the form of same-type and multi-type library networks, with membership based on geographical proximity, on collection strengths, and on shared customer profiles.

An early example of a powerful library alliance is RLG (Research Libraries Group), a cooperative formed by Yale, Harvard, Columbia, and the New York Public Library in 1974. Today, RLG is an international network with some 150 members, including universities and colleges, national libraries, archives, historical societies, museums, independent research collections, and public libraries. In 2006, RLG was absorbed by OCLC, but still has its own presence for some things under the OCLC brand.

Resource sharing in all its forms is the backbone of library services as it enables agencies to share personnel, to centralize cataloging and processing efforts, to lobby for improved purchasing power from vendors, and to provide patron access to a greater number of materials.

National Awareness of Libraries

The American Library Association first adopted its Library Bill of Rights in 1948 (see Appendix B) to establish guidelines for the rights of library users. Based on our nation's First Amendment to the Constitution, which guarantees the freedom of expression in speech, writing, reading, access to information, and so on, the Library Bill of Rights has been supplemented with interpretive statements several times to reflect new issues regarding the freedom to access information, censorship, and multimedia formats. Many libraries formally adopt this statement as part of their official policy.

U.S. libraries of all types benefited from legislation in the 1950s and 1960s that provided financial aid for collection development and facilities building. The Bicentennial Celebration of 1976, with its commemoration of the historical roots of our country, shined a new spotlight on libraries and archives, underscoring the need to preserve documentation of our national, regional, and local history.

The library boom years of the 1950s and 1960s contrast with later observations made by the National Commission on Excellence in Education in their

1983 report *A Nation at Risk.* This study determined that the educational system in the United States was slipping in terms of quality and effectiveness and that publicly supported institutions such as library systems had fallen far behind as well.[30]

The American Library Association reports more than 117,000 libraries in the United States as of 2007. Although the funding levels can be counted on to vary widely among these diverse types of libraries, the new technological leaps and fresh challenges of the 21st-century promise to keep libraries and information centers in the spotlight as they continue to provide information access to their clientele.

STUDY QUESTIONS

1. Describe some of the historical information needs that have driven the collecting of written materials.

2. Compare what we know of the Great Library at Alexandria to a modern library facility.

3. What was the impact of Gutenberg's new technology on reading and printing at the time in Europe?

4. Describe the service philosophy of early American colonial college libraries. How does this compare to your current college or university library's philosophy?

5. What were the major contributions of Melvil Dewey to the library profession? How did his accomplishments dovetail with other events in the field in the late 1800s?

6. What impact did Andrew Carnegie's program have on American communities? Are there similar privately funded grant programs in place for helping libraries and information centers today? Name some major ones.

7. Describe the historical rivalry between the writing mediums of papyrus and animal skin. Can you draw any comparisons between the current competition between the printed book and electronic dissemination of information?

8. How do political instability and war—such as World War I or II or the current Middle East conflicts—affect cuneiform collections and other ancient treasures (such as those found in Baghdad's Iraq Museum) that document humanity's common cultural heritage?

RESOURCES

Print Resources

Carnegie Corporation. "Public Buildings: A Postcard Collection: Public Libraries, Carnegie Libraries." *Carnegie Reporter* 4, no. 2 (Spring 2007): http://www.carnegie.org/reporter/14/backpage/back_story.html. Reprinted from *Planning Commissioners Journal* (Winter 2001).

Casson, Lionel. *Libraries In the Ancient World.* New Haven: Yale University Press, 2001.

Harris, Michael H. *History of Libraries in the Western World.* 4th ed. Metuchen, NJ: Scarecrow, 1995.

Jones, Theodore. *Carnegie Libraries Across America: A Public Legacy.* New York: John Wiley, 1997.

Polk, Milbry and Angela M. H. Schuster, eds. *The Looting of the Iraq Museum, Baghdad: The Lost Legacy of Mesopotamia.* New York: Abrams, 2005.

Swerdlow, Joel. "The Power of Writing." *National Geographic,* August 1999, 110–32.

Thorpe, James. *The Gutenberg Bible: Landmark in Learning.* 2d ed. San Marino, CA: Huntington Library, 1999.

Van Slyck, Abigail A. *Free to All: Carnegie Libraries and American Culture, 1890–1920.* Chicago: University of Chicago Press, 1995.

Wiegand, Wayne A. *Irrepressible Reformer: A Biography of Melvil Dewey.* Chicago: American Library Association, 1996.

Web Sites

Cary Collection: Before the Printing Press

http://wally.rit.edu/cary/cc_db/before_press/index.html

(accessed January 19, 2008).

This Web site from the Cary Graphic Arts Collection at the Rochester Institute of Technology has photographs illustrating several early forms of bookmaking technology, including cuneiform tablets and papyrus scroll fragments

The Cuneiform Digital Library Initiative (CDLI)

http://cdli.ucla.edu/about_cdli.html

(accessed January 19, 2008).

The CDLI is a scholarly international effort by museum curators and historians to make available on the Web the content and analysis of early cuneiform tablets from leading cuneiform collections around the world.

Illuminated Manuscripts at the Getty Museum

http://www.getty.edu/art/

(accessed January 19, 2008).

The J. Paul Getty museum has a leading collection of illuminated manuscripts dating from the ninth to the 16th centuries and representing many styles. Located in Los Angeles, California, the museum regularly features stunning public exhibitions from its illuminated manuscript collection.

Project Gutenberg

http://www.gutenberg.org/

(accessed January 19, 2008).

Project Gutenberg is a pioneer in the distribution of full-text, noncopyrighted classics of literature on the Internet. More than 18,000 electronic-text titles are available for free downloading.

Jefferson's Legacy: A Brief History of the Library of Congress

http://www.loc.gov/loc/legacy/toc.html

(accessed January 19, 2008).

This site is an illustrated Web version of the book by John Y. Cole (also available in print) that discusses the early years of our national library and Jefferson's key role in the collection's development.

Videos

A Tour of the Library of Congress. (21 min.). Washington, DC: Library of Congress Information Office, 1986.
This video provides an overview of the founding and historical development of our national library.
Richest Man in the World: Andrew Carnegie. (120 min.). Produced and directed by Austin Hoyt. Boston: PBS/WGBH, 1997.
The *American Experience* series looks at the rags-to-riches story of controversial steel magnate Andrew Carnegie.

NOTES

1. P. J. Huffstutter and Kasri Naji, "Antiquities Stuck in Legal Limbo," *Los Angeles Times,* July 13, 2006.
2. "Large Cache of Mesopotamian Tablets Found," *Los Angeles Times,* December 29, 1987.
3. Jean Key Gates, *Guide to the Use of Libraries and Information Sources* 7th ed. (New York: McGraw-Hill, 1994): 5.
4. Lionel Casson, "Triumph from the Ancient World's First Think Tank," *Smithsonian* (June): 158–68 (1985).
5. Dr. Sohair F. Wastawy, Chief Librarian Bibliotheca Alexandrina, e-mail to authors, April 29, 2006.
6. Will Durant, *Story of Civilization, Part III: Caesar and Christ* (New York: Simon & Schuster, 1944), 159.
7. Ibid., 360.
8. G. Morley Sylvanus and George W. Brainerd, *The Ancient Maya* 4th ed. (Stanford, CA: Stanford University Press, 1983), 513.
9. Ibid.
10. Jean Peters, ed., *The Bookman's Glossary* 5th ed. (New York: R. R. Bowker, 1975), 130.
11. *Encyclopædia Britannica Online*, s.v. "Bray, Thomas," http://search.eb.com/eb/article-9016283 (accessed March 30, 2006).
12. Elizabeth W. Stone, *American Library Development, 1600–1899* (New York: H. W. Wilson, 1977), 94.
13. John Y. Cole, *Jefferson's Legacy: A Brief History of the Library of Congress* (Washington, DC: Library of Congress, 1993), 12.
14. Ibid., 13.
15. Elizabeth W. Stone, *American Library Development, 1600–1899* (New York: H. W. Wilson, 1977), 153.
16. Ibid., 127, 128.
17. Fremont Rider, *Melvil Dewey* (Chicago: American Library Association, 1944), 6.
18. H. W. Wilson Co., "John Cotton Dana Library Public Relations Award-About John Cotton Dana," http://www.hwwilson.com/jcdawards/about_jcd.htm (accessed January 21, 2008).

19. Carl A. Hanson, ed., *Librarian at Large: Selected Writings of John Cotton Dana* (Washington, DC: Special Libraries Association, 1991).

20. Richard A. Peterson, "Philanthropic Phoebe: The Educational Charity of Phoebe Apperson Hearst," *California History* 64, no. 4 (Fall 1985): 287.

21. Alexandra M. Nickliss, "Phoebe Apperson Hearst's Gospel of Wealth," *Pacific Historical Review* 71, no. 4 (November 2002): 585–6.

22. Andrew Carnegie, "Wealth," *North American Review* 148 (June 1889): 653–64.

23. Carnegie Corporation of New York, "About Carnegie Corporation: Biography of Andrew Carnegie," http://www.carnegie.org/sub/about/biography.html (accessed January 21, 2008).

24. Abigail A. Van Slyck, *Free to All: Carnegie Libraries and American Culture, 1890–1920* (Chicago: University of Chicago Press, 1995), 22.

25. Nancy Smiler Levinson, "Takin' It to the Streets: The History of the Book Wagon," *Library Journal*, 1 (May 1991): 43–45.

26. OCLC United States, "About OCLC," http://www.oclc.org/about/ (accessed January 21, 2008).

27. *OCLC Abstracts* 9, no.27 (July 17, 2006), e-mail to author, July 17, 2006.

28. John Carlo Bertot, Charles R. McClure, and Paul T. Jaeger, *Public Libraries and the Internet 2004: Survey Results and Finding* (Chicago: Bill & Melinda Gates Foundation and American Library Association, 2005), http: www.ala.org/ala/washoff/oitp/GatesFinalJun05.pdf (accessed January 21, 2008).

29. World Internet Usage Statistics News and Population Stats, "Internet Usage Statistics: The Internet Big Picture," http://www.internetworldstats.com/stats.htm (accessed January 21, 2008).

30. United States National Commission on Excellence in Education, *A Nation at Risk: The Imperative for Educational Reform: A Report to the Nation and to the Secretary of Education* (Washington, DC: U.S.G.P.O., 1983).

Types of Library Job Opportunities

This book presents an overview for those who are considering a career in libraries and library-like organizational settings. Before addressing specific career possibilities, one must have some common understanding of the varieties of organizational settings in which these career opportunities can be found.

It is clear in the 21st century that the entire landscape of libraries and information gathering is evolving with accelerating speed. Many question whether libraries will continue to exist as we knew them in the past century. However, the basic purpose of libraries to organize and disseminate information is needed now more than ever. No prognosticators have a crystal ball clear enough to convince us that they really know how this evolution will play out during the working lives of those now beginning a career. Two observations, however, are very clear: those who see themselves as the keepers of books will be shelved themselves, and those who demonstrate that they can help solve other people's information, imagination, and inspiration problems will always be in demand. This chapter is intended to help the latter group build an understanding of the organizational environments in which they are likely to work.

WHAT IS A LIBRARY?

What is a library? There are hundreds of different kinds of libraries and library-like organizations. In some ways, every library is different. In other ways, they are all the same. This chapter covers some of the differences. Subsequent chapters cover some of the similarities.

To the uninitiated, all libraries are the same, just as all library workers are the same. The uninitiated realize that some libraries are bigger than others and that library buildings look different from each other, but they believe that

39

the differentiation ends there. Even fairly sophisticated library users generally do not understand the range of libraries that exist or that almost every library is different. Each library's clientele is different; therefore, each library's mission is different. Also, libraries' collections are different; therefore, their services must differ.

What is it that makes an organization a library? Traditionally, libraries have been defined as organizations that acquire, organize, and disseminate information. This is certainly true, but it does not differentiate libraries from many other entities. For example, newspapers are among the many other kinds of organizations that meet each of these criteria. More will be said about the unique attributes of libraries in succeeding sections.

EACH LIBRARY IS DIFFERENT

Libraries are generally divided into four major categories:

- public libraries
- school libraries
- academic libraries
- special libraries

Each type of library has a distinct mission and a specific group of customers to serve. There are many distinct subcategories within each of these four groups, and some libraries overlap more than one category. Often, the different types of libraries specialize to such an extent that students training for the field consider them to be almost separate career tracks that, once embarked upon, are difficult to switch from. The balance of this chapter discusses how the different types of libraries have missions that are sometimes similar to—and sometimes distinctly different from—each other, and how they are shaped by the needs of the clientele they serve.

The four types of libraries mentioned are only the primary kinds. In reality, many libraries are combinations or blends of more than one basic type. This is somewhat analogous to having variations of 16 or even 256 colors created from only three primary colors.

HOW MANY LIBRARIES ARE IN THE UNITED STATES?

It is estimated that there are almost 130,000 libraries of all types in the United States that employ paid staff. These libraries range in size from small libraries with several hundred books, a single part-time staff member, and limited operating hours, to the world's largest facility, the Library of Congress, with about 138,000,000 items and thousands of employees. Table 3.1 breaks out libraries in the United States by type.

TABLE 3.1 How Many Libraries Are There in the United States?

Academic Libraries		3,617
Less than four years	1,334	
Four years and above	2,283	
Public Libraries		16,592
Centrals	9,050	
Branches	7,542	
School Libraries		99,623
Publicly Supported	82,569	
Privately Supported	17,054	
Special Libraries		9,236
Law	1,515	
Medical	2,017	
Religious	1,070	
Industry	1,649	
Nonprofits, etc.	2,028	
Government	957	
Total Libraries		**129,068**

Note: These statistics do not take into account the potentially vast number of libraries that are operated totally by volunteers for a few hours each week in churches and other not-for-profit organizations.

HOW MANY PEOPLE WORK IN LIBRARIES?

According to the ALA it is not easy to attain an exact figure, but the number of people working in libraries may approach 400,000. The library workforce includes librarians and other professionals, paraprofessionals, and clerical and technical personnel. Statistics are not consistently collected for each category of personnel in each type of library. The figures in table 3.2 piece it all together and present a reasonable estimate of the paid library workforce early in the 21st century:

The numbers in the table do not include individuals with library training and skills who work for library networks and regional cooperatives that supply services to individual libraries, but who do not directly provide services to individuals.

Vendors, who develop and market products and services to libraries, like to hire persons with library training, library experience, or both. The number of individuals who are employed in this capacity is not known. Often there is a revolving door through which individuals move between employment with vendors and employment in libraries. At other times, it is a one-way move from not-for-profit libraries to the for-profit sector. Consultants and freelance and temporary library staff comprise another arena of employment that is growing but that is very hard to measure.

TABLE 3.2 Types of Libraries, Librarians, Other Paid Staff, Total Staff

	Librarians	Other Paid Staff	Total
Academic Libraries	26,469	67,121	93,590
Public Libraries	46,185	94,257	140,442
Schools Libraries	61,701	30,785	92,486
Special Libraries	18,535	31,946	50,481
Total	**152,890**	**224,109**	**376,999**

PUBLIC LIBRARIES

The public library is the one major type of library that serves every citizen at every stage of life. In the United States, public libraries seem to take seriously the admonition of the Declaration of Independence that our citizens should be able to pursue life, liberty, and happiness. Thus, in addition to helping individuals learn how to earn a living and lead their lives, helping them enjoy recreational activities is also a legitimate function for the collections and services of public libraries. Historically, public libraries have served as a resource for succeeding generations of immigrants to learn how to function as effective citizens, both economically and politically.

Public libraries serve a wider range of needs and objectives than most other libraries. They serve the leisure-reading needs of people from toddlers to senior citizens and the information needs of patrons from first-graders to scholars. The public library has even been termed the *people's university* because people can pursue their own search for knowledge in the library's treasure house of literary works and scientific and technical information. Because public libraries are so important, they exist in more than 16,000 locations in communities both large and small throughout the United States.

Public libraries have the broadest mission because they have to be all things to all people. In some ways, their children's and young adults' departments supplement local school libraries. In some communities, the merging of school and public libraries is being explored. Their reference departments and periodical and nonfiction collections supplement local academic libraries. Joint public/academic ventures have also appeared in public libraries. The business and adult services departments of public libraries often provide services to local people, businesses too small to maintain their own libraries, and larger companies that need information services outside their primary economic focus. In addition, public libraries provide Internet access—often the only such access to this important source of information for those on the wrong side of the digital divide. As seen in chapter 8, this relatively new service often places public libraries at the forefront of political disputes as the public's right to know collides with the need to protect children.

Library educator Kathleen de la Pena McCook describes the mission of the public library today as follows:

> The public library in cities and towns and rural areas across the United States is a community center for books and information. In any community, the local public library provides a sense of place, a refuge and a still point; it is a commons, a vital part of the public sphere and a laboratory of ideas. The public library supports family literacy, fosters lifelong learning, helps immigrants find a place, and gives a place to those for whom there is no other place to be. The public library provides a wide-open door to knowledge and information to people of all ages, abilities, ethnicities, and economic station.[1]

The service areas of public libraries are defined by a local geographic area, usually a city or county. The lines of this traditionally defined "home turf" are becoming blurred. Some states are introducing statewide borrower cards that can be used in any public library in the state. In other areas, consortia of libraries of all types have reciprocal agreements to honor each other's registered customers. State-wide licensing of databases is becoming common. These trends, combined with the ubiquitous nature of the World Wide Web, are redefining all library services, with public libraries often taking the lead.

Typically, a public library is part of the municipal government and often is a department of the city or county government, with the library director reporting to the mayor, city manager, county executive, or similar authority. In other cases, the library is semi-autonomous, with a governing board appointed by the chief executive of the municipality. In this case, the chief librarian is responsible primarily to the library board and only secondarily responsible to the chief executive of the municipality. In rare cases, a public library is its own autonomous unit of municipal government, with its own elected governing board and independent taxing authority. In this case, the chief librarian is responsible solely to the elected library board.

The mission of the public library is to meet the needs of its particular community. It may carry out that mission through a single facility or through a sprawling system of libraries with scores of service locations. Even within the same city or county, different branches may require very different hours of operation, different collections of materials, and different patterns of service to meet the needs of their clients. For example, the socio–economic level, ethnicity, and average age of the clientele served by a particular facility dictates the solutions to the information needs of the community served by that facility. A community of young families would need different services than a community made up primarily of retirees. A community heavily saturated with recent immigrants would have different needs than a community in which most are native-born English speakers.

The urban or rural nature of the community and the predominant economic activity of the region also have major impacts. In congested urban areas, libraries must be conveniently located near public transportation. In the suburbs, ample parking is essential. Rural areas may require that libraries come to their patrons in the form of a bookmobile that makes regular rounds to reach the dispersed population. Finally, the level of technological penetration in the community will suggest the priority with which services must be delivered over the Web.

Public Library Objectives

As community needs have changed over the years, American public library objectives have changed to keep pace. Through much of the 19th century, education (adult education in particular) was the foremost objective of the public library. Late in that century and early in the 20th century, recreational reading and reference were added. The recreational reading was initially added to create new readers who could be converted to more serious endeavors. However, leisure reading gradually became a legitimate end in itself. The heightened social consciousness of the 1960s accelerated efforts of public libraries to help poor and uneducated people fit into a highly scientific and technical society, a trend that is currently receiving new emphasis.

In the 21st century, public libraries are mobilizing again to meet new community needs. The Web exploded into our society during the last few years of the 1990s. It has fundamentally changed the way Americans view information. This has caused librarians to re-examine whether the library is a place or a function. Should information be served to customers any time and any place they want it? If so, what role does the library have in selecting and organizing the electronic information thus distributed? To what extent should digital social networking play in the library's efforts to meet community information, imagination, and inspiration needs? How can the public library provide access for those who do not have independent access to the information available on the Web? These questions pose great challenges to the future of libraries and to future librarians. The extent to which libraries overcome these challenges will determine the relevance of libraries to society in the future.

The biggest challenge for public libraries will be developing and delivering Web-based services while continuing to maintain current in-building services to those who are better served in the latter mode. Libraries are neither cyber nor paper. They are both at the same time, and that is expensive in terms of resources, staff, and time.

Public Library Standards

The major direction for today's public libraries was set when the ALA published its post-war *Standards for Public Libraries* in 1943. These standards emphasize that a public library should provide free library service to the residents of a particular community. This direction was expanded in 1966 with the publication of the *Minimum Standards for Public Library Systems*, which included the concept that "service to all" is the reason that a library exists. This enhanced concept meant that libraries were looking beyond their typical library patron—the married, middle-class, educated, adult female who represented only a minority of the population—and toward the unserved one-third of the population who had never used a library and the millions of Americans who had no access to free public library service because they lived in rural communities or because of their race.[2]

The emphasis in these standards for library systems was on the quality of library service provided rather than on the quantity of library materials. The standards required the public library to develop written selection policies and choose accurate materials that included opposing views and appealed to all members of the community. Materials were to be purchased and discarded on a planned basis. Services and programs were to be developed to satisfy the needs of all individuals and groups. Standards for services to many of these groups, such as children, young adults, and people who are blind or physically disabled, were developed and published in separate standards by the responsible divisions of the ALA.

Although library systems are based on qualitative standards, librarians had long recognized the public relations value of stating these standards in quantitative terms. They found that government and community leaders could relate to standards that stated, for example, that a certain amount of "money per capita should be spent to support library services." Thus, the 1966 standards also included quantitative standards for such areas as services, materials, and staffing. These standards recommended that local community libraries be open at least six days a week and that bookmobile services be provided to areas without libraries; staff should include one-third professional and two-thirds support staff. Minimum numbers of staff were identified based on the population served. The number and types of materials to be provided were also identified by population served, and community library collections were backed up by a larger collection at the library headquarters.

These quantitative standards were not meant to be definitive, but were intended as guidelines that libraries should strive to meet. Although some libraries quickly and easily surpassed the standards, many libraries took 5 to 10 years to reach them, and others have yet to achieve them.

As librarians were striving to meet these quantitative standards, they also began to recognize that each library had its own unique characteristics that sometimes did not fit into any standard formula. The Public Library Association (PLA) assisted librarians in meeting this challenge by publishing *A Planning Process for Public Libraries* in 1980.[3] This process stressed that an analysis of an individual library and its community, by community members, library board trustees, and library staff members, could be used to help identify library needs and set directions for library services.

Although many librarians welcomed this emphasis on local community needs, they still felt a need to maintain some quantitative standards against which they could evaluate their library's level of services and materials. They recognized that many community leaders and governmental authorities were impressed by statistics such as the number of people who used the library and its materials and services. To help meet this need, the PLA published another document, *Output Measures for Public Libraries: A Manual for Standardized Procedures,* in 1987.[4] It gave specific instructions for measuring library uses, such as the number of library visits or reference questions per capita. Use of the collection was measured in circulations per capita and the turnover rate (i.e., the number of total items in the collection divided by the items checked out). Even the availability of library materials was measured to determine how many material requests were filled and how long it took to fill them. These output measures could be used in conjunction with more traditional input measures (such as the number of items added to a collection) to quantify a library's services. By comparing their own results with those from similar libraries, librarians could assess their library's effectiveness. Many states provide aid to encourage libraries to improve their standings in these measurements.

Public Library Services

Once libraries selected the roles of service they would strive to fulfill, they developed differing material collections, programs, and services within these roles to satisfy their individual communities' needs. Perhaps the greatest differences between libraries were in the variety of library collections developed to fulfill specific roles. For example, to fulfill the role of providing popular materials, some libraries developed ample collections of popular materials, and others developed ample collections for children and young adults. Still others developed ample collections of media and computers, and some developed strong collections of ethnic literature and culture. In fulfilling the formal education support center role, most libraries provided public access computers, others provided multiple or reserve copies of materials needed by schoolchildren, and still others supplied supplementary materials to their local schools for classroom use.

In addition, libraries also expanded their collections to include a wide variety of materials. The traditional print materials of books, magazines, and newspapers were expanded to include large-print books and magazines, college catalogs, pamphlets, business reports, and updated reference or financial services such as *Facts on File* and *Value Line.* Audiovisual materials became included in the mainstream of library services and were made available to patrons as readily as were print materials. Outdated audiovisual materials, such as films and records, were often replaced in the collection by audiocassette tapes, CDs, videotapes, DVDs, computers, and computer databases. Some libraries even produced their own radio and TV programs or ran their own cable TV channels to reach all segments of their populations.

Age-Specific Services

In addition to developing diverse collections to satisfy different roles of service, libraries established a variety of programs and services to meet the differing needs of various populations. For example, most public libraries provide collections, programming, and staff for children's services. Collections in these library departments usually include picture books, audiotapes and videotapes, and DVD kits, puppets, developmental toys, games, and animals (both live and stuffed). These materials are sometimes housed in separate preschool rooms, where children can climb on playscape equipment or sit quietly looking at books. They can listen to stories read aloud by their parents, watch mock puppet shows, or take part in a learning or craft activity without distracting other library patrons. Preschool story hours and puppet shows are presented to children at the library and at preschools, day care centers, and play groups. Parenting materials and child development programs also are sometimes provided.

Libraries provide programs and services for school-age children, too. In many of these libraries, circulation of all children's materials can be as much as one-third to one-half of the library's total circulation. To encourage such use, some libraries extend their former summer reading clubs to year-round programs. They combine them with contests, such as Battle of the Books, which offer prizes and awards. Regular monthly programs often feature puppet shows, magic shows, animal acts, or visiting performers.

Another group of library patrons who use the library frequently after school is teenagers from age 12 to age 17. Libraries provide programming for these young adults, which includes informational programs such as baby-sitting clinics, child development classes, homework clubs, and college entrance examination preparatory classes. Libraries also provide paperback collections containing multiple copies of books on topics of particular interest to young adults. Some libraries hire young adult librarians and establish young adult advisory councils or peer homework support groups.

Reference Services

Most public libraries emphasize reference service as one of their major roles. To support this service, libraries develop collections that contain general reference encyclopedias, directories, dictionaries, yearbooks, handbooks, atlases, and indexes. Depending on their communities' needs and interests, libraries might also develop specialized subject reference collections. These could be business and financial collections, genealogical and local history collections, or special interest collections, such as art history, hunting and fishing, or gardening and landscaping. In addition to books, many collections traditionally contain such media as weekly or daily updating services, periodicals on microform, and online and local government archives. To help their patrons use these materials more effectively, libraries provide individual or group instruction about use of the library and its collections.

Libraries also provide reference staff to help patrons locate information. Such reference help includes remote ready-reference service (via telephone, e-mail, or live chat), on-site assistance in using the library's reference tools, database searching, and securing additional information through inter-library loan. The range of services depends on the library's size and resources. Large public libraries operate banks of telephones to receive and answer many questions at one time as the staff members disseminate information located in their special-subject collections. Small libraries use computer and telephone links to headquarters or system libraries to locate answers to patrons' questions that cannot be answered using the local resources. The newest mode of reference service is e-reference, where patrons e-mail queries, complete requests on the library's Web page, or engage in online chats with reference staff members. Library staff then answer these questions electronically. Almost half of all library patrons use some form of these services.[5]

Libraries develop large collections of current fiction, including multiple copies of bestsellers and genre books, such as mysteries, graphic novels, and biographies. They also promote these materials with book lists and book discussion groups, library displays, and merchandising techniques such as face-out display shelving similar to that found in bookstores. In addition to books, other popular library collections include feature videotapes, popular as well as classical CD and DVD recordings, art prints, and sculptures. Programs for adults range from book discussions and informational lectures to how-to programs, such as cooking or photography classes, to travel-film or feature-film programs. Most libraries provide programs and services for persons with special needs, such as senior citizens or the homebound. Libraries also include materials and services for physically impaired individuals, and features such as captioned videotapes for the hearing impaired, talking books (recordings of books read aloud to the blind), Braille materials, large-print materials, and computer terminals that display text in larger fonts that are more readable to the user.

Outreach Services

Many libraries further serve the independent learning needs of their adult customers. Some librarians serve as examination proctors for distance-learning courses or make their meeting rooms available for private or group study. In cooperation with other educational institutions and community agencies, libraries help individual patrons study for credit courses or take high school equivalency tests, such as the General Education Degree (GED). Sometimes adult education classes are conducted at the library, or video courses or computer software are made available to library patrons. Also in support of adult independent learning, libraries attempt to reach beyond their traditional middle-class educated patrons to their underserved populations. In keeping with the push for national literacy, which gained momentum in the 1980s and 90s, libraries participate in adult literacy programs by providing adult basic education materials and study rooms for literacy students and their volunteer tutors. Some libraries provide foreign-language collections for their foreign-speaking populations and host classes in English as a second language. When the economic climate of their communities dictates it, some libraries establish job placement centers to help unemployed patrons.

In trying to meet the needs of their underserved populations, libraries also design outreach services for persons who cannot get to a main or branch library. Bookmobiles travel rural highways and city streets to deliver popular materials to all ages. In inner-city areas, bookmobiles are painted in bright, attractive designs and stocked with easy reading material, paperbacks, and magazines to help attract nonreaders. "Mediamobiles" tour inner-city areas to deliver library programs to children and young adults on their own street corners.

The Read Rover is a bookmobile that was specifically designed with the day care community in mind. The Read Rover, with its brightly painted kangaroo on the outside, visits day care centers, home day care providers, and pre-kindergarten classes in Baltimore County. The children come on board the truck to enjoy story time, and then the teachers or providers have a chance to select material to keep in their centers until Read Rover returns the following month.

As libraries reach out to serve these underserved patrons, many establish storefront branches or place materials collections in urban housing developments and local ethnic or senior citizen centers. Prefabricated kiosk-type libraries are erected in such diverse communities as small rural hamlets or sophisticated urban shopping malls to provide quick and easy access to library materials. Local community members staff these facilities, and foreign-language-speaking librarians develop collections and services that meet the needs of the community's various ethnic populations. In addition, libraries work with other agencies to provide voter registration, notary publics, income tax forms, tax assistance for seniors and people with low income, and health-testing programs. Libraries make their meeting rooms available for community and government organizations to present public information programs or for cultural groups to present lectures, concerts, and art exhibits.

Libraries provide community information centers to help residents find agencies that meet a variety of needs. In this role, libraries gather information about community organizations, businesses, and governmental agencies and make the information available to the public. This information often is shared with other agencies, published in directories, or made available through computer databases or Web links. Libraries work with social service, health, educational, business, governmental, and economic agencies and organizations to locate and provide information to help people resolve health, housing, family, and legal problems. As referral agents, librarians present available alternatives to patrons.

Library Management

Although many consider the public library to be an institution basic to civilization, public library collections and services are always affected by economic conditions. National and local economic recessions impact library services, as do the local community's political and social situations. As agencies that serve all persons from cradle to grave, public libraries sometimes try to be all things to all people. Public library staffs attempt to provide equal service to patrons of all ages and interest groups in their communities. They consider the ups and downs of library budgets, the availability of electronic technology, and the capabilities of networking with other libraries as they develop library programs and services to satisfy the needs of all their patrons.

Of primary importance to public libraries in the development of their programs and services is their vulnerability to economic changes in their own communities. With their almost total reliance on public property taxes, public library revenues are controlled by the allocation of tax revenue. In some states and cities, the public library's ability to increase tax revenue is limited by legal or political considerations. In others, libraries have to appeal to the voters to get approval for increasing their tax limits, and these appeals are not always successful. To minimize their dependence on such sources, libraries have begun to explore additional sources of income and to develop creative and innovative sources to finance their services and programs.

Public libraries in growing communities have begun collecting developer impact fees from real estate developers to help finance library services to owners of new residences. Libraries have joined the Public Library Foundation or similar investment pools to increase the interest paid on their library funds. Many

Figure 3.1. Friends' groups help to support a library through promotion, fund raising, and by increasing the level of community involvement.

libraries have formed nonprofit Friends of the Library support groups (see figure 3.1). Such organizations conduct used-book sales, library auctions, or sales of library-related merchandise to raise additional funds. A few libraries even allow profit-making ventures, such as restaurants or friends-of-the library-operated retail shops, within the library building. Such activities serve to raise the library's visibility in the community, as well as garner some supplemental financial support.

Overdue fees, charged by a majority of public libraries, have been increased, and many libraries charge higher or additional processing fees for lost items. To help ease their economic plight, some libraries have initiated fees for formerly free services, such as placing book reserves and inter-library loans. Others also charge fees for expensive services, such as database searches, or the loan of premium materials, such as DVDs, best sellers, and equipment. These latter fees cause considerable debate within the library profession. Opponents of such fees claim that the income raised from them is not a sufficient reason to deny access to library materials and services to patrons who cannot afford them. In the final analysis, the revenues raised from all of these various methods account for only a small portion of the average public library's budget. Furthermore, libraries must be careful not to get involved with revenue schemes that can divert more staff time and energy from the direct provision of services than can be replaced in terms of additional revenue.

Cooperative library networks have had a positive effect on the ability of libraries to stretch their budgets and share their resources. By sharing the costs of automation technology, even small libraries can afford to join bibliographic cooperatives with circulation, cataloging, and inter-library loan capabilities. Regional and statewide resource networks allow these libraries to share their materials and services with other libraries as materials are sent from library to library by van delivery systems and mail systems. Increasingly, these delivery systems are supplemented by facsimile and online computer transmissions. In addition to exchanging materials, libraries exchange their patrons, too.

Reciprocal borrowing agreements among libraries enable patrons to visit and check out materials at other libraries throughout a regional system or state. Another benefit to cooperative agreements is that patrons can use computers, either in the library or in their homes, to see which libraries have the materials they want and whether the materials are available. All types of libraries participate in many such cooperative networks. Therefore, public libraries are able to provide the desired service to all, and, at the same time, expand the resources to which their primary clients have access.

In providing library service to all of their patrons, library administrators and their staffs take great care to ensure that everyone is treated alike—whether the patron is a city council member, a library board trustee, or a young child. Library governing boards generally adopt the ALA *Library Bill of Rights* (see appendix B) and the American Film and Video Association's *Freedom to Read and View* statements and institute policies and procedures to protect the freedom of intellectual inquiry for their patrons. Such policies include free access to the library's collections by children and also provide protection of patron records from public inquiry.

Staffing

As libraries develop new roles and goals of service, their staffing needs change. Computer literacy to varying degrees has become essential in almost every position. Children's staff have been expanded to include specialists who are knowledgeable about the psychological and educational growth and development of their patrons. Filling these changing staff positions, however, is often difficult. The supply and demand of such specialties is not always well balanced. These library staffing needs vary greatly depending upon the size of a library and its location. Public libraries range from one- or two-person branches to main libraries with 50 to 100 staff members. Medium-to-large libraries usually have a large range of library positions at all levels filled with appropriately trained personnel. They might have many specialized librarians responsible for administration, reference and readers' advisory services, collection development, and programming. Paraprofessional library technicians and clerical staff perform supportive tasks in such areas as access services, children's services, bookmobiles, outreach, and technical services.

Smaller libraries might have only one or two librarians to handle reference and children's services. In very small libraries, branches, or on bookmobiles, staff members tend to be generalists who share all the jobs from checking out materials to helping people find books. There may not be a great differentiation between library positions in these very small libraries, and the person in charge may be a technician with or without formal library education.

As libraries grow in size and complexity, their staff members tend to become more specialized in their responsibilities and their job classifications more distinct. Many of these staff members have advanced education, although they might not have masters' degrees in library science. Their education and training is often in specialties other than library science. Graphic artists, TV technicians, computer programmers, and specialists in information science or public relations are just a few of the varied types of personnel found in public libraries. There is also a very definite pattern of specialization among library personnel in larger library systems.

It is not unusual for library employees to work many years in one particular area of either public or technical services. For example, in the circulation department, one clerk may be responsible for reserves, one for overdue collections, one for stacks maintenance, and others for checking materials in and out. These clerks may be supervised by a library technician or by a librarian, and they may also be supported by library pages or shelvers.

To organize these varied staff members most effectively, public library administrators need to examine and evaluate their personnel policies and procedures. Library administrators recognize that they should take the personal needs of their staff members into account as they design these policies. Nowhere is this need more evident than in scheduling staff for the public service desks. It is not unusual for a public library to be open from 9:00 A.M. to 9:00 P.M., Monday through Friday, 9:00 A.M. to 5:00 P.M. on Saturday, and 1:00 P.M. to 5:00 P.M. on Sunday. Library administrators and supervisors find it challenging to schedule the 60- to 80-hour weeks that require one and one-half to two separate staffs working 40 hours each. In addition to making sure the library is well staffed, supervisors try to consider their staff members' personal preferences for the hours they work.

Many recent developments in public libraries have centered on the revolutionary impact of the World Wide Web on information exchange. Two of these events, e-rate legislation and the involvement of the Gates Foundation, have been highly visible factors in helping extend access to the Web to almost every public library in the country. This almost universal implementation of this transforming technology has led to one of the dominant public debates of recent times—to filter or not to filter public access Internet terminals. That issue is discussed later in chapter 8.

The E-rate

E-rate, or education rate discounts on telecommunications charges, was established as part of the balancing act when the Telecommunications Act of 1996 deregulated many of the services of telecommunications carriers. According to the ALA, more than 30,000 schools and libraries soon completed the application process to benefit from the fund, which was set up to ensure universal access to the Web.[6] E-rate was funded by some of the windfall profits realized by telecommunications companies as a result of partial deregulation of their operations set forth in the Telecommunications Act.

E-rate is certainly no panacea, but it is another revenue stream that can make a critical difference in funding, because the deepest discounts go to the most needy schools and libraries. In 1996, only one in seven public library systems was able to offer public access to the Web, with the primary obstacle to providing Internet access being the ongoing cost of telecommunications charges.[7]

A sampling of the 30,000 e-rate applications shows 33 percent for telecommunications services, 4.4 percent for Internet access, and 63 percent for inside wiring. The latter is not surprising given the number of classrooms that lack Internet access. More than 50 percent of discount requests for internal connections come from the neediest schools and libraries eligible for 80–90 percent discounts....FCC [Federal Communications Commission] rules prohibit discounts from being spent on workstations, applications software, training, or other purposes.[8]

E-rate has made a valuable contribution to our society because the public library is often the Internet option of last resort for those who do not have access at home or at work.

The Gates Foundation

The Gates Library Foundation has provided a nice counterbalance to e-rate. Although the amount of money provided does not approach the $2 billion generated by e-rate, the foundation does provide a source of funds to pay for the items that e-rate does not provide. During the first round of funding, the foundation worked with approximately 1,000 libraries, with a special emphasis on those serving low-income communities. Grants were used to provide new computers for library patrons and for staff technical training and support. First-year grants ranged from $4,000 for a small rural library requiring only one computer to $30,000 or more for larger library buildings that received 10 or more computers. Like e-rate, the foundation targeted libraries in the most needy states and communities, using U.S. Census statistics and a study conducted by the ALA on public libraries and poverty to establish eligibility guidelines.[9]

Public Library Use

Are public libraries used now, and will they be needed in the future? Evidence is accumulating that public libraries are not just surviving; they are thriving in the 21st century in spite of—or because of—the Internet. A September 2008 Harris Poll revealed the following findings:

- 68 percent of Americans have a library card—up from 66 percent in 2006 and the highest since this started being measured in 1990.
- 76 percent of card holders visited their local library in the past year.
- In that same time period, 41 percent of card holders visited the Web site of their local library—up from 23.6 percent in 2006.

Americans say they view their local library as:

- an important education resource (92 %);
- a pillar of the community (72 %);
- a community center (71 %);
- a family destination (70 %); and
- a cultural center (69 %).

In the 2008 report of the ALA on the State of American's Libraries, the association stated,

Libraries play a key role in learning and development: Public libraries are engines of economic growth, studies show, libraries provide an excellent return on investment, have a measurable positive impact on the local economy and contribute to the stability, safety and quality of life of their neighborhoods. Specifically:

- Americans check out more than 2 billion items each year from their public libraries; the average user takes out more than seven books a year
- Patrons also go to their libraries to borrow DVDs, learn new computer skills, conduct job searches and participate in the activities of local community organizations
- Average cost to the taxpayer for these services is $31 a year
- New studies show that the nation's public libraries are engines of economic growth, contributing to local neighborhood and community development through early literacy programs, employment services, and small business information resources. [10]

Later that year, as the economy soured, ALA President James Rettig added, "As the nation continues to experience a downturn in the economy, libraries are providing the tools needed to help Americans get back on their feet. From free homework help to assisting with resumes and job searches, now more than ever libraries are proving they are valued and trusted resources."[11]

Whether public libraries will continue to succeed in meeting patron needs is subject to conjecture. Visions of the public library in the year 2025 range from the library as a fully automated and robotized institution to one that completely disappears. Some library futurists see the library as a place where wondrous and exotic adventures can be experienced, whereas others see it replaced by home access to information and entertainment.[12] However, whether the public library as we knew it in the last century will survive until 2025 will depend greatly on the effort, imagination, and perseverance of everyone connected with it, from the library board and director to the newest library clerk.

There should be openings for those seeking jobs in public libraries in the next decade. Between 2002 and 2007 the number of individuals employed in public libraries increased by 8.9 percent. Whether or not that trend continues, the baby boom bulge in retirements is expected to significantly thin the ranks. Of those librarians employed in public libraries in 2007, one-third of them expected to leave by 2012, and one-half of current incumbents expected to leave by 2017.[13] Similar statistics are not available for those in nonlibrarian positions, but it is not unreasonable to expect similar turnover in those positions.

SCHOOL LIBRARY MEDIA CENTERS

A school library is an integral part of a school that educates students in kindergarten through the twelfth grade. School libraries may be either private or public and are frequently called library media centers or school media centers.

These libraries, as well as academic libraries, are responsible for supporting the curriculum of the institutions to which they belong. Improving basic literacy is a key function of the library media center. In addition, school libraries also share with academic libraries the responsibility for promoting information literacy. It is important for library staff members in schools and academic libraries to teach students the process of how to find and evaluate the information they need, rather than to find the information for them. This process is essential for students if they are to become lifelong learners and function effectively as citizens in the economic and political arenas.

In many of today's schools, a well-run library media center may very well be the most active room in the entire school. Individual children go there to choose books, use computers, view DVDs, or listen to audio materials. Entire classes go to learn how to use the media center or to locate information for their reports. Groups of students may come for help in making *PowerPoint* presentations, designing Web pages, or producing videos for class projects. Professional librarians or media specialists, library media technicians, and clerks assist these students. These active media centers have shown how important they can be in a modern educational system. Yet it is amazing that school library media centers have taken so long to become basic parts of the educational institutions of this country.

The Beginnings

Not until the 1950s did most secondary schools have libraries, and even in the 1970s many elementary school libraries were just getting started. What took the educational system so long to recognize that libraries are necessary components of the educational process? The answer to this question lies in the schools' educational goals and methods. In the early centuries of our country's history, school consisted primarily of students memorizing information presented by a teacher. There were few textbooks, and students were not encouraged to become intellectually curious. In the 19th century and the early part of the 20th century, emphasis was on subject content, which was mainly learned from textbooks. In the 1920s and 1930s, the emphasis shifted to the learner, and finally, in the 1940s, the emphasis was placed on life adjustment and the education of all youth for their future roles.[14]

However, the space race of the 1950s and 1960s placed new emphasis on subject mastery so that U.S. education would be equal to education in the Soviet Union. To achieve this end, the 1960s emphasized the education of individual students according to their needs and abilities to prepare them for participation in American society. Unfortunately, economics often prevented schools and libraries from meeting these commendable goals. The situation became so grave that the U.S. National Commission on Excellence in Education published a report, *A Nation at Risk,* in 1983 that identified the United States as just that. This report determined that the United States had let its formal educational system deteriorate to a very dangerous level.[15] In response to this report, librarians drafted *Alliance for Excellence,* a statement that identified the important steps school libraries should take to reverse this deterioration process.[16]

Standards

At the turn of the 20th century, accreditation associations provided the major impetus for the development of centralized secondary or high school libraries. The purpose of these associations was to rate high schools so that colleges could compare graduates of one high school with graduates of another. Because libraries were included in the criteria listed by the associations, schools that wanted to become accredited had to develop libraries that met the standards of the accrediting associations.

In the 1920s, accrediting associations and the ALA began to develop standards for school libraries. However, these standards were not widely adopted. Instead, the major type of library service that schools provided, particularly below the high school level, consisted of traveling library collections from state agencies. In many cases, public libraries provided school collections to classrooms and public librarians who visited the schools. Sometimes the public library was actually part of the school system or housed branches in the school buildings. These services seemed to be satisfactory for those school systems that still considered learning to be largely classroom oriented.

As educators in the 1940s began to recognize that students should be involved in the discovery of learning based on study and inquiry, they realized also that library services and materials were needed to support the expanded curriculum. To help identify needed library services and materials, the ALA published standards for school library service in 1944, entitled *School Libraries for Today and Tomorrow*.[17] The ALA also identified qualitative and quantitative standards for library resources and services that should be provided by a professional staff in a centralized library. Although these standards were applied in some high schools, very few elementary school libraries were established, and, on the whole, the concept of library services envisioned by the standards was seldom implemented.

To encourage library development, in 1956 the ALA published a policy statement that identified the important role the school library should play in a school's total instructional process. For the first time, the library was envisioned as a central school library that included all types of learning materials available to both students and teachers. The concepts of this statement were translated into new standards, *Standards for School Library Programs*, in 1960.[18] Adoption of these standards was greatly facilitated by the country's interest in the educational system after the Russian satellite *Sputnik* was launched in 1957. In addition, the National Defense Education Act (NDEA) of 1958 provided funds for schools to buy print and nonprint materials and equipment. Some states also used these funds to hire school library supervisors at the state level to help local libraries purchase these materials.

The standards helped usher in a new era for library services. Educators began to recognize that libraries should be an integral part of the educational curriculum. Central libraries that contained all types of learning materials began to be developed in elementary, junior, and senior high schools. Librarians were recognized as teachers whose subject specialty enabled them to help students and teachers use such materials as books, audiotapes, records, films, filmstrips, transparencies, and programmed instruction. These materials were used in both the classroom and the library to help students learn. The concept of a school library changed to that of instructional materials center (IMC), where many learning activities took place simultaneously.

In an IMC, students and teachers could listen to or view the library's media, or they could produce their own. Students and teachers could also work in the library on group projects, hold meetings in its conference rooms, or study independently in the quiet areas. Library technical and clerical staff were hired to provide instruction in the use of the library and its resources or to help students learn independently. Librarians were able to perform such professional tasks as offer in-service training to teachers in the use of audiovisual materials and equipment. They became active members of curriculum committees and teaching teams. In many school districts the modern school library finally arrived in the 1960s.

With IMCs well on their way to becoming part of many local school systems, new standards were proposed in 1969 by the American Association of School Librarians (AASL) and the Association of Educational Communications and Technology (AECT). These *Standards for School Media Centers* carried the IMC concept one step further.[19] They proposed that schools develop media programs and services that integrated all types of media into the curriculum based on their contributions to the educational program of the school, rather than on their formats. The standards also proposed replacing the terms *library, librarian, audiovisual center,* and *audiovisual specialist* with the new terms *media center* and *media specialist* to better identify the integration of all forms of media.

From Library to Library Media Center

The concept of a media center caused great consternation in the educational and library worlds in the 1960s and 70s. Many school systems enthusiastically endorsed this concept and combined their library, audiovisual, video, and graphics operations and programs into one media department. Titles for such new departments varied from "media center" and "library media center" to "learning resource center", "instructional media center", "instructional resource center", or "resource center". However, no matter what their titles were, they all attempted to provide the media services recommended in the standards. Other librarians and audiovisual specialists had difficulty adjusting to this new concept, which required them to alter their thinking and their focus. Often, they, as well as many educators, believed that the standards were utopian rather than practicable. To add to this confusion, the economic crisis of the 1970s practically wiped out the federal monies that had been used to develop library services. To provide direction in this chaotic time, the AASL and AECT published new standards in 1975.

The 1975 standards, *Media Programs, District and School,* expanded the concept of media programs beyond the individual school to include services and facilities that could be provided at the district level.[20] The standards were based on the principle that media were a central part of the learning process and that if schools were to meet students' needs, they must provide quality media programs. These programs were seen to be a combination of district-wide and building-level services tailored to fit the educational goals and objectives of each individual school system. Although quantitative standards were included, the emphasis was on the qualitative aspect of the programs.

This emphasis was extended in 1988 with AASL's and AECT's publication of *Information Power: Guidelines for School Library Media Programs.* These standards responded to issues that had been raised in the U.S. National

School library media services

1. Offers a sequential program of library skills instruction.
2. Coordinates library skills instruction with classroom instruction.
3. Informally instructs students in the use of various types of materials and equipment.
4. Conducts in-service education for teachers in the effective evaluation, selection, and use of media.
5. Assists curriculum committee in selecting appropriate materials and media program activities for resource units and curriculum guides.
6. Helps individual teachers to coordinate media program activities and resources with subject areas, units, and textbooks.
7. Helps teachers to develop, select, implement, and evaluate learning activities requiring various types of media.
8. Provides teachers with information about new educational and media developments.
9. Provides reference assistance to teachers.
10. Assists students in locating information and resources valuable to their educational needs and to the growth of their personal interests and ability.
11. Helps students and teachers find and use relevant information sources outside the school.
12. Provides inter-library loan services to students.
13. Provides inter-library loan services to teachers.
14. Provides reading/listening/viewing guidance to students.
15. Helps parents realize the importance of assisting their children to understand the benefits of reading, listening, and viewing for pleasure as well as for gaining information.
16. Coordinates in-school production of materials required for instructional use and other activities.
17. Provides technical assistance to students in the production of materials.
18. Provides technical assistance to teachers in the production of materials.
19. Coordinates textbook selection, ordering, and distribution program in school.
20. Coordinates school-operated radio station.
21. Coordinates video production activities in school.
22. Coordinates cable or other TV transmission and utilization activities in school.

From *Information Power: Guidelines for School Library Media Programs.* Reprinted by permission of AASL, Appendix A, p. 1160. © 1988 by ALA.

Commission on Excellence in Education's report, *A Nation at Risk,* and answered in librarians' *Alliance for Excellence* statement.[21] In particular, *Alliance for Excellence* identified important steps that school library supporters should take to develop quality library services and resources for every school library. For example, the statement said that libraries should incorporate their services and resource collections into their schools' curricula. They should provide access to, and instruction in the use of, information resources both within and outside the library. Each library should be well funded and staffed by well-educated and well-paid library media specialists. These library media professionals would actively indoctrinate teachers and administrators in the appropriate role and activities of the school library.

Information Power provided the guidelines and directives to help library media personnel carry out these recommended steps. The publication described the library media program's vital role in helping students gain the information skills they needed to function in a learning society. The document's primary focus was to help the building-level library media specialist develop a team partnership with administrators and teachers to identify and establish the best instructional programs.

The guidelines reinforced the role of the library media specialist as that of an information specialist, teacher, and instructional consultant working with teachers to fulfill curriculum needs. Access to information outside the library would be provided via inter-library loans, multi-library networks, and electronic technologies. A strong emphasis on intellectual freedom and intellectual access to diverse viewpoints was also encouraged. Finally, extensive guidelines were presented for the development of library media facilities designed specifically to serve individual school and curriculum needs.

Implementation of these guidelines was affected by both the educational and economic conditions. The majority of teachers continued to rely on lecturing that did not require strong library media support. In addition, many administrators and teachers did not expect much involvement by library media specialists in the school's educational process. In such an educational climate, some school library media specialists felt uncomfortable adopting these new roles and becoming agents of change. The economic climate was also not conducive to the development of such comprehensive school library media programs. Although *A Nation at Risk* recognized the need for a strong educational program, local communities were often reluctant to finance such programs. To encourage these communities to implement strong school library media programs, most states adopted statewide school library media standards by 1990. Many of these states required local schools to meet these guidelines if they wanted to receive state or federal monies. Strong regional accreditation associations also encouraged the development of strong library media programs through their accreditation standards and local self-study requirements.

Library Media Programs

Although state and national guidelines have had some impact on the development of school library media programs, such development has also been

strongly influenced by the philosophies, objectives, and economics of the individual school systems served. In many school systems, the library media
programs not only stopped growing during the late 1980s and 90s, but also
began to stagnate or shrink. In other school systems with excellent educational programs, outstanding library media programs were developed. These
superior library media programs are no accident, however. The more successful and effective programs are based on stated philosophies and objectives
carefully designed by everyone concerned. Library media center staff, administrators, teachers, students, and parents have worked together, sometimes in
advisory committees, to develop library media programs and activities to meet
the needs of individual students.

Many of the resources provided in library media centers now include much
more than the traditional print and film resources of the 1970s. Many books,
magazines, newspapers, pamphlets, and catalogs are also available in foreign
languages or in formats that students with disabilities can use. Multimedia
formats include art prints, realia, compact and laser discs, and, more recently,
DVDs. Technological advancements have also enabled library media centers to
provide access to information in new ways. Many library media centers provide
computers for the students' use as well as for computer-assisted instruction
and computer-based catalogs. Library media centers provide online access to
local, regional, and national union library catalogs and bibliographic and full-
text databases. Some centers provide cable television, interactive video, and
satellite and online distance learning programs.

To make these library media resources more readily available to students
and teachers within the schools, library media centers adopt flexible scheduling to accommodate both classes and individualized instruction. They expand their programs to include access to resources outside the school. Library
media centers have joined with other schools and other types of libraries in
networks and consortia to share their resources through inter-library loan
networks; access to special collections, such as film collections; and facsimile
transmission of materials, such as magazine articles. Access to other collections is extended through direct loans to schools, student access to other
libraries, and cooperative collection development.

In addition, businesses and corporations have become involved in local
adopt-a-school programs to help schools and library media centers expand
their programs. Some national companies, such as Apple and IBM, offer educational discounts and programs. Other corporations make news broadcasts
on channels such as CNN (Cable News Network) and Channel One available to
schools without cost. Through these and other cooperative activities, library
media specialists find that they can stretch their budgets. At the same time,
this increased access to additional resources and information expands the
library media program's impact on the educational process.

This impact is further heightened by library media specialists, who take
on the roles of teacher, information specialist, and instructional consultant.
As teachers and instructional consultants, library media specialists not only
teach library skills, but also work with teachers to integrate these skills into
curriculum projects. Many of these specialists not only develop computer laboratories, but also teach students, teachers, administrators, and parents how
to use these resources. Specialists work with students and teachers to develop

such resources as independent learning programs or packages on specialized subjects using all types of media. Games and kits are developed and produced by students and teachers to encourage students to think.

As information specialists, library media specialists also work with teachers to emphasize literature and the enjoyment of reading. Programs such as reading incentive programs, reading clubs, and contests are developed with teachers, administrators, parents, and other libraries to encourage and reward students for increasing their reading. To further encourage participation in these programs and to disseminate information about the total library media program, media specialists also publicize their programs through newsletters and public relations campaigns.

The library media center itself is also changing. Many school systems with more than one school have established library media programs at the district level to assist the building-level library media center staff. In such systems, district library media centers often provide centralized services such as ordering, cataloging, and processing; graphic production and duplication; television or radio production; and the distribution of expensive media collections, such as films, kits, and live animal exhibits. In the 1980s and 90s, these services were automated and expanded to include the centralization of other library operations, such as circulation, media bookings, and bibliographic and administrative support. The district library media staff also helps building-level library media personnel develop programs to meet the educational goals of their individual schools.

The organization of building-level library media centers depends upon the educational programs of the schools they serve. Some library media centers are centralized in one geographic area, whereas others have a central library media center supported by satellite subject resource centers. These satellite centers may be adjacent to the central facility or adjacent to classes in their subject areas in other parts of the building. Some schools adopt an open concept of learning that produces media centers without walls. Others develop library media centers that include small rooms for study groups as well as classrooms large enough for coordinated library-subject instruction. However, it is not the pattern of organization alone but the program's ability to become fully integrated into the school's curriculum that determines how effective such a program is.

Library Media Personnel

The development of quality library media programs depends on the development of qualified library media staff to direct and operate these programs. Most states require that teacher-certified personnel must be in charge whenever children are present. Thus, teacher-certified library media specialists staff the majority of library media centers. These specialists usually have either an M.L.S. degree or a master's of educational media degree, and many work under district media coordinators. Some media staffs also include other professionals with varied backgrounds and experiences. At the building level, media specialists often work outside the media center as integral members of the educational staff.

In fact, the success of the library media program in each school often depends on the specialist's acceptance by the other teachers as an important member of the educational team. For specialists to be able to fulfill this role beyond the walls of the library, they need well-trained paraprofessionals and clerical staff who are capable of operating the library hour by hour or even day by day—freeing the specialist to participate in school activities beyond the physical library. Librarians plan services and coordinate programs with their staff and with teachers and administrators. When such a team is in place, students learn.

However, the commitment to adhere to professional standards for certification varies considerably from state to state. For example, although 77 percent of the public school head librarians in the United States are state certified, the percentage of public school head librarians who are certified by their states as librarian media specialists varies from a low of 25 percent in California to a high of 90 percent or more in Alabama, Arkansas, Georgia, Kansas, Kentucky, Missouri, Nebraska, North Carolina, South Carolina, South Dakota, Tennessee, Virginia, and Wisconsin.[22]

Funding for hiring librarians for school libraries also varies widely from community to community and from state to state:

> In 1995, public schools nationwide employed an average of only two librarians for every 100 teachers. Wyoming (2.03), Alaska (1.99), and Colorado (1.98) were the most typical states in this regard. Arkansas and Montana topped the list at approximately three-and-a half (3.60 and 3.45, respectively) librarians per 100 teachers. California ranked lowest in this statistic, with less than one librarian for every 100 teachers (0.39 per 100).[23]

Readers are advised to check the situation in their own localities.

As library media specialists become more successful in their educational role, they turn the day-to-day operations of the library media center over to their support staff. Encouraged by national and state guidelines, many schools develop full-time media center staff based on a ratio of one specialist to one technician and one clerk. At the building level, this means that library media technicians often supervise clerks, students, and volunteers in checking materials in and out. Library media technicians also supervise building resource centers that are separate from the main library media center. In some smaller schools, library media technicians operate building-level media centers under the direction of a system-wide media specialist.

In larger school systems, staff in the building-level library media centers are often backed by district library media staff who provide further professional or technical expertise. Specialists and technicians in such specialized areas as graphics, television, cable, audiovisual production, and computer technology can be found in district library media centers. These staff members produce resource materials to be used in classrooms and building-level media centers. District-wide processing centers provide centralized support staff to order and process materials for the individual media centers. Centralized booking services for films and computerized learning are usually staffed by clerks, technicians, or both, as are many of the centralized automation services.

Although many of the technical duties in these library media centers require specialized skills (e.g., computer literacy), formal library training has not always been a prerequisite for library media clerical and technical personnel. This was due in some cases to the economic recession of the 1980s, which saw the decline of library media technician training programs. In other cases, it was because of the constant availability in earlier years of a large pool of untrained but talented workers. These workers were usually homemakers willing to volunteer or work at very low wages so they could have work hours and vacations that coincided with the schedules of other family members. However, the economic need for people to earn more than the minimum wage has almost eliminated this pool of workers. Thus, if school library media centers are going to meet their growing need for library media support staff with more specialized skills, they will have to change their hiring patterns. They will have to seek out and pay well-trained technical and clerical staff to fulfill their schools' missions.

Library Media Centers Help Students Achieve

Emphasis on accountability in education is receiving increasing emphasis. Generally, the method used to establish this accountability is to link performance on standardized tests with rewards and/or penalties for schools. Early in the administration of President George W. Bush, *The No Child Left Behind Act of 2001* was passed. Although this law remains controversial, one of its major aims was to establish such a system. A growing body of research supports the long-held intuitive belief that good library media centers have a positive impact on student performance on such tests.

Apparently, there is no substitute for professionally prepared librarians backed by well-trained LTAs and clerks. And the level of professional preparation really does matter. Four decades ago, Lucille Wert established that school librarians who held an M.L.S. offered more services and spent less time performing housekeeping tasks than did those who had undergraduate minors in library science and teaching credentials.[24] More recently, Lance and associates correlated these services and staff qualifications statistics with significantly higher student performance:

> Students in schools with appropriate and sufficient library collections and qualified library personnel tend to perform better on standardized tests, especially in reading, according to studies of school library programs in Alaska, Colorado, and Pennsylvania. Making the school library an integral learning center and encouraging teachers and librarians to collaborate on lesson plans and classroom assignments could help raise student achievement, the report suggests.[25]

When library media center "predictors are maximized (e.g., staffing, expenditures, and information resources and technology), CSAP reading scores tend to run 18 percent higher in fourth grade and 10 to 15 percent higher in seventh."[26] These predictors of academic achievement cannot be explained away by

- school differences, including:
- school district expenditures per pupil,

- teacher/pupil ratio,
- the average years of experience of classroom teachers, and
- their average salaries; or
- community differences, including:
- adult educational attainment,
- children in poverty, or
- racial/ethnic demographics.[27]

These results would appear to provide powerful ammunition to secure increased resources for school library media centers; however, that outcome is yet to be achieved in the political arena.

Library educator and consultant Ester G. Smith more recently extended these findings, "that while socioeconomic and school variables have the greatest impact on student achievement, library media program components explained a significant portion of the variance in state-wide...testing."[28] More specifically Smith showed that:

> library media program variables explained 3.4 % of the variance in...reading and 3.2% in...language arts performance at the elementary level.
>
> At the middle/junior high school level they explained 9.2% of the variance in...reading performance.
>
> At the high school level, they explained 7.9% of the...reading variance and an even higher percentage—19%—of the...language arts variance. At the high school level, the impact of a quality library media program was almost 7 percentage points greater than the impact of the socioeconomic variables.
>
> Programs that were well staffed, especially programs that had full-time professional and support staff, exhibited a greater impact on student academic performance.[29]

Taken together, studies from 16 states have shown similar findings about the power of school libraries.[30]

ACADEMIC LIBRARIES

Academic libraries are found in public and private post-secondary institutions of higher education—that is, colleges and universities. Although logic might lead one to consider high school libraries to be academic libraries, they do not fit within this definition. The mission of an academic library is to support the faculty, students, and staff of the college or university and in so doing help achieve the mission of the parent institution within which the library is located. This mission varies considerably from institution to institution.

For example, a community college has the mission to teach lower-division undergraduate students (i.e., students in their first two years of college). The curriculum generally includes academic programs to prepare students to transfer to upper-division programs at four-year colleges as well as vocational training programs to prepare students for direct entry into the workforce.

As junior colleges have evolved into colleges of the community and for the community, their missions have expanded to include support of community economic development and support of lifelong learning, including emeritus courses for seniors. Thus, the mission of the community college library has also expanded from that of just classroom support to include service to the community users enrolled in noncredit courses and other tailor-made training courses. Distance learning courses are expanding and challenging libraries to keep pace with the information needs of geographically scattered students.

The library of a four-year institution, including those with graduate degree programs, will have a much different focus than a two-year college library. The funding levels, scope of collections, and often highly technical materials will contrast greatly with a community college facility. A large university will maintain many separate departmental libraries (e.g., biological sciences, music, art, business) and may also have distinctive library facilities serving undergraduates and graduates. At times these branch libraries will resemble special libraries (discussed in the next section) as much as they do traditional academic libraries.

An important development that had it roots in the 1970s, but did not fully blossom until the 1990s, is that of academic libraries changing from storehouses of books to learning and research centers, providing access to information in all of its varied forms. Previously, an academic library's volume count had defined prestige. By the turn of the 21st century, access to, rather than ownership of, information resources had become the criterion against which academic libraries were being measured. With this change came a change in library services and the roles of staff within academic libraries.

Types of Academic Libraries

The library world, as mentioned previously, defines an academic library as a library in an institution that provides education beyond the high school level. This level of education is called post-secondary or higher education. There are more than 3,600 libraries at this level in the United States. They are found in four-year colleges and universities, community colleges, junior colleges, and technical institutions. The number and levels of degrees granted by an academic institution greatly impact its library development.

Within higher education circles, institutions are categorized using the Carnegie Classification, which has evolved over the past three decades. The 2000 version of this system has the following major categories:

- Doctoral/research universities
- Master's colleges and universities
- Baccalaureate colleges
- Associate's colleges
- Specialized institutions
- Theological seminaries and other specialized faith-related institutions
- Medical schools and medical centers

- Other separate health profession schools
- Schools of engineering and technology
- Schools of business and management
- Schools of art, music, and design
- Schools of law
- Teachers' colleges
- Other specialized institutions
- Tribal colleges and universities[31]

These classifications attempt to describe the breadth and depth of programs. Some institutions seem to straddle two or more classifications. In fact, doctoral/research universities are likely to include many of the other categories within their structure. However, the purpose of including this taxonomy here is not to discuss such fine distinctions, but to highlight the different philosophies of library service that may be appropriate within the range of categories.

Although community service is at least paid lip service in the mission statements of all levels and categories of higher education, this role generally does relatively little to shape the basic collections and services of academic libraries. What really defines the different approaches taken by academic libraries is the extent to which their parent institutions emphasize the creation of new knowledge.

All educational institutions are engaged in disseminating knowledge to their students. However, some colleges and universities have an expectation that new knowledge will also be created and added to the knowledge base of humankind. The extent to which an institution focuses on this mission will affect its library in two distinct ways. Supporting cutting-edge researchers in a discipline calls for very different collections and services than does supporting novice learners in that same discipline. Researchers at the leading edge of their specialty need to know everything possible about their specialty, including what has happened in the last five minutes. This requires very specialized sources of information not just for the discipline, but also for the narrow sub-discipline within which the scholar is working.

Therefore, library collections of millions of volumes are not uncommon. Information sources are generally specialized refereed journals, and even these do not publish new results fast enough to be of great use to those dedicated to enhancing the knowledge bases of their fields. Scholars do not want to waste their time duplicating work that, unknown to them, has just been completed by another researcher somewhere in the world.

Lower-division undergraduates, on the other hand, are just assimilating an overview of their discipline and some of its basic vocabulary and concepts. They need much more basic information than leading-edge researchers. One of the myths of academic librarianship is that if you have a collection rich enough to support researchers, you must have more than enough resources to satisfy the needs of the undergraduates studying that same discipline. This is not the case. Undergraduates are not generally prepared to understand and benefit from the highly technical vocabulary and specialized context of discourse at the leading edge of their disciplines. At this stage in their learning experience, a much smaller but tailored collection, measured in tens of thousands, may be most appropriate for lower-division undergraduates; for upper-division under-graduates, a library collection of a few hundred thousand appropriate volumes may suffice. Support for the curriculum being taught in the classrooms is the measure of a good library at this level.

Faculty roles, and, therefore, librarian roles differ within these institutions as well. Within the community colleges, faculty assignments are weighted al-most exclusively toward classrooms and laboratories. Evaluation of instruc-tors is centered on how well they help students learn—as are rewards, such as promotion and tenure. In research universities, faculty members are expected to bring exciting new nuggets from their research to class to enhance the learning environment. Evaluations leading to promotion, tenure, or termina-tion are focused on progress in research and publication. Although lip service is paid to student learning, it is truly a publish or perish world.

If librarians have faculty status, then these same expectations carry over to them as well. In an undergraduate college that is focused almost exclusively on teaching and learning, librarians have educational backgrounds compara-ble to those of classroom faculty. The role each plays in helping students learn is also similar. In this environment, it is appropriate for librarians to share the same status and meet the same performance expectations.

The college library staff is generally much smaller than that of a university library. College libraries are likely to be staffed by 5 to 10 professionals who are supported by paraprofessional, clerical, and student personnel. Univer-sity libraries require many more, often highly specialized, staff members to acquire, process, and disseminate the information contained in much larger collections, which can range from several hundred thousand to millions of volumes. These larger libraries may be staffed by as few as 25 and as many as several hundred professional, associate, technical, and clerical personnel who are supported by sometimes hundreds of student helpers. Also, university li-braries generally have large collections in almost every subject area, whereas college libraries tend to concentrate on the general arts and sciences with a strong emphasis on humanities, social sciences, and the physical and biologi-cal sciences.

Development of College and University Libraries

The majority of academic libraries began as mere adjuncts to the class-room, housed in small rooms and administered by part-time faculty members. Further library development was accelerated by the rapid expansion of the world's known information. As late as the 1920s, even the largest university libraries were no bigger than those of a modern-day medium-sized college. As published knowledge began to expand rapidly, academic libraries expanded their collections accordingly. During the mid-20th century, the collections of research university libraries doubled every 17 to 20 years. The large influx of students after World War II, largely funded by veterans' benefits, also placed a demand on libraries to provide materials in great quantities.

A typical academic library of the 1950s would have contained only print ma-terials (books, serials, and pamphlets) housed in an architectural monument named after some benefactor. Universities often kept most of their collections in closed stack areas, to which only graduate students and faculty members were admitted. Undergraduates had to ask for books at a circulation desk and wait for the materials to be paged or delivered to them. Many universities attempted to help the first- and second-year students adjust to the wealth of library materials by providing separate undergraduate libraries.

The primary objective of academic libraries was to contribute to the goals and philosophy of the academic institutions the libraries served. Because the academic institutions were still largely faculty, graduate student, and research oriented, library objectives also leaned in that direction, rather than focusing directly on the students' need for support of classroom learning.

The sudden increase of published information made it clear that no library could meet all of the needs of their faculty and students. This encouraged co-operation with other libraries so that mutually they could strengthen library resources available to all. Still, the inter-library loan process mainly targeted faculty and graduate students. Undergraduate students rarely had access to materials their college or university did not own. Undergraduates were also hampered by not knowing how to find materials the library did own, because library instruction was often limited to a single orientation tour for freshmen during their first week on campus.

Learning Resource Center Programs and Services

As their parent institutions changed, academic libraries also changed to support new educational programs. Many libraries began to experiment and to expand their library collections beyond the traditional print materials. The media explosion that impacted elementary and secondary schools expanded to include higher education. Some libraries began to incorporate all types of media into their collections and programs, including audiotapes; videotapes; microforms; transparencies; films of all forms, shapes, and sizes; programmed learning; and computer-assisted instruction. The academic library became more student-oriented.

The growth and development of these new types of libraries and library services in the 1960s encouraged the development of new academic library standards over the past three decades of the 20th century. Whereas previous academic standards had emphasized traditional library materials and services, the new standards emphasized quality learning resource programs and student access to all media within the library. The Association of College and Research Libraries (ACRL) adopted standards for all types of academic libraries. The most recent versions of these are *Standards for Community, Junior, and Technical College Learning Resource Programs* (1994);[32] *Standards for College Libraries* (2000);[33] and *Standards for University Libraries* (1989).[34] However, rather than setting the pace for library services as the school standards had done, these academic standards seemed to follow rather than lead the development of innovative library services.

The current *ACRL Standards* (2004) take a different approach from the quantitative measures for the past. In so doing they follow the lead of regional

accrediting agencies in their emphasis on accountability for achievement output measures, defined as student learning outcomes and institutional effectiveness. The attempt is being made to shift the focus from what is taught to
what is learned—a subtle but profound change. The preamble of the new
document states:

These standards differ from earlier ACRL library standards in four significant respects.

1. They are intended to apply to all types of libraries in higher education,
   from technical institutes to research universities.
2. The standards and key principles are designed as a tool to help libraries establish individual goals within the context of their institutional
   goals.
3. They focus on documenting the library's contribution to institutional
   effectiveness and student learning outcomes.
4. The standards provide suggested points of comparison for peer and
   longitudinal comparison, and encourage the development of other
   measures. Some measures of quality and quantity are used in this
   document, as well as questions to provide guidance for assessing each
   element of library operations and the provision of library services.[35]

The paradigm shift envisioned by the accrediting bodies and these standards will take time, effort, and soul searching before any transformation
can truly be achieved. However, that journey is underway. This shift would
change the entire character of academic library service. Previously, the focus,
particularly in university libraries, had been on serving the needs of faculty
and advanced graduate students. As the needs of undergraduate students
gained more importance, it became more obvious that this group needed professional assistance to identify and interpret the information resources that
were most appropriate to meet their needs. As a result, the information contained in the books and other materials gradually became an increasing focus
for public services staffs. Amassing large collections in anticipation of what
someone might need in 20 years was no longer enough. The books, though
still important, were no longer the end in themselves—they increasingly became the means to the end of conveying information. This new focus on information takes on new meaning with the advances in technology that are now
affecting libraries.

Other library services and procedures are changing to match students'
needs. Many new university library buildings house their major book collections in open stacks that are being made accessible to undergraduates for
the first time. The interiors of these buildings are also changing. Group study
rooms that allow for conversation and collaboration are now a prominent
feature of academic libraries. Larger, flexible open spaces known as *learning
commons* allow for activities such as group meetings, rotating exhibitions, art
galleries, public speaking, in-library cafes, and more. Library hours are more
flexible, with some libraries staying open until midnight, while others feature
reading rooms that remain open 24 hours a day. Professional staff members

are often available for student assistance whenever the library is open, including during traditional holiday or semester breaks. The academic library has removed some of the physical barriers that had restricted student access to its collection.

Technology

Academic libraries have also taken advantage of the emergence of relatively reliable and affordable computer technology to develop automated systems for library operations. Some of these libraries were so successful in this development that they sold their products commercially under labels such as UTLAS (University of Toronto), BRS (Bibliographic Retrieval Services, State University of New York), and NOTIS (Northwestern University). As technology became more sophisticated, computer systems grew from single-purpose systems for internal operations (e.g., circulation or cataloging) to integrated library systems. Integrated library systems, such as Illinois's Library Computer System (ILCS), included not only circulation and cataloging but also online public access catalogs (OPACs). Students and faculty from a cooperating academic institution could use the database as an online union catalog to locate and borrow materials through direct borrowing (i.e., in person) or by requesting that an inter-library loan be delivered to their home campus library. Some systems included serials control systems (e.g., Serials of Illinois Libraries [SILO]), online search systems (e.g., BRS), and materials acquisitions systems that were also used for collection analysis and development.

In addition to providing automated services for the library, academic libraries took the lead in intra-campus and inter-campus networking. In some cases, institution-wide computer centers and programs were added to the academic library's service roles. Computer labs were made available in libraries for students' homework use, and some schools, such as Carnegie-Mellon, made computers available in students' dormitory rooms. OPACs were made accessible to students and faculty in their dormitories, offices, or homes. Libraries promoted inter-campus networking with link-ups for teleconferencing and two-way audio and video telecourses via satellite or TV, and, more recently, asynchronously online on the World Wide Web.

Libraries marketed their services to community business and economic leaders. Services such as business library cards, journal photocopying services, document delivery, computer search services such as DIALOG, and professional librarian consulting services were made available for a fee or in exchange for business donations. Many institutions made their resources available for a fee to any citizen either in the library or outside the library. An example of such comprehensive services is found at the University of Southern Florida, where the library and information services department is responsible for the library, the computer center, all information flow on campus, and the use of campus information resources by the business community. However, these quasi for-profit ventures were not uniformly successful.

Academic libraries also took the lead in developing resource-sharing networks with other libraries. These libraries had recognized many years previously that they must share their resources, both bibliographically and physically. This sharing originally began on an informal basis, with academic libraries in the same geographic area sharing materials or allowing reciprocal borrowing among their patrons. In the 1970s, library budgets failed to keep up with the publication explosion that produced more materials than a single library could buy. These informal arrangements became formal agreements for inter-library cooperation. This cooperation took many forms and provided many varied services. Some academic institutions joined consortia to formally share their educational resources and prevent costly duplication of subject specialties. Another type of cooperative endeavor is illustrated by the Center for Research Libraries, which provides cooperative storage facilities of little-used materials for its members.

This expanding wealth of access options placed renewed emphasis on the need to teach students how to make efficient use of them. In addition to giving orientation tours of the library, librarians developed computer and media programs that explained parts of the library or individual library resource tools. Librarians also taught credit and noncredit bibliographic instruction courses. This was not a new activity. Some progressive institutions, such as Iowa State University, offered library instruction throughout the 20th century. However, these programs have received new emphasis. In some cases the courses were competency based, and students were required to pass them to become upperclassmen or to graduate. Libraries also established programs to help nontraditional students overcome their reluctance to use the library as a learning tool. Some libraries developed ongoing programs to help retain these students and worked with high school enhancement programs or programs for under-achieving students.

Academic librarians have long had the urge to promote library use to undergraduates. However, such direct marketing efforts are rarely successful. Students have so many demands on their time that most can direct their attention to only what is absolutely necessary to preserve their academic status. Indirect efforts aimed at the faculty have a much better chance of success. Almost any course in a college or university can be taught so that students can earn an "A" without ever having to darken the door of a library. On the other hand, those same courses can be structured in such a manner that the students must be in the library every week to have a chance to survive the course with a passing grade.

Academic Institutions in the 21st Century

In the 21st century, academic libraries face the dilemma of keeping up with new electronic forms of information. Electronic products offer opportunities to provide library services in ways that were not previously possible—information can now be delivered anytime to any place. However, these services cannot be offered without funding for the infrastructure and the staff needed to support these innovations. At the same time, it is not often possible to stop providing services in the traditional manner. There is little evidence that the rest of the academic world is ready to move uniformly to embrace these new services as a replacement of the traditional. Textbooks, lectures, and assignments from library reserved-book collections continue to be at the heart of most college teaching by faculty who themselves are not always comfortable in libraries.[36] It is understandable then that a study by the Carnegie Foundation of 5,000 undergraduate students showed that 65 percent of them used a library for only four hours or less per week, whereas one-quarter of the students did not use the library at all.[37] A more discouraging commentary for libraries was that most of these students used the library only as a place for quiet study—even though this is a legitimate and necessary library function.

The Carnegie Foundation has provided some momentum for the change that is underway by suggesting that the quality of colleges should be measured by the resources they offer for learning on campus and the extent to which their students become independent, self-directed learners.[38] As higher education slowly moves in this direction, libraries have opportunities to become more integrated into the total learning experience.

This expands the concept of the library as a physical place. As mentioned previously, more information services can now be provided remotely. These include:

- electronic reserves
- e-books
- full-text (and even better, full-image) periodical articles
- remote media booking services
- online information competency tutorials
- online public access catalogs (OPACs)
- other online indexes and databases
- online reference assistance
- online inter-library loan requests

So far, studies have been mixed as to whether these enhancements in service reduce or increase the likelihood that students and faculty will visit their campus libraries. One group of results suggests that it is no longer necessary to come to the bricks and mortar library to get needed information and services any longer. Other studies suggest that users are more likely to come to the library if they can check online in advance and determine that there is information of relevance or customized personal assistance awaiting them at the library.

Library Management

Generally speaking, the library director is a dean of learning resources who reports to an academic vice president. The library dean is not only the administrator of a large department and budget, but is also active in the council of deans and the total university administration. This expanded administrative role often strengthens and solidifies the library's place in an academic institution.

Increasingly, librarians are freed from supervising in-house library operations so that they can serve on faculty and institution committees and work with their faculty colleagues. Supervision of in-house library activities is being delegated to technical support staff, because libraries have discovered that technicians can operate most library functions on a day-to-day basis once service parameters are established and policies are set. These developments give impetus to librarians' quest for faculty status, tenure, and pay equity. Their success in achieving such demands depends on their success in becoming an integral part of their academic institutions beyond the walls of the library facility.

The reality that funding for publicly supported academic institutions is based on political considerations is not lost on academic librarians. Many of them serve on higher education advisory committees at the state level. They join forces with librarians from other types of libraries to lobby for recognition and funding from local, state, and national library and higher education governmental agencies. However, as important as funding is, Richard DeGennaro reminds us that "the greatest challenge facing academic libraries is not funding or technology, but leadership and administrative ability."[39] Library leaders must be committed to making their libraries more productive, innovative, and entrepreneurial to fulfill their major roles of developing information-literate students, integrating libraries into the academic curricula, and providing access to all the information students and faculty need without regard for its location or format.

Additional library workers will need to be recruited to meet these challenges. Academic library staffs increased by more than 10 percent between 2002 and 2007.[40] Of those in librarian positions in 2007, almost 30 percent of them expect to leave those positions by 2012, and 48 percent expect to have left academic libraries by 2017. If these projections hold, a massive change of personnel is going to be taking place in the next decade. The baby boomers will take a large amount of experience with them into retirement.[41] This will create the need for new workers at all levels to continue to provide the combination of traditional and innovative library services needed by academe.

SPECIAL LIBRARIES AND INFORMATION CENTERS

Special libraries include corporate, medical, law, religious, governmental, prison, not-for-profit organizational libraries, and many other highly specialized collections. A few very different examples include the small Hearst Castle Staff library, the Smithsonian Institution's research library, and the voluminous LDS (Mormon) library of family history in Utah. Often, the term *special library* is used as a catch-all term to refer to any library that is not a public, school, or academic library. A common thread, though, is that collections and services are very narrowly focused to support the activities of the library's parent organization.

The lines between special libraries and other types of libraries are not precise. Often, the subject-specific departmental libraries within large university library systems or within large public libraries function more like special libraries than they do like general academic or public libraries. The professional orientation of the staff may be more toward the subject matter than to the type of library in which the particular departmental library is located. For example, music librarians often have their primary allegiance to the Music Library Association (MLA) rather than to the broad-based ALA. Some special librarians have dual expertise and are actively involved in scholarship or practice of their libraries' subject discipline specialties as well as in librarianship.

Even within a specialized subdivision of special libraries, there is unlimited variation in the types of libraries and the opportunities for employment. Although the following discussion uses law libraries to illustrate the point, similar illustrations could be given within almost any other sector of special libraries.

One of the authors formerly taught in a library technician-training program in the Los Angeles area. In the introductory course, a panel of law librarians was invited to address the students. The panel was composed of the following:

- a librarian from a very large law firm in downtown Los Angeles
- a librarian from the Los Angeles County Law Library
- a librarian from the University of Southern California School of Law library
- a librarian from the Ninth District Court of Appeals library
- a librarian who had left traditional library employment and organized a personnel agency that specializes in placing temporary and permanent employees in law libraries

All of these librarians work within the context of law librarianship. However, the commonality ends there.

The librarian of the large firm and the court librarian serve no one other than those within their own organizations. For the firm this is a competitive issue: it is in business to make money, and its information resources are among its most valuable commodities. The firm does not want competitors to know what it is researching, let alone make it easy for those competitors to do similar research. In the case of the court library, confidentiality and privacy, more than competitiveness, are the driving forces. The entire clientele of the library comprise the judges and their immediate staffs. The judges need to be able to complete their research without being exposed to the prying eyes of others or the interruptions of chance encounters with parties to the litigation they are adjudicating.

At the opposite extreme, the Los Angeles County Law Library functions almost as a public library. Its collections make it the largest law library west of the Mississippi River. Although LA County's primary clientele are judges, lawyers, and their staffs, the general public constitutes more than 30 percent of its customers.

Dress codes are another area in which law libraries differ greatly from each other. The general rule of thumb seems to be that staff members dress just slightly more conservatively than the typical clientele. One large law firm took the dress code one step further. It required all nonlawyers to wear a uniform. The firm was so large that not everyone knew the other employees who worked there. The lawyers felt the need to be able to walk into a room and immediately know who the members of their team were. Therefore, the company bought staff members blue blazers and gray skirts or slacks to wear on the job. Many of this firm's clients were bankers and others in the financial community who dress very conservatively.

Employees at other law libraries in Los Angeles dress less formally. Firms that specialize in entertainment law encourage their staff to dress more casually to blend in better with the customary attire of most of their clientele. And then there are the law school libraries where the primary clientele are college students and faculty. Again, the rule of thumb is to dress just slightly more conservatively than the customers.

With all this diversity, is there a unifying theme or common core that ties all of these libraries together? The term *special library* is used as an umbrella term to describe many different types of libraries. There have been many attempts to define what special libraries really are. What could a large scientific library with thousands of volumes and many paid staff members have in common with a small local historical museum library with 1,000 books and a photographic collection cared for by volunteer staff members? What characteristics of these two libraries would enable one term to be used to define both?

Of the characteristics that are most common to these libraries, the primary one is that their collections include materials that relate to specialized subject areas. Second, these libraries gather their collections and design their services to directly support and further the objectives of a parent organization, rather than to support a curriculum as school and academic libraries do. Finally, these libraries are primarily concerned with actively seeking out and providing information that the parent organization's clients or patrons need rather than just acquiring and preserving information in a collection. In other words, special libraries provide special and even individualized services for their patrons. These three characteristics are key elements of any special library or information center.

There are more than 9,000 different libraries in the United States that fit this definition of a special library.[42] Usually, they are libraries devoted to special subject areas, such as music and art libraries; libraries devoted to special forms, such as map libraries and archives; and libraries devoted to special clientele, such as medical patient libraries and prison libraries. Special libraries can also be identified by their parent organizations or institutions, such as bank or insurance libraries, church libraries, and federal libraries. However, these designations are far from comprehensive. If there is an organization, corporation, institution, or group of people with a special need for library and information services, then a special library has probably been developed to address these needs.

Although most librarians are attracted to faddish terms, special librarians seem especially susceptible. Perhaps this is because of their need to constantly market their services as being at the cutting edge. For example, special libraries are often referred to as information centers. The term *knowledge management* is associated with some special libraries. Each of these terms communicates a slightly different image of the services of the library and its relevance to the parent organization.

The growth and development of special libraries has varied widely. Yet for all of their variety in funding, type, subject, and clientele, special libraries and information centers continue to have more similarities than differences. Their financing, governance, resources, and services are strongly affected by their importance to the well being of their parent organizations. Therefore, their fortunes can change quickly, as the fortunes of their parent organizations either flourish or falter.

Research Libraries

Research libraries are some of our most important special libraries. Because they have been developed to support the research needs of the world's scholars, they have traditionally been allied with academic libraries. Most are actually part of large universities, but many can be found outside academe. The New York Public Library has its own, mostly privately funded, research library as its central library. (The branches are tax-funded public libraries.) Most research libraries were originally established and endowed by wealthy benefactors. Limited funds have forced most research libraries to limit and refine their subject interests, but, through careful purchases, many libraries have been able to develop definitive collections in narrow subject areas.

Independent research libraries are unique because they do not belong to any other institution and exist for their own sake. Generally, they have been established by wealthy benefactors, are governed by their own self-perpetuating boards of directors, and manage their own facilities and endowment funds. In some cases, the focus of the library may be based on the private collection of the library's benefactor, such as the Folger Shakespeare Library, or it may be chosen to coordinate with other research libraries. For example, the subjects of the Newbery Library (humanities) and the John Crerar Library (physical and natural sciences) in Chicago were chosen to complement each other and those of the Chicago Public Library (social sciences). Sometimes these libraries may lose their independent status, as the John Crerar Library did when it was absorbed into the University of Chicago in 1984. Although these libraries have been called independent research libraries, they have become important—and often unique—links in the network of national information resources.

Federal Libraries

Federal government libraries also important links in our national information resources. They include national health, agriculture, technical, and institutional libraries, as well as academic (e.g., the Air Force Academy), school (e.g., on federal reservations), and quasi-public (e.g., military base) libraries. However, all federal libraries are considered to be special libraries because they serve the goals of their parent institutions and their users are usually members of these institutions. There are more than 1,500 federal libraries serving the various departments and agencies of the U.S. government. About 40 percent of these are scientific and technical (including health and medical) libraries that serve the special objectives of the agencies to which they belong. Almost as many serve as quasi-public libraries for persons at military installations, veterans' hospitals, and federal prisons. About 20 percent of all federal libraries serve the educational needs of personnel in U.S. armed forces, the military academies, and military–dependent schools overseas.

The importance of federal libraries to our national information resources is seen in the extensive research and subject collections found within them. The most comprehensive federal collections are contained in the three national libraries: the Library of Congress (LC), the National Library of Medicine (NLM), and the National Agriculture Library (NAL). These three libraries not only provide extensive research collections in all forms of media, but also represent one-third of the total federal collections, one-half of all federal library expenditures, and two-fifths of all the personnel in federal libraries. The LC alone has a staff of almost 5,000 employees.

> The enormous size and variety of its collections make the Library of Congress the largest library in the world. Comprised of approximately 138 million items in virtually all formats, languages, and subjects, these collections are the single most comprehensive accumulation of human expression ever assembled. True to the Jeffersonian ideal, the collections are broad in scope, including research materials in more than 450 languages, over 35 scripts, and in many media.[43]

These national libraries provide library services to the nation and serve as national information resource centers. The NLM and the NAL have developed subject collections in medicine and agriculture and their allied fields; the LC covers all the other subjects.

Serving as a national library is still an unofficial function of the LC, although it has been steered in this direction by two important events. The first was Congress's purchase of Thomas Jefferson's collection, which contained materials on a great variety of subjects. Over the years, librarians of Congress continued to strengthen these subjects. The second event was the passage of the Copyright Law in 1870, which required that two copies of every copyrighted work be submitted to the LC. This national library function was further enhanced in the early 1900s, when the library began to sell its classification schedules and catalog cards. The *National Union Catalog* (NUC) and the *Union List of Serials* (ULS) also enabled libraries to share the LC's collection as well as the collections of the largest libraries in the United States. Finally, the LC became the national resource for materials for blind or physically disabled people.

In spite of these services to the nation, the primary purpose of the LC is still to serve as a legislative library for Congress. Librarians of Congress have judiciously nurtured this relationship, and their skillful public relations have helped gain unparalleled financial support for the library and its programs. This financial support has enabled the LC and the other national libraries to provide leadership in the development of internationally significant library automation programs. For example, the LC-developed format for exchanging computerized cataloging information, MAchine Readable Cataloging (MARC), has, with minor variations, become the standard worldwide.

By the early 1990s, the actual LC catalog became available online to other libraries. Recent initiatives have digitized rarely held materials that are in danger of disappearing because of the deterioration of the paper on which they are printed. One of the earliest of these projects, *American Memory,* is a gateway to rich primary source materials relating to the history and culture of the United

States. The site offers "more than 13.6 million items from more than 90 historical collections." More items are being added at a prodigious rate.[44]

The LC is not the only national library to have made its collection readily available to the world. The NLM developed *MEDLARS*, an online service that made 25 medical literature databases accessible to its 30,000 users by the early 1990s. The NLM's computerized cataloging information in the biomedical area was made available to medical libraries on *CATLINE*. Citations and indexes to articles were made available through *Index Medicus* or online through *MEDLINE* for the field of biomedicine. Because many of *MEDLARS*'s users were individuals, the NLM also provided *Grateful Med* software to allow health professionals access to more than 13 million references and abstracts via their personal computers. *PubMed*, a service of the National Library of Medicine, provides access to "over 18 million citations from MEDLINE and other life science journals for biomedical articles back to 1948. PubMed includes links to full text articles and other related resources."[45] In addition, the NLM provides document delivery to medical libraries and health professionals and establishes regional medical libraries throughout the country to serve as resource centers. In-depth consumer health information is provided as well.

The NAL also took its place as a national leader in providing library and information services to the agricultural community. As early as 1970, the NAL made its computerized database, *AGRICOLA* (AGRICultural On Line Access), available to other libraries. The NAL was an active member of *AGLINET*, a voluntary association of 27 agricultural libraries. It was also active in *USAIN* (U.S. Agriculture Information Network), a national forum to discuss agricultural information issues. Because the success of any agricultural effort often depends on worldwide climatic conditions, the NAL also became an important part of the international agricultural information network, which has developed interconnecting resource centers that provide electronic access to data, documents, and computer files throughout the world. This network was made available so that both the scientist and the layperson could understand its information. Access to this international agricultural network was also made available via computer link-ups to users, such as farmers, at the local level.

Another rich special library system within our national government is the National Archives and Records Administration (NARA) with its headquarters facility in the capital and 14 regional branches in urban centers throughout the country. This agency preserves and makes accessible important historical and legal documents produced by the federal government.

Corporate Libraries and Information Centers

The private world of business and industry has kept pace with the government in developing libraries and information centers to support research needs. Almost all businesses and industries, including banks, insurance companies, utilities, advertising agencies, newspapers, chemical companies, and aerospace corporations, have their own libraries. Though these companies' products may vary considerably, their libraries and information centers are similar in that their collections and services are completely correlated with the objectives of their parent organizations. Figure 3.2 depicts a corporate library from the 1950s.

Figure 3.2. The 1957 movie *Desk Set,* starring Katharine Hepburn and Spencer Tracy, takes place in a "modern corporate library." Notice the state-of-the-art computer in the background.

Because large corporations are now so multifaceted, completely different libraries are often found within the same organization. For example, Kaiser Permanente, a large health care organization, has medical libraries at each of its hospitals. However, it has a business library at its administrative center that focuses on management issues. The Art Institute of Chicago maintains at least three separate libraries: (1) a research library used by staff and other qualified researchers to authenticate and establish the provenance (chain of ownership) of items of art; (2) an educational center for the museum's children's programming that includes resources for school teachers of art; and (3) a library (including a media center) for the School of the Art Institute.

Businesses such as law firms, communications media, insurance companies, advertising agencies, and high-tech and marketing firms are so dependent on the quick retrieval of information that they provide well-funded collections and trained staff in their libraries to support their own business purposes. For example, law firms subscribe to expensive legal databases, such as *Lexis* or *WestLaw,* that make current court decisions instantaneously available upon release, rather than weeks later in printed form. Other types of businesses, particularly smaller businesses, might consider information services as peripheral to their profit goal and cut their libraries' staffing, materials, and funding when profits begin to sag. Thus, a library's or an information center's success in convincing upper management that it is contributing to the parent corporation's bottom line is essential to guaranteeing its continued existence.

The need to successfully contribute to the corporation's profit by providing information is so vital that corporate libraries have become information centers rather than bona fide libraries. Although there is no precise defining difference between the two, the information center tends to be more involved in the flow of internally generated information, which may not be intended to see the light of day outside the organization. Information specialists and other employees who have subject and library expertise and a solid grounding in the corporation's objectives and organization staff these information centers.

The Special Library Association describes such workers as follows:

An Information Professional ("IP") strategically uses information in his/ her job to advance the mission of the organization. This is accomplished through the development, deployment, and management of information resources and services. The IP harnesses technology as a critical tool to accomplish goals. IPs include, but are not limited to, librarians, knowledge managers, chief information officers, web developers, information brokers, and consultants.

Information Professionals work for information organizations, which are defined as those entities that deliver information-based solutions to a given market. Some commonly used names for these organizations include libraries, information centers, competitive intelligence units, intranet departments, knowledge resource centers, content management organizations, and others.[46]

The diverse responsibilities that Information Professionals may have include:

- developing and maintaining a portfolio of cost-effective, client-valued information services that are aligned with the strategic directions of the organization and client groups;
- building a dynamic collection of information resources based on a deep understanding of clients' information needs;
- gathering evidence to support decisions about the development of new services and products;
- maintaining current awareness of emerging technologies;
- assessing and communicating the value of the information organization, including information services, products, and policies to senior management, key stakeholders, and client groups; and
- contributing effectively to senior management strategies and decisions regarding information applications, tools and technologies, and policies for the organization.[47]

Information specialists have developed collections that include resources in all types of forms. This information may be contained in externally published materials, such as books, microforms, serials, patents, and conference reports, or in internally generated materials, such as research and technical reports, corporate and product indexes, correspondence, and market surveys. However, it is not the format of the information but its currency that is of primary importance in special libraries and information centers. In fact, the most important service any information center provides may be rapid access to journal articles and research data through extensive serial collections or electronic databases.

To facilitate easy access to relevant data, information centers usually collect and index everything written or published, either externally or internally, about the corporation, its products, and its competitors. Because their collections are used by every division in the corporation, information centers also include information about the corporation's clients or customers, competitors, business indicators, economic factors, and business administration. In cataloging these materials, information centers often devise simplified classification and subject-heading systems because many documents do not have the necessary information for standard cataloging.

Information centers also provide in-depth indexing for information of interest buried within relevant book chapters, periodical articles, and specific subjects, rather than just providing traditional bibliographic descriptions of whole books or periodicals. Access to these materials has been further enhanced by recent technological advancements, which enable information centers to make digital images of their materials available to any member of the corporation anywhere in the world.

The economic model on which the special library is based is very different than that of other libraries. The special library's customers are on the company payroll, unlike the school and academic library (and to some extent the public library), where student or patron research time is not a cost to the institution. Therefore, special libraries cost companies, no matter whether researchers gather their own information or have information center staff gather it for them. It is generally more cost-effective for information center staff to perform this activity because they are more skilled and may also be paid less per hour than other specialized employees of the organization. As a result, the staff members in special libraries will go much further than those of other libraries not only to locate bibliographic citations, but also to obtain the documents, read and analyze them, and write a report for the requesting department. In some corporations, information specialists join with department teams to work as researchers on corporate projects. Such active participation in a company's programs helps prove the library's worth to many corporate executives.

The information specialist may also save corporate personnel valuable time, and, at the same time, improve the competitive position of the organization by providing individualized and specialized services, such as current alert services, which search current literature according to profiles tailored to an individual's or group's specific needs. Current alert services can be among the most productive services for keeping researchers abreast of new research developments in their fields. Information specialists usually interview a patron to determine what specific type of search or information is desired. The specialist then identifies subject descriptors or subject headings to create a profile for that person. This profile is run against new information sources as the company acquires them, and the researcher is notified of any relevant matches.

Most corporate information centers circulate books, publish and distribute bibliographies and acquisitions lists, provide abstracting and translating services, supply RSS feeds, publish information bulletins, and provide copies of relevant articles or patents. Through these many services, the corporate information center attempts to improve the corporation's efficiency and profits by taking an active part in its day-to-day operations.

Other Special Libraries

Some of the more common examples of other special libraries are museum libraries, association libraries, and organization libraries. Within each of these areas, there are numerous variations based on the subject areas or organizations or institutions that a library serves. For example, about 3,000 libraries are located in historical museums, art museums, science museums, and other museum-type establishments such as zoos, arboretums, historic houses, and national parks. All of these libraries vary in size and are funded by both private and public agencies. Although a few of them have large collections and well-trained staff, most have small collections (1,000 to 5,000 items) and may be staffed by volunteers who may or may not have library training. Museum-type libraries are primarily open during regular business hours to serve the staff and researchers at their institutions as well as qualified off-site scholars and researchers.

Other kinds of institutions served by special libraries include associations and agencies. Professional associations such as ALA, the American Dental Association, and the American Medical Association are just a few of the associations that provide libraries for their executive staff and their members. State and local government agencies provide libraries to serve their staff, although these are not nearly as extensive as federal libraries. Publicly operated law libraries are located in practically every county in the United States.

Access to archival materials is also made available by many governments, institutions, and organizations through limited reference service, photo duplication, and lending policies. Such library-like services are encouraged by the Society of American Archivists (SAA), which provides a voluntary certification program for archivists. As with the other types of special libraries, these archives serve the major objectives of their parent organizations and institutions by providing both in-depth research and current information to their members as quickly and efficiently as possible.

One type of institution, the hospital or health care center, is unique because it often has two types of special libraries or one library that provides two distinct types of services. The first type is the patient library, which provides recreational and leisure reading for patients. These libraries usually have very flexible circulation routines, and services may be provided by volunteer staff rather than by paid technical or professional staff. In many cases the services have to be taken to bedridden patients rather than expect them to come to the library. The second type serves the research needs of the medical and other professional staff. On rare occasions a library staff member in this latter type of library has been credited with making a difference between life and death. The typical example is that of a surgical team operating on a patient and discovering something totally unexpected. At that point, time and accuracy are certainly of the essence if additional technical information is required.

Among the other institutional libraries are prison libraries, which serve their incarcerated populations. The goals of prison libraries have varied throughout the years as the philosophy of prison reform has changed. The first prison library collections contained moral and religious works to help prisoners see the error of their ways. Next, prison collections became important in supporting the educational system in the prison, and, finally, prison libraries became a part of the prisons' rehabilitative function. By the 1990s, literacy programs had become a major activity in many prison libraries. The biggest growth in prison libraries, though, has been in the area of legal information. Since the 1970s, federal courts have required that prisons provide adequate legal information that inmates can consult for drafting legal papers and briefs. As a result of this requirement, prisons have developed their own law libraries. In some states the department of corrections employs more library workers than any other state agency.

Many subject specialty libraries are connected with universities and colleges. These can be as numerous and varied as the university departments themselves. To support these diverse libraries, special library associations have developed. These include associations for art, architecture, agriculture, astronomy, documentation, film archives, geography and maps, law, medicine, music, social science, sound archives, and theater. In addition, there are religious associations such as the theological, Jewish, Catholic, and Lutheran library associations.

Library and Information Management

The management and staffing of special libraries and information centers are more varied and distinct than those in other types of libraries. Often, the administrator responsible for the library or information center is not a librarian, but a director or officer of a major department or division. In business and industrial libraries, the directors of research and development or the vice presidents of marketing may be given responsibility for administering the library or information center. These administrators usually hire library and information staff who support their own conceptions of library services. Thus, if a research and development (R&D) director considers library services important, then that person will provide a sufficient number of well-trained staff members to support the R&D function. Such a library might have a staff of information professionals supported by technicians and clerks. If another R&D director considers the materials more important than the services, the library staff might consist only of clerical workers. If either director were replaced, the services in that library or information center might be changed once again to fit the new director's viewpoint.

Personnel working in special libraries and information centers usually have more varied backgrounds than do staff in other types of libraries. Ideally, personnel should have both library and subject expertise. The special librarian or information specialist may have a degree in a subject specialty as well as in library science, and the staff may also include subject and language specialists. In fact, this subject expertise may be so important to companies and businesses that they may prefer a technician with subject specialization to a professional with a master's degree in library or information science. Large libraries often include professional librarians or information scientists backed up by subject specialists, technicians, programmers, and clerks.

In reality, however, sometimes the only staff member in a special library may be a secretary who has been put in charge of a collection of books and magazines. In other special libraries, someone who is a librarian or information specialist in name only may supervise several clerks and technicians. This manager may have a degree in the subject specialty of the parent corporation or institution, but may not have much knowledge of library or information science. In other cases, technicians may be offered a high wage to perform professional responsibilities for which they are not fully prepared. At the opposite end of the spectrum, professional librarians or information specialists are often offered technician-level wages. Sometimes library services are outsourced (i.e., provided on a contract basis by an outside agency or vendor). Some organizations hire professional library consultants to set up a library that is then turned over to lower-paid personnel who are charged with carrying out daily operations.

Because the major purpose of the parent corporation is to make a profit, the major purpose of the corporate library is to collect, organize, and put to use the knowledge in its collections for the greatest efficiency of the corporation. It is this characteristic that distinguishes corporate business and industrial libraries from other special libraries. The profit-making motive may be one of the most influential factors in the makeup of a business or industrial library. In private sector corporations, libraries are sometimes operated as profit centers, rather than being treated as general overhead, and, therefore, cost centers.

Psychologically, this changes the entire equation. Such libraries must continually demonstrate their worth by generating a profit similar to other divisions of the organization. This is a foreign concept throughout much of the library world. Charge for library services? Although, intellectually, most library workers believe in the value of information, few of us expect to put this belief to the test in the marketplace.

The way this works in some firms is that the librarian/researcher's time is billed out for the hours he or she works on a client's project. This billable time is inflated to cover all of the overhead costs associated with the research—collections, facilities, technology, supplies, subscriptions, support staff, and so forth. Therefore, billing rates in excess of $100 per hour are necessary to cover the costs of the services provided to the client. Often, these costs are billed directly to the client, along with the chargeable time of other professionals in the firm, such as lawyers, accountants, scientists, engineers, and consultants.

This constant financial focus has forced special libraries and information centers to be entrepreneurial. Special libraries often charge back their services to the corporate department end user, such as the engineering or marketing departments. In addition, by the 1990s, some firms, such as law and engineering firms, began passing through, or billing the costs of such library and information services to the end-user client. Also, many special libraries and information centers began to provide fee-based services and consulting to external corporate or individual users who were not members of their own organization. Fees were charged for services such as online searches, reference service, and document delivery.

These fees often enabled a library or information center to provide additional services for its primary clients. In contrast with public and academic libraries that have to face freedom-of-access concerns when charging similar fees, the special library or information center has to ensure that the benefits of providing such fee-based services do not reduce services to its primary clientele.

Sometimes, rather than working in a special library, librarians or information specialists may prefer to use their problem-solving skills to become an information broker. An information broker is an independent or freelance librarian or firm who searches out and provides information on a profit-making basis. The information broker provides services ranging from searches of computerized databases, to translations, to market surveys. An information broker's clients may include corporations and individuals who do not have access to information centers. Or, the clients may be libraries or information centers that need specific information outside the realm of their collections. Information brokers' ability to specialize and produce results in a short span of time has made them invaluable resources for libraries and information centers.

Special libraries are the one area of the library industry where it appears the workforce has been shrinking since the beginning of the 21st century. Between 2002 and 2007 the number of paid staff in such libraries appears to have declined by about 7 percent.[48] Only time will tell if this is a continuing trend or if there is any correlation between staffing levels in special libraries and the services provided by independent information brokers.

SUMMARY

Although those in the library business categorize all libraries into four groups, (i.e., public, school, academic, and special), many of the almost 130,000 libraries in the United States have properties of more than one of these types. Approximately 400,000 library staff members attempt to serve the unique needs of the communities or organizations of which they are part.

Public libraries serve all citizens at every stage of life, whether they live in a large city or in the most remote rural area. Public libraries have developed collections, programs, and services to help them fulfill their principle of service to all. Each library examines its community to identify and provide and co-ordinate programs and services with other community agencies and services. In this process, each library's success in meeting its own community's needs is significantly affected by prevailing economic and political conditions at the local, state, and national levels.

School libraries play an important role in helping students learn. To emphasize that all forms of media are available to help students learn both inside the classroom and beyond, many school libraries refer to themselves as instructional materials centers or media centers. Similarly, school librarians and audiovisual specialists have taken the titles of media specialists and are supported by media technicians and clerks. As librarians become more involved in curriculum development and are assisted in daily operations by well-trained support staff, student achievement levels provide growing evidence that good school libraries make a significant difference.

Academic libraries have grown and evolved over the years to meet the changing educational objectives of their parent institutions. Along with school libraries, they have put increasing emphasis on building information literacy by teaching students how to find and evaluate information. Collections have been expanded to include all media, and library services have become more student-centered. Computer technology has expanded library resources and services and has placed additional strain on budgets. Academic libraries have joined networks with other libraries to acquire, preserve, and share their resources.

Special libraries and information centers provide services in a narrowly defined subject area or in a specialized format for a homogeneous clientele. They are more varied and distinct than any other type of library. Special libraries often have extensive information collections as well as extensive staff and services to support the research needs of their parent organizations. Staff members go further than other types of libraries to anticipate, locate, and even synthesize the information needed by other members of the organization.

All libraries exist to meet the objectives of their parent institutions or their communities. Their fortunes mirror the economic health of those institutions and communities. The libraries that thrive are those that convince the leaders of their institutions and communities that they actively facilitate reaching the goals of the larger body.

In the early 21st century, the number of library workers was increasing significantly in public libraries and academic libraries, but declining slightly in special libraries. This was before the results of the 2008 recession could be measured. Economic swings definitely affect library staffing levels over the short run. However, over the next decade almost half of the currently employed librarians are expecting to retire. This creates a great opportunity for those seeking entry to and fast advancement in a dynamic field.

LIBRARY VISITS

Document your visits to at least four libraries. They should be libraries of the type you think you might like to work in some day. At a minimum, collect the information needed to answer the following questions for each of the libraries you visit:

1. What is the library's complete name, address, telephone number, and Web site address (uniform resource locator or URL)?
2. How easy is it to find the library?
3. How easy is it to find parking nearby?
4. How readily available is public transportation?
5. How is the library's primary clientele defined? What special information needs do the library's patrons have?
6. Is the library open to the public? If so, on what basis?
7. How many clients are eligible for service?
8. How many clients are served?
9. What is the budget of the library?

10. To which governing body or to which official does the head of the library report?

11. What special services are offered to clientele?

12. What hours is the library building open?

13. Describe the nature, size, and scope of the library's collection.

14. What is the nature and size of the staff?

15. What staff did you observe? What impression did you get of the staff? Were they businesslike, courteous, sloppy, friendly?

16. What technology is used in the library?

17. What is the size and adequacy of the library's physical facilities?

18. Describe the adequacy and attractiveness of staff work areas.

19. When you first enter the library, stop and look around. Is it obvious without consulting the staff where the following are located:

    the circulation/reserve desk?

    the reference/information desk?

    the library catalog (OPAC)?

    the Internet terminals?

    the hard copy periodicals?

    the restrooms?

    the photocopiers and printers for computer workstations?

    the change machines?

    the elevators and stairs (if the library has more than one level)?

    the water fountain?

20. What kind, number, and variety of seating is there for library users?

21. Does the library have an attractive and functional Web presence?

22. What traditional library services can be accessed over the Internet?

23. What new services has the Internet allowed?

24. Have any social networking techniques been employed to interact with established or potential users?

25. Are there group study rooms and public meeting rooms?

26. Into what cooperative arrangements with other libraries has this facility entered?

27. What public programming, educational offerings, and other outreach activities are offered?

28. What most impressed you about this library?

29. What most concerned you about this library?

30. Would you feel comfortable using this library in the future, both in person and online?

31. Do you think you would like to work here? List and discuss the pros and cons and come to a conclusion.

STUDY QUESTIONS

Public Libraries

1. Identify the roles of library service that a public library might select.

2. Identify some of the major services libraries provide to fulfill these roles.

3. State the underlying philosophy of library service for public libraries as presented in the PLA planning documents.

4. Identify the levels of input and output measures recommended by the state library agency for the state in which you live.

5. Visit a public library you have not visited before. Compare the objectives with those found in PLA documents. Are services of this library aligned with those discussed in the text? Also, compare the library's input and output measures in question number 4 with the staff, collections, and so forth.

6. How are public libraries using the Internet to deliver traditional and new services to long-standing or new audiences?

School Libraries

1. Identify the major objectives of school library media center programs.

2. Briefly describe school library media development from the classroom library to school library to library media center.

3. How has the Internet affected school library operations?

4. Compare your own state's standards with the guidelines presented in *Information Power.*

5. Identify the kinds of media that can be found in a school library media center.

6. Describe some services and programs provided in successful library media programs.

7. Identify duties of the different levels of staff in the modern library media center.

8. Visit a school library media center and compare its objectives, staff, collection, and services with those described in this chapter.

Academic Libraries

1. Define an academic library and describe some of the major types of academic libraries.

2. What are the main objectives of an academic library?

3. Describe the changes in academic libraries from libraries to learning resource centers.

4. What are some of the major services academic libraries provide?

5. What are some of the changes in staff development brought about by the installation of automated library services?

6. List some examples of cooperative academic library resource-sharing and networking programs.

7. Visit a local academic institution and compare it with the objectives and services discussed in this chapter and the standards identified for that type of library.

8. Visit two types of academic institutions, such as a community college and a four-year college or university, to compare and contrast their libraries.

9. How are academic libraries serving the needs of distance education students?

10. What kind of information literacy activities are being offered in academic libraries?

Special Libraries

1. Identify the major objectives of special libraries and information centers.

2. Describe the relationship of a special library or information center to its parent institution.

3. Describe the scope and services of the three U.S. national libraries.

4. Describe the kinds of materials usually included in corporate libraries and information center collections.

5. List 10 examples of special libraries or information centers.

6. Visit one or two special libraries or information centers and compare their objectives, services, and collections to those discussed in this chapter.

RESOURCES

Workforce in all Libraries

The Future of Librarians in the Workforce—What will it look like? This massive study should be posting final reports on many types of libraries during 2009: http://www.libraryworkforce.org/tiki-index.php

Occupational Outlook Handbook (OOH): http://www.bls.gov/OCO/

Librarians: http://www.bls.gov/oes/2007/may/oes254021.htm

Library Technicians: http://www.bls.gov/oes/2007/may/oes254031.htm

Audio Visual Collections Specialists: http://www.bls.gov/oes/2007/may/oes259011.htm

Public Libraries

Future of the Public Library. Conference proceedings of OCLC Online Computer Library Center, Dublin, OH, March 20–22, 1988.

Giacoma, Pete. *The Fee or Free Decision: Legal, Economic, Political and Ethical Perspectives for Public Libraries.* New York: Neal-Schuman, 1989.

Griffiths, José-Marie and Donald R. King. "The Future of Librarians in the Workforce: Status of Public Libraries." June 2008. http://sils.unc.edu/research/publications/presentations/2008.06.27ALAPubLibfinal.pdf

Ihrig, Alice B. *Decision-Making for Public Libraries.* Hamden, CT: Shoe String, 1989.

Lee, Pat W. "Managing Public Libraries in the 21st Century." *Journal of Library Administration* II nos. 1, 2 (1989).

Mayo, Diane. *Wired for the Future: Developing Your Library Technology Plan.* Chicago: American Library Association, 1999.

McClure, Charles R., et al. *Planning and Role-Setting for Public Libraries. A Manual of Options and Procedures.* Chicago: American Library Association, 1987.

McClure, Charles R. & Paul T Jaeger. *Public Libraries and Internet Service Roles: Measuring and Maximizing Internet Services* ALA Editions, 2009.

McCook, Kathleen De la Pena. *Introduction to Public Librarianship.* New York: Neal-Schuman, 2004.

Nelson, Sandra S., Ellen Altman, and Diane Mayo. *Managing for Results: Effective Resource Allocation for Public Libraries.* Chicago: American Library Association, 2000.

Nelson, Sandra S. *The New Planning for Results: A Streamlined Approach.* Chicago: American Library Association, 2001.

Palmour, Vernon E. *A Planning Process for Public Libraries.* Chicago: American Library Association, 1980.

Public Library Association. *Minimum Standards for Public Library Systems, 1966.* Chicago: American Library Association, 1967.

Public Library Mission Statement and Its Imperatives for Service. Chicago: American Library Association, 1979.

Sager, Donald J. *Managing the Public Library.* 2d ed. Boston: G. K. Hall, 1989.

Shuman, Bruce A. *Beyond the Library of the Future: More Alternative Futures for the Public Library.* Englewood, CO: Libraries Unlimited, 1997.

Van Horn, Nancy, et al. *Output Measures for Public Libraries: A Manual for Standardized Procedures.* 2d ed. Chicago: American Library Association, 1987.

Webb, T. D. *Public Library Organization and Structure.* Jefferson, NC: McFarland, 1989.

School Libraries

AASL. *Realization: The Final Report of the Knapp School Libraries Project.* Edited by Peggy Sullivan. Chicago: American Library Association, 1968.

AASL/AECT. *Standards for School Media Centers.* Chicago: American Library Association, 1969.

AASL/AECT. *Media Programs: District and School.* Chicago: American Library Association, 1975.

AASL/AECT. *Information Power: Guidelines for School Library Media Programs.* Chicago: American Library Association, 1988.

ALA Yearbook: A Review of Library Events. Chicago: American Library Association, 1976–2001.

Haycock, Ken, ed. *Foundations for Effective School Library Media Programs.* Englewood, CO: Libraries Unlimited, 1999.

Kulleseid, Eleanor R. *Beyond Survival to Power: For School Library Media Professionals.* Hamden, CT: Library Professional Publications, 1985.

Lance, Keith Curry, Marcia J. Rodney, and Christine Hamilton-Pennell. *How School Librarians Help Kids Achieve Standards: The Second Colorado Study.* San Jose, CA: Hi Willow Research & Publishing, 2000.

Liesener, James W. "Information Power: A Broader Perspective." In *School Library Media Annual, 1989.* Englewood, CO: Libraries Unlimited, 1989.

Loertscher, David V., May Lein Ho, and Melvin M. Bowie. "Exemplary Elementary Schools and Their Library Media Centers: A Research Report." *School Library Media Quarterly* 15 (Spring 1987): 147–53.

Parsons, Larry A., comp. *A Funny Thing Happened on the Way to the School Library: A Treasury of Anecdotes, Quotes, and Other Happenings.* Englewood, CO: Libraries Unlimited, 1990.

Prostano, Emanuel T. and Joyce S. Prostano. *The school library media center.* 5th ed. Englewood, CO: Libraries Unlimited, 1999.

"School Libraries in the '90s." *Illinois Libraries* 72 no. 7 (1990).

School Libraries Work!. Third Edition. Scholastic Publishing, 2008. http://www2.scholastic.com/content/collateral_resources/pdf/s/slw3_2008.pdf

Smith, Ester G., *Student Learning Through Wisconsin School Library Media Centers: Library Media Specialist Survey Report, 2006.* http://dpi.wi.gov/imt/pdf/finallmssurvey06.pdf.

Standards for School Library Programs. Chicago: American Library Association, 1960.

Woolls, Blanche. *The School Library Media Manager.* 4th ed. Englewood, CO: Libraries Unlimited, 2008.

Academic Libraries

Association of College and Research Libraries. "The Mission of a University Undergraduate Library: Model Statement." *C&RL News* (October 1987): 542–44.

Association of College and Research Libraries. "Standards for University Libraries: Evaluation of Performance." *C&RL News* (September 1989): 679–91.

Association of College and Research Libraries. *Standards for Community, Junior, and Technical College Learning Resource Programs, 1994.* http://www.ala.org/acrl/guides/jrcoll.html (accessed December 6, 2001).

Association of College and Research Libraries. *Guidelines for Media Resources in Academic Libraries.* http://www.ala.org/acrl/guides/medresg.html (accessed December 6, 2001).

Association of College and Research Libraries. *Standards for College Libraries 2000 Edition.* http://www.ala.org/acrl/guides/college.html (accessed December 6, 2001).

Association of College and Research Libraries. *Standards for Libraries in Higher Education.* 2004. http://www.ala.org/ala/mgrps/divs/acrl/standards/standards libraries.cfm.

Breivik, Patricia Senn and E. Gordon Gee. *Information Literacy: Revolution in the Library.* New York: American Council on Education, 1989.

Breivik, Patricia Senn and Robert Wedgeworth. *Libraries and the Search for Academic Excellence.* Metuchen, NJ: Scarecrow, 1988.

Budd, John. *The Changing Academic Library: Operations, Culture, Environments.* Chicago: Association of College and Research Libraries, 2005.

Cohen, Laura B., *Library 2.0 Initiatives in Academic Libraries.* Chicago: Association of College and Research Libraries, 2007.

Courtney, Nancy. *Academic Library Outreach: Beyond the Campus Walls.* Westport, CT: Libraries Unlimited, 2008.

Dowell, David R. and Gerard B. McCabe, eds. *It's All about Student Learning: Managing Community and Other College Libraries in the 21st Century.* Westport, CT: Libraries Unlimited, 2006.

Griffiths, José-Marie and Donald R. King. "The Future of Librarians in the Workforce: Status of Academic Libraries." June 2008. http://sils.unc.edu/research/publications/presentations/2008.06.27ALAAcadfinal.pdf

Lynch, Beverly P., ed. *The Academic Library in Transition: Planning for the 90's.* New York: Neal-Schuman, 1989.

McCabe, Gerard B. and Ruth J. Person, eds. *Academic Libraries: Their Rationale and Role in American Higher Education.* Westport, CT: Greenwood Press, 1995.

Spyers-Duran, Peter and Thomas W. Mann, Jr., eds. *Issues in Academic Librarianship: Views and Case Studies for the 1980s and 1990s.* Westport, CT: Greenwood Press, 1985.

Van House, Nancy A., Beth Weil, and Charles R. McClure. *Measuring Academic Library Performance: A Practical Approach.* Chicago: American Library Association, 1990.

Veaner, Allen B. *Academic Librarianship in a Transformational Age: Programs, Politics and Personnel.* Boston: G. K. Hall, 1990.

Special Libraries

Bierbaum, Esther Green. *Museum Librarianship.* 2d ed. Jefferson, NC: McFarland, 2000.

Bulletin of the Medical Library Association. Chicago: Medical Library Association, 1911–2001.

Griffiths, José-Marie and Donald R. King. "The Future of Librarians in the Workforce: Status of Special Libraries." June 2008. http://sils.unc.edu/research/publications/presentations/2008SLAFFinal1.pdf

Journal of the Medical Library Association. Chicago: Medical Library Association, 2002–.

Larsen, John C., ed. *Museum Librarianship.* Hamden, CT: Shoe String, 1985.

Larsgaard, Mary Lynette. *Map Librarianship: An Introduction.* 3d ed. Englewood, CO: Libraries Unlimited, 1998.

Matthews, Joseph R. *The Bottom Line: Determining and Communicating the value of the Special Libraries.* Westport, CT: Libraries Unlimited, 2002.

Medical Library Association. *The Medical Library Association Guide to Managing Health Care Libraries.* Edited by Ruth Holst, Sharon A. Phillips, and Karen McNally Bensing. Chicago: Author, 2000.

Porter, Cathy A., et al. *Special Libraries: A Guide for Management.* 4th ed. Washington, DC: Special Libraries Association, 1997.

Russell, Keith W. and Maria G. Piza, eds. "Agricultural Libraries and Information." *Library Trends* 38 (3): 327–38 (1990).

Special Libraries. Washington, DC: Special Libraries Association, 1910–2001.

Strauss, Lucille J., et al. *Scientific and Technical Libraries: Their Organization and Administration.* 3d ed. Melbourne, FL: Krieger, 1991.

White, Herbert S. *Managing the Special Library: Strategies for Success Within the Larger Organization.* Boston: G. K. Hall, 1984.

NOTES

1. Kathleen De la Pena McCook, *Introduction to Public Librarianship* (New York: Neal-Schuman, 2004), 1.

2. Public Library Association, *Minimum Standards for Public Library Systems, 1966* (Chicago: American Library Association, 1967).

3. Vernon E. Palmour, Marcia C. Bellassai, and Nancy V. DeWath, *A Planning Process for Public Libraries* (Chicago: American Library Association, 1980).

4. Nancy A. Van House, et al., *Output Measures for Public Libraries: A Manual of Standardized Procedures* 2d ed. (Chicago: American Library Association, 1987).

5. Glenn R. Wittig, "Some Characteristics of Mississippi Adult Library Users," *Public Libraries* 30 (1): 30 (1991).

6. "The E-Rate," *ALA Fact Sheet,* November 1998, http://www.ala.org/pio/fact sheets/erate.html (accessed March 30, 2001).

7. Ibid.

8. Ibid.

9. "Gates Library Foundation Releases Grant Guidelines," ALA Press Release, October 28, 1997. http://www.ala.org/news/gatesgrants.html (accessed March 30, 2001).

10. "Public Library Use," *ALA Library Fact Sheet Number 6,* http://www.ala.org/ala/aboutala/hqops/library/libraryfactsheet/alalibraryfactsheet6.cfm

11. Ibid.

12. Bruce A. Shuman, *The Library of the Future: Alternative Scenarios for the Information Profession* (Englewood, CO: Libraries Unlimited, 1989), 116.

13. José-Marie Griffiths and Donald R. King, "The Future of Librarians in the Workforce: Status of Public Libraries," (June 2008), http://sils.unc.edu/research/publications/presentations/2008.06.27ALAPubLibfinal.pdf, pp. 11 & 13.

14. Jean Key Gates, *Introduction to Librarianship* (New York: McGraw-Hill, 1968), 220–21.

15. United States National Commission on Excellence in Education, *A Nation at Risk: The Imperative for Educational Reform: A Report to the Nation and the Secretary of Education, United States Department of Education* (Washington, DC: The Commission, 1983).

16. *Alliance for Excellence: Librarians Respond to a Nation at Risk: Recommendations and Strategies from Libraries and the Learning Society* (Washington, DC: U.S. Department of Education, Office of Educational Research and Improvement, Center for Libraries and Education Improvement, 1984).

17. Committee on Postwar Planning, *School Libraries for Today and Tomorrow: A Statement of Standards Prepared by the Committee on Postwar Planning of the American Library Association, Division of Libraries for Children and Young People and its School Libraries Section* (Chicago: American Library Association, 1944).

18. American Association of School Librarians, *Standards for School Library Programs* (Chicago: American Library Association, 1960).

19. Joint Committee of the American Association of School Librarians and the Department of Audiovisual Instruction of the National Education Association, *Standards for School and Media Programs* (Chicago: American Library Association, 1969).

20. American Association of School Librarians, *Media Programs: District and School* (Chicago: American Library Association, 1975).

21. American Association of School Librarians and Association for Educational Communications and Technology, *Information Power: Guidelines for School Library Media Programs* (Chicago: American Library Association, 1988).

22. William Chaney Bradford, *School Library Media Centers, 1993–94* (Washington, DC: U.S. Dept. of Education, Office of Educational Research and Improvement, 1998), A-130.

23. "Librarians, Teachers & Librarian/Teacher Ratio in U.S. Public Schools: State Variations & Trends, 1989–95," *Fast Facts: Recent Statistics for the Library Research Service* (April 8, 1999, ED3/110.10/No. 159), http://www.lrs.org/documents/fastfacts/159lmctrends/pdf

24. Lucille Mathena Wert, *Library Education and the High School Library Services* (Ann Arbor, MI: University Microfilms, 1970).

25. Kathleen Kennedy Manzo, "Study Shows Rise in Test Scores Tied to School Library Resources," *Education Week on the Web* (March 22, 2000), http://www.educationweek.org/ew/ewstory.cfm?slug = 28libe.h19 (accessed April 1, 2001).

26. Keith Curry Lance, et al., *How School Librarians Help Kids Achieve Standards: The Second Colorado Study* (Denver: Colorado Department of Education, 2000), 5.

27. Ibid.

28. State of Wisconsin—Department of Public Instruction, *Student Learning Through Wisconsin School Libraries: Executive Summary* (2007), http://www.dpi.wi.gov/imt/pdf/SLMP2.pdf.

29. Ibid.

30. *School Libraries Work!* Third Ed. (Scholastic Publishing, 2008), http://www2.scholastic.com/content/collateral_resources/pdf/s/slw3_2008.pdf

31. "The Carnegie Classification of Institutions of Higher Education," *The Carnegie Foundation for the Advancement of Teaching* (2000), http://www.carnegiefoundation.org/Classification/index.htm (accessed April 5, 2001).

32. Association of College and Research Libraries, "Standards for Community, Junior, and Technical College Learning Resource Programs," (July 1994), http://www.ala.org/acrl/guides/jrcoll.html (accessed December 6, 2001).

33. Association of College and Research Libraries, "Standards for College Libraries 2000 Edition," (January 2000), http://www.ala.org/acrl/guides/college.html (accessed December 6, 2001).

34. Association of College and Research Libraries, "Standards for University Libraries: Evaluation of Performance," (February 1989), http://www.ala.org/acrl/guides/univer.html (accessed December 6, 2001).

35. Association of College and Research Libraries, *Standards for Libraries in Higher Education* (2004), http://www.ala.org/ala/mgrps/divs/acrl/standards/standardslibraries.cfm

36. Patricia Senn Breivik and Robert Wedgeworth, *Libraries and the Search for Academic Excellence* (Metuchen, NJ: Scarecrow, 1988), 29–32.

37. Ibid., 7–8.

38. Ibid., 13–24.

39. Richard DeGennaro, Foreword to Allen B. Veaner, *Academic Librarianship in a Transformational Age: Programs, Politics and Personnel* (Boston: G. K. Hall, 1990), xiii.

40. José-Marie Griffiths and Donald King, *The Future of Librarians in the Workforce: Status of Academic Libraries* (June 2008), 11, http://sils.unc.edu/research/publications/presentations/2008.06.27ALAAcadfinal.pdf

41. Ibid., p. 13.

42. José-Marie Griffiths and Donald King, *The Future of Librarians in the Workforce: Status of Special Libraries* (June 2008), 4.

43. Library of Congress, "About the Collections," http://www.loc.gov/about/generalinfo.html#2007_at_a_glance (accessed January 13, 2009).

44. Ibid., "American Memory: Historical Collections for the National Digital Library," http://memory.loc.gov/ammem/index.html (accessed January 13, 2009).

45. National Library of Medicine, *PubMed,* http://www.ncbi.nlm.nih.gov/sites/entrez?db=pubmed (accessed January 13, 2009).

46. Special Library Association, "About Information Professionals," http://www.sla.org/content/SLA/professional/index.cfm. (accessed January 13, 2009).

47. Ibid.

48. José-Marie Griffiths and Donald King, *The Future of Librarians in the Workforce: Status of Special Libraries* (June 2008), 17.

Chapter 4

Collections

When it comes to assessing the quality and resources of a library or information center, one of the major aspects to consider is the facility's collection of materials. Today, that no longer means just what a library physically owns, but, increasingly, what it provides access to, regardless of the format. Collections now consist of hard-copy books, magazines, newspapers, videos, CDs, CD-ROMs, and DVDs, along with free and subscription-based documents, periodicals, images, and multimedia that are available electronically to patrons of that library. New formats of information packaging are emerging regularly to add to the list.

Regardless of delivery formats, library collections are acquired, cataloged, processed, and supplied to customers based on well-thought-out collection development policies, user profiles, organizational principles, and price considerations. This often comes as a surprise to patrons. Unlike the highly visible services of the reference and circulation departments, the selection, purchasing, cataloging, and processing of items usually does not involve the public directly but rather takes place behind the scenes. Typically, the division where these activities take place is called the technical services department.

It is probably fair to say that the development of library collections is one of the least understood aspects of library work to outsiders. When one of the authors worked in an urban public library, a patron was quite upset when she discovered that a particular new title was not in the collection. "Why don't you have it?" she complained. "I thought publishers sent libraries free samples of all the new books." False!

USER NEEDS

Every library has its own distinct set of user needs that influence the development of its collection. As the staff endeavor to make a collection as responsive as possible to those information needs, they turn to direct patron input (e.g., user surveys, patron suggestions, and item requests), demographics of their client base, staff observations, and usage patterns. Publishing trends, new product releases, and current events are also factors to be considered as library staff members attempt to meet ongoing needs and anticipate future demands.

Advisory committees or library boards may also contribute their input on collections. Of course, the library or information center's budgetary resources also greatly impact overall purchasing decisions. Many state university or college systems and other academic library cooperatives are able to form a buying consortia and negotiate a group rate with a particular vendor. This qualifies all of their member libraries to special pricing from vendors of key products such as subscription databases. And this arrangement simplifies the billing and other paperwork for the vendors since they do not have to bill each member separately.

The end result is that no individual library or information center collection is alike. And their primary users wouldn't want them to be. For example, academic library collections typically reflect the curriculum offered in their educational institutions. Thus, a polytechnic university with large science, engineering, and architecture departments can be expected to have significant library holdings in those areas, as well as a broad-based collection to support lower division, general education classes. A local public library will provide recreational reading and offer a wide range of popular materials on business topics, consumer information, regional history, and local government issues suited to its users' demographics. An art museum research library can be expected to collect overview information on art history and material on the museum's specific art holdings, periods, and artists, as well as data on interpretation, preservation, and curatorial techniques.

Libraries and the Role of Social Networking

A new aspect of the Internet that is influencing library collection building is the use of social networking tools to gather and share patron reading preferences and to build a feeling of community among all stake-holders of a library.

The phenomenon known as social networking began in 2002, and emphasizes the power of the Web to build community—among strangers as well as friends, family, and colleagues. Early sites promoting social networking were *Friendster, MySpace, Facebook, Flickr*—all of which have become household names and incredibly popular, especially among teens and those in their 20s and 30s. Blog (short for "Weblog") hosting is often a part of social network sites. Much like instant messaging (IM) and the earlier chat rooms, social networking represents not only a new, fast, convenient way to connect and to maintain relationships, but another venue where people elect to spend their time, both recreationally and professionally. For those hooked on sites such as *MySpace,* checking one's personal site multiple times per day for posts from family, friends, and newbies, is as much a part of the daily routine as checking traditional e-mail or brushing one's teeth.

There has been much recent discussion in the library world as to how these social networking sites can be best integrated into library services and how they can be successfully used as tools to build community among library patrons. A few examples of libraries that have integrated *MySpace* accounts into their library Web sites include Brooklyn College Library, Denver Public Library, and the Public Library of Charlotte and Mecklenburg County (North Carolina). Emphasis is on promoting library services such as digital reference and online resources, providing free podcasts and other information on featured authors, and connecting teens to the library and to each other.

The use of library blogs and interactive commenting is a feature of the Ann Arbor District Library's recent Web site makeover. Another innovative social networking service that is growing in use among libraries is online book clubs. This is where a commercial company such as Dear Reader.com sends regular e-mail snippets of text from newly released books to subscribed library patrons, who then share their comments about their reading experiences and their favorite titles with others in the club. The online reading club promotes the sharing of good reads, builds friendships, and also encourages library use, circulation of materials, and overall readership.

A Glut of Information

For years we have been hearing of the information explosion that surrounds us, and there is no sign of it letting up any time soon. And although computer technology has made great inroads (especially in the library field) in the storage and retrieval of massive quantities of information, there does not seem to be any reduction in the volume of data, but, rather, the contrary. Trying to estimate the size of the entire Web is rather difficult due to its highly dynamic nature. An often cited statistic from early 2000 estimated the size of the Web in 1999 to be 1.5 billion individual Web pages, with a growth rate that would double every year.[1] As of late 2006, a survey by the British company Netcraft counted 105 million Web sites (which would each include many individual pages).[2] Any way you try to measure it, the exponential growth of the World Wide Web only adds to the information glut that already engulfs us

At the same time, U.S. book production has been on the rise in recent years with a record-setting total of over 190,000 new titles and editions released in 2004, according to the yearly industry analysis provided in the *Bowker Annual.*[3] It does seem rather overwhelming. How will a researcher ever find the Web site, book, article, or item of data that he or she needs? How will an information specialist know which quality products to add to their information center?

SELECTION TOOLS

Although there are no comprehensive magic lists, librarians rely on industry tools, along with direct user input and their own professional judgment, to make selection and purchasing decisions. These may include reviewing media, core collection lists or bibliographies, lists of award-winning titles, and industry listservs.

Review Media

Critical or evaluative reviews of books, as well as those of magazines, videos, DVDs, audio CDs, and computer software, are published by many sources for the retail trade and for the library business. Such reviews help library professionals decide on relevance and quality before making a purchase. Because it would be impossible to preview, read, or listen to each individual item under consideration, perusing reputable review media is a time-saver. Bear in mind that there are many items in print and multimedia that are never reviewed. Whether an item garners a favorable review, poor review, or no review, the decision to acquire it is still up to the library's selector.

Listed below are some of the established reviewing sources for books and other media commonly in use by library collections staff:

Major reviewing media for adult titles

Booklist

Choice

Kirkus Reviews

Library Journal

New York Times Book Review

Publishers Weekly

Science Books & Films

Major reviewing media for children's titles

Booklist

Hornbook

School Library Journal

Besides being well respected, these publications devote the bulk of every issue to reviews, each covering thousands of releases annually. Many other specialized and nontraditional periodicals with critical reviews exist as well, although the numbers of reviews included in each of these are much smaller. For most titles listed, the current trend is for the reviews to be available only by paid subscription both in the print periodical version and the online Web site. Some of the Web sites offer free features like Best Book Lists or current articles as teasers or samples of the full online version; most offer free 30-day trials of their online sites.

Some weekly newspapers, such as the *New York Times*, offer Web access to a searchable archive of book reviews (in the case of the *New York Times*, since 1981). Other newspapers offer their current weekly book reviews on a free RSS (really simple syndication) feed so that readers can easily receive them as regular updates that they access via a news feed reader or aggregator. This is becoming a popular way to receive ongoing current Web content without having to remember to check each site manually or having an e-mail inbox swamped with individually sent articles. No doubt policies and access will continue to change as electronic distribution and subscription models evolve. In addition, many online booksellers post in-house editorial comments, excerpts from published critical reviews, and reader/customer opinions free of charge on their Web sites.

Core Collection Lists

Vendors, library trade associations, and publishers produce core collection lists or bibliographies. These serve as a starting point for establishing an opening-day collection or for updating an existing one. Such lists may or may not be annotated or contain reviews. However, inclusion in such a list is usually an implied recommendation. The following are just a few representative core lists—there are many more available. Full citations are listed in the resources section near the end of this chapter.

Periodicals

Magazines for Libraries

Reference collections

Recommended Reference Books for Small and Medium-Sized Libraries and Media Centers

Children's collections

Best Books for Children: Preschool Through Grade 6

Best Books for Middle School and Junior High Readers, Grades 6–9

Best Books for High School Readers, Grades 9–12

Medical libraries

Print Books and Journals for the Small Medical Library

Academic libraries

Choice's Outstanding Academic Books, 1998–2002

Award Winning Titles

There are many literary awards given out each year in various categories, such as children's literature, young adult (YA) literature, adult works, and so on. Some of the most prestigious awards include the Newbery Medal for the most outstanding contribution to children's literature, the Caldecott Medal for the most distinguished picture book, and the Coretta Scott King Book Award for works by African-American authors/illustrators for the children's and teen levels. Representative adult awards include the Pulitzer Prize and the National Book Awards, both of which recognize several categories of fiction, non-fiction, and drama.

In terms of collection development, award winning titles and even runner-up titles automatically garner a lot of media attention, and for libraries this translates into patron curiosity and demand. Such award winners are often "must buys" for libraries, or are at least favorably considered for purchase as they relate to the collection development criteria for each particular library or media center. Start-up collections for new school libraries or for new public library branches routinely include back lists of prestigious award winning titles, since the receipt of a literary prize is seen as an indicator of high quality literature and likely of enduring value. See the resources section at the end of the chapter to locate lists of current and backlist award recipients.

Industry Listservs

Listservs or electronic discussion groups that focus on a particular type of library or information center can be helpful because they often include reviews by group members. These are best used as an augmentation to perusing the major reviewing media because the quantity of items covered on listservs is very limited. Listserv reviews can be a good source for discovering publications by small publishers, specialty items, or items written by colleagues in the field.

WHO SELECTS?

Responsibility for the selection process varies considerably depending on the size of a library or information center and the number of professional librarians on staff. Large university and research libraries with collections numbering in the millions of items will have many subject specialists, resource coordinators, or bibliographers who are experts in their field. Each librarian specialist has responsibility for the selection of materials within his or her area of expertise; for example, French language and literature, environmental sciences, architecture and city planning, American literature, and so forth.

For smaller libraries, areas of responsibility are usually delineated among staffers. In a medium-sized public library, selection assignments might be divided up as follows: children's materials, young adult materials, current fiction, general reference, business reference, medical reference, local history, art and architecture, and so on. Sometimes staff assignments are based on classification system divisions (e.g., 000s, 100s, and so on for collections using the Dewey Decimal scheme). Branch librarians may have direct responsibility for building their own collections, or they may work with a centralized system-wide selection team.

For the solo librarian or technician operating a small special library independently, selection is just one of the many tasks to be juggled.

COLLECTION DEVELOPMENT POLICIES

Most well-run libraries and information centers have a written statement that articulates their vision and policies for developing their collection. Two terms in frequent use for this statement are *materials selection policy* and *collection development policy*. Although sometimes used interchangeably, they

are different. Oregon State University Acquisitions Librarian, Richard Brumley, put it succinctly:

> A materials selection policy is much more limited: [It discusses] what cri-
> teria are used in purchasing (or accepting gift) books, journals, CDs, vid-
> eos, etc., for a library. A collection development policy is much broader:
> in addition to criteria for selecting materials, it will include such things
> as collection assessment, weeding criteria, preservation and conserva-
> tion, balance of monographs to serials, switching formats (print to CD to
> Web), liaison to academic departments, serials cancellation projects, etc.
> One is more apt to use the term *collection development policy* in academic
> libraries or large research libraries, while the term *materials selection
> policy* has a greater public library connotation.[4]

Written Selection Policies

Why do we need material selection or collection development policies in our
libraries and media and information centers? Having a written selection policy
has many advantages, including the following:

It formalizes a plan for selecting materials. By drafting a document, library
staff members are forced to plan ahead and to think critically about their
selection procedure. What are the library's collection goals? What does the
library intend to acquire? By making the policy statement formal, the staff is
guided in making selection decisions and discouraged from making frivolous
purchases. A written policy is taken more seriously than an informal, verbal
one. It also gives the agency a starting point for continuous review and revision. As with any effective policy, periodic updating is needed.

*It provides a chance to draft a new mission statement for the library or revisit
an existing one.* In the past, many library agencies placed most of their efforts
into the routines of day-to-day operations, such as assisting patrons, stocking and restocking materials, essentially keeping the "store" open. Long-term
planning efforts were minimal or overlooked. A written document forces staff
to identify or draft a mission statement, which is a vital first step in the planning process.

Whether beginning the design for a new facility or updating a policy for
an existing library, a mission statement provides a focal point for ensuing
discussion and reflection. To begin with, review of the parent agency's mission statement is necessary. From that, the library's own mission statement
evolves. This can be a thought-provoking exercise that leads staff to discuss
the purpose of the organization, its clientele, its objectives, and other visionary
and organizational concepts.

It prioritizes areas for purchase. As discussed previously, both materials selection and collection development policies describe priority areas for purchase
as well as delineate limitations or types of material not collected. For example,
public libraries may indicate that they do not collect comic books, textbooks,
or workbooks, considering these consumable items best purchased by patrons
for their individual use. Smaller college libraries may indicate that they only
purchase materials related to class offerings. A corporate information center

may decline to purchase fiction or popular bestsellers, focusing instead on technical, work-related materials.

It establishes responsibility. A written policy usually spells out which staff positions are charged with selection and also who has the final responsibility for what is on the library's shelves, network, or Web site. For schools and other publicly accessible libraries, policy should also delineate who has the authority to approve or deny removal of a challenged title.

It becomes official policy. A formal policy statement may need to be reviewed by a governing board or council. This process allows for input and review from other employees or the library's constituents. In the best case, this process helps build support and understanding of the library's role at all levels.

It protects library and staff in cases of complaint or controversy. When a complaint arises and a citizen, parent, or patron questions the appropriateness of an item in the collection, a written policy gives the library or information center credibility. With an approved plan in hand, staff can respond that the purchase meets the selection criteria, is an award-winning book or resource, has received positive reviews, is age appropriate, and so on. A thorough policy should set out specific requirements for the process of challenging an item for removal from the collection.

Criteria for Selection

As part of their written collection development policy, many libraries will delineate specific criteria that they look for when considering materials for purchase. These criteria should also be applied to donations that are accepted for the collection, as well as to items culled during discarding. Some commonly used criteria include the following:

1. Topic: Is this a subject area that the library collection focuses on?
2. Reading level: Is the level appropriate for the library's clientele?
3. Currency: Is the information up to date and timely?
4. Demand: Is much demand anticipated for the topic or for the author; is it tied in with other media?
5. Cost: How does the price compare with other similar items? *Bowker Annual Almanac* tracks average pricing in many categories.
6. Author's credentials: Does the author seem to be credible and knowledgeable on the topic?
7. Publisher or producer's reputation: Is the publisher a small, specialty, or vanity press or a major publishing house; what other titles have they produced?
8. Features: Does the item have extras; for example, an index, bibliographies, special appendices, a CD-ROM, companion Web site, and so forth?
9. Resource sharing: Will other local libraries purchase it?
10. Available in other media: Which version is the most appropriate: print, multimedia, or electronic?

CENSORSHIP

No treatment of libraries and information centers in the United States would be complete without a discussion of censorship and the concept of the freedom to read. Guaranteed by the First Amendment of the Constitution, the right to free speech and expression has been broadly supported by library trade associations, the publishing industry, retail bookstores, and by many individual librarians. For staff this has meant discouraging censorship, advocating patrons' freedom to read or view materials, stocking a diversity of information from different viewpoints, refraining from limiting library materials because of personal beliefs, and remaining neutral when providing access to information.

The ALA devised its *Library Bill of Rights* (see appendix B) in 1948 to interpret library services in light of the First Amendment. Within ALA, its high profile Office for Intellectual Freedom (OIF) is charged with educating librarians and the public about the importance of freedom of expression. The OIF Web site is an excellent source of information on the office's activities and on the promotion of free access to libraries and library materials. Other groups also advocate an individual's right to view or read; for example, the American Film and Video Association's "Freedom to View" statement supports the access rights of minors and adults to multimedia materials. Such statements share the belief that it is the right of each individual to make his or her own decision regarding what to read or view. In the case of minors, these policies explicitly state that it is the responsibility of a parent to supervise and monitor children's choices. Many library agencies and information centers have incorporated these concepts into their own policies.

In practice, academic and research libraries and corporate information centers are more realistically able to support full access and to take an uncompromising anti-censorship stance because their clientele is adult. Those in public and school libraries regulate access to controversial materials and have long been creative in their strategies, from locking book cases, to requiring parental permission slips for access, to avoiding the purchase of controversial books or videos. In some schools, sensitive materials may be housed as special reading and require a counselor's or teacher's referral for access.

What Is Censorship?

What, then, is censorship? A broad definition of censorship is *the practice of suppressing or deleting material considered to be objectionable.* As it most often applies to public or school libraries, censorship is the act of removing titles from the library collection. Typically, books are challenged because they have been selected as required school reading for a certain class or grade level. Parents or other interested parties will often protest a choice as objectionable and seek to have it removed from the reading list, and, perhaps, also from the library.

Classics, dictionaries, contemporary novels, nonfiction works, picture books (the familiar as well as the lesser known) all show up on the list of titles banned, removed, or challenged. Steinbeck's *Of Mice and Men;* Maya Angelou's autobiographical *I Know Why the Caged Bird Sings;* many of Judy Blume's pre-teen titles; the popular Harry Potter novels by J.K. Rowling; the *American Heritage Dictionary;* and Mark Twain's *Adventures of Huckleberry Finn* are perennial targets for removal. See *Banned in the USA* by Herbert Foerstel (listed in the resources section) for a detailed treatment of this heated topic, and see also chapter 8 (Ethics in the Information Age).

Challenging books generates a hotbed of controversy and media coverage for public and school libraries, with much debate ensuing on both sides of the issue. Ironically, challenging a book also stirs up much interest and curiosity about the item in question, which frequently results in increased readership of a controversial title. In the challenge process, library staff members are called upon to support their criteria for having purchased the title, and this often translates into submitting their selection policy to public scrutiny. Most savvy library and school administrators will have in place a detailed process to be followed in consideration of the withdrawal of a title. Based on a Supreme Court ruling, one of the elements of the formula for determining obscenity is to measure an item against the community standards of each specific locality. In other words, each local area sets its own standard for considering items objectionable or appropriate based on the collective opinion of the citizens of the community. This can be a rather imprecise measure for settling a challenge case.

Another twist on censorship that doesn't draw media attention but is all too familiar to library staff is the stealthy actions of individual patrons to censor materials they deem offensive. Some library customers take it upon themselves to remove these materials by ripping out the offending pages, mutilating pictures, or stealing the items in question.

Censorship versus Selection

Naturally, the question arises: how does the selection philosophy and process that takes place in libraries differ from censorship? As discussed previously in this chapter, the selection process is based ideally on articulated criteria for purchasing the highest quality and most appropriate material for a given collection and is not used as a means to ban information.

Librarians and information managers have a professional responsibility to be inclusive, not exclusive, in their collection development, and to refrain from withholding topics because of their own personal beliefs. At the other end of the acquisitions continuum, weeding also should not be seen as a means for removing controversial items. Ideally, libraries and information centers, as nonpartisan suppliers of information, should support in their holdings a wide range of ideas and viewpoints for their customers to access, leaving the customers to draw their own conclusions.

Selection policies might include prioritized categories for purchase or, conversely, areas to be omitted in the collection process. Although some might argue that this is censorship, the intent is to prioritize purchases based on established local needs, because few libraries can afford to buy everything.

The following quotation from longtime American library school educator and scholar on intellectual freedom issues, Lester Asheim, is over half a century ago old now, yet it still rings true in trying to define the ideal spirit of professional library staff as they approach this sensitive responsibility.

Liberty or Control?

Selection, then, begins with a presumption in favor of liberty of thought; censorship, with a presumption in favor of thought control. Selection's approach to the book is positive, seeking, its values in the book as a book, and in the book as a whole. Censorship's approach is negative, seeking for vulnerable characteristics wherever they can be found-anywhere within the book, or even outside it. Selection seeks to protect the right of the reader to read; censorship seeks to protect-not the right-but the reader himself from the fancied effects of his reading. The selector has faith in the intelligence of the reader; the censor has faith only in his own.[5]

What About the Internet?

But now, we have the Internet. This is a relatively new medium against which librarians must apply and test the freedom-of-access philosophy. And the quandary is that the old laws don't apply. The concept of selecting quality materials based on local criteria doesn't apply because, unless effective filters are in place, the Web is not acquired piecemeal. It's an all or nothing acquisition. Official government sites, online retail stores, personal home pages, and more abound, all with text, colorful images, photographs, sound, and video. It just happens that this same environment works equally well for distributing pornographic material as it does for federal tax forms. So although the Internet vastly expands the research sources available to patrons, it also introduces new problems.

The Internet knows no geographical boundaries per se, so the old rule of relying on community standards to determine what is offensive cannot be applied. The federal government has been unable to successfully place limits on pornographic content on the Internet through the so-called decency acts and other similarly intentioned bills.

Librarians are coping by implementing policies that discourage viewing of pornographic material, such as placing terminals in full view of staff, installing privacy shields on computer monitors, requiring parental signatures on consent forms, and posting acceptable use policies. School libraries often make use of filtering software to restrict access to predetermined pornographic sites and also to block searches using offensive keywords. Many public libraries fall back on their support of the freedom to read and view policies, warning all adult patrons that it is up to them to screen and monitor their children's use of the Internet just as they would with DVDs, CDs, books, and other materials.

As library staff would be the first to admit, this is straddling a difficult line—promoting access to information while dealing with concerns about viewing pornography in a public place. But there is something very different about a patron peering at a full-color screen of pornographic images in plain view of children and others, as opposed to a solitary reader perusing an art book of nude figures while tucked away in a corner cubicle. The freedom to read and view has become an even more complex issue, with no easy answers.

WEEDING

Mention weeding to most library staff and they will either groan or reply virtuously that they never have enough time to get to it. Although it is everyone's least favorite task, weeding or de-selecting is an essential aspect of maintaining a relevant, appealing, and timely collection of materials.

Weeding is defined as evaluating existing library holdings for possible replacement, repair, updating, or discarding. It is often carried out in conjunction with an inventory project, a move into new quarters, bar coding installation, or conversion to an automated system.

It's doubtful that any other library can rival the mission statement of the Library of Congress, which is "to sustain and preserve a universal collection of knowledge and creativity for future generations."[6] Nonetheless, even that venerable institution, with its more than 130 million items, does not maintain everything. Although many large research, academic, and special libraries do maintain serious, scholarly, historical collections of great breadth, all collections still need periodic, and often regular, weeding. Thoughtful de-selecting of obsolete, damaged, superseded, or otherwise inappropriate materials complements the care given to the selection of new materials at the beginning of the collection development process.

Another driving force behind the need to cull collections is shelving or storage limits. Floor and stack space are often at a premium; thus, it's not efficient to clutter costly space with unneeded materials. One of many advantages of the digital revolution in publishing is the potential savings in storage or display space that online editions bring. However, this potential is achieved only with careful planning and hard work.

The decision to transfer to a Web-based document, a CD-ROM, or another electronic version of a print title needs to be evaluated by each library or information center. The answer may differ depending upon client preferences and use, the facility's space needs, and cost considerations.

A colleague's recent quandary over how to best provide access to current general encyclopedias exemplifies the typical decisions facing librarians as they renew, purchase, or weed familiar sources each year. With her college library about to undergo a major remodel, our colleague was in the midst of a large weeding project to eliminate unneeded volumes prior to relocating the entire contents of the library's stacks. This caused her to consider the viability of a traditional print reference source, *Encyclopaedia Britannica*. A multi-volume source well known to many public, academic, and school libraries, the *Encyclopaedia Britannica* has been published for over a hundred years and is the oldest continuously published English-language encyclopedia. It takes three full shelves to house this set of 32 oversized volumes, and the set under consideration was more than five years old. The retail price for a new hard copy set in 2006 was about $1,200, a one-year subscription renewal to the full *EB* Web version was $1,140, while access to the limited *EB* Web version on the "teaser" site was free.

Our colleague was pressed to consider discarding the print set and replacing it with a new one; discarding the print volumes and renewing the full Web version; or, as a cost-saving measure, relying entirely on the free teaser site and other limited free online encyclopedia Web sites.

After weighing the options, soliciting staff input, reviewing the history of use (number of access hits) for the online encyclopedia, and carefully reviewing the contents of each version, she reached her decision. She decided to discard the older print version on the shelves and to renew the full Web version because of its superior content over that of the free teaser site and other similar free online encyclopedias. When it comes time to pay for next year's online renewal, the decision will have to be reconsidered.

As with selection, the issues to consider in weeding are many. Cost, currency, physical or electronic storage space, ease of use, and customer preference are critical considerations.

CHANGING FORMATS OF INFORMATION

In the Information Age, librarians and information specialists can be sure of one thing: that is, that information will continue to be repackaged, often at a rapid and overwhelming pace. Other current trends include the continuing merger of large national and international publishers, an emphasis on converting print reference titles to Web-based products, and reliance on the Web for subscriptions to full-text periodical databases. Electronic publishing of textbooks and original book-length works (called e-books) continues to grow, but the lack of a standard delivery platform and the medium's lukewarm acceptance by students and readers has kept this format from meeting its touted promise/popularity. Publishers will continue to produce new works and to repackage old ones—sometimes those already owned by a library. Each must be critically evaluated.

The huge, high profile project underway by search engine giant and innovator Google called Google Book Search plans to digitize the world's books and make them available online. Including partnerships with over a dozen major academic and research libraries (Harvard, Princeton, University of California, Oxford, and others), the project has generated lots of attention as to the potential revolutionary results, as well as controversy among publishers and authors who do not want their copyrights violated. Corporate competitors envision parallel projects, but so far have not produced comparable results.

As publishing formats continue to morph, a problem faced by many libraries attempting to maintain in-depth research or historical back files is the inevitable gap between leasing temporary access and permanent ownership. Renting electronic access means that libraries no longer possess their own copies of books, periodicals, or other works. Rather, they are at the mercy of publishers who may or may not change their access policies or begin charging additional fees for access to archives. For serious research and larger libraries, this uncertainty often means maintaining dual subscriptions—both print and electronic—to ensure access to the complete run of a periodical or reference title. Thus, collecting a comprehensive collection can be expensive.

Once touted as the cost-saving answer to the problem of mushrooming materials costs for libraries, electronic publishing does provide significant added value over print equivalents with its instant delivery, convenience, and many sophisticated searching enhancements. But electronic reference products and services rarely provide cost savings over print versions. And the unspoken reality is that traditional allocations for book budgets keep shrinking as funds are used to pay for electronic editions.

In an era of changing information formats that is at once both exciting and confusing, perhaps the touchstone for collection managers is to adhere to the old adage of knowing their collections—both hard copy and virtual—while continuing to seek out the customers' changing needs.

STUDY QUESTIONS

1. Find a copy of the mission statement for your college or university library. Where did you find it published (e.g., on the library's Web site, in the college catalog, elsewhere)? Do you agree with the mission as stated? Why or why not?

2. Study the collection development policy for a library of your choice. Is it up to date? Does it specify guidelines for weeding as well as collecting new materials? Discuss the similarities and differences between these two processes. Does the collection development policy include the process for handling challenges or requests for removal of materials?

3. Some libraries are posting their collection development policy on their Web sites. What are the pros and cons of publishing these policies on the Web?

4. What is Banned Books Week? Who sponsors it and what is its purpose?

5. Are you aware of any recent attempt to challenge a book at your local public library? Describe the circumstances and the outcome.

6. Does your local public library use social networking tools (e.g., My-Space, Flickr, online reading clubs, etc.) as community-building tools? In your opinion, is this successful? Does the library consider it to be a successful effort?

7. Is your university library a participant in the Google Book Search project? What kind of news reports or press releases can you find on this project?

PRINT RESOURCES

Barr, Catherine and John T. Gillespie, eds. *Best Books for Children: Preschool Through Grade 6.* 8th ed. Westport, CT: Libraries Unlimited, 2005.

Bartlett, Rebecca Ann, ed. *Choice's Outstanding Academic Books, 1998–2002.* Chicago: American Library Association, 2003.

Foerstel, Herbert N. *Banned in the U.S.A.: A Reference Guide to Book Censorship in Schools and Public Libraries.* Revised and Expanded edition. Westport, CT: Greenwood Press, 2002.

Gillespie, John T. and Catherine Barr, eds. *Best Books for High School Readers, Supplement to the First Edition, Grades 9–12.* Westport, CT: Libraries Unlimited, 2006.

Gillespie, John T. and Catherine Barr, eds. *Best Books for Middle School and Junior High Readers, Supplement to the First Edition, Grades 7–10.* Westport, CT: Libraries Unlimited, 2006.

Hysell, Shannon Graff, ed. *Recommended Reference Books for Small and Medium-Sized Libraries and Media Centers.* 2007 ed. Westport, CT: Libraries Unlimited, 2007.

Laguardia, Cheryl, ed. *Magazines for Libraries: For the General Reader and School, Junior College, College, University, and Public Libraries.* 15th ed. New York: R. R. Bowker, 2006.

Web Sites

ALA Youth Media Awards

> http://www.ala.org/ala/pio/mediarelationsa/factsheets/youth mediaawards.htm

(accessed March 22, 2007)

Provides overview information on the many annual awards presented by the American Library Association (ALA) honoring books, videos, and other high quality materials for children and teenagers. Names and describes the major awards, including the Newbery, Caldecott, Coretta Scott King, Michael L. Printz, Margaret A. Edwards, and several others. The site also has links to news of current award winners and backlists of all winners through the years.

Brandon/Hill Selected Lists-Levy Library-Mount Sinai School of Medicine

> http://www.mssm.edu/library/Brandon-hill/small_medical/index. shtml

(accessed February 7, 2007)

Web-based version and 2003 update of the classic hard copy bibliography by Alfred N. Brandon and Dorothy R. Hill, *Selected List of Books and Journals for the Small Medical Library.*

Collection development on Library Journal.com

> http://www.libraryjournal.com/community/891/ Collection+Development/42796.html

(accessed February 28, 2007)

A new Web site compiled by one of the industry's leading periodicals, *Library Journal,* this is an interactive toolkit featuring a variety of recent bestseller and other recommended lists from libraries and other sources.

Library Resource Guide

> http://www.libraryresource.com

(accessed February 7, 2007)

A paid advertising site operated by publisher Information Today, Inc. This Web site contains alphabetical and categorical listings for many supply companies, publishers, and industry vendors.

New York Times

  http://www.nytimes.com/pages/books/

(accessed February 7, 2007)

Searchable, online archive of book reviews from the respected *New York Times* daily and Sunday sections.

National Book Foundation

  http://www.nationalbook.org/nba.html

(accessed March 22, 2007)

Since 1950, this foundation has presented their prestigious annual awards to "enhance the public's awareness of exceptional books written by fellow Americans, and to increase the popularity of reading in general." View press releases on current awards and lists of past prizewinners.

Office of Intellectual Freedom

  http://www.ala.org/alaorg/oif/

(accessed February 7, 2007)

From ALA's Office of Intellectual Freedom. An extensive resource of updates, policies, and interpretations on the freedom to view and read as it affects libraries, librarians, and patrons.

NOTES

1. David Lake, "The Web: Growing by 2 Million Pages a Day," *The Industry Standard* (IDG Publications, February 28, 2000), http://www.thestandard.com/article/0,1902,12329,00.html (accessed December 6, 2001).

2. *Netcraft: Web Server Survey Archives,* http://news.netcraft.com/archives/web_server_survey.html (accessed December 14, 2006).

3. Dave Bogart, ed., *The Bowker Annual: Library and Book Trade Almanac,* 51st ed. (Medford, NJ: Information Today, 2006), 516.

4. Richard Brumley, e-mail to author, January 27, 1999.

5. Lester Asheim, "Not Censorship But Selection," *Wilson Library Bulletin* 28 (September 1953): 67.

6. Library of Congress, "Mission and Strategic Plan of the Library (Library of Congress)," *Mission of the Library of Congress,* http://www.loc.gov/about/mission/ (accessed February 7, 2007).

Chapter 5

Preparing Materials for Use

The careful selection of library items described in the preceding chapter is just the first of multiple stages in the preparation of materials for use by customers. Further steps include acquisition, cataloging, classification, and, for hard copy formats, physical processing of each requested item. Although every library develops its own routine for handling these operations, there are many shared activities and functions common to both the largest and smallest of collections.

ACQUISITION

Selection is the systematic process of choosing materials relevant to a library or information center, whereas acquisition is the nuts and bolts of procuring titles and paying the companies that produce or supply the items. As with selection, acquisition is usually under the umbrella of Technical Services in a library and takes place out of the public eye.

According to *Bowker Annual: Library and Book Trade Almanac,* more than 190,000 book titles alone were produced in the United States in 2004.[1] These were the products of over 3,500 American book publishers.[2] The relationship of buyer and seller closely binds libraries and publishers together.

There are numerous types and sizes of publishers, with many now offering multimedia and electronic works in addition to the more traditional print titles. Most libraries and information centers select books and other publications from a variety of publishers in order to fill their collection needs. Publishers may include large corporate publishers owned by powerful media outlets; university presses, which produce more scholarly and esoteric titles of limited appeal; regional publishers specializing in a geographic area; children's publishing houses; and small or alternative presses, which produce limited print runs on a variety of material, including poetry, literature, health, religion, and other topics. Some publishers narrowly limit the subject areas in which they produce titles, or focus on a particular age group or other demographic.

Reference book publishers closely target the library market and may include library professionals as editorial consultants to develop relevant and timely products. Trade publishers direct their products at a particular professional or industry group. Seasoned librarians develop name recognition of and an appreciation for many specific publishers as they purchase their materials over the years. This is helpful in the selection process because a publisher's reputation can influence a decision of whether or not to buy an item.

As in the rest of the corporate world, mergers are occurring in the publishing industry, both nationally and internationally. This trend tends to make library professionals and others worry about the resulting tight control of what gets published and the quandary of having too few outlets to allow for varied voices and points of view. An additional concern is the consolidation of multiple media under one roof; for example, print, TV, and online, as exemplified by the America Online and Time Warner merger in 2001, or the acquisition of the venerable *Wall Street Journal* newspaper by Rupert Murdoch's News Corp. media empire in 2007. Such mergers further narrow the information sources to which the public is exposed.

To gain an overview of the North American publishing industry, browse the annual reference work *Literary Market Place (LMP)*. A comprehensive directory of that region's publishing industry, *LMP* is essential for locating and identifying information about publishers and ancillary services, such as jobbers, bookbinders, electronic publishing services, and so forth, and includes a classified index to publishing houses by specialty. Some publishing companies depend exclusively on regional sales personnel to market and sell their products. The sales representatives may regularly call on libraries in their territory to promote and vend their title list. Many other publishers work either directly with libraries and retail outlets or through middlemen known as *jobbers* to sell their products.

The Services of a Jobber

Libraries, media, and information centers most commonly use jobbers or wholesalers to acquire materials. Jobbers and wholesalers are industry middlemen who supply books, videos, CDs, DVDs, and other materials to retail stores and libraries from hundreds of individual publishers. Familiar industry names include Brodart, Baker and Taylor, Ingram, BWI, Mook and Blanchard, Blackwell, and many more. For library science students and novices to the world of libraries, conferences and industry trade shows also provide good opportunities to visit jobbers' booths and find out about their many specialized services.

Jobbers pass on to libraries a discount from the publisher on the suggested retail or list price of an item. Typically, discounts range from a low of five percent to a high of 40 percent. Other services offered by wholesalers include customized processing and cataloging of materials, special heavy-duty bindings, MARC records, foreign language titles, bar codes, standing orders, and opening-day collections.

Although the majority of library purchases are handled through jobbers for convenience, efficiency, and cost savings, some small presses and specialty producers may require that an order be placed directly with them, thus by-passing jobbers. For libraries purchasing thousands of titles each year, relying on jobbers for the bulk of acquisitions is a necessity. Because *direct orders* are more time-consuming for a library staff to handle and track, these are typically kept to a minimum.

Most libraries work with a number of different wholesalers to acquire the variety of materials their collection demands. Just as there are general and specialty publishing firms, there are jobbers that handle mainstream current releases of print and nonprint titles and those that deal exclusively with medical or legal titles or only with periodical subscriptions. Thus, most libraries have accounts with multiple wholesalers to procure all the materials they need. And even with various jobbers to choose from, many libraries and information centers make purchases from their community or online bookseller because of immediate need, exclusive distribution, or other considerations. The growth and success of online booksellers has also contributed to the trend of libraries buying slightly used copies (in good condition) of books through these sites rather than paying a higher price for a brand new copy even with the jobber price breaks.

Order Plans

Many jobbers and individual publishers offer an acquisitions service known as an *approval plan.* When subscribing to an approval plan, a library submits a detailed profile of its selection criteria to the jobber, who then automatically ships materials matching the profile to the library. Items are still subject to approval by the acquisitions librarian or other designated staff. After review, undesirable items are returned. The objectives are to save staff time in the selection and ordering processes for certain predictable subject areas, to be able to select with the book in hand rather than relying solely on a review, and to expedite the receipt of materials. Generally, approval plans work best for very large libraries, which are likely to purchase the majority of titles released by designated publishers anyway. If much more than five percent of the titles received on approval are being returned, the library's profile needs to be adjusted.

Standing orders or continuation plans are another time-saver for libraries and good business for publishers or wholesalers. With a standing order contract, a library indicates that it will automatically purchase each new edition of a title; there is no need to be on the watch for an upcoming edition. Upon release, the publication is immediately supplied and the library is billed. Standing order status is most likely to be applied to standard reference works and sets, where a library is confident it wants each new edition of a must-have title.

Another service offered by some companies is book rental, as opposed to outright purchase. For example, the McNaughton Books service by Brodart, which allows libraries to lease a certain quantity of new releases, is a popular choice, particularly among public libraries. The staff pre-selects titles from a monthly catalog of forthcoming titles. This provides a steady infusion of new titles that can either be returned when their popularity has waned or, if needed, purchased to add to the permanent library collection.

This service provides an effective solution for meeting the rush of interest that often accompanies the release of highly promoted titles and popular best-sellers. Multiple copies of such a title can be rented at a savings, and, because the service provides the books as shelf-ready, staff processing time is saved as well. Rental plans can improve customer satisfaction while saving the staff time and money. Some libraries pass on the cost of such a program to patrons, charging daily rental fees for these books; others choose to absorb the cost and circulate them free of charge.

Many jobbers and vendors employ professional librarians to enhance their customer service and provide innovative ideas for products. As a job seeker, you may want to explore employment opportunities among the many industry wholesalers, product vendors, and supply companies.

Although a company may sometimes function both as a wholesaler of materials and a seller of library-specific supplies, there are many firms that vend only the unique equipment, furnishings, shelving, housing, security devices, and other supplies targeted for the library industry. A few examples of library supply and equipment companies are Demco, Gaylord, Highsmith, Library Bureau, and Metal Edge. There are many others.

Leasing

Many business, financial, and marketing publications, such as telephone company crisscross directories and corporate directories, have long been available to library collections not through outright purchase but rather through lease agreements. This keeps older, used copies from being retained or resold, thus allowing the publishers tighter control over the use of their valuable data and final published products.

Licensing

As libraries' reliance on electronic sources of information, or e-collections, grows, so does the importance of negotiating the licensing agreement with the publisher, now a standard part of the acquisitions process. Commonplace with the purchase of computer software, then with CD-ROM products, and now with Web-delivered sources, licensing is a growing area of library responsibility. The procurement of online sources may be handled directly with the company that produces the database, periodical index, full-text books, or other information product, or the resources may be procured through a library purchasing consortia

In some cases, when library consortia such as academic library systems have negotiated group purchase deals, an intermediary agency may serve as a bursar or third party in implementing the leases. This third-party arrangement gives libraries more leverage in bargaining with large corporations. A license will specify the terms of access that the library or information center is agreeing to with their purchase; this may vary from annual pricing for just one year's access to the more expensive ongoing access with retrospective access rights.

Licenses are arranged for specific periods of time—typically on an annual basis, though it is sometimes possible to negotiate multiple-year agreements. Access to the e-collection, once the license period is over, varies depending on the terms of the agreement. In some cases, if the contract is not renewed or paid, access to the e-collection vanishes overnight, with nothing to show for the library's past investments. Thus, the licensing concept is a very significant one for libraries, with access rather than ownership as a core issue.

Publishers use licensing as a legal means of controlling the use of their products. Thus, licensing agreements are legal contracts that bear scrutiny by the acquiring party, in this case, the library (licensee). Generally, the seller (or licensor) prepares the contract with the terms of the agreement. In many cases, individual libraries do not have a level negotiating position in dealing with large content providers. In this situation, libraries run the risk of giving up certain rights that they and their patrons would have enjoyed if the rights had been defined by copyright laws that allow for fair use, particularly in educational settings. Care should be taken to make sure that the library understands what it is being asked to agree to when it negotiates a license.

Fees are usually determined by the approximate number of users allowed access; for example, the number of employees in a corporation, the size of a school's student body, the current enrollment of a university, or the population served by a public library. A site license may include access for multiple offices, branches, or campuses affiliated with the main library agency, or the agreement may require additional site licenses to provide access to these other physical locations. In some agreements, a password allows users remote access from off-site, such as from home or from another location. In other cases, access is restricted to onsite computers only, based on a range of authenticated IP (Internet Protocol) addresses that uniquely identify the computers in the licensee's library. Although providing value-added service and an ever-increasing number of convenient options, typical licensed electronic products, such as indexing and abstracting services and full-text databases of journals, are not cheaper than their print equivalents. In fact, they often cost substantially more. In some cases, the publisher imposes restrictions or conditions along with the electronic access, such as requiring the licensee to maintain simultaneous print subscriptions to their products, although this practice appears to be waning.

Consortia Efforts

As statewide and regional library consortia in the United States mature, a high priority for them is to seek site licenses to make selected electronic resources available to their entire membership. These consortia may include libraries of similar size and type, such as an academic library group, or may be a regional, multi-type network with everything from prison libraries to school media centers to museum research facilities and more. An example of an academic library group is the Community College Library Consortium. This cooperative buying group represents the largest system of higher education in the United States—the 109 public community college campuses in California—and actively negotiates consortium pricing and licensing agreements for online database subscriptions and e-book collections. In Britain and other European countries, national site licensing is being piloted for all the university and polytechnic libraries of an entire country. This means that all current students and all faculty members within a particular country have access to certain products in electronic form.[3] For all such library groups or consortia, negotiated contract rates for library regions, university systems, or other memberships can often provide significant price breaks.

Library Concerns

Besides the expense of electronic subscriptions and the slippery issue of perpetual access, there are other challenges to e-collections. Especially noticeable with periodical databases is that, to appeal to the widest possible range of potential library clients, publishers often mix scholarly and popular titles into one product. The result can be an unfocused mishmash—something that does not occur with customized, individual print subscriptions. And the library cannot narrowly refine its collection within an e-journal product as it could with individual hard copy subscriptions; an electronic subscription is a package deal.

Some vendors are now talking about allowing individual libraries to tailor the list of titles they want to include in the index along with the full-text offered to patrons. It remains to be seen if this trial option will be judged as commercially viable. It is much more labor intensive, both for the vendor and for the library. It is easier to try to make one size fit all. However, from the researcher's point of view, it might be best to have an index to all electronic and print holdings for which full text is immediately available—whether online or onsite. Why tantalize customers with citations if the documents are not readily available?

Other concerns include licensing restrictions on what librarians consider standard library services and practices, such as providing interlibrary loans for periodical articles from an electronic resource. Also, there is no guarantee that the particular titles found in an e-collection today will, in fact, be there tomorrow. The arrangements between the actual periodical publishers and the producers of the e-product are subject to change and revision, resulting in the addition and deletion of titles without notice to subscribers.

Some good guidelines and active discussions of the issues surrounding e-collections can be found by visiting the Web sites of the leading trade associations and by joining listservs that focus on licensing issues. The licensing of electronic resources is very much an evolving area where the old rules don't apply. Library staff responsible for acquiring these resources and for negotiating licenses will want to keep up-to-date on the issues and should be encouraged to actively lobby publishers to make their collection needs known.

Finally, never accept publishers' definition of what *copyright* or *fair use* means. This is one of the few issues on which publishers and librarians have divergent viewpoints and conflicting interests. Many publishers use license agreements in an attempt to get librarians to give up rights inherent under the fair use clause of the copyright law. On the other hand, many publishers are very generous in granting libraries, particularly those in educational institutions, rights to use their materials in ways that may well go beyond what copyright laws mandate.

Electronic Ordering Systems

Compared to the neighborhood book dealer, the chain store at the mall, or your favorite online bookseller, the local library has always been plagued with an abysmally slow turnaround time in making hard copy materials available for patrons. Many of the services offered by jobbers focus on speeding up delivery and outsourcing processing and cataloging tasks. The end result should mean faster provision of materials to library customers.

The advent of Web-based order placement has delivered on the promise of speed at that starting point in the acquisitions process. Established customers can quickly place an order by accessing the Internet, and, with the click of a mouse, instantly submit their order to the jobber. The old, tedious task of generating paper order cards, then filing and tracking them, has been left behind. Figure 5.1 shows an Acquisitions Ledger from the 1940s.

At the heart of today's ordering systems is the International Standard Book Number (ISBN). A unique number assigned before publication to a book or specific edition of a book, the ISBN identifies the work's national, geographic, language, or other group, and its publisher, title, edition, and volume number. ISBNs are critical when ordering a specific title and are the key identifier for electronic acquisitions systems both in libraries and in the retail world.

Originally a 10-digit number when it was first adopted in 1969, the ISBN was expanded to a 13-digit sequence in 2007 to accommodate the future need for more numbers. Today, the two sequences are being referred to as ISBN-10

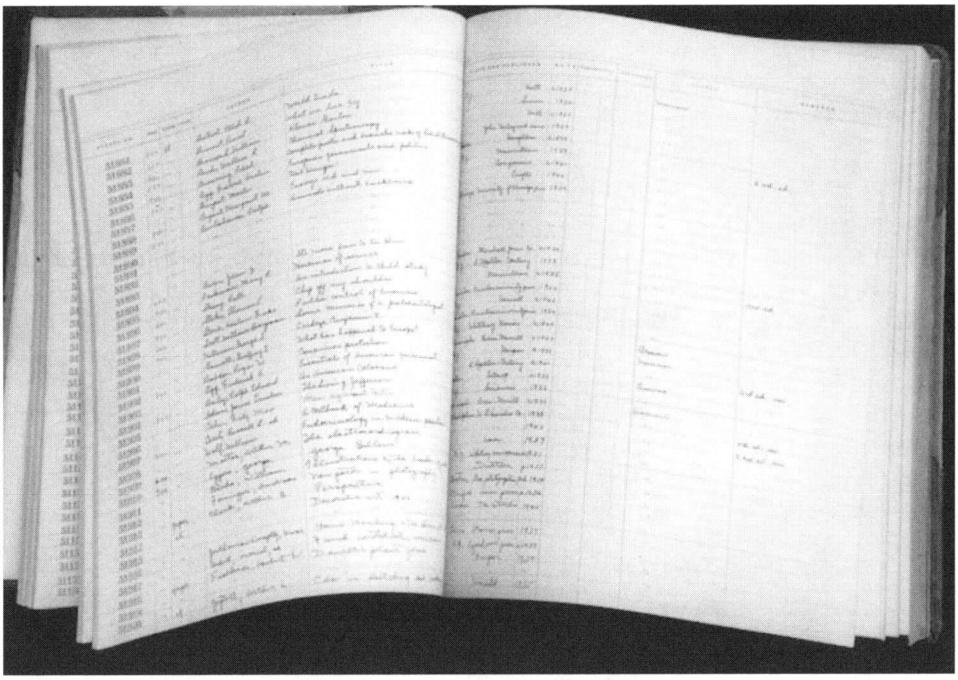

Figure 5.1. Before the era of automated library operations began in the 1960s, acquisitions and circulation data were often logged by hand into large ledgers. This Acquisitions Accession Book is from Pasadena Junior College, circa 1940.

and ISBN-13 to differentiate between them. The revision of the ISBN has impacted publishers, distributors, booksellers large and small, libraries, and vendors, as they have had to adjust their workflow to deal with the new, longer numbers.

To take full advantage of doing business in a Web-based ordering environment, library staff may be required to use a bank credit card for payment. Many e-businesses are set up to accept credit cards only. Parent institutions may need to be educated about the advantages of allowing library staff to commit funds in this manner, which appears to bypass some of the fiscal safeguards that are typical in the workplace. As an added incentive to customers using Web-based ordering, some vendors may offer discounts when a credit card is used because this method frees them from complicated billing procedures.

In addition to the advantages of paperless orders and swift submission of those orders, Web-based acquisition consolidates what were once several separate, time-consuming clerical tasks. Most bibliographic verification can now be accomplished through browsing publishers' or retailers' Web sites. By toggling back and forth between a bibliographic utility, the library's automated system, and the jobber's Web site, order requests can be checked quickly against current holdings, then the verified order submitted. Accounting records are generated easily, and the MARC record for an on-order item can be added immediately to the library catalog, giving patrons a status report on the title that is being acquired.

The standardization of Web technology is an improvement over earlier, automated ordering systems, which relied on software and hardware that was specific to each vendor. With a Web interface, the process is familiar, easy, and doesn't require disks or CDs. The speed, ease of use, and consolidation of tasks that have resulted from Web-based ordering frees up staff time for learning new technologies, computer maintenance and troubleshooting, special projects, and other tasks.

Out-of-Print Materials

Books, videos, DVDs, individual periodical issues, and other materials in demand by researchers and needed as replacement copies for library collections often may be out of print. This means that the publisher is no longer producing the item, and no new copies are available for order. Out-of-print status may be temporary or permanent. Either way, a library in need of an out-of-print title may contact a search service or query an out-of-print dealer to attempt to procure a copy. Out-of-print and second-hand book dealers abound online now, and, of course, there are the traditional "brick-and-mortar" dealers as well. Surcharges added by dealers vary considerably.

CATALOGING AND CLASSIFICATION

As new items arrive in the Technical Services area, they are unpacked, checked against packing slips, and examined for defects. If there are no problems with the order, the items are ready for the cataloging staff to handle. The purpose of cataloging materials is twofold: (1) to provide a shelf address or location for each book, CD, DVD, video, e-book, or other item, and (2) to provide specific information for the library holdings database. After Technical Services staff assign classification numbers (more commonly referred to as call numbers), determine subject headings, and provide descriptive information on an item, all is entered into the library's database, known as an OPAC (online public access catalog). This database of information provides a master inventory of holdings and allows patrons to search the automated catalog, whether on site or off site. It answers the following questions, among others: "What books or resources does the library carry on my topic?" "Does the library have a specific book or resource?" "Where is it located?" "Is it available now?" "Is it a hard copy book I can check out; or is it an e-book that I link to?"

The two most common classification systems in use in North American libraries are LC and Dewey Decimal. LC evolved from the original organizing scheme that U.S. President Thomas Jefferson used for his own book collection before selling it to the new national library. An alpha–numeric system, LC is in use mostly in larger libraries, such as academic and research facilities. Melvil Dewey's decimal-based scheme was introduced in 1876 and remains the standard among public and school libraries. It has been translated into many languages and is commonly used outside of the United States. An example of a more specialized classification is the Superintendent of Documents (SuDocs) system, used for large government document collections. SuDocs divides a collection into subgroups of documents based on the agency that issued or produced them.

The automation of library bibliographic records began with the invention of the MARC record. MARC records are a standard way of recording and sharing information about a bibliographic item. By using three types of content designators—tags, subfield codes, and indicators—the information is stored electronically and can be retrieved and interpreted by any other computer in the world that is programmed to read MARC records. For example, anyone reading a MARC record can assume that information found in the 245 field is information about the title and author, listed exactly in the form as it is shown on the title page of the book. Variant title information, such as the spine title, would be in the 246 field. The records can contain all the information displayed in OPACs as well as additional information that is useful to librarians. It is beyond the purpose of this text to fully explain the intricacies of the actual MARC coding. Readers who seek a deeper level of understanding should refer to the resources section at the end of this chapter for a citation to a tutorial.

Once a library has cataloged a book or another real or virtual bibliographic item and has coded the resulting cataloging data into MARC format, that data can be passed on to other libraries and read by their cataloging software without human intervention. This allows libraries to acquire cataloging data from the Library of Congress and other libraries with respected cataloging standards without repeating the labor-intensive effort of original cataloging. The receiving library has only to verify that the MARC record actually describes the item in hand and not some other edition or variant.

MARC format was originally developed by the Library of Congress in the 1960s, but quickly evolved into the international standard for exchanging bibliographic data. For example, the Diet Library in Tokyo serves many of the functions of the national library of Japan. Japanese books are cataloged there and coded into MARC format. The resulting MARC records can be used by libraries the world over who want to have Japanese vernacular records for the Japanese books in their collections. As the Internet has raised the bar for searching over the last decade with sophisticated natural language searching and meta data tagging common to today's powerful search engines, a heated debate within the library field is whether MARC is still viable. In response to this concern and to the changing standards for accessing information, the Library of Congress has developed a framework for working with MARC data in a xml (Extensible Markup Language) environment called the MARC21 XML Schema. The concept is to retain MARC record elements, but to be able to use them in newer, more flexible and sophisticated ways.

One influential thinker and librarian outside of the United States was the Indian scholar Shiyali Ramamrita Ranganathan (1892–1972), whose major contributions to library science centered around classification and indexing theory. Ranganathan's Colon Classification (CC) system was developed as an attempt to improve on the Dewey Decimal system. Its name comes from the use of colons to separate facets in class numbers.

In addition, Ranganathan's 1931 treatise *The Five Laws of Library Science* is considered a classic in the field; it is still referred to and has been re-examined to explore how it applies to ideals of library service in today's Information Age. For example, Ranganathan's First Law, "BOOKS ARE FOR USE," can still inspire a spirited debate—on a blog or in a face-to-face discussion—on contemporary access and copyright issues.

Descriptive versus Subject Cataloging

There are two types of cataloging that take place for each item in a collection. *Descriptive cataloging* delineates the physical characteristics of a book, video, data file, or other material. Depending on the format, this may include data such as size and physical dimensions, number of pages, length of running time, accompanying leaflets or CD-ROMs, and so forth. *Subject cataloging* focuses on content by identifying the primary subject or subjects of an item and then assigning the best subject headings and classification number to reflect this. The goal is to allow researchers to search an OPAC by keyword, author, title, subject, or other access point to locate an item of potential interest based on the carefully assigned headings and call numbers.

At one time, most cataloging was done on a one-by-one basis, with each individual item scrutinized and cataloged from scratch. This was a labor-intensive activity and resulted in massive duplication of effort. With the invention of many time-saving solutions, such as the catalog card distribution program at the Library of Congress, the ability to purchase digital cataloging data from jobbers, and today's cooperative catalogs and worldwide bibliographic utilities, there has been a sizeable reduction in the amount of original cataloging required by library staff. Instead, copy cataloging has become commonplace for a large majority of items.

By searching a large, reliable database of completed MARC records, such as those on OCLC (Online Computer Library Center), a library cataloging technician can locate the data for a specific item, then download or copy that information to use in local records. The customary placement of Cataloging-in-Publication (CIP) data in new releases, a joint effort since 1971 by Library of Congress and publishers to standardize cataloging data, is another helpful tool to expedite cataloging. Check the verso page (i.e., the reserve side of the title page, which will be a left-hand page) to find CIP data in many books.

Cooperative databases, such as the substantial OCLC holdings referred to previously, are built from records submitted by the Library of Congress and supplemented by member libraries, museums, and other research agencies. As of 2007, OCLC's record count exceeded 74 million,[4] and the WorldCat database grows by nearly one new record every 10 seconds.[5] Even video, DVD, and nonprint titles are increasingly represented on this database. Thus, the need for labor-intensive, original cataloging still exists, but on a decreasing basis.

A significant amount of original cataloging does take place in larger academic and research libraries with collections that include government documents, manuscript and archival materials, foreign language titles, scholarly serials, and scientific proceedings. In these facilities, there are often many language specialists among the Technical Services staff whose responsibility it is to catalog all items in their area (e.g., Romance languages, Slavic languages, Asian languages).

Along with the decrease in the need for original cataloging, the automation of most libraries' card files has also meant the elimination of many of the previous tedious, repetitive tasks of old such as updating and filing of cards in the physical catalog drawers and in the accompanying shelf list. Cataloging operations have changed dramatically over the last 35 years. The authors have observed that most libraries now provide original cataloging for less than 10 percent of their acquisitions, and many smaller libraries can find acceptable cataloging copy for all but one or two percent of new materials. These exceptions in need of original cataloging might include items such as local government documents and the occasional title from a small publisher. Rather than reinventing the wheel at each library around the world, the cataloging process has become much more streamlined.

Processing

The last step in the chain of events before stocking the shelves for customer use is to physically process each item. Although many aspects of Technical Services are highly automated, the processing that must take place before an item is shelf-ready remains a low-tech operation. Stamping materials with library ownership stamps, adhering call number labels and label protectors, installing magnetic security tapes, applying protective book jacket covers, and other tasks are necessary to protect materials from theft and to make them accessible on the shelves.

Larger libraries have separate acquisitions and cataloging divisions within the technical services department, where head librarians oversee each operation and the library technicians, clerks, student assistants, and volunteers. Many library employees who have a preference for limited public contact find their niche in the predictable workflow of acquisitions and cataloging. They also take much satisfaction in the ongoing stocking of the library, previewing new materials, and knowing that they are providing patrons with a steady incoming flow of the resources they need.

Physical processing requires an exacting attention to detail and an ability to follow through on lengthy, complex tasks where accuracy is critical. In larger research libraries, a knowledge of foreign languages is often required, as is an understanding of the subdivisions of fields of knowledge. In these facilities, the processing of monographs may be an entirely separate operation from the processing of serials and periodicals, with different departments maintained to acquire, catalog, and physically prepare each category for researchers' use. In the largest Technical Services departments, workflow may be assigned based on the language or subject of the material being processed. In contrast, one person does it all in the smallest of branch libraries or information centers—from the most menial to the more intellectually challenging tasks.

SPECIAL MATERIALS

Certain types of information formats that libraries collect don't conform to the standard acquisitions, cataloging, and processing model described previously. In fact, within research, university, and larger public libraries, it is typical to find separate departments organized around formats such as periodicals, manuscripts, rare books, institutional archives, local history, microforms, and government documents. Each of these materials has unique housing, display, and access needs that warrant the organization of its own discrete department.

Periodical Collections

Any discussion of *periodical* collections must take into account the definitions of the terms *periodical* and *serial.* Based on the authors' experiences and conversations with colleagues, there is considerable ambiguity as to the precise meanings of the terms. Added to that, there are many localized variations of use in the workplace that are often dependent on the size of the library's collection.

Arlene Taylor uses the following definitions in her classic textbook *Introduction to Cataloging and Classification:*[6]

> **Serial:** A publication issued in successive parts at regular or irregular intervals and intended to continue indefinitely. Included are periodicals, newspapers, proceedings, reports, memoirs, annuals, and numbered monographic series.
>
> **Periodical:** A publication with a distinctive title, which appears in successive numbers or parts at stated or regular intervals and which is intended to continue indefinitely. Usually each issue contains articles by several contributors. Newspapers and memoirs, proceedings, journals, etc., of corporate bodies primarily related to their internal affairs are not included in this definition.

As is apparent from the definitions, *serial* is a much broader term than *periodical*, and in very large research and academic libraries with sizeable holdings of scientific proceedings, annuals, and so on, the distinction will have great significance. For purposes of general discussion, this book will use the more common term *periodical.*

Periodicals account for a critical part of any library, media, or information center's research collection. In many disciplines, particularly scientific and technical, periodicals form the primary and almost exclusive means of communicating new knowledge. Published with predictable frequency, which may be weekly, monthly, quarterly, or at other intervals, periodicals provide a continual flow of fresh information into the library collection.

Periodical publications differ in concept and coverage from books. Also known as monographs, books are single works, although they may come out in multiple parts or volumes, are not intended to continue indefinitely, and tend to treat a topic in more depth than an article. The term *monograph* also has a more narrow, technical meaning, but in this work the term will be used in its generic sense. Periodical issues are numbered consecutively with sequential volume and issue numbers to differentiate between each unique part and to reflect their publishing order.

Frequent fluctuations in the publishing of periodicals, such as title changes, title splits, mergers, acquisitions, cessations, and other events, require special cataloging expertise to properly compile and revise holdings records for them.

In addition, many periodicals now maintain companion Web sites that differ in many ways from their corresponding hard copy formats. These companion Web sites may offer free Web access to current and back issues, Web access for paid subscribers only, or a combination of the above where some content is free to all and the rest available only to subscribers. Most periodical companion Web sites share a common trait in that they are updated more frequently than their print versions.

Categories of Periodicals

Periodicals are typically divided into several categories based on their targeted audience and technical level. *Magazines* tend to be written for the layperson, use vocabulary easily understood by the average reader, and are glossy, full-color publications replete with advertisements and photographs. Think of the familiar publications found on newsstands and in doctors' waiting rooms—those are magazines.

In contrast, *journals* are written for a particular academic or professional audience. Scholars and professors in the field are the major contributors. Articles and studies may be reviewed or juried by an editorial board of highly respected peers before being accepted for publication in a particular journal. Journals assume that their readers have specialized vocabulary and knowledge, often at a highly technical level. Expect journal articles to be signed; that is, the author or authors are given an obvious byline with their professional credentials noted. At the end of the journal article, there is usually an extensive bibliography, list of works cited, or other documentation for further reference.

In terms of physical appearance, journals are not as eye-catching as magazines because they do not try to appeal to the general public. Often, they have few ads and few illustrations. Graphs or charts that are included often require some technical knowledge on the part of the reader.

Trade periodicals fall in between the two previous categories. These tend to be written for a specific professional or industry group, such as nurses, librarians, electricians, network managers, and so forth. Their content is narrowly focused on the given field, but the reading and vocabulary level is usually discernible to the layperson.

Then there is the *newspaper*—perhaps the publication most familiar to the reading public. Newspapers range from prestigious national dailies to weekly rural papers. They focus on current events, weather, and sports, among other topics. Note that according to the definitions above, a newspaper is technically a serial rather than a periodical. In practical usage in the workplace, newspapers are treated, processed, and housed much like the periodicals described previously.

It is important to note that with the rapid growth of periodical publishing on the Internet, the distinctions between categories so obvious in the hard copy counterparts are becoming blurred.

Hard Copy Needs

Because of their ongoing publication, relatively small size, and often time-sensitive value, hard copy periodicals require much labor-intensive handling before they make it onto the library's shelves for patron access. In large library facilities, tracking the receipt of each issue, individual labeling, security tattle-taping, shelving, and eventual binding can employ dozens of library technicians and student assistants.

Some of the processing needs that often require a separate periodicals department include the following:

The currency of contents requires a very short turnaround time in making the periodicals available to customers.

The slim size makes periodicals vulnerable to theft, so care must be taken in attaching security targets (tattletapes) to each issue.

The high use and vulnerability to theft often require a closed stack or reserve collection, which increase both space and staffing needs.

The ongoing publication requires the claiming of lost or missing replacement issues to maintain a complete title run.

The wear and tear on the paper copies often necessitates binding into annual volumes for durability and retention.

The temporary housing of current, high-interest issues in display shelving, rather than stacks, for customer convenience increases overall handling requirements.

In summary, periodicals add a vital element of timely material covering an incredible diversity of subject areas to any library collection. They require labor-intensive processing and a high level of maintenance to ensure access and complete back files.

Even though today's libraries rely increasingly on electronic access to periodical indexes and full-text article databases for their current subscriptions, the majority maintain a mix of paper copies and electronic versions. In some cases, this translates into purchasing simultaneous subscriptions to the same title to ensure access to periodical archives or back runs. In other cases, publishers require a paper subscription before they will grant access to an e-subscription. The model varies, but hard copy periodicals are still a key component of library collections.

Staffing

Larger libraries of all types may employ professionals whose primary responsibility is overseeing the periodicals collection. A periodicals, or serials, librarian will typically coordinate the selection, acquisition, processing, organization, and management of the library's periodicals collection. In large research libraries, which receive thousands of subscriptions, several serials assistants are employed in the check in, claiming, and cataloging of periodicals to get them to the public as near to the time of arrival as possible.

New products, publishing trends, title changes, and emerging patron preferences in this rapidly changing area make such a job more dynamic and challenging than it was in the past, when emphasis was often centered on balancing tight budgets with collection needs as subscription prices spiraled upward. That fiscal challenge has not disappeared. Rather, it has morphed into the question of how to maintain existing collections with budget dollars split between hard copy titles and electronic subscriptions, and then, in addition, possibly adding new subscriptions to electronic periodical resources—all set against the backdrop of static funding levels.

Special Collections

Collections of original manuscripts, photographs, architectural drawings, diaries, first editions, realia, institutional archives, and other unique materials usually with an historical focus are often centered in a section of the library known as the *special collections department.* Such a department focuses on the acquisition, management, storage, preservation, and user access of these special holdings, just as a general library unit operates its general book and multimedia collection. In the biggest of libraries there may be multiple special collections departments (e.g., archives, manuscripts, rare books, local history). How these collections are differentiated depends on local needs. Typically, *archives* refer to documents generated by the organization itself in the daily course of doing business (e.g., by the college or municipality or corporation of which the library is a subordinate unit). Similar documents originating from outside the organization might be housed in an entirely separate unit called *manuscripts.* Care and organization of the materials is very similar. rare books and local history departments are less distinct divisions and tend to blend many of the characteristics from general collections with those of special collections.

Even the largest of libraries severely limit the scope of the manuscripts they collect. For example, the library at the University of Illinois–Urbana is the third largest university research library in the United States; its Rare Book & Manuscript Library has over 300,000 books and more than 7,130 linear feet of manuscript materials; however, there are only a handful of topics for which it attempts to collect any scrap of information, regardless of the format. Among those topics earmarked for comprehensive collecting are materials by and about President Abraham Lincoln and author/poet Carl Sandburg. This is an example of the general practice of collecting policy being determined by the curriculum or research focus of the parent institution.

Sources for Acquiring Materials

Because of the unusual nature of the materials in special collections, the acquisition, processing, and cataloging aspects of these items are handled very differently from more traditional library materials. In terms of acquisitions, an institutional archive will receive selected noncurrent records from other departments within its agency. For example, older publications, photographs, architectural plans, and transcripts of presidential speeches (for a college or corporation), or mayoral speeches (for a municipality) will be transferred to the archival repository. In addition, retired faculty or staff often make donations of materials after leaving their positions with the agency.

The institutions that have substantial acquisitions budgets for manuscripts are usually limited to large, scholarly research and academic libraries. Materials may be purchased from manuscript vendors who work in the subject areas in which the department collects (e.g., Californiana, New Jerseyiana, Civil War, John Steinbeck, women authors, American children's literature). Often, dealers very familiar with a collection's focus will suggest relevant items of interest from their inventory to special collections staff for possible purchase.

Materials also frequently come from private sources, often as donations. As a result, the cultivation of potential donors plays an important role in the ongoing collection development efforts of a special collections department. Careful record keeping in the form of deeds, appraisals and correspondence follows each donation of materials. A deed documents the legal transfer of ownership, specifies any restrictions on use or reproduction, conveys literary and other rights, and verifies the provenance or origin of a collection.

Materials may be acquired as large collections, in small lots, or singly. The special collections department at Cal Poly University, San Luis Obispo, recently received the personal and business papers of a locally prominent, pioneering mercantile family. Before processing, the donation comprised some 100 cartons along with hundreds of loose ledgers, maps, drawings, and other oversized items. In contrast, the same department just purchased a slim, handwritten 1849 Gold Rush-era diary from a rare book and manuscript dealer.

MARC Format, Encoded Archival Description, and Finding Aids

Another distinction of special collections is found in the accessing and cataloging of materials. Unlike book materials, each item is not individually indexed in an OPAC. For example, a manuscript or archival collection consisting of correspondence, historical photographs, and ephemera might contain 5,000 individual pieces; rather than devising a cataloging record for each scrap of paper or image, the bibliographic record describes the collection as a unit. A distinct MARC record protocol—MARC-AMC (Archival and Manuscript Control) was devised for cataloging archives and manuscripts, but it has since been superseded by MARC 21. All prior separate formats, such as the AMC bibliographic format, have been fully integrated into MARC 21. The ability of MARC format to handle archival and manuscript materials means that collection-level bibliographic records for these collections can be added to a library's OPAC. Compiling such a record may be a joint effort between special collections personnel and cataloging staff. In the largest libraries, there may be staff whose sole job is to catalog rare books or manuscript materials.

In addition to the MARC record, special collections are accessed in much more detail through an archival tool known as a *finding aid* or *descriptive guide.* A finding aid or guide describes and provides an inventory of materials (manuscripts, papers, photographs, multi-media, etc.) within a collection.

Typically, this includes some narrative material describing the history and significance of the collection and its creator(s), biographical notes on the creator(s), and the physical arrangement, size, and formats of materials. A brief inventory or container list of the holdings follows. In terms of physical and intellectual organization, each collection is broken down hierarchically into series, subseries, boxes, and folders. The organizational framework for each individual collection within the department reflects the unique contents of that collection, and, wherever possible, is based on the provenance or origin of the materials. Today, many libraries routinely publish their finding aids online to assist researchers in preparing for an onsite visit to their special collections. This may take the form of html Web pages or pdf files on a library's Web site, or as an xml encoded finding aid hosted by a regional archival cooperative, such as the OAC, Online Archive of California (http://www.oac.cdlib.org/).

Encoded Archival Description (EAD) using *Extensible Markup Language (xml)* is the current standard for use with archival finding aids. Like other markup languages, SGML xml prepares documents for publishing on the Web, with varied display and search options. Preparation of an online finding aid can be completed in-house with the help of an authoring program or by contracting with a mark-up vendor.

Traditional book classification systems such as LC or Dewey are not generally applied to special collections materials. Because of their varying shapes, sizes, and often fragile condition, materials found in special collections are also housed differently than books, videos, CDs, DVDs, or other physical packages of information that can literally stand on their own. Manuscripts, photographs, and the like are placed inside special acid-free storage boxes, folders, and sleeves of varying sizes, which house them and also contribute to their preservation and stabilization. The original condition of each historical item is closely guarded; no library ownership stamps, sticky call labels, Post-it® notes, or colored dots are allowed on the materials. It is likely that the staff of the special collections department handle all processing for these materials.

Emphasis on Preservation

Special collections departments take seriously their preservation mission. Controlling the environment within the department, much like a museum does, is an important element of ensuring long-term access to unique, histori-cal materials. Temperature and humidity extremes are to be avoided because they can advance decay or deterioration of materials. Sophisticated air control systems or *HVAC* (heating ventilation and air-conditioning), treated window-panes, dehumidifiers, humidifiers, and meters that measure temperature and humidity, called *thermohygrometers,* are all used to monitor the environment. The use of acid-free storage containers and file folders, Mylar® sleeves, and other stable protective housing is standard procedure.

Research etiquette also emphasizes preservation. Special collections de-partments are closed stack areas where materials are paged or retrieved by staff for onsite review and study by researchers, one box or folder at a time. Patrons are often required to wear white, cotton gloves when handling original items. This prevents the transfer of oil from the hands to the historical mate-rials. Writing implements are restricted to pencils only—again, to protect the special materials from any permanent damage or defacing. Materials are non-circulating, and there may be photocopying limitations to minimize handling of fragile, original items or because of deed restrictions. Figure 5.2 depicts research etiquette.

Because of the unique nature of the materials and their potential value on the retail market, special collections items are especially vulnerable to theft, so greater security precautions and restricted user access are the norm. Photo identification, research credentials, or other documentation may be required of patrons prior to accessing materials. For some large, scholarly, independent institutions such as California's Huntington Library or the Folger Shakespeare Library in Washington, DC, letters of recommendation and an application

Figure 5.2. Researchers in special collections or archives departments may be re-quired to wear cotton gloves when viewing manuscripts or other fragile materials.

may be required of potential researchers before access privileges are granted. Building or reading rooms are equipped with security systems to control and monitor access.

Conservation Efforts

At times, conservation techniques must also be applied in an attempt to reverse water or smoke damage, to stabilize deterioration as from high acid content in paper, or to mitigate other problems with documents. Some very large research and university libraries have their own conservation labs on site—such as the Library of Congress, Los Angeles's Getty Museum, and Yale University. The majority of libraries send their conservation work to outside specialists because of the highly skilled and labor-intensive nature of such work.

It is tempting to think that the expensive and time-consuming effort of preserving original documents can be abandoned now that information can be digitized easily. However, every storage medium has a different shelf life, and, in many cases, these are not known until some time has passed. Although today we herald the wonders of computers, it remains to be seen what the life span of digital storage will be. On the other hand, high quality "permanent paper" buffered and with low acid content still remains the most durable and reliable medium, with a life span of approximately 500 years.

In addition to the breakdown of the storage medium itself, the obsolescence of the playback equipment (e.g., microfilm reader, computer programs and drives) can also prevent access to information and necessitate its transfer from one medium to another. After all, how many libraries still have film loop readers? And zip disk drives are no longer standard equipment in current personal computers, let alone the much earlier floppy disk drives. Equipment for reading data stored on the 8-inch and 5¼-inch floppy disks is difficult to find, and accessing 3½-inch diskette and zip disks presumes library ownership of older model computers. When considering the transfer of information from its original format (e.g., paper, photograph, 16mm film, floppy disk) to a newer medium, archivists are also aware that, for some scholars, the container is as much a focus for research as is the information within.

Institutional Repositories

As the Web continues to mature, an application that is growing in widespread acceptance and popularity is that of the *institutional repository*. Often this type of effort originates in the library of an institution, or it might also be a project assigned to a library department such as a special collections unit. What is an institutional repository? The earliest applications were in large universities where they aspired to capture and make available the scholarly publishing (lectures, periodical articles, conference papers, theses, dissertations, data sets, etc.) of their faculties via the Web. Model programs include the University of California's California Digital Library (http://www.cdlib.org/), University of Rochester's UR Research (https://urresearch.rochester.edu/), and Purdue University Libraries' E-Scholar (http://e-scholar.lib.purdue.edu/).

In addition to publicizing and making scholarship electronically accessible, such repositories—also called digital repositories—serve a valuable role by promoting the institution as a whole, as they provide free, publicly available information to the public at large, to students, to staff and faculty, and to alumni and potential donors. Preservation of material is another major motivation behind most institutional repositories, as library managers look to this as a method for preserving and enhancing access to local history materials, photographic and other visual media, manuscript and archival collections.

Some of the key issues involved in the start-up and maintenance of institutional repositories are winning "buy-in" to the project from faculty and other potential contributors, setting policy standards for content submission, dealing with copyright and licensing issues, finding appropriate software to manage such collections (e.g., CONTENTdm, DSpace, Fedora, Embark, and others), and, of course, securing overall funding and ongoing support.

Staffing

Staff who work in special collections may be called librarians and library technicians, or they may be termed archivists and archival technicians. Thus, professional training requirements vary accordingly. It is fair to say that a degree in history, or a least an affinity for history, is an important requirement for those considering a career in this area. A national certification program for archivists was implemented in 1989. The independent, not-for-profit Academy of Certified Archivists provides standardized certification through an examination process. For those interested in further exploring these specialties, the Society of American Archivists' Web site is listed in the resources section at the end of this chapter.

Although some would argue that librarians and archivists are entirely different breeds, the authors (both of whom have worked in special collections settings) choose to differ with that point of view. The careful selection of materials according to a plan, preparation of items for researchers' use, and access and reference services are all required in both arenas. Emphasis on electronic access to information, especially digital imaging and institutional repositories, is very timely and is transforming special collections, just as it is impacting other areas of library services.

Microforms

Microforms have come in many different sizes and variations since their initial use in libraries during the 1930s. Microfilm and microfiche remain the two types most commonly found in libraries, archives, and research centers today. Microfilm editions are photographs of each page of an original periodical, newspaper, thesis, or other document. The images are produced on rolls of film, typically 35 millimeters in size. To read the miniaturized document, which is not legible to the naked eye, the film must be loaded into a microfilm reader, which enlarges the tiny, reduced-size print to legible size. Microfiche editions are cards of 16-millimeter film. Common sizes include 3 inch by 5 inch, 4 inch by 6 inch, and 3 inch by 7 inch. These are all significantly reduced and must be placed in a microfiche reader machine to magnify the text. Most modern readers also produce photocopies of the document. Other types of microforms in use over the years have included aperture cards, microcards, ultrafiche, and other variations of microphotography.

For more than half of the 20th century, microforms were a major storage medium in libraries and information centers of all sizes.[7] Advantages to this miniaturized format include the preservation of hard copy data, reduction in shelving and space needs, and, in its high quality form, stability and a long life span as a reliable storage medium. Archival quality microfilm (also called silver halide microfilm) will last for approximately 200 years.[8] Microfilm has been particularly well suited to interlibrary loan because its compact size makes it easy to ship, and playback machines are standard worldwide, thus eliminating concerns about incompatibility between libraries.

Making Microforms Accessible

For approximately 50 years, libraries building retrospective collections have purchased mainstream periodical and newspaper titles in microfilm from special microform vendors who work exclusively with that medium. For in-house or smaller local publications, libraries contract with other companies to produce microfilm records of these unique titles.

Once received by the library, the film requires special, labor-intensive processing before it is shelf-ready. This includes inserting stoppers at the end of each reel and labeling the film leaders and storage boxes. Special storage cabinets are used for both microfilm and fiche; they are rarely shelved on regular-sized book stacks.

As for user access, the library must provide patrons with multiple readers or printers and to keep them in good working order. Staff assistance in the use of the machines is also required and often results in an additional service desk devoted to microforms. In large microfilm reading rooms, such as those found in the National Archives' regional branches, trained volunteers are available to help with equipment use and problems. Student assistants and interns are also often posted in microform rooms to troubleshoot problems. And, of course, all of this requires dedicated library space.

National cataloging standards call for separate cataloging records to be made for different formats of a title. So, in theory, where microform holdings form archives or backups of hard copy titles, they require additional work from a cataloging perspective. (In practice, many libraries cut corners on this standard by adding holdings data in different formats to the main bibliographic record.)

Patron Resistance

Although accepted among staff, microforms have never been a favorite among patrons. For researchers, eyestrain and repetitive use syndrome are physical discomforts that result from long hours in front of a reader. Another source of frustration (to the library staff as well as to patrons) is the breakage of microform reader parts, which occurs with frequent use. Also, poor quality film can be blurry and illegible. Anyone who has done genealogical research and has accessed early 19th-century newspapers and census records on mi-microfilm will empathize.

Most younger students today are quite unfamiliar with microforms, not having been exposed to the medium in junior or senior high school. In an introductory library skills module, it is not unusual for college professors to give students an assignment to locate the front page of a major newspaper from their birth date to introduce them to the mysteries of microfilm.

Future of Microforms

Today, microfiche and microfilm are still viable media for the archival preservation of large periodical back files and other historical materials, especially those with low usage. Prior to the advent of electronic information storage, microforms were hailed as the solution to the never-ending library-space dilemma. But the Internet revolution has significantly impacted the longstanding practice of storing noncurrent periodicals and newspapers on microfilm, and, less frequently, on microfiche. As Web-based periodical archives begin to reach back more than a decade or two, many libraries have canceled their microfilm subscriptions and are relying solely on their online holdings. Although perpetual access (that is, the guaranteed, continued access to retrospective holdings online) remains an unsettled issue, it is likely that microform publishing may decrease significantly.

During its first decade, the distinct emphasis of the Web was the provision of current materials. But new trends are emerging with the digital conversion of some large, key microform historical collections: the National Archives and the Church of Jesus Christ of Latter-Day Saints' (Mormons) vast family history facility in Salt Lake City have both been almost exclusively microform-based collections for decades. Between the two, they house a major percentage of the world's genealogical and historical resources and are used extensively by professional and lay researchers daily.

Enhanced digital access to these popular collections is being developed. For example, leading for-profit genealogical publisher, Ancestry.com, has digitized the heavily-used U.S. Population Censuses held in the National Archives, taking almost 10 years to complete the conversion process. The huge (and amazing) searchable database is now available to paid subscribers as part of Ancestry's digital family history collection. (The censuses on microfilm are still available for free perusal to researchers at National Archives branches.) An initial digitization effort by the LDS is their Family History Archive at the Harold B. Lee Library, Brigham Young University, which when completed will make available some 100,000 family histories on the library's Web site.

Similarly, publisher ProQuest/UMI has digitized a century's worth of Sanborn Insurance Fire Maps as well as the leading U.S. national daily newspapers *The New York Times* and *The Los Angeles Times* covering a similar time span. Previously, newspaper articles older than about 20 years were only available for viewing on microfilm, with very limited indexing to provide access points. While the search interfaces and the display options for some of these digitized collections leaves room for improvement, they remain attractive products. These digitization efforts are all very labor intensive and require up-front capital, and the product pricing of these subscription databases reflects that start-up investment, which is most often made by private sector companies.

Although not inexpensive, another alternative for enhanced viewing of microfilmed documents exists. Special digital microfilm scanners can digitize film or fiche images for distribution over computer networks to desktop computers, allowing for e-mail or fax distribution. This conversion process combines photographic and electronic imaging technologies. Leaders in the use of this conversion technology so far have been corporate libraries and their record management centers.

It remains to be seen whether the further retrospective conversion of microfilm holdings into online formats and databases will be lucrative enough for commercial publishers to pursue fully. Even if the demand is there and the numbers play out, it is likely that the oldest and most obscure titles will remain in library collections on their microfilm rolls and fiche cards. Historians and other researchers, as well as library staffers, will continue to use microfilm for accessing retrospective titles.

The current microform holdings of retrospective titles represent a significant investment for the average library facility with limited resources and will not soon be discarded. Because this format is still viable, and, for most collections probably represents low-use items, many libraries will keep their extant microform holdings, but will look to new technologies to access current materials and to archive them as they become noncurrent.

Government Documents

Although they represent an enormous wealth of data on almost any subject imaginable, government documents tend to be overlooked by the average researcher as sources of information. "Gov docs," as they are nicknamed by library staff, are those publications produced by or for a government agency; this includes international, federal, provincial, state, county, parish, city, or other jurisdictions. In the United States, the Government Printing Office (GPO) is the agency charged with producing, distributing, and selling documents for all three branches of the federal government. As such, the GPO is one of the world's largest publishers. According to its Web site, they have some 250,000 titles publicly available on the GPO Access Web site (www.gpoaccess. gov), with hard copies of more than 5,500 of those documents available for purchase.

Many of these titles tend to be of high interest to consumers. Compared to commercially published books that often have attractive, attention-getting packaging and professionally designed covers, government publications are often plain and drab in appearance. However, the lack of frills also keeps the price down, and, as a whole, government publications are very reasonably priced—sometimes they are even free. The variety of topics covered and the diverse audiences for which these publications are written are wide ranging. A short pamphlet on good parenting skills, a checklist of resident bird species at a national park, a technical report from the Surgeon General on second-hand tobacco effects, or the multi-volume, annual *U.S. Budget* are all examples of documents produced by national government agencies. Government publications are often critical and sometimes sole sources for detailed statistics on many aspects of life, from the population census to motor vehicle fatalities, to the number of fish netted, to precise rainfall tallies.

GPO Access Web Site

Creative and efficient dissemination of information has always been a point of pride and a mandate for the GPO. Over the years, this has meant using new technologies to package and distribute documents from federal agencies. The GPO was an early adopter of producing publications in CD-ROM format. Then, beginning in 1994, they implemented an information-rich Web site for the public called GPO Access (see figure 5.3), and continue to improve and enhance its features. GPO Access provides links to many services, including their *Catalog of Publications,* and a searchable database and ordering system

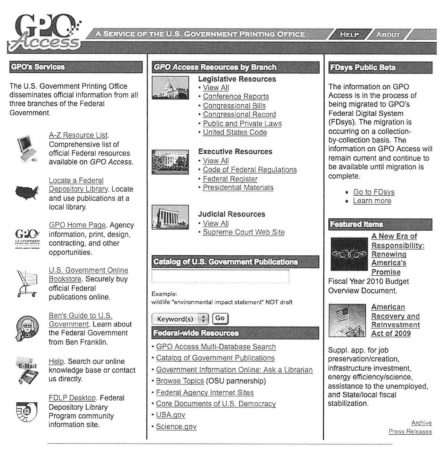

Figure 5.3. The Government Printing Office (GPO) Access Home Page provides links to many of the agency's services of interest to libraries and offers online ordering of federal publications.

for titles from the *Consumer Information Catalog.* The extensive site also serves as a gateway to many other federal government Web sites.

Federal Depository Program

Since 1813, the federal government has designated depository libraries to ensure consumers access to many of its publications. Today, the Federal Depository Library Program (FDLP) consists of over 1,250 participating libraries throughout the nation. These libraries are designated at one of two levels for the regular receipt of information in print, multimedia, and electronic formats: (1) regional, and (2) selective. Materials are sent to the library at no cost. In return, the depositories provide organization, housing, and professional reference assistance, available to all citizens who want access. Publications received as part of the federal depository arrangement may have mandatory retention schedules, and they cannot be weeded in the usual fashion. Instead, they must first be offered to other depositories, and, if there are no takers, only then can they be discarded.

Through the depository libraries, the federal government disseminates key information to the public at large. Many state governments also have depository arrangements with libraries to provide convenient access to their documents for citizens.

Diversity of Formats to Process

A hallmark of government documents (especially those from the federal government) has been the diverse formats in which they are produced. Printed materials include monographs, technical reports, periodicals, booklets, pamphlets, brochures, maps; multimedia ranges from videos to CD-ROMs to DVDs. The online publishing of government information dramatically increased in the 1990s, and the Web continues as the primary distribution channel for government data.

Nonetheless, from a processing point of view, the diversity of formats of the hard copy materials can be a bit problematic. Irregular sizes, spiral bindings without spines for labeling, and the constantly changing formats for a single title require additional staff time and special handling before they are shelf-ready. In addition, there are depository status labeling requirements and retention mandates to which depository libraries must adhere.

The steady flow of depository products means a serious space commitment for the library, and the diverse formats need various styles and sizes of shelving to accommodate them all. Many government publications are new editions of standard titles that replace older versions, and, thus, constant weeding of superseded items is required.

Although publishing of many government documents on the Web is a major convenience in access and distribution, it presents a new question in terms of long-term, archival access. Currently, there is no policy for preserving or capturing digital documents, which can be very ephemeral in nature. Just as the federal depository system has provided a system for preserving public access to publications in print, microfilm, and other formats, a policy needs to be implemented to ensure permanent access for digital documents.[9]

Why House Government Documents Separately?

In many larger library facilities, government documents are housed separately from the main collection. There are a variety of issues that play into this decision. A significant one is that federal documents have their own distinct classification system called SuDocs, which is often used in place of the more common Dewey Decimal or Library of Congress codes. When the SuDocs classification is applied, a separate shelving sequence is required. If the collection of documents is large, then this requires a sizeable commitment of both floor space and shelving. Additionally, there are many special indexes produced, both commercially and by the government, that provide exclusive access to government documents. It is both convenient and practical to house a collection of documents in proximity to their accompanying special indexes and finding aides.

Cataloging issues also often argue for providing a separate reading room or department for government publications. Because they originate from hundreds of different agencies, there is no standardized format for producing government documents. And with each new presidential administration, there is often a reorganization or renaming of federal agencies, which further confuses the collection of publications. As a result, government documents are notorious for their lack of basic bibliographic data so critical for compiling library cataloging records; often, no author is cited, there may be several variant titles on the work, a publication date may be lacking, and so forth.

Federal documents are in the public domain; thus, no dated copyright statement is required on the work. (Copyrighting of state-produced materials varies for each state.) Hence, performing full MARC cataloging and adding each record to the library's OPAC is an expensive and labor-intensive task. In fact, government documents are often relegated to the last priority by the cataloging staff because of this. It is not unusual to have government publications in a sort of cataloging limbo, where they are put out on the shelves for public access and use but are not included in the OPAC. Although government publications may be inventoried in a departmental index, this practice obviously limits full access for researchers who believe that the library catalog is comprehensive.

Somewhat new on the scene is the arrival of cataloging services specific to government publications. One such firm is Marcive. Drawing from a library's designated profile of government documents received, the company supplies the cataloging record and accompanying labels and processing data. The ability to rely more on this type of outsourcing service could make a great difference in reducing the traditional cataloging backlog of government document departments.

Another reason for maintaining a separate documents room for government documents is that it allows for specialization among staff. By focusing primarily on the complexities of the documents collection, professional and support staff are able to hone their expertise and provide high-quality service to customers using these specialized materials.

Proponents for integrating government documents into the main library collection argue that keeping them separate only contributes to their being overlooked. And the use of yet another mysterious classification system only further intimidates and confuses researchers, presenting one more obstacle to overall access. There is no argument that maintaining a separate department and another service desk is an added expense in the library's budget. With all of these considerations, both for and against separation, the trend is for larger collections of documents to be situated and managed as discrete departments.

Acquisition Choices

There are several approaches to obtaining federal documents. As with books and other more familiar library materials, there are jobbers who specialize in providing government publications, such as the long-time documents wholesaler Bernan. Participation in the depository library program, as described previously, is another option.

In recent years, the GPO has phased out its network of 20 retail bookstores in major cities that used to sell popular hard copy titles and has replaced them with the all-online U.S. Government Bookstore site.[10]

Another acquisitions approach is to use the *Catalog of U.S. Government Publications (CGP)*. The CGP is the finding tool for federal publications, and includes descriptive records for historical and current publications as well as direct links to those that are available online. This replaces the old standby *Monthly Catalog of U.S. Government Publications*, which over the years has morphed from unwieldy print and microform versions to online ordering on the Web.

At the regional and local government levels, library staff often acquire materials directly from the issuing agencies by being placed on a mailing list or by direct query. Although this approach may be necessary for local publications, any library with a significant collection of government documents will try to maximize the use of jobbers for acquisitions because it would be prohibitively labor-intensive to contact all levels of government agencies in this manner.

With any of these methods for gaining awareness of and eventually ordering government publications, there is very little reliance on reviewing media. Only a few periodicals cover the release and review of government documents and government Web sites for librarians. A current cross-disciplinary title is the *Government Information Quarterly*, a periodical published by Elsevier Inc. to which major academic libraries with large document collections subscribe.

For an historical overview of the world of government documents, see Joe Morehead's *Introduction to United States Government Information Sources*, 6th edition. For a discussion of the sweeping changes brought on by the evolution of the Web, the terrorist attacks of 9/11, and the U.S. Patriot Act, see the *Changing Face of Government Information: Providing Access*, edited by Suhasini L. Kumar

DIVERSE JOB OPPORTUNITIES

The library activities, such as acquisitions, cataloging, and processing, that take place behind the doors of technical services offer many interesting career paths, at both the technician and professional levels for those who excel in detailed work, possess strong computer skills, and prefer limited public interface.

Certain library materials, such as periodicals, special collections, micro-forms, and government documents, often require a separate department to properly handle the special needs that these formats bring with them. Such departments also afford diverse career opportunities—many of which are over-shadowed by the higher profile public service jobs in reference and circulation. Those who enjoy variety in their daily work life—a blend of selection and acqui-sition, processing, and reference service to users—are encouraged to investi-gate these areas of specialization.

Associations such as the ALA have professional sections devoted to technical services areas, such as serials, acquisitions, and collection management, along with round table groups for government documents, federal government librari-anship, and students. The Society of American Archivists supports member sections focusing on such issues as electronic records, digital imaging, preser-vation, and reference, as well as sections for students, college and university ar-chives, business archives, and more. Connecting with working professionals as mentors is an effective way to explore an area of specialization within the field.

STUDY QUESTIONS

1. Check the current edition of the *Bowker Annual: Library and Book Trade Almanac* to see whether the number of hard copy books being published is increasing or declining. What trends in the publishing in-dustry do you think are affecting the production of hard copy titles?

2. Outline the stages that a book passes through to get onto the shelves of your college library. What is the typical turnaround time from initial order to receipt by the library? How long does it then take to be ready for public use? How does a CD or DVD compare?

3. Find out the names of five jobbers active in the library trade. How are they different in the services they offer? How are they similar?

4. Find both a popular magazine title and a scholarly journal title of your choice. For each publication, find out in what formats it is currently available (e.g., hard copy, full-image Web, full-text Web). How does the pricing of each format compare?

5. Visit a special collections department, such as a university archives, a manuscript department, or a local history room. Describe some of their major holdings. What security precautions are in place when you visit them in person? Do they offer digital images or digitized manu-scripts from their collection online?

6. Since the inception of the World Wide Web, catalogers, reference librar-ians, and other library staff have been discussing and experimenting with various methods for cataloging the Web. What current methods in this direction do you think are particularly effective?

7. Go to a U.S. government portal site like http://www.usa.gov/ or http://www.gpoaccess.gov. Browse the site and then visit five fed-eral agency Web sites. Did you discover any agencies that you had no knowledge of before?

RESOURCES

Print Resources

Drake, Miriam A. Scholarly Communication in Turmoil. *Information Today*, February 2007.

Evans, G. Edward and Margaret Zarnosky Saponaro. *Developing Library and Information Center Collections*. 5th ed. Westport, CT: Libraries Unlimited, 2005.

Fox, Michael J, Peter L. Wilkerson, and Suzanne R. Warren. *Introduction to Archival Organization and Description: Access to Cultural Heritage*. Los Angeles: Getty Trust Publications/Getty Information Institute, 1999.

Hafner, Katie. 2007. "History, Digitized (and Abridged)." *New York Times*, March 11.

Hunter, Gregory S. *Developing and Maintaining Practical Archives: A How-To-Do-It Manual*. 2nd ed. New York: Neal-Schuman Publishers, 2003.

Ketcham-Van Orsdel, Lee, and Kathleen Born. Serials Publishing in Flux. *Library Journal*, April 151999.

Morehead, Joe. *Introduction to United States Government Information Sources*. 6th ed. Westport, CT: Libraries Unlimited, 1999.

Schellenberg, Theodore. R. Modern Archives: Principles and Techniques. (SAA Archival Classics Series) Chicago: Society of American Archivists, 2003.

Taylor, Arlene G. *Wynar's Introduction to Cataloging and Classification*. 10th ed. Westport, CT: Libraries Unlimited, 2006.

Web Sites

Bancroft Library, University of California, Berkeley

http://bancroft.berkeley.edu/

(accessed June 25, 2007)

One of the West Coast's leading primary source repositories has an extensive Web site and provides electronic access to finding aids for many of its special collections as part of the Online Archive of California.

Cal Poly University Archives/Special Collections

http://www.lib.calpoly.edu/specialcollections/

(accessed June 25, 2007)

An example of a university special collections department Web site. The department posts their mission statement, department hours, access information, a list of manuscript collections, reference services provided, and reproduction rules.

The Five Laws of Library Science

http://dlist.sir.arizona.edu/1220/

(accessed June 25, 2007)

Contains the full text of each chapter of the class work *The Five Laws of Library Science* by the Indian scholar S. R. Ranganathan. First published in 1931.

Getty Conservation Institute

http://www.getty.edu/conservation/institute/

(accessed June 25, 2007)

Part of the J. Paul Getty Center in Los Angeles, the Getty Conservation Institute.

Web site features a newsletter, publications information, and relevant links.

GPO Access

http://www.gpoaccess.gov/about/

(accessed February 22, 2007)

GPO Access Web site is a service of the U.S. Government Printing Office (GPO) that provides free electronic access to a wealth of important information produced by the Federal Government. Find lists of GPO bestselling publications, place orders for federal documents at the Online Bookstore, locate a Federal Depository Library, view an online *Consumer Information Catalog* for publications from the Pueblo distribution center.

How to Decipher Call Numbers: Tutorial

http://www.lib.monash.edu.au/vl/callno/callcon.htm

(accessed June 25, 2007)

Australia's Monash University has developed a site that describes the basics about Dewey Decimal system call numbers. The tutorial teaches users and staff what a call number is, how they are created, and how to use them in locating library materials.

Introduction to the Dewey Decimal Classification

http://www.oclc.org/dewey/versions/abridgededition14/intro.pdf

(accessed June 25, 2007)

OCLC, which publishes the Dewey Classification volumes, provides an overview of the Dewey Decimal system, summaries of the tables, and information on ordering Dewey publications.

Library of Congress Classification System

http://www.usg.edu/galileo/skills/unit03/libraries03_04.phtml

(accessed June 25, 2007)

This site explaining how to read LC call numbers was developed as a tutorial for college students at the University System of Georgia.

Library of Congress: Conservation Division

http://www.loc.gov/preserv/conserv.html

(accessed June 25, 2007)

Provides an overview of our national library's Conservation Division, which has been a world leader in developing many modern conservation practices. Programs featured include Environmental Housing of Rarities, Book and Paper Conservation Section, and Preventive Preservation Section.

Northeast Document Conservation Center

http://www.nedcc.org/home.php

(accessed June 25, 2007)

This highly regarded, non-profit regional conservation center specializes in preservation of paper-based materials. They assist libraries, archives, historical organizations, museums, and other repositories without their own facilities in conservation efforts. In addition, they are a leader in the preservation and conservation fields.

Society of American Archivists

http://www.archivists.org/

(accessed June 25, 2007)

The leading national archival professional association, SAA, provides a site that includes membership information, continuing education opportunities, employment links, and more.

Understanding MARC Bibliographic

http://www.loc.gov/marc/umb/umbhome.html

(accessed June 25, 2007)

Authoritative tutorial written by Betty Furrie and reviewed and edited by the Network Development and MARC Standards Office, Library of Congress. For those wanting a more thorough knowledge of the MARC record.

NOTES

1. *Bowker Annual: Library and Book Trade Almanac*, 51st ed. (New Providence, NJ: R. R. Bowker, 2006), 516.

2. *Statistical Abstract of the United State: 2007* (Washington DC, U.S. Department of Commerce, 2006), 707.

3. *E-collections* listserv, e-mail to author, April 3, 2000.

4. OCLC, Inc., *OCLC Abstracts*, Vol. 9, No. 41 (October 23, 2006), e-mail to author, October 23, 2006.

5. Ibid.

6. Arlene Taylor, *Introduction to Cataloging and Classification*, 10th ed. (Westport, CT: Libraries Unlimited, 2006), 541, 544

7. Allen B. Veaner, "Microforms," in *Encyclopedia of Library History*, Wayne A. Wiegand and Donald G. Davis, eds. (New York: Garland Publishing, 1994), 435.

8. Karen Kaplan, "The Culture's Immortal, But Not the Disk," *Los Angeles Times*, February 16, 1998.

9. "Science Information in Peril," *Los Angeles Times*, March 1, 2000.

10. Nikki Swartz, "NARA Taps Lockheed for Archives Project," *Information Management Journal* (Nov/Dec): 7 (2005).

Chapter 6

Circulation

Just as in a retail establishment, efficient inventory control and good customer service are important elements in managing a successful library. Each individual book, video, CD, DVD, map, pamphlet, course reserve reading, or other material needs to be tracked as it circulates via remote access, within a reading room, in and out of a department, or is physically removed from the library for use elsewhere. In addition to offering desirable products, friendly and professional assistance is also critical in generating satisfied repeat customers. It does not matter how well other areas of the library function; if the connection to the customer is not made successfully, the library has not served its purpose. Both inventory control and customer service fail or succeed largely based on the effectiveness of the circulation department.

The most visible sign of a library's inventory control or circulation efforts is the service counter, where the official charging and discharging of library materials takes place—and which, most often, is a hub of activity. Besides the obvious checkout transactions, many other activities go on at a circulation desk, including referral to other departments, answering directional questions, patron registration, fines collection, and more. As with the location of cashier stations in retail stores, the careful positioning of a circulation desk is a critical part of the inventory control operation. Strategic placement helps deter theft, provides the ability to count and view inbound and outbound traffic, and offers convenience to customers as they enter and exit the facility.

For many customers, regardless of the type of library, circulation desk employees are often the first and only staff with whom they come in contact as they visit the library. Thus, the public relations value of all interactions at the circulation counter should never be underestimated. And first impressions—positive or negative—leave a customer with lasting memories. As the old adage says, "You never get a second chance to make a first impression."

Most customers and novice staff see the circulation department as being synonymous with only those operations that take place at the service counter. But, in fact, there are other circulation-related responsibilities that come take place away from the physical space of the service desk. These operations may include shelving, management of reserve collections, document delivery and

145

interlibrary loan services, collection inventory and maintenance, and library security.

In small libraries, branch outlets, or other facilities staffed by a solo librarian or technician, the circulation desk also doubles as a reference counter or all-in-one service desk. Larger libraries have a separate service counter dedicated just to circulation functions and typically positioned adjacent to the main exit. Departmental collections, such as government documents, local history, children's room, and others, may handle their own circulation, and thus a large library may have several checkout counters on different floors or locations in various departments.

ACCESS TO LIBRARY MATERIALS

The designation *Circulation Department* is a popular one, but such a department may also be named borrowers' services, loan services, or access services, particularly in larger university, public, or research facilities. These latter names clearly reflect the department's emphasis on making library resources available to borrowers. Traditionally, that has meant physically loaning out materials to qualified borrowers so that they can take them home, to school, to the office, to work, and use them off site.

As electronic access to resources continues to grow dramatically, the actual loaning out of a physical item is only one type of access. Increasingly, libraries provide remote access to holdings data and the actual documents themselves for their qualifying clientele. Typically this includes e-books and electronic reserve collections (e-reserves), databases, indexes, and full-text periodicals. In some cases, access is free to all interested users; in others, access is limited to qualified borrowers who receive a password, subscription number, or other code that lets them log on to the library's electronic holdings.

Circulation Terminology

When discussing the loaning out of library materials, there are several commonly used terms that tend to confuse library users. These terms define the circulation status of the book, video, government document, or other physical item. Materials that do not leave the premises of the library or information center include those designated as reference, rare books, and other specially identified items that, because of age, condition, or value, may call for restricted use. Available for in-house use only, *reference* materials tend to be multi-volume sets, handbooks, dictionaries, indexes, and other works that can be consulted briefly for facts or overview information. They may also be expensive, or frequently used, or both; the implication being that patrons can study them on site or photocopy the needed pages, whereas the volumes themselves remain in the library at all times to maximize their use by the greatest number of individuals.

In contrast to the restrictions of the reference status, materials designated as *circulating* may be checked out to registered borrowers. In the majority of libraries and information centers that stress full service and maximum access to materials, it is typical for the bulk of the collection to circulate. However, in the case of specialized materials, such as those discussed in chapter 5 (e.g., microforms, special collections, current hard copy periodicals, maps, and other unique items), circulation may be very limited, or the entire collection may be for reference use only.

Reserve status is normally found in school media centers and academic library environments. Reserve materials are high-use items required for study by classes during a semester or school term; the number of copies is less than the number of students, so shared use must be enforced. Examples of reserve materials include copies of required textbooks, supplementary course readings, sample tests and assignments, or other curriculum-linked items. The materials may be part of the permanent library collection that has been transferred temporarily to reserve status, or they may be the property of an instructor who has loaned them to the library for the duration of the course. Public and special libraries will also, on occasion, classify materials as reserve to meet the requirements of seasonal school assignments or in-house training needs.

The electronic provision of reserve collections is growing, especially in academic libraries. Newer releases of OPACs feature an e-reserve module for seamless delivery of required readings, lecture notes, sample quizzes, and so forth to authorized users (e.g., enrolled students). Copyright permission must be obtained whether from the professor—in the case of quizzes, notes, and study packs—or from the commercial publishers of texts and other books.

Deciding on Loan Periods and Circulation Status

Library policies today are a far cry from the chained books and closed stacks of earlier times. Although total anytime–anywhere access is not yet a reality for most researchers, the current emphasis on maximizing access can be seen in innovative services such as extended operating hours, remote access to databases, e-books, OPACs, online renewals, electronic reserve collections, and e-mail reference assistance. However, there are legitimate reasons why the circulation of certain physical materials may to be limited or denied. Some items that typically have limited circulation include the following:

- Sets or series (e.g., multi-volume encyclopedias or print periodical indexes where a missing volume lessens the value of the set as a whole)
- One-of-a-kind items (e.g., the only copy of an out-of-print item)
- High-demand items (e.g., class-required items)
- Reference materials (e.g., items not designed for reading cover to cover that can be briefly referred to or sections photocopied)
- Fragile or rare items (e.g., manuscripts, maps, or photographs that could be damaged by extra handling)
- Expensive items (e.g., items that are costly to replace)
- Items with a record of being stolen (e.g., these are certain topics in every library that are considered "hot;" anything dealing with these topics is prone to theft).

- Items with copyright and security issues (e.g., lending software may violate copyright laws and can also spread viruses).
- Items that require special playback equipment (e.g., microfilm).

Once a collection or an item has been reviewed, if it warrants checkout but with limitations, there are other options for limiting status in addition to the basic reference and reserve categories discussed previously. The library's standard loan period (e.g., two days, two weeks, or a month) can be modified so that material is returned earlier and is available sooner for other users. Limiting the renewal of materials is another option. For example, policies for certain materials may be that no renewals are allowed or that only one renewal is possible.

Restriction by user type is another standard circulation policy. For example, in an academic environment it is not unusual to limit the borrowing of DVDs to instructors only or to restrict the checkout of reserve items to currently enrolled students. Also, in a college or university library, alumni or community cardholders may have only partial borrowing privileges, whereas current students and staff enjoy full privileges. Loan periods may also differ by user type. In a corporate setting, permanent employees may have longer borrowing periods for materials, whereas temporary or contract employees may only check out materials for short intervals. College professors are often able to borrow materials for an entire term, whereas their students are limited to a two- or three-week loan period.

Circulation restrictions according to a user's age may be in place in school media centers or in public libraries. Although a broad reading of the First Amendment, as is advocated by the ALA's "Free Access to Libraries for Minors: An Interpretation of the Library Bill of Rights,"[1] argues against such age restrictions, they are, in fact, common. Local public library systems in particular may limit the checkout of videos, CDs, DVDs, and CD-ROMs to those over 18 years old; the rationale for this type of policy may be based on content, on the need for special care of multimedia materials, or because of an item's replacement cost.

Though not frequently advertised, many libraries and information centers will modify loan policies at the discretion of the librarian on duty. These loans tend to be allowed on a case-by-case basis and usually consist of waiving the standard circulation status or extending the loan period of an item based on special circumstances.

With all of these circulation policy options, balancing the individual's access needs with those of the library's clientele as a whole is a key concern. Additionally, the security of library materials is a consideration in decision making. As with all policies, circulation rules need to be revisited and revised on a regular basis—especially as new formats or services come along—to keep them current with borrowers' needs and usage patterns. So, a healthy dose of common sense helps keep policies reasonable.

As the online renewal of books by patrons becomes more commonplace, many libraries are revising their standing renewal policies to work in this new environment. In some cases, telephone renewal is being replaced by the online option, with an eye toward eventually eliminating phone-in renewals. Online renewal offers convenience to users, and, once implemented, reduces the overall amount of staff time spent on renewals. However, a negative issue is that users do not always notice when an online renewal attempt has been denied. Denial of a renewal might occur because of a recall or hold on the title, outstanding patron fines on library materials, or other reasons. The result is that the patron keeps the book for an additional loan period, erroneously thinking that he or she is acting legally. Instead, the item accrues overdue fines, and, upon return, an unpleasant situation could arise.

E-book collection vendors often have a different method of restricting circulation, or, more precisely in their case, electronic access to titles. Often, only one subscriber at a time may open an e-book to view its contents; there may be a time limit for viewing or check-out (for example, 24 hours or some other time period). Once the first reader has checked the e-book back in, it becomes available for other subscribers to view.

Overdue Fines

Whether at the corner video store or the local public library, a familiar practice is to charge borrowers a fee for the late return of materials. Although this may seem like an annoying penalty for the tardy customer, the rationale behind these fees is to gather materials back so that they are available to the rest of the user population. In other words, assuring timely access for all is the motivation behind the fines. Contrary to popular opinion, few libraries get rich off their overdue fines.

Overdue fine policies and fee schedules usually must be approved by the parent organization of a library, such as a school board, city council, board of supervisors, advisory board, or other governing body. Once approved, it is good customer service to clearly post and publicize these fee rates. As first-time borrowers are registered with a library, the overdue policies and fees should be explained, along with the borrowers' new privileges.

The collection of overdue fines is a time-consuming task. When a library or information center is able to link outstanding overdue fines to their parent organization's operations, the process becomes more efficient. University and college libraries track outstanding fines as part of a student's overall account at the institution. When fines remain unpaid, other key services, such as registration for courses, retrieval of grades, or transcript requests, are blocked, often resulting in timely payment of library fines. Although they seldom charge overdue fines, school library media centers often contact parents directly about overdue or lost material, meanwhile limiting library privileges and postponing the release of report cards.

An increasing number of library systems hire collection agencies to follow up on delinquent or long overdue accounts. This get-tough stance represents a more efficient method than previous in-house efforts because collection agencies have access to customer data and credit records and are in the business of delinquent accounts collection.

At the other end of the policy spectrum, some libraries choose to waive overdue fees altogether. After calculating the cost of tracking, processing, and collecting overdue fines on their own or through a collection agent, they decide to discontinue the practice. Rather, they emphasize the safe return of materials and charge only replacement costs if the item is lost. The positive public relations value of a no-fines policy is another consideration that may convince some libraries and information centers to take that route. (The popular online movie rental service Netflix also takes this tack, with no late fees or even due dates for their subscribers.)

In the past, amnesty weeks or fine-free weeks have been popular, especially with public libraries. These are often timed to coincide with National Library Week in late April or with an individual library's anniversary, new branch opening, or other special event. No questions asked; no fees assessed. Just bring 'em back!

Other Fines

Although library overdue fines get the most attention, there are other fines commonly assessed to borrowers. When patrons lose or damage library materials, they may either be charged the actual replacement value of the item (or, if out of print, something comparable), or the library may have set a flat fee for various categories (e.g., adult hardback book, $30; children's hardback book, $20; bound journal, $150). Many libraries add a processing fee to the replacement charge as a revenue recovery method for processing time and supplies. These fees typically can be as little as $5 or more than $30, with academic libraries on the high end. This type of charge is similar in concept to a restocking fee charged by some retail stores for returned merchandise.

Although the hard and fast rules surrounding library fines have been the butt of countless jokes and newspaper cartoons, in fact, many agencies employ alternative methods of accepting payment for those who cannot pay in cash. Volunteer time in the library or the donation of like material plus a processing fee may sometimes be accepted in lieu of outright payment.

Whether overdue fines and lost/damaged fees are recovered from patrons or not, all libraries need to build into their budgets regular, ongoing funds for replacement and repair of materials. To not do so is to be in a state of denial.

Patron Registration

Patron registration is the opening of a new account for a qualified library customer. It is a process very similar to walking into a department store, such as Macy's or Nordstrom's, and signing up for a store credit card. In this case, the library card takes the place of the charge card. Libraries vary greatly in the way they handle the registration process. Public libraries tend to have the most stringent procedures for registering new patrons and verifying their identification. This makes sense, because their patron base is large, ever changing, and not intimately known to them. Many public libraries are experimenting with online patron registration forms that allow customers to fill out the required information and e-mail the form to the library. Library staff members process the form, then wait for the patron to appear in person with the appropriate photo identification before issuing the new library card.

Academic libraries may rely on official campus identification cards and draw from enrollment databases for patron verification. Special libraries may vary from not requiring registration at all, on the one hand, to a very formal process involving security clearance, on the other.

School libraries consult class lists supplied by teachers or the administrative office at the beginning of the academic term to open student accounts for a given school year.

In the case of some private research facilities or university libraries, community members with no affiliation to the institution may be able to purchase access privileges. In this case, the registration process involves payment of a fee in addition to the collection of name, address, and other identifying information.

Why Register Patrons?

There are many valid reasons for a library or information center to register its patrons. Some of the major reasons include the following:

To verify that a person qualifies to use the specific library

To determine the person's level of borrowing privileges, once qualified

To establish a record of who borrowed what items

To have contact information to locate patrons with overdue materials

To collect demographic information on customers for planning purposes

To be able to recall items needed for reserve use

Privacy of Patron Records

Once patron data have been gathered and becomes part of the library's database of customer information, it is very important for staff to realize that this personal data is private. Industry ethics and laws in some states advocate that such confidential information be afforded both internal and external privacy protection. This means that neither personal data gathered nor an individual's circulation records are to be shared with outside agencies; nor are these records accessible to library staff other than those who are assigned to work with them.

This issue and others relating to workplace ethics are discussed more fully in another section of this book in chapter 8, "Ethics in the Information Age."

Stacks Maintenance

Maintenance of the library's collections is crucial to an efficient operation. In most libraries, collection maintenance tasks are managed by the circulation department as an extension of their primary mission to provide access to and track the loan of materials. Admittedly, these are housekeeping tasks and tend to be somewhat tedious chores that must be done to maintain quality library service.

Some of the key maintenance tasks include shelving and shelf reading; cleaning, repairing and rebinding items, and inventorying items. Although the accurate and rapid reshelving of all materials is an ongoing, daily activity in any library, the other tasks take place on a more periodic basis. Many libraries and media centers that are closed to students for holiday or summer breaks select that time to conduct an inventory of their collections. For those libraries and information centers that do not close for extended periods of time, collection inventorying or shifting of collections in the stacks may be done in phases, with parts of the collection temporarily out of circulation while the process is underway.

LIBRARY CIRCULATION SYSTEMS

Today most libraries, information centers, and school media centers have an automated circulation system in place. Modern systems link a database of bibliographic records with patron use records to form an integrated OPAC. Most of today's systems provide a module that is accessible on the Web, allowing anytime–anywhere searching by patrons and staff. In addition, those OPAC systems that are fully Z 39.50 compatible allow a user to simultaneously search catalogs from two or more different libraries, even if each catalog is running software from different vendors. *Z 39.50* is a protocol by which one OPAC transfers a search inquiry or other data to another OPAC, without the user being required to reenter the information, using the precise search keys of the second OPAC. Since the Z 39.50 protocol predates Web technology, there are various efforts underway to modify it so as to better mesh with the modern Web-based environment.

For many larger academic and public libraries, the current system may be a fifth- or sixth-generation system. Early use of computerized library circulation systems began in the 1960s at large, academic facilities. Many of these libraries had been experimenting in the prior decade with key punch cards to tabulate circulation.[2] Before the advent of commercial software packages, some of these libraries developed their own homegrown automated circulation systems, usually in concert with campus or municipal computer departments. In the early 1970s, CL Systems, Inc. (later to become known as CLSI) was one of the first commercial vendors to begin selling turnkey library circulation systems. They were soon followed by many other companies offering software solutions for basic library circulation tasks.[3]

These early automated systems were limited to circulation control functions—check-in and check-out transactions, calculation of fines, printing of overdue notices, and placing of items on hold—all of which are time-consuming, laborious, and repetitive, but necessary tasks for accurate inventory control and library operation. Typically, these early turnkey and homegrown systems were not integrated to include bibliographic look-up functions for the public. Thus, the wooden card catalog, with its numerous drawers filled with index cards, remained the tool for patron access to a library's holdings. Maintenance of the card catalog required an ongoing effort of detailed, repetitive, painstaking work by cataloging department staff.

The first OPACs, which married the patron records with a detailed database of the library's holdings and were geared for public use, arrived on the scene in the early 1980s.[4] As OPACs matured and became commonplace in the next

15 years or so, that longtime staple of libraries, the card catalog, was superseded by a computer screen. Across the nation and around the world, libraries
began closing their card catalogs. Even the venerable *New Yorker* magazine
noted with mixed emotions this passing of a cultural icon. In a much read
1994 article, staff writer Nicholson Baker caused quite a stir in the library
world as he mourned the closing of Harvard's card catalog and questioned the
need for installation of its automated system, HOLLIS.[5]

Although there have certainly been growing pains associated with the initial transfer to OPACs, most library staff will overwhelmingly attest to the
benefits that automation has brought both to patrons and to employees. For
customers, this has meant improved, decentralized access and convenience,
user-centered features, and the demystification of library processes. OPACs,
by providing precise title location and availability data, have also allowed customers to play a more active role and enabling patron-initiated placement of
holds. For library staff, integrated computer systems have automated many
tedious, repetitive tasks associated with circulation's record-keeping functions
and technical services' cataloging operations.

There are some patrons who still lament the conversion to computer access and feel at a loss. An older, longtime library user recently said to one of
the authors, "I feel like I have lost the college library since the installation of
computers. Without the card catalog, I don't even want to come to the library."
A renewed effort to assist and train reluctant computer users is one approach
to mitigating this discomfort, but realistically, there will always be some researchers who resist any change from the familiar.

Since the early OPACs of the 1980s, there have been many advances and
improvements in the product, most parallel to developments in computer hardware and software technology overall. Currently, Web interfaces are the state
of the art for automated library systems. These contemporary card catalogs
are remotely accessible and offer to the general public value-added features,
such as online renewal and personal account checking.

Automation of library systems does come with a hefty price tag. Installation
of a new system is regarded by library agencies as a capital expenditure, and
often costs in the six-figure price range. For most public sector library agencies, this translates into a competitive bid process with vendors submitting
complex responses to library-generated requests for proposals, or RFPs.

OPACS in Common Use

At the beginning of the new millennium, OPACS were in common use across
the United States. Exact statistics for all types of libraries are not available,
especially for schools and for special libraries for which data gathering tends
to be difficult, but trends are visible to practitioners in the field. One such observation by Dick Boss, a respected library automation consultant, estimated
that nearly 100 percent of the nation's 2,000 largest libraries were automated
by 1999.[6]

Those libraries that are still relying on a manual system for their circulation and other operations tend to be smaller, rural, poorly funded, and not
members of any type of library network or consortium. These typically include

smaller special libraries, such as those found in churches, museums, historical societies and archives, non-profit organizations, or obscure government agencies.[7] School libraries in smaller private or parochial schools, as well as those located in isolated and rural public school districts, are other examples of libraries often without automated systems. Because these libraries are without partners, are minimally funded, are often staffed by volunteers or temporary help, have limited telecommunications infrastructures, and have done little to convert existing paper records to machine-readable formats, the roadblocks to installation of an OPAC are many.

Two approaches that are helping isolated libraries and information centers make progress toward automation are grant funding from private sources and membership in state-funded, multi-type library networks. Although no single grant will provide a ready-to-use OPAC on a silver platter, the receipt of specific grants can assist a library in laying the groundwork needed before conversion from a manual to an automated system can take place. Various state and national telecommunications measures have provided infrastructure funding for needy schools and libraries, and grants from the private Gates Foundation provide updated hardware, software, and staff training. By partnering with state-funded, multi-type library consortia, a once-isolated library can gain much needed expertise, access to consultants, and reduced pricing as part of a larger group.

Early Circulation Methods

Ledgers were the earliest method used in libraries for tracking information on borrowers and the items they borrowed. For the system to function well, multiple ledgers were required. Each transaction for a business day was noted in chronological order in a daybook. Later, data from the daybook was copied into separate ledgers, which provided access by patron name and book title.

The ledger that contained the borrowing record of each patron was arranged alphabetically by the borrower's last name and several pages were allowed to record ongoing entries. The third ledger listed each book in the collection and several pages were reserved to record successive borrowers and their respective due dates. Between them, the three logs provided three different access points to circulation data. The daybook provided a daily transaction log, but to verify a patron's account, the alphabetical patron ledger needed to be consulted. To ascertain the whereabouts of a particular book, the book ledger needed to be viewed. Ledgers were in common use in American libraries until about the time of the American Civil War.[8]

An earlier variant method, which eliminated the need for multiple ledgers, was the so-called dummy system. Wood dummies—that is, blocks with lined paper attached to them—were used to represent each book; as a patron checked out a book, his or her name and the book's due date were noted on the side of the book dummy. The dummy was then placed in the empty shelf space to indicate that the book was charged out. A variation of this was to have a dummy represent each patron. The correct block was then placed on the shelf as the book was removed; book title and due date were then written on the dummy.[9] An obvious limitation of this version was that each patron was limited to borrowing one book at a time.

These early tracking systems worked successfully only when small numbers of both borrowers and circulating items were involved. Once the number of patrons, the volume of use, and the collection size increased, these methods quickly became cumbersome and inefficient.

Improvements on the ledger method of tracking circulation led to various systems that used paper slips. These transaction slips functioned like receipts and were inserted into a book pocket attached to the inside of each tome. Further improvements on the slip system led to the two-card method. One pre-prepared card held key bibliographic information about a book, such as author, title, call number, and copy number, and was tucked inside the book pocket. The second card contained borrower identification and was kept at the charging desk for a borrower's signature at checkout. Both cards were stamped with the due date when an item was checked out.

The Newark System, so called because of its first use by the Newark, New Jersey, Public Library in 1896, became a popular example of the two-card system and was in widespread use for several decades. Approximately 30 years later, a refinement of the two-card system, known as the Detroit Self-Charging System, raised efficiency with the use of preprinted due date cards and library identification cards.[10]

Although these systems seem archaic today, in times of lengthy periods of electrical outages or computer malfunctions, library staff may need to revert to these manual systems to try to maintain some order over circulation. A library technician intern in a local school district encountered just such a situation recently. Besides being unfamiliar with the manual system, not all of the elementary school children were able to sign their names, which presented further complications during the outage period.

In the latter half of the 20th century, many systems for printing due date cards, book cards, charge cards, and borrowers' identification cards were developed to replace the earlier manual tasks of typing, stamping, and signing. Borrower identification cards ranged from paper to embossed plastic to the now common cards with optically readable barcodes.

The Library Card as a Symbol of Opportunity

Though the details surrounding the first borrower's card issued to a customer are lost to history, the concept of possessing one's own library card remains a symbol of opportunity and lifelong learning. A library card is the key to the free public library services that are a right for all citizens in the United States.

For residents, retirees, and immigrants new to a community, the initial trip to the public library to sign up for a user's card is a first step in accessing local programs and services. It is a fact well-known to public library staff that for ex-convicts and others returning to mainstream society, signing up for a library card in their new town is a recommended early step in their rehabilitation. A library identification card is equated with attaining literacy; the pursuit of pleasure reading; exploration of resources for study, research, and job search; Internet access; cultural programs; a sense of belonging to a community; and more.

And for young readers, a first library card is a proud possession that encourages them to grow in their reading skills. Recent ALA promotional ads, released in conjunction with National Library Card Sign-Up Month each September, remind parents "that a library card is the most important school supply of all" and is usually free. Such a campaign emphasizes the important and multifaceted community resource that a library is to its customers and the vital role it plays in the education and development of children.

Characteristics of an Automated Circulation System

Upon examination, the key characteristics of a modern automated circulation system are not too different from the basic inventory control needs of the 19th-century manual systems briefly described previously.

At minimum, a circulation system needs to do the following:

Be efficient and easy to use for both staff and patrons in all of its modules. Just because library staff may think that a system is wonderful and efficient does not mean that the public interface is equally convenient and intuitive.

Record and track three key elements relating to collection circulation: (1) the person who borrowed the item, (2) the exact item borrowed, (3) the time the item was borrowed and (4) when it is due back.

Track the status of all items in the collection individually. Accuracy and detail are important aspects of an efficient inventory control system, and thus are of primary importance in a library circulation system. At a minimum the system must record, whether items are charged-out to a patron, overdue, lost, missing; loaned to another library; out of circulation for repair or binding; or on the shelf and available for use. Most newer systems also indicate the status of items on order from vendors and materials that are being processed but are not yet available for use by the public.

Track the status of all patron accounts. This includes all registered borrowers, either active or inactive, and especially those with overdue items, outstanding fines, blocks, or other problems with their accounts.

Match requests for holds with incoming items. Upon patron or staff request, the system must be able to flag the record of an item that is charged out and then acknowledge that the requestor is next in line to receive the desired title when it is returned.

Provide statistics relating to the circulation of items. Key statistics include, at a minimum, the number of times a particular item has been checked out; overall circulation by week, month, or other period; circulation by individual library outlet, branch, department, or entire system; and circulation by call number.

Since the coming of the Internet, there is a new characteristic that is currently essential and can be added to the list above. A modern, integrated circulation system must offer a Web interface option in its OPAC module. Web access for an OPAC serves a very utilitarian purpose because it is the same platform upon which many other key library services and research tools are now delivered. In addition to taking advantage of all emerging Web technologies, such an interface provides customers the convenience of easy toggling between a library OPAC and other Web resources.

Other hallmarks of Internet access that provide added value and convenience to a Web-based OPAC include anytime–anywhere access, patron authentication, patron-initiated holds, interlibrary loan requests, and account tracking.

A rule of thumb for all library automation systems is that every system should receive serious review at least every seven years, with replacement of the system and a change in vendors possibilities to be considered. In the interim period, there will probably be upgrades (e.g., new software releases) to the system provided by the vendor every year or two to reflect new features and capabilities.

Automation Resources

Although settling on an automation vendor is a daunting task, there are currently many reputable sources to help a library manager or other staff with the selection of vendors and products. For more than 20 years, Pamela Cibbarelli, a leading analyst and writer in the field of library automation, has published a bi-annual directory that lists software packages, Web sites, consultants, and other key resources related to the automation of North American libraries.[11] The trade periodicals *Computers in Libraries* and *Information Today* regularly include articles analyzing major integrated library system companies

Another respected industry periodical, *Library Journal*, features the results of its own annual library automation marketplace survey every April. The published results in *LJ* focus on the performance of major library automation vendors and include profiles on each company with data such as market niche, number of installations, market share, and new products and services. *Library Technology Reports*, a bi-monthly periodical published by the ALA, is another authoritative source for information on library systems and equipment.

Professional conferences aimed for the library generalist, as well as those that specifically target technical staff, also prove extremely valuable for data gathering, both from automation vendors and from library and information center colleagues. Examples include, but are by no means limited to, the Internet Librarian, annual meetings of state and regional library associations, the annual and midwinter sessions of the ALA, the National Online Meeting, and the Special Libraries Association conferences. Typically, at the exhibit hall of the conference, the major automation vendors host booths staffed by sales and technical representatives who are there to answer questions and demonstrate their software products.

User groups of a particular automation package (e.g., Voyager, Millennium, SIRSI) help provide a different perspective to balance the vendor's point of view. These groups are comprised of customers, and they communicate through a listserv or blog and often hold periodic regional workshops. Querying user groups before making a purchase decision or when drafting the specifications for an RFP can be a valuable way to evaluate products and customer satisfaction. Once a system has been chosen, participation in a user group provides support, shared expertise, and strength in numbers when lobbying the vendor for improvements. With Web access to most OPACs a given, another means of testing the performance of a potential system is to anonymously use it just as a patron would do. In addition, in-person visits to library sites provide a unique chance to watch multiple users at work on a system and to consult with technical services staff.

With the great strides gained in computerized systems over the past four decades, library routines have become increasingly streamlined with each new generation of automated systems, especially in the area of circulation functions. The once standard tasks of manually date-stamping books or calculating overdue fines by hand are now seen as quaint and old-fashioned routines that show up in classic movies. The trend of personalizing one's Web account, so popular on retail Web sites like Amazon.com and with college campus portals (MyCalPoly, MyCuesta, etc.), is also becoming commonplace with the newer releases of OPAC software. Such customization may allow patrons to save past OPAC searches, submit and track ILL requests, suggest titles for library acquisition, get e-mail alerts or RSS alerts, and take advantage of other time-saving and convenient functions.

LIBRARY SECURITY

Thieves in an archive? Violence in a library? How dare they! There are many patrons, members of the general public, and even novice staff members who cherish the concept of a library as a safe haven from the woes of the outside world. Unfortunately, libraries, archives, and media and information centers are prone to purposeful theft, vandalism, and other crimes. Just as there seems to be more news media coverage of violent events in general, libraries have their share of shootings, seemingly senseless attacks, and other crimes that make the evening news.

Because the circulation or loan services department is responsible for the largest part of the library facility, the broader issues of library security and crime also tend to fall under its jurisdiction. Generally, there are two categories of security issues. The first category is offenses involving library property. This includes the theft of library materials or equipment, mutilation or intentional damage to library materials or equipment, and vandalism to the building. The second category is offenses against people—staff or patrons—that take place in the library building. Examples of such offenses include abusive conduct, assault, and indecent exposure.

Security in libraries is not a new concern. During the Roman Empire, it was the custom for a conquering army to pillage library buildings as they swept through a city, taking library books as spoils of war. In more modern times, a notorious library thief, Stephen Blumberg, was convicted in the 1990s and served a prison term for the theft of approximately 24,000 volumes from libraries in 45 states.[12]

Theft

The most common incidents of crime are theft or mutilation of library materials. The perpetrator may be a student with no money for a photocopy machine, a kleptomaniac, a self-appointed censor, or a professional thief out to make a profit. It could also be a library employee.

Electronic theft detection systems were first installed in libraries in the 1960s. By the 1980s, all but the smallest libraries and information centers were using some type of security system to deter theft. Once the library market was saturated, vendors targeted retail stores to find additional customers for their security products. Known in the industry as *materials control systems*, the most commonly used systems are found in libraries, supermarkets, and retail stores. Although not foolproof, they do lower losses through the concept of deterrence. Many would-be thieves, seeing a security gate or locking turnstile at an exit point, are discouraged from attempting to steal an item. Setting off an alarm and being confronted with possession of an unauthorized item in a public place is embarrassing at the least.

Such systems in and of themselves are by no means infallible. But when combined with vigilant staff efforts, security systems have generally reduced pilferage by about 80 percent over that experienced by a library with no security devices in place, according to 3M, a major vendor of such systems.[13]

Figure 6.1 depicts a library patron passing through an electronic security portal.

There are various models of materials control systems; some work on radio frequency, others on electromagnetism. Typically, a screen or gate detects

Figure 6.1. Security equipment positioned at checkout counters and building exits can help discourage library theft.

sensitized items. Each item—such as a book, magazine, videocassette, or DVD caddy—carries a hidden or disguised target. When properly checked out, the item is desensitized and the target turned off, and the patron passes through the security gate uneventfully. When an item has not been checked out properly and has not been desensitized, passing it through the gate triggers an alarm and locks the gate or turnstile. Options to the turnstile include the addition of flashing red lights or loud, recorded messages to increase the visibility of an unauthorized exit. Larger library facilities may place gates on every floor or at all reading room exits. When in use, these detection system turnstiles and gates must comply with the Americans with Disabilities Act (ADA) so as not to present a physical barrier to access for those in wheelchairs.

Pass around systems are another variation on security arrangements. This alternative, which is used in large video stores such as Blockbuster and other retail chains, is most likely to be used in nonacademic library settings where patrons are unlikely to bring items back into the building until they are ready to relinquish them. In such a system, the item is never desensitized. Instead, it is passed around the security gate by a staff member, after being checked out, and handed to the customer who is standing outside the security zone.

Preventive Measures

Attention to overall library security increases the effectiveness of materials control systems. A good place to begin is with a survey of the library's security. Conduct the survey with security or police personnel to gain their expert input. Assess vulnerable areas, such as unsecured windows and unalarmed delivery or staff entrances that allow one to circumvent the secured entrance. Control all exits with gates, alarms, locks, cameras, electronic keypads, or guards to minimize such security gaps.

Internal library procedures should also be considered. For example, how long do new materials lie around in the technical services area before a security or tattletape target is applied to them? Who has access to the new, unprocessed materials? Don't overlook library, custodial, or other building staff. Taking active measures, such as locking down computers and peripherals, TV monitors, DVD players, and other property can help prevent equipment loss.

When building a new library from scratch, staff have the advantage of taking security issues into consideration with the architect and designing a facility to deter theft and crime. Attention to preserving visual corridors in reading rooms and stack areas that allow for surveillance by personnel from service counters can increase the security of collections, staff, and patrons. Minimizing the presence of poorly lit stack areas and dark, remote corners in the library is also very important. Similar safety and design concerns apply to the library building itself and to adjacent parking areas. Although not often discussed in the literature on library security issues, the safety of these adjacent areas is an important issue. If unsafe, it can provide a barrier to patron access to the library and its services.

Within existing library structures, there are various methods for augmenting security, such as increased lighting, video surveillance cameras, a library security guard to patrol the building, staff visibility at all service points, and enhanced materials controls systems. Attempting to offer reasonable loan periods on library materials is another consideration that could impact theft and mutilation. For example, if an item can be checked out for only two days and patrons need the material for a longer period, they may think that stealing it is the best answer to satisfy their needs.

Realistic Policies

As with most security systems, a determined or practiced thief will find a way around them. So the bottom line for library staff is that losses to the collection will occur. Therefore, realistic administrators need to allow for some shrinkage in the collection and to budget funds for the replacement of stolen or damaged items. Also, setting aside funds to periodically upgrade or replace security systems is a necessary planning strategy. To be cost-effective, the overall cost of the security measures should not exceed the amount saved by having those procedures in place.

Having a policy in place with the library's parent organization for penalizing a perpetrator is a necessary step. Typically, in an academic library, students can be fined, placed on probation, or at least sent to the dean's office for a warning. In school settings, disciplinary action can be taken and parents notified. Public libraries will want to have good working relations with their local police departments to provide them needed support with security issues. Library staff should not attempt to physically restrain suspected thieves or perpetrators, but should summon the assistance of police or trained security personnel.

As with many other elements of a library or information center (relevancy of collections, helpfulness of staff, public hours, and so on) the library's reputation for safety will be known in the community and will affect patron satisfaction and usage levels.

Mutilation

The purposeful act of mutilation may involve cutting out a section of a book or magazine with the intent of taking just those pages needed by the irresponsible patron. Or it may involve destroying pages or tearing whole volumes from their spines in an effort to eliminate offensive photographs or text. Because mutilation typically occurs inside the reading room or library building, security systems are of little help in catching perpetrators in the act. If a security target remains attached to the pages that were removed and the perpetrator attempts to pass through the exit gate, they can be caught at that time and dealt with. Sadly, however, the damage to materials is already done. Sometimes the purpose of the mutilation is simply to defeat the security system.

In a school or academic setting where much usage is linked to topical assignments, informing faculty of the problem can help catch a potential mutilator. Some libraries periodically mount displays of damaged and mutilated materials in an attempt to educate patrons and perhaps deter would-be mutilators.

People Problems

Those libraries that are open to the general public are the most apt to encounter problem patrons. Because these facilities are open for long hours (often including evenings and weekends), and provide warm, comfortable shelter, they are inviting places of shelter for homeless and other needy people. No identification is required to enter, and there is an abundance of free entertainment available, along with restrooms and hot, running water.

Most problem patron behavior can be characterized as falling into the following categories: nuisance behavior (e.g., lonely or elderly people who monopolize reference personnel or carry on long-winded monologues); criminal behavior (e.g., vandalizing materials, stealing materials, performing sexually lewd acts); and various types of behavior that are often bizarre, unpredictable, and threatening and exhibited by mentally disturbed patrons.

Many libraries provide special staff training conducted by outside experts or local law enforcement personnel in dealing with problematic individuals. Such training usually includes conflict resolution, safety issues, defusing difficult situations, and other techniques. Dealing with problem patrons in the course of a workday is a genuine issue for most library staff, and they deserve access to this training to best prepare them for handling such interactions.

Disaster Preparedness

Another aspect of library security is disaster preparedness. Also referred to as emergency preparedness, this is a related but much larger security issue that focuses on making a library facility and its staff ready in the event of a natural disaster, such as flood, fire, earthquake, tornado, or the like. Disasters perpetrated by criminals or terrorists, such as bombs, arson, and hostage-taking, are also included in emergency preparedness. Just as with theft, libraries do not have a special immunity from disasters.

To have a viable disaster plan, much advance footwork, preparation, and coordination is needed. An up-to-date, written library disaster plan is probably part of a larger campus, school district, corporate, city, or other agency's overall plan. Typically, a disaster plan should specify the chain of command for decision making and include data such as maps and floor plans, evacuation routes, and procedures. Highest priority collections for removal or safeguarding should be indicated. Computer data backups, especially all OPAC files, should be housed at an alternate, remote location in case onsite files are unrecoverable.

A thorough discussion of disaster preparedness is beyond the scope of this textbook. Many comprehensive books have been written about this topic, and certain library industry Web sites provide helpful emergency checklists. The ALA Web site features a Disaster Preparedness and Recovery section developed by the group's Washington Office (http://www.ala.org/ala/washoff/woissues/disasterpreparedness/distrprep.cfm)

Features include a template for the creation of a comprehensive disaster plan, actual disaster plans submitted by other libraries and archives, and photos of damage sustained by Gulf Coast libraries from the devastating hurricanes in 2005.

Whether the responsibility of a library director managing a multi-branch system or the solo librarian operating a small, special library, disaster preparedness training is a topic to be taken seriously.

INTERLIBRARY LOAN SERVICES

Interlibrary loan (ILL) is an important service whereby individual libraries agree to share their collections and to supply materials to one another for patron use. Upon the receipt of a patron's request, the borrowing library asks another facility to supply a needed book, video, or copy of a periodical article for a minimal fee (typically $10 to $20), or sometimes free of charge. Often, agreements are drawn up among member libraries belonging to regional networks or consortia that formalize this cooperation. But, typically, those libraries that receive public funds—state colleges and universities and public systems—will automatically accept requests from other libraries without a formal cooperating agreement, though they may impose fees or restrictions. In contrast, special libraries that are part of private corporations or institutions, such as those in law firms and businesses, and that do not belong to any networks, are under no obligation to loan out their materials. And, in fact, for reasons of competitive intelligence, they may not want to do so because it might assist a rival business.

In state-funded library networks, all libraries that want to receive services must provide some level of access to their own collections as a prerequisite to membership. This may take the form of providing onsite use, ILL services, access to specialized reference services, or even direct borrowing to qualifying customers affiliated with the network.

Often, ILL services are under the umbrella of a circulation department because each external loan, though it requires special handling and attention, is just another type of borrowing transaction. The net result of this sharing of materials is better service for library customers. Specifically, patrons have access to a much-expanded resource base. Even in the information-rich age of the new millennium, no single library can have it all. Through the use of ILL, the boundaries of a single library's collection, or even a system's, are extended far beyond its own hard copy and electronic holdings.

The *Interlibrary Loan Code for the United States*, a document compiled by the Reference and User Services division of the ALA, serves as a guideline for libraries in general and for any systems or networks that want to develop their own ILL policies.

As the Explanatory Supplement to the Code states:

Interlibrary loan is intended to complement local collections and is not a substitute for good library collections intended to meet the routine needs of users. ILL is based on a tradition of sharing resources between various types and sizes of library and rests on the belief that no library, no matter how large or well supported, is self-sufficient in today's world. It is also evident that some libraries are net lenders and others are net borrowers, but the system of interlibrary loan still rests on the belief that all libraries should be willing to lend if they are willing to borrow.[14]

Regarding the involvement and reciprocity implied in such a nationwide effort, the Code notes:

> The effectiveness of the national interlibrary loan system depends upon participation of libraries of all types and sizes.[15]

Implied by the code and as discussed in the supplement is the premise that libraries of all types and sizes should be willing to share their resources liberally so that a relatively few libraries are not overburdened.

For researchers in the know, ILL is one of the best-kept secrets of libraries. There are rarely big, bright signs offering this extended service. Rather, it has always been suggested to patrons on a case-by-case basis as the reference interview progresses or when the request for information cannot be filled locally. The ILL service is similar to a special order in a retail store. When the color, size, and label of the jacket you want (say, black, size 12, Liz Claiborne) is not available, your local department store might offer to call other regional branches to see if they stock the exact jacket desired and can send it to your local store.

The first formal mention of ILL in America was in a letter to the editor in *Library Journal*'s premier issue in 1876. ILL became common in the 1920s, although cooperative loaning between libraries had already been taking place for some time prior to that.[16] With the adoption of the first ALA *Interlibrary Loan Code* in 1919 and the growing number of union or shared catalogs of library holdings, ILL became firmly established.[17] Standardized forms were developed mid-century and were in common usage until the advent of OCLC's ILL model, faxing, and then e-mail in the 1990s rendered the multipart paper forms obsolete.

Limitations on ILL Requests

Certain types of library materials may not be available for interlibrary loan because of their physical size, shape or condition, copyright restrictions, or local demand. Typically, these materials include, but are not limited to, computer software; rare, very old, or valuable books; most newly released books; the hard copy issue of a journal in its entirety; audiovisual materials; and reference books. Each library sets its own limitations on what materials it will and will not loan out. In addition, copyright law restricts the number of articles that can be photocopied from the same journal without incurring royalty fees.

An important concept of ILL is that the service is to locate and obtain a specific book or article citation; thus, ILL is not a subject search for materials but a search for a supplying library that owns a precise title not available at the local level. The ILL service is considered to be a supplement to the onsite collection. On the other hand, ILL should not be mistaken as a substitute for collection development in individual libraries. If an item is repeatedly requested through ILL, it is an indication that there is a local need for that item, and purchase for the permanent collection should be seriously considered. Repeat requests for ILL may also provide data for cooperative collection development efforts among libraries.

When requesting an item through ILL, there is a direct correlation between the accuracy and completeness of the book, DVD, or journal article citation provided and the likelihood of the material being located. Staff from the borrowing library search large databases such as OCLC to locate an item that matches the citation provided by the customer. So when a patron submits a citation with the author's name misspelled or omitted, incomplete publishing data, or other inaccuracies, the chances of locating the material are diminished substantially.

Once a supplier is located, the borrowing library queries the potential lender as to the item's availability for loan. It may take queries to several libraries that own the item before a successful loan actually happens. There are many reasons that multiple queries may be required, including the following: the item in question may be checked out or may have been sent out to the bindery; if it is an older publication, it might be in a remote storage facility and require a longer delivery time; ILL departments in academic libraries are often closed for two to three weeks during holiday or semester breaks. Many times, diligent library technicians who process ILLs will shop around until they find a free supplier so they can save the patron from having to pay a service charge.

Patrons frequently ask, "How long before my ILL request will come in?" The reality of ILL is that the turnaround time for receiving the desired material varies with each specific request. For researchers and students using this inexpensive but often slow service, the caveat is "submit your request as early as possible" before a project deadline. Anecdotal evidence and the disclaimers on many library Web sites indicate that, for libraries using modern methods of ILL processing, the bulk of requests arrive within a two-week period. But on a case-by-case basis, the turnaround time can be unpredictable. And, certainly, international loan requests may take considerably longer to fill.

Abuse of the ILL Service

No discussion of the benefits of interlibrary sharing would be complete without mention of the abuses and imbalances that can arise. Many libraries have limits on the number of active ILL requests that a patron can have at any one time. One of the authors remembers an eager nursing student at a community college who, during a single library visit, submitted requests for 25 articles from specialized health periodicals. From that time on, that small college library instituted a limit of 10 ILL items at once, per patron.

Staff time is a consideration when setting reasonable limits on ILLs, as is the estimated cost of each ILL transaction. One estimate conducted at a metropolitan public library put the minimum cost in staff time for processing an ILL request to borrow an item at an average of $10 per unit.[18] Calculating the cost of an ILL transaction can provide a basis for determining a fee schedule in an effort to recover the costs of the service. One source for computing costs is Boucher's *Interlibrary Loan Practices Handbook*.[19]

Another consideration is that completed ILL requests often lie on the hold shelf of the requesting library, never to be picked up by the patron. The reasons that library patrons neglect to pick up these items vary, but it might be that they found another supplier, refused to pay any ILL changes, simply forgot, or lost interest in the material that was once so urgently needed. Placing a limit on the number of simultaneous ILL requests per patron helps balance the needs of borrowing and supplying libraries. Remember that in the case of a borrowed book or video, when it is sent out on loan, the item remains unavailable to local readers for three to four weeks.

Because of their vast resources and the breadth of their collections, large university and research libraries have traditionally been deluged with requests for technical, medical, and other materials not available in small, generalized library collections. This can create quite an imbalance, with large facilities constantly being asked for material and small libraries rarely receiving loan requests. For this reason, early ILL codes recommended that "the requesting library should avoid sending the burden of its requests to a few libraries. Major resource libraries should be used as a last resort." The current code stays away from such a recommendation, but it remains a common sense guideline among practicing ILL library technicians.[20]

As a means of remedying this transaction imbalance, some states have set up a system of ILL reimbursement within their boundaries. This means that a public library receives a set dollar amount as reimbursement for supplying an ILL requested for a library patron from outside its jurisdiction. According to a study in January 2000 by Himmel and Wilson (library consultants on such reimbursement programs), of the 45 states responding to the survey, 22 received some type of state reimbursement for ILL, whereas the same number did not. (One state did not respond to the question.)[21]

The widespread use of automated library catalogs, especially union catalogs that delineate holdings of multiple libraries, along with other advances in technology in the last decade or so, have greatly enhanced the process of identifying potential ILL suppliers. Locating those libraries that hold a desired title is now faster and easier overall. Plus, the ability to identify various libraries—small or large, well-known or lesser known, in state or out of state, helps to spread the resource sharing more equitably.

How It Works

Here is a recent illustration of how the service works typically. One of the authors received (through ILL) a request for an obscure Canadian local history book, *The History of the County of Guysborough, Nova Scotia.* The request was placed with the Cuesta College Library's loan services department, using its Web-based ILL form. The request form (see figures 6.2 and 6.3) is part of the library's Web site and is accessible to campus students, staff, and faculty (http://library.cuesta.cc.ca.us/illoan.htm). Because the college subscribes to the bibliographic utility OCLC, its expansive international database of members' holdings was searched for this title. More than 15 potential supplying libraries were identified. Several libraries were queried unsuccessfully before the University of Windsor in Ontario, Canada, agreed to supply the title. A hard copy volume was shipped fourth-class library rate to the borrowing library, along with an invoice of $10. The patron was allowed to check the book out for two weeks and promptly paid the fee directly to the loaning library.

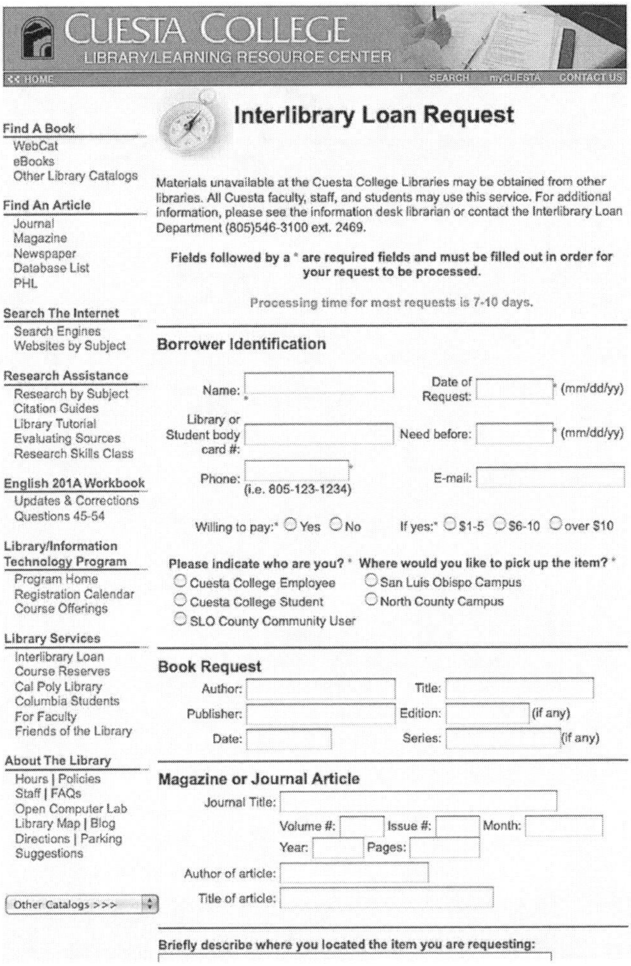
CUESTA COLLEGE
LIBRARY/LEARNING RESOURCE CENTER
<< HOME | SEARCH myCUESTA CONTACT US

Find A Book
WebCat
eBooks
Other Library Catalogs

Find An Article
Journal
Magazine
Newspaper
Database List
PHL

Search The Internet
Search Engines
Websites by Subject

Research Assistance
Research by Subject
Citation Guides
Library Tutorial
Evaluating Sources
Research Skills Class

English 201A Workbook
Updates & Corrections
Questions 45-54

Library/Information Technology Program
Program Home
Registration Calendar
Course Offerings

Library Services
Interlibrary Loan
Course Reserves
Cal Poly Library
Columbia Students
For Faculty
Friends of the Library

About The Library
Hours | Policies
Staff | FAQs
Open Computer Lab
Library Map | Blog
Directions | Parking
Suggestions

Other Catalogs >>>

Interlibrary Loan Request

Materials unavailable at the Cuesta College Libraries may be obtained from other libraries. All Cuesta faculty, staff, and students may use this service. For additional information, please see the information desk librarian or contact the Interlibrary Loan Department (805)546-3100 ext. 2469.

Fields followed by a * are required fields and must be filled out in order for your request to be processed.

Processing time for most requests is 7-10 days.

Borrower Identification

Name: * Date of Request: * (mm/dd/yy)
Library or Student body card #: Need before: * (mm/dd/yy)
Phone: * (i.e. 805-123-1234) E-mail:
Willing to pay:* Yes No If yes:* $1-5 $6-10 over $10

Please indicate who are you? * Where would you like to pick up the item? *
Cuesta College Employee San Luis Obispo Campus
Cuesta College Student North County Campus
SLO County Community User

Book Request
Author: Title:
Publisher: Edition: (if any)
Date: Series: (if any)

Magazine or Journal Article
Journal Title:
Volume #: Issue #: Month:
Year: Pages:
Author of article:
Title of article:

Briefly describe where you located the item you are requesting:

Figure 6.2. Many college, university, and public libraries now provide online interlibrary loan forms as a convenience for patrons. This one is from Cuesta College in San Luis Obispo, California.

Compared to the expense of trying to obtain a copy of this out-of-print title, or, even more costly, having to journey cross-country to read the book in a Canadian library, the small fee was well worth the convenience of having the book shipped to the customer's library.

Initiating an ILL Request

For many patrons, an ILL request is prompted by a visit to their library. Often such a request begins at the circulation desk when a patron realizes that a desired item is not held locally. Frequently, it may also develop as the final step of a reference interview, as local resources are explored and found to be inadequate. For patrons who search a library's OPAC remotely and are familiar with the ILL service, a request might be submitted via e-mail

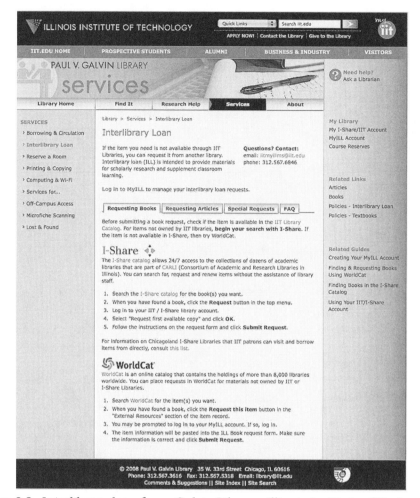

Figure 6.3. Interlibrary loan form; Galvin Library, Illinois Institute of Technology.

or telephone. Conveniently, many libraries now have complete ILL forms available on their Web sites. Again, each library will determine how it accepts an ILL request. Often, ILL services are limited to valid, card-carrying patrons, so that whatever form the request takes—an e-mail inquiry, a completed ILL form submitted from a Website, or an in-person request—some verification of the patron's account is performed.

Historically, an important aspect of ILL is that the transaction is library to library. It is true that changes are now on the horizon that will make online, customer-initiated ILL requests more commonplace within official library networks, but patrons will still need to be members in good standing at one of the participating libraries. Authentication of their status will be part of the log-on interface. At the current time, at the majority of libraries in the United States, patrons cannot initiate a request on their own, independent of a home library affiliation. The borrowing library, whether placing the request or authenticating a subscriber to place a request themselves, in effect, vouches for the patron's careful use of a supplied item. Affliation with a home library also helps to ensure the prompt return of borrowed items to the lending library and the collection of any service fees charged. In many cases, the loaned item—once delivered—does not leave the borrowing library. For example, loaned microfilm must be used on site in the requesting patron's library. Often, unique or older books, such as local history titles or reference books, are loaned with the understanding that the customer must read them on site.

Direct Borrowing

Direct borrowing is a variation on the interlibrary loan services described previously and one that many seasoned library users have yet to experience. In library consortia where direct borrowing is an agreed-upon service, patrons from one participating library can walk into any other member library and check out items. The computer system of the lending library verifies that patrons are in good standing with their home library before authorizing the transactions. The home library generally is responsible for enforcing loan periods. In some arrangements, the patron must return borrowed items to the lending library. In others, the items can be returned to any participating library.

One of the authors had the opportunity to use direct borrowing when he worked at an engineering university in Chicago, the Illinois Institute of Technology (IIT). That university participated in a consortium with more than 30 other academic libraries in Illinois. Because the author's personal research interests were centered in the social sciences, the library resources that met his needs were more likely to be found in the collections of other consortium members than they were on the shelves of the library at his own institution.

The OPAC of IIT was linked with those of the other libraries in the consortium. Therefore, the author could easily check to determine which members of the group held the desired titles. Because the circulation systems were also linked, it was possible to determine if any of those titles were missing, checked out, or restricted from circulation by virtue of being categorized as rare, reference, or reserve materials. Generally, the author found titles of interest to be available at the libraries of two comprehensive universities that were both along his daily commuting path. With this as the case, he had three options:

1. Stop at a holding (lending) library on his way home, hoping that no one had checked out the book in the meantime.
2. Request that the item be pulled from the shelf and immediately charged out to him and held at the lending library until he could pick it up.
3. Request that the item be charged out to him and delivered to his home library by means of a state-funded delivery service if he could wait a few days for the item.

Although direct borrowing has never been nearly as commonplace as the library-to-library loan method, the current growth in distance education courses may see both of these services become staples for the far-flung, off-campus student who needs anywhere–anytime access to course-required materials or supplemental resources.

Document Delivery Services

There are a variety of sources that provide what is referred to as *document delivery,* a service similar in concept to interlibrary loan. Most of these sources are commercial firms, although many larger university libraries also offer such a service to the general public on a fee basis. Document delivery differs fundamentally from traditional interlibrary loan in four ways:

1. The service is not restricted to library card holders; any individual with a valid credit card can patronize a document delivery firm.
2. The service uses a broader array of suppliers, including libraries, private firms, individuals, publishers, and others to procure the desired item.
3. The emphasis is on speed in procuring the requested item.
4. The service can be costly.

Document delivery firms are often located in communities with large academic or research libraries, and they may employ regular as well as contract employees in their effort to quickly locate, retrieve, photocopy, and deliver the desired materials. Examples of large, established document delivery vendors include Ingenta (http://www.ingentaconnect.com/), the U.S. Department. of Commerce National Technical Information Service (NTIS; http://www.ntis. gov/), ISI Document Solution (http://ids.isinet.com), and Information Express (http://www.ieonline.com/docdel.html). A scan of the Yellow Pages in most telephone or business directories will often reveal smaller, local document deliveries firms as well.

Like many other vendors in the library business, document delivery companies may be specialized. Some may supply only medical sources, others may specialize in patent data, and other firms may provide access to a wide range of subject area materials, ranging from newspaper and periodical articles, to monographs, to foreign language materials.

Special libraries, such as those in law firms and corporations—where competitive intelligence and other time-sensitive business decisions often influence rush information requests—have traditionally been frequent users of document delivery vendors. In these scenarios, whenever possible, the cost of document delivery transactions is billed to a client or charged back to a specific department within the organization.

Well-funded academic libraries often have accounts with commercial document delivery firms and pay all or part of the fees to supply items to their faculty, currently enrolled students, or both. In this case, the end user cannot distinguish between an item acquired through the traditional ILL process or one procured through a commercial firm. The cost and means are transparent to the satisfied patron.

Future of ILL

Although the interlibrary loan service to date has been primarily used by serious researchers, faculty, genealogists, and seasoned library patrons, there are many indications that the service may soon undergo a renaissance as a result of the Internet's many applications.

ILL may soon be discovered by new groups of students and researchers. Distance education, where students (regardless of geographical location) use the Web to access course materials online and never meet in any physical classroom or visit a brick-and-mortar library, is projected to be a growth industry for colleges and universities. These academic institutions must make required and supplementary materials available to their far-flung students in a convenient manner. This often means providing them with full ILL services and subsidizing all or part of any costs. Requested books or DVDs might be physically delivered to a student's home or office; or articles and readings may be delivered via e-mail or viewed on the Web with password access. Commercial document delivery firms may also be used to provide materials to students in a speedy manner, with the cost absorbed, or at least subsidized, by the university.

The increase in multi-type library consortiums with shared holdings lists will also encourage interlibrary loan activity by making holdings data more readily available to patrons. After checking a holdings list online, qualified researchers then turn to an ILL request form that is also online. Quickly, conveniently, and at the point of need, the patron can then submit a timely request for a needed ILL item. In addition, many college and university libraries now feature sophisticated electronic ILL request accounts for registered patrons that are accessible via a Web page login. Advantages for the patrons include more accuracy and speed in handing requests, since all ILL data is held in a searchable database, as well as the ability to log on for a status check of a requested item; for library staff, such a system allows for more efficiency in managing requests and easier tabulation of ILL statistics. See the DeWitt Wallace Library at Macalester College for an example of this type of process. (http://www.macalester.edu/library/about/policies/interloan.html). In another interesting development, the Library of Congress is experimenting with using the Internet to provide digital ILLs for certain short, fragile works from its collection that are in the public domain. Rather than photocopying or mailing out such items, the Library of Congress scans the contents and notifies the requesting library agency that the item will be available for online digital viewing at a specific time.[22]

Commercial document delivery may also benefit from technological advances and from a general increased awareness of such services. The need to supply distance education students with required materials may also impact the fee-based alternatives to traditional library-to-library transactions.

STUDY QUESTIONS

1. In your college library, what is the name of the department that handles circulation and interlibrary loan? How many people are employed in this department, and at what job levels are they employed (e.g., student assistants, pages, library technicians, librarians, managers)?

2. What is the distinction between the designations *reference* and *reserve* for library materials?

3. What are some of the considerations that must be balanced when setting circulation policies for the loan of a library or information center's materials?

4. What is your opinion about limiting access to library materials according to a patron's age? In a public library? In a school media center?

5. Are overdue fines a necessary evil in the management of a library's collection? Explain why or why not.

6. Name the key functions of a modern automated circulation system. What are some other features that provide added value?

7. Why are libraries, media centers, archives, and information centers vulnerable to theft? Name some basic preventive measures that can be taken to deal with theft problems.

8. Have you placed an interlibrary loan request in the past year? If so, were you satisfied with the materials obtained and the overall service? Explain why or why not.

9. How do interlibrary loan and document delivery services differ? How are they alike?

RESOURCES

Articles

Bishop, George. "Library Security At Its Best." *Media & Methods* 16 (September/October, 1998).

Crawford, Walt. "The Card Catalog and Other Digital Controversies." *American Libraries* (January): 52–58 (1999).

Hamilton, John Maxwell. "Is There a Klepto in the Stacks?" *New York Times Book Review,* 18: 1, 48–49 (November 1990).

Jones, David and Geoffrey Larkin. "Securing a Good Design: A Library Building Consultant and an Architect Consider Library Security." *APLIS* (December): 164–70 (1993).

Khong, W. K. "A Security Flaw in Barcode Self-Charging Systems." *Library & Archival Security* 15 (1): 91–94 (1999).

Linderfelt, K. A. "Charging Systems." *Library Journal* (June): 178–82 (1882).

Manzano, Roberto J. "Library Guards Await Limited Police Power." *Los Angeles Times,* July 15, 2000.

Nelson, Jesse. "Security in the Schools." *Media & Methods* (May/June): 12 (1997).

Plummer, Mary W. "Loan Systems." *Library Journal* (July): 242–47 (1893).

Scott, Janny. "No Longer a Refuge for Readers." *Los Angeles Times,* 10 (August): A-1, 14 (1993).

Shuman, Bruce A. "Designing Personal Safety into Library Buildings." *American Libraries* (August): 37–39 (1996).

Thompson, Amy. "The Next Chapter in Library Security." *Security Management* (August): 61, 63–64 (1997).

"3M Introduces Digital Identification System, Model 3500 Detection System; Demonstrates Pikiosk." *Information Today* (September): 47, 49 (1999).

Vogel, Brenda. "Making Prison Libraries Visible and Accessible." *Corrections Today* (April): 120, 122–24 (1994).

"With Millions of Dollars in Overdue Items, Librarians Get Tough." *New York Times,* Late Edition (East Coast), May 21, 1995.

Books

Boucher, Virginia. *Interlibrary Loan Procedure Manual*. 2nd ed. Chicago: American Library Association, 1997.

Kahn, Miriam. *Disaster Response and Planning for Libraries*. Chicago: American Library Association, 1997.

McNeil, Beth, and Denise J. Johnson. *Patron Behavior in Libraries: A Handbook of Positive Approaches to Negative Situations*. Chicago: American Library Association, 1995.

Morris, Leslie. *Interlibrary Loan Policies Directory*. 6th ed. New York: Neal-Schuman, 1999.

Shuman, Bruce A. *Library Security and Safety Handbook: Prevention, Policies, and Procedures*. Chicago: American Library Association, 1999.

Switzer, Teri R. *Safe at Work? Library Security and Safety Issues*. Metuchen, NJ: Scarecrow Press, 1999.

Willis, Mark. *Dealing with Difficult People in the Library*. Chicago: American Library Association, 1999.

Web Sites

Lyall, Dr. Jan. "Disaster Planning for Libraries and Archives: Understanding the Essential Issues." *Provenance: The Electronic Magazine* 1 (2): 1996.

http://www.netpac.com/provenance/vol1/no2/features/lyall1.htm

(accessed January 18, 2001)

NOTES

1. "Free Access to Libraries for Minors: An Interpretation of the Library Bill of Rights," (Chicago: American Library Association, 2004), http://www.ala.org/alaorg/oif/free_min.html (accessed August 10, 2007).

2. Wayne A. Wiegand and Donald G. Davis, Jr., eds., *Encyclopedia of Library History* (New York: Garland Publishing, 1994), 143.

3. Ernest Muro, *Automation Services for Libraries: A Resource Handbook* (Annandale, NJ: Vendor Relations Press, 1991), 5, 6, 14, 24, 25.

4. Ibid., 25, 26.

5. Nicholson Baker, "Discards," *New Yorker*, April 4, 1994.

6. Dick Boss, e-mail to the author, March 15, 1999.

7. Arlene G. Taylor, *Organization of Information* (Englewood, CO: Libraries Unlimited, 1999), 24.

8. Nevada Wallis Thompson, *Circulation Systems for School Library Media Centers: Manual to Microcomputer* (Littleton, CO: Libraries Unlimited, 1985), 4–12.

9. Wayne A. Wiegand and Donald G. Davis, Jr., eds., *Encyclopedia of Library History* (New York: Garland Publishing, 1994), 142–43.

10. Ibid.

11. Pamela Cibbarelli, ed., *Directory of Library Automation Software, Systems, and Services: 2006–2007 Edition* (Medford, NJ: Information Today, 2006).

12. Laurie Becklund, "Man Writes Novel Chapter in Annals of Library Thefts," *Los Angeles Times*, Home Edition, April 28, 1991.

13. *3M Quality Guaranthree* (St. Paul, MN: 3M Library Systems, 2001), 1.

14. ALA Reference and Users Services Association Interlibrary Loan Committee, "National Interlibrary Loan Code for the United States," last revised January 2001, (Chicago: American Library Association), http://www.ala.org/rusaTemplate.cfm? Section=referenceguide&Template=/ContentManagement/ContentDisplay. cfm&ContentID=31579 (accessed August 13, 2007).

15. Ibid.

16. Arthur Curley and Dorothy Broderick, *Building Library Collections,* 6th ed. (Metuchen, NJ: Scarecrow Press, 1985), 174.

17. Wayne A. Wiegand and Donald G. Davis, Jr., eds., *Encyclopedia of Library History* (New York: Garland Publishing, 1994), 285–86.

18. Nancy O'Neill, Santa Monica Public Library, e-mail to author, September 28, 2000.

19. Virginia Boucher, *Interlibrary Loan Procedure Manual,* 2d ed. (Chicago: American Library Association, 1997), 220–32.

20. ALA RASD MOPSS Interlibrary Loan Committee, "National Interlibrary Loan Code for the United States, 1994," last modified March 28, 2000 (Chicago: American Library Association), http://www.ala.org/rusa/stnd_lnc.html (accessed October 6, 2000).

21. *Supporting Interlibrary Loan and Direct Loan Services in California's Multitype Library Environment* (Milton, WI: Himmel and Wilson Library Consultants, 2000), 7.

22. "Library of Congress Interlibrary Loans Delivered Online," *Ancestry Daily News,* December 4, 2000, http://www.ancestry.com/library/view/news/articles/2999.asp (accessed December 15, 2000).

Chapter 7

Reference Service

What is reference service? The centerpiece of reference service is an individual reference transaction. The transaction occurs when highly trained staff members provide walk-in, telephone, e-mail or live interactive chat consultation with library customers. The consultation is generally one on one and therefore can be specifically targeted to resolve the information or research needs of individual patrons. Thus, the primary activity of a reference unit is to directly aid specific customers in their quests for information and in the effective use of resources.

Although all divisions of a library or information center ultimately serve the customer, reference service is one of the most direct and visible efforts regardless of the type of library environment.

A 2006 study of public library usage conducted by KRC Research & Consulting for the ALA showed that 63 percent of adults had library cards, and that 54 percent of those surveyed who had visited a public library recently had consulted a librarian for assistance. Thus, reference is also a well-used service.[1]

A reference service counter may also be called Research Services, the Information Desk, the Help Desk, or other similar names, all connoting the provision of assistance. In most libraries these terms are used interchangeably. Popular terms for virtual reference services—which are also referred to as digital or electronic reference—are Ask the Librarian, E-Reference, AskNow, and other phrases implying real time interaction or at least a speedy response time.

In very large libraries there may be multiple service desks, each with a very specific function. For example, in such a library, the Information Desk may be found in a very visible and readily accessible location, such as a first floor or entrance area, where general and directional referring occurs. More specialized problem-solving would then take place in subject-oriented locales (e.g., the Fine Arts section or the Science and Technology section), often as a result of a referral from the Information Desk.

In such arrangements, the rationale is for the Information Desk staff to screen patron requests, answer the routine questions, and refer the more complex ones to more highly trained and often subject-specialist librarians.

In some ways this would be similar to nurses screening patients and referring the more serious problems to doctors while handling routine matters themselves. However, in most libraries, all reference activities take place at one service point.

Each community of information seekers has its own distinct set of needs. Whether that community is an affluent suburban population, attorneys in a legal firm, middle school students, or university students or professors, they will interact uniquely with the reference department serving them by requesting different information. Because of the ongoing interaction between reference staff and patrons, this department often has a pulse on those local information needs—at least those that are articulated and expressed to the staff.

In addition to providing research guidance, a secondary goal of reference service in many libraries is to teach users how to conduct searches and to use resources in an effort to become self-sufficient in their investigations. Reference staff spend much of their time instructing customers on how to navigate their way through the ever-growing virtual sea of information. This may be achieved through face-to-face, one-on-one tutoring, with self-paced online tutorials, or by more formalized classroom-like education.

The goal of helping customers become self-sufficient is both a necessity and a mission for most libraries. Academic and school libraries, like their parent institutions, have a teaching mission. Information literacy, as well as literacy in traditional reading, writing, and arithmetic, is critical to students' success in all aspects of their lives. In addition, libraries are not generally staffed at levels that allow reference staff the luxury of actually doing the research for each customer, even if it would be faster and more enjoyable for all concerned. The needs of other customers must also be met. Also, once customers have learned one information skill, they may be able to perform it unaided the next time they need similar data. They will then return to the reference staff with more complex and more interesting challenges, having been able to solve the more mundane problems on their own.

A question that often comes up in today's Information Age is: "With so much information available on the Internet, why would anyone need to use a Reference Librarian?" A 2006 study from the University of Michigan's Comprehensive Cancer Center reported that cancer patients looking for medical information about their particular disease found more information by seeking assistance from a reference librarian than by searching on their own.[2] Overall career experience, as well as the daily frequency of searching and access to subscription databases not available to the general public were all factors in making librarian-mediated searches more productive.

In contrast with academic and school library settings, within many special libraries the goal of teaching patrons some self-sufficiency in their searching does not apply. In this setting, the primary customers are highly specialized and highly paid professionals. It is more cost-effective for the library staff to collect and synthesize the information than it is to train the specialists to do their own research. For example, in a law firm library, the library staff time spent on a particular case may be billed directly to the client instead of just being absorbed as overhead. Even if the client is being billed $60 to $100 per hour for library research, this is considerably less than the hourly billing rate for attorneys in the firm. In addition, the library staff can probably find the information more efficiently than the attorneys can. Thus, the clients save money and perhaps get better service as well.

THE EVOLUTION OF REFERENCE SERVICE

Up until the last decade of the 20th century, the mark of a superior reference librarian was a comprehensive, working familiarity with sources—standard titles, their contents, scope, frequency of publication, and their counterparts on various free and fee-based databases. With the phenomenon of the World Wide Web and the continuing proliferation of electronic sources, this ability to "know it all" has changed significantly. Because of its very nature, the contents of the Web are limitless, highly dynamic, and defy memorization. Some reference books may have online editions similar to or the same as their print versions; some have interactive, continuously updated versions online; and some refuse to have a Web presence, remaining available in print form only. Information publishing has changed dramatically and will continue to move in new directions that may defy conventional wisdom.

The Modern Reference Desk

Despite an active industry watch against negative and demeaning stereotypes of librarians, the image of a stern, white, middle-aged, single female with glasses and dowdy clothing is a perennial one in the media. (One humorous rejoinder to that stereotype has been the popularity of The Action Librarian plastic figurine, which depicts a middle-aged librarian and is found on many a library reference countertop.) In reality, library reference workers are a diverse, technologically savvy, and very people-oriented group.

Reference technicians and librarians typically staff a service desk where the tools of the trade consist of several formats. A computer workstation with a Web-based library catalog and periodical databases, full Internet access, a fax or data modem, printer, scanner, and e-mail, all networked to the local area network, is the centerpiece of the reference desk. Swivel-screen computer monitors allow for shared viewing of a search with patrons. A telephone, of course, remains an essential resource. Also, key-ready reference print resources are often very close at hand with access to a larger reference collection of print materials in an adjacent area.

Surrounded by an ever-changing array of resources, reference librarians or technicians spend their workdays adeptly toggling back and forth between electronic tools and physically moving from computer workstations to print resources or even historic runs of microforms as each question demands. Today's reference worker is equally at ease in the worlds of print and electronic information.

An ongoing challenge for the modern reference librarian is knowing which is more important in a given search, an Internet-based resource or a print source. An important factor is whether the library relies only on free online resources or has been able to purchase or subscribe to additional electronic resources beyond the free Web. Another variable is the issue of whether to purchase electronic versions of print resources; generally, electronic versions—while more sophisticated and with value-added search capabilities—tend to be more expensive than their print counterparts. The majority of libraries are currently looking closely at past preferences for purchasing print versions of books based on cost savings. The enhanced value of electronic versions, the growth in distance education courses, and the increased demand by the public for remotely-accessible, online library sources all are strong driving forces behind the re-evaluation of maintaining hard-copy editions of many former classic reference books.

One reference librarian, Tina Lau, recommends: "Sometimes, the Internet resource is all you have in a subject area unless you work at a very large library. The same criteria of authority, accuracy, objectivity, coverage, and timeliness apply to an Internet resource as to a print resource. A great set of guidelines for evaluating webpages can be found at http://www.lib.berkeley.edu/TeachingLib/Guides/Internet/Evaluate.html."

Although the reliance on electronic tools increases as we speak, computers do crash occasionally, and there are days when power outages mean that library staff must rely solely on print sources in the library. Also, for those patrons still reluctant to use computer-based resources because of age, disabilities, reticence, or learning style preference, print tools may be their preferred medium.

No Question Too Trivial

Seasoned reference librarians and technicians attest that a major stimulus of the job is the wide spectrum of reference questions they encounter each day. During the course of one week in the authors' county, the following questions were asked at the local reference desk of public, academic, and special libraries:

I want to start a muffin company. Can you help me research the market for such a venture?

Do you have Cliffs Notes for *Hamlet*?

Do you have a repair manual for a 1976 Ford Mustang?

My child is doing a report on Kwanzaa. What do you have?

I'm trying to find the original street names in our city's historic downtown area.

Where do I find current census data for the tri-counties, especially breakdowns by ethnicity?

I'm doing a stock market report and need the beta for Pepsi.

My term paper is on the history of sewers and water management systems on campus and in town. Where do I start?

Although an unusual or difficult request may be memorable because of the challenge it poses or because of its novelty, within each type of library or information center there are well-defined patterns to the reference questions asked. And some degree of predictability or recurrence can be expected for a certain percentage of the queries. For reference staff, it is this mix of the familiar and the exotic that keeps them on their toes.

Job Skills for Reference Service

What are the job skills needed to effectively perform reference services in a library, school media center, or information center? The following combination of communication skills, personal attributes, and technical competency are highly recommended for reference staff:

- *Interpersonal skills.* With a high level of customer interaction in reference, it is essential to have strong people skills, enjoy public contact, and be approachable and patient.
- *Knowledge of information sources.* Keeping current with print and electronic resources and keeping pace with their many rapidly changing formats and contents is critical.
- *Perseverance.* Searches often require sustained effort and creative thinking in the hunt for information.
- *Sense of curiosity.* It may seem low tech, but a good reference librarian should enjoy playing detective and be motivated by the hunt for information, regardless of the specific query or subject or information format.
- *Ability to work as a team player.* As one member of the library's reference team, most staff will likely work independently as well as with other staff. Collegiality in sharing information and search techniques, referring patrons, or in training reference desk assistants makes the job go more smoothly.
- *Training skills.* Providing on-demand instruction for customers in the use of various print or technology-based tools is an important and ongoing task. The ability to do this in multiple mediums—in person or via e-mail or live chat—is now becoming a required skill for reference staff.
- *Verbal and written communication skills.* Many patrons are researching sensitive topics and may be hesitant or unable to articulate their information requests clearly. An ability to deal sensitively with customers while ferreting out their needs is a must. This applies to in-person reference service as well as virtual interactions. An additional skill for the virtual medium is fast and accurate keyboarding.

Evaluating Information

Along with instructing library customers and helping them locate data, reference librarians and technicians also assist them in evaluating the credibility and relevance of what they have found. This role is becoming increasingly more visible in the era of instantaneous electronic information and the easy access to self-publishing present via the Internet. Many industry leaders see this as the librarian's most significant role in the future. As with the old saying, "Just because it's in print, don't believe it," even more scrutiny must be applied to digital sources. Many of the traditional elements relied upon for evaluating a book—for example, a publisher's name and location or an author's credentials—may not be present on a Web site. The very act of publishing on the Web is accessible to anyone with no editing or review process required at all.

Wikipedia

A new twist on the online publishing front is wiki software (derived from the Hawaiian word *wiki,* to hurry), which allows the content on a Web site to be easily and quickly contributed and edited by any reader, unlike pages marked-up with traditional html or xhtml. A well-known example of a wiki is found at the free "people's" encyclopedia *Wikipedia,* begun in 2001. Wikis have many uses, especially for collaborative writing, but in the case of Wikipedia it is highly controversial as a reference tool because the content is not necessarily from credible sources.

Many reference librarians have strong feelings about using Wikipedia because of this lack of credibility; one commonsense approach is to avoid using it as a stand-alone source, instead using it in conjunction with another more traditionally edited, quality-controlled source.

Another interesting point about Wikipedia is that there are many *locked* entries (submission of content is blocked) due to purposeful submissions of false or inflammatory content. Entries for current political figures, celebrities, and controversial issues often become hot button topics and editing may be disabled for a while until the debate subsides.

Primary and Secondary Sources

Another important distinction in assisting researchers to locate or evaluate information is whether the material is a primary or secondary source. Secondary source materials are probably most familiar to novice researchers and students. Compilations and summaries of information, such as encyclopedias, fact books, almanacs, and textbooks, are considered secondary sources. This is because the information is a generation or more removed from the original source; it may have been abridged, paraphrased, abstracted, critiqued, translated, or otherwise interpreted by various authors and editors. To those unfamiliar with a subject area, secondary sources can be easier to understand because another person has tried to place the material within a meaningful context.

In contrast, looking at a primary source enables researchers to study first-hand accounts and to draw their own conclusions from these original documents. Primary materials include original letters, diaries, maps, scientific studies, speeches, and photographs and are especially favored by historians, other scholars, and professional writers for study or perusal. Consider the difference between browsing George Washington's actual words and thoughts as conveyed in his personal letters compared with reading a summary of his point of view in a biographical account; studying an original, hand-drawn town site map versus reading a textual description of the location of an ancestor's property; consulting the actual data table in a scientific study versus reading a newspaper account or hearing a TV news sound bite summarizing it. Therefore, primary sources carry greater credibility than do secondary sources because people have not filtered their content.

Whether with print, multimedia, or electronic sources, or whether the sources are primary or secondary, reference staff guide users through the evaluation process. Questions to ask when evaluating information include the following:

Credibility:
- Is it clear who is responsible for creation of the document? Is an author's name, a group name, or another sponsor credited on the document?
- Can the credentials or authority of the author or publisher be clearly identified?
- Is current contact information for the author or publisher provided?
- Is the author affiliated with an established publisher, business, university, or other organization?
- Does the URL of a Web site provide any clues as to the sponsoring group?
- Is there a print or Web counterpart to the information at hand?
- Is the information supported with a bibliography, work cited page, or footnotes?

Bias:
- Can any political, philosophical, religious, or other bias to the information presented be detected?
- Are all points of view presented on the topic, or only a single view?
- Is the source trying to sell a product, idea, or service?

Currency:
- Does the document have a date on it? Can one locate when it was published, posted, last updated, or created?
- Does it seem that the information is updated regularly?

Appropriateness:
- Does the information meet the customer's need?
- Is the reading level appropriate for the customer?
- Is the level of technical information appropriate?
- Is the coverage or length adequate?

The Best Source for the Job at Hand

With the prevalence of personal computers at home, work, school, and in the library, many users (especially younger patrons) think that the Internet is the only tool available or the only source needed for all possible research. Patrons may also assume that the first computer they walk up to houses all the programs and tools that the library has to offer. This may or may not be the case.

These common scenarios reinforce the importance of another advisory role of the reference librarian: recommending the best tool for the research need at hand. The Web's wonderful explosion of access to information can also translate into a confusing welter of options for a library customer: "Do I check the Web, the electronic card catalog, the library portal, the subscription databases, or just use Google?" As an information advisor, the reference librarian or technician is well equipped to direct a user to the best tool, which means time saved and a less frustrating research experience for the customer.

REFERENCE INTERVIEW

Step back for a moment and think of the all-too-common frustration level that you feel when you come away empty-handed or unsatisfied from a visit to a retail store, a municipal agency, a physician's office, or another service venue. With your information quest unsatisfied or perhaps only partially filled, you go away thinking, "They didn't give me any answers. That was a waste of time. I still don't have what I need." This can be the case for people who patronize a library or information center.

But reference librarians are not psychics. Thus, before they can advise customers on the best source or guide them in the use of tools, a crucial exchange must take place: the reference interview. This interview is a unique interaction between the reference librarian or technician and the library user. In many cases, the successful outcome of the user's visit to the library will be based on a careful reference interview. Often, this conversation determines not only where the answer can be found, but also what the specific question or need is. Respected library educator and author William Katz defined this interaction as a dialog "between the librarian with expert knowledge and the layperson in need of information."[3] Ideally, this dialog takes place before beginning a search, thus providing the librarian with key data for interpreting the question in terms of library resources.

Reference Interview Steps

The following outline delineates the typical sequence of a reference interview. This is not always a linear model; it may be necessary to return to the second step if no appropriate source is located. The model applies to walk-in and telephone reference requests as well as to virtual reference interactions.

1. *Initial question:* Customer poses query to reference librarian or staff.

2. *Clarification of the question:* Staff initiates a dialog to attempt to clarify the actual needs of the customer and to try to elicit more information, such as the level or format required, the amount of data needed, an applicable deadline, and so forth. This conversation between reference staff and the customer may be brief or it may continue throughout the search itself.

3. *Translating the question into potential library sources:* Library staff take the lead by suggesting potential sources and finding out what has already been consulted before formulating a search strategy.

4. *The search:* The reference librarian or technician guides the patron through the physical search of appropriate sources. Simultaneously, they implement point-of-use instruction with each tool consulted so that the patron gains some knowledge for future independent searching.

5. *Follow up:* This is an important closing element that is often overlooked, but that is essential from a customer service point of view. As the search progresses, the librarian should query the patron—"Is this what you needed?"—to be sure that the search is on track. As patrons are left to evaluate the located material on their own, reference staff should offer, "Let me know if you need more help." This leaves the door open for a renewed search or other additional help.

Categories of Reference Questions

When is a reference interview necessary? To answer this, it is first helpful to consider the types of questions reference librarians typical encounter. Although there are many methods for analyzing queries, the following all-purpose division devised by William Katz is logical.[4] This scheme classifies queries into four general categories: *directional, ready reference, specific search,* and *research.* With the increased dependence on computer use for delivery and access of information, a fifth category has since emerged that we will add to Katz's list and call *technical assistance.* Of course, as with any attempt to categorize things, not all reference questions will fit neatly into one of these five divisions, but may be hybrids of one or more categories.

Directional Category

These are straightforward questions that deal with location or existence of a service or resource. Typically, it is not necessary to spend time delving further than what is asked. Staff knowledge of the building, services, and policies are sufficient to answer these queries.

Examples of directional questions include the following:

"Where is the photocopy machine?"

"Do you have wireless Internet access here?"

"Where is the children's department?"

"Where do I get a library card?"

"Where is the printer for this computer?"

Ready Reference Category

Quick, single-fact queries, ready reference requests are reminiscent of questions from Trivial Pursuit® board games or TV quiz shows. They often deal with isolated statistics or facts that require verification and fact finding. To answer these queries, turn to online and print sources such as encyclopedias, almanacs, statistical compendiums, directories, dictionaries, as well as quick Web searches using regular or meta search engines. Google's definitions search, phone book search, and other features are very useful for many basic ready reference questions such as spelling look-ups, personal names, business names, phone numbers, and address listings. Some ready reference queries may require a reference interview for clarification.

Examples of ready reference questions include the following:

"Which U.S. president was never married?"

"I need the Web address for the National Archives."

"I need the birth and death dates of Elvis Presley."

"How do you say good morning in Spanish?"

An example of a ready reference question in a reference interview is as follows:

Patron: I need the current population of New Jersey.

Staff: How current does the population figure need to be?

Patron: The most current available.

Staff: Do you need a total population, or breakdowns by county, sex, or ethnicity?

Specific Search Category

This is a more involved and time-consuming level of inquiry than the isolated fact finding required of ready reference questions. Gathering overview or background information may be the first step, followed by further delving into the subject. A patron may want to browse materials and read about a topic to become familiar with it, then eventually refine the search further. Specific search queries require a reference interview to elicit facts and identify a direction for the search. Sources used may range widely from encyclopedias at the start, to books, periodicals, government documents, and Web sites as the search progresses.

Examples of specific search questions are as follows:

"What do you have on swimming pools?"

"I'm doing a term paper on Julia Morgan, the architect. Do you have information on her?"

"Do you have information about the history of the AIDS epidemic?"

"We need cultural guidelines for business travelers in Indonesia."

"I need everything there is on our competitor's new CEO."

Examples of specific search questions in a reference interview are as follows:

Patron: I need information on becoming a ranger.

Staff: What kind of information do you need? Do you need a job description or perhaps a job exam study book?

Patron: Hmm. Maybe both.

Staff: What type of ranger? Park ranger, forest ranger, Texas Ranger, or something else?

Research Category

Although the word *research* is often used quite loosely (e.g., "I want to research the phone number for this company"), it is used here to convey a sophisticated level of inquiry that implies in-depth study of a topic or issue. Research queries may require ongoing investigation, with multiple trips to the reference desk. They will probably entail using a variety of primary and secondary sources and may use interlibrary loan or document delivery services. Accessing technical and fee-based databases may be appropriate. After in-house sources have been exhausted, referrals to other libraries, information centers, or agencies will be needed. The research level of investigation is characterized by the synthesis and analysis of information, not merely the copying of it. A reference interview at this level could be fairly lengthy because the librarian will need to ascertain the topic, determine what previous research has been completed or sources consulted, figure out the technical level of information needed, and so on.

Examples of research questions include the following:

"I'm studying the effects of sun exposure on skin cancer and need recent scientific studies about it."

"What are the latest theories on the disappearance of Amelia Earhart?"

"I'm writing a journal article on the medical uses of aromatherapy in the United States and in Europe."

Technical Assistance Category

This is a relatively new and ever-growing category of reference questions. The complexity or simplicity of answering or resolving such questions varies greatly. As with all other reference queries, technical assistance questions come from both patrons inside the library reading room and virtual patrons querying reference staff by telephone, e-mail, or e-reference. In some cases, a library might refer the more complicated technical questions to an onsite or remote Help Desk that is staffed specifically to deal with technical support.

Examples:

How can I log on to the library databases from home?

How do I logon to *WebCT*?

I forgot my password; how do I get a new one?

How do I use your online interlibrary loan request form?

How do I print from this computer?

Can I use my flash drive in the library's computer?

How do I connect my computer to your Wi-Fi access?

Do I need any special software to view e-books?

Reference Interview Techniques

There are several straightforward techniques that practitioners can employ to help carry out successful reference interviews with customers. The following is a brief overview of these techniques. For more in-depth coverage, refer to works listed in the resources section at the end of this chapter.

Open-Ended Questions

Whenever possible, ask an open-ended question to allow for more than a staccato yes or no answer. When you engage a customer in a dialogue, clues about their information needs should emerge to help carry out the search.

Patron: I want something for a paper on Shakespeare.

Staff: What kind of project are you working on?

Patron: It's a term paper on *Hamlet.*

Staff: How long does your paper need to be?

Patron: Ten pages with 15 sources cited.

Staff: Where have you looked so far?

Asking the two-part question can be also helpful. For example:

Patron: I need something on Amelia Earhart.

Staff: Are you interested in her life story or in a particular flying record?

Active Listening

Whether on the job or in our personal lives, the art of listening is a skill that we often take for granted. Active listening takes a conscious effort, and, when used effectively, is a technique that can be vital to anyone staffing a service desk or involved with customer interaction. Active listening means paying close attention to a speaker's comments and hearing the speaker out, rather than jumping in or cutting the person off. In the interest of saving time, it is easy to feel compelled to second-guess a need and quickly recommend an appropriate source without fully hearing the query. An active listener resists that temptation.

Trained reference employees apply active listening to the reference interview by giving the patron full attention and maintaining eye contact. While directing the interview, they indicate their understanding by responding to the patron's explanation with nods and short "yes" and "OK" responses. Then it is useful to paraphrase the query back to the patron to ensure both parties that they are on the same wavelength.

Putting the Customer at Ease

Asking for assistance in a library setting is not something that everyone feels comfortable doing. Putting into play some basic tenets of good customer service can help alleviate some of that discomfort. When staff present a friendly, informal, yet businesslike demeanor, people sense that library staff are there to help them. (This same combination of friendliness and efficiency has been cited as being helpful in successful virtual reference exchanges as well.) Moving out from behind the reference service counter and walking to the computers or stacks with the patron removes the physical barrier of a desk or counter. The increasing use of large, thin computer screens with swivel capability also decreases barriers and facilitates the sharing of search results between librarian and patron. Keeping the reference desk clear and free from clutter also sends the message that staff are available and not otherwise distracted. Many reference librarians and technicians wear name tags indicating their job title and company logo while on duty. This encourages customers to approach them, instead of a student aide, volunteer, or other library staff not specially trained in reference assistance.

Nonverbal behavior, or body language, also plays an important part in putting the customer at ease. A pleasant, even tone of voice—not too loud or condescending—is optimal. A patient and courteous manner is much more welcoming than an abrupt, easily annoyed demeanor. Unconscious gestures such as placing hands on the hips or folding the arms can be interpreted as negative, aggressive gestures. Prefer a neutral stance, with both hands to the side or placed behind the back in the "actor's grip."

Maintaining eye contact is an important cue that expresses interest and a willingness to assist. In contrast, averting eye contact with a customer conveys the distinct feelings of inattention or boredom. When a staff member and a patron are at different levels, making eye contact can be difficult; for example, when the staff member is seated at a desk and a customer is standing, or, conversely, when a staff member walks up to assist a wheelchair patron or a customer seated at a computer. Computer screens themselves, though indispensable, can also present a barrier to eye contact. Instead of directly communicating with one another, all eyes are on the monitor. Selecting counter height reference desks and computer tables is one method of putting both parties on the same eye level.

Being aware of cross-cultural differences is of growing importance as the library-using community increases in diversity. Issues such as personal space, reluctance to approach strangers for help, reluctance to make eye contact with a perceived authority figure, and other cultural customs or behaviors can prevent direct communication. Some libraries with distinctive ethic populations provide cultural sensitivity training to staff as a means of breaking down such barriers.

Burnout is a problem in any public contact job. At a busy reference desk it is important to schedule staff for shifts that reduce the chance for burnout. Usually two hours without a break or without a variety of other tasks is about the longest most staff can maintain the highest level of service orientation. Occasionally, longer shifts may be tolerable, but, over the long haul, prolonged shifts lead to stressed staff members and less than optimal service. Many libraries offer their virtual reference as part of a geographically dispersed consortium in order to share coverage of evening, night, and weekend service hours. Digital reference shift patterns and problem areas are still emerging, but issues such as repetitive use syndrome and patron rudeness to reference staff in the (anonymous) virtual environment have been identified to date. Potential for burnout also applies here as well.

Learning the Reference Interview

One of the best methods for novices to learn the ins and outs of the interview process is to observe reference librarians in action. If possible, shadowing, or following the librarian-patron interaction from the initial query to the completion of the search, is particularly helpful. Afterwards, discussing the search strategy chosen and its pitfalls or successes will reinforce the actions observed. Shadowing more than one staff person is especially valuable because each individual has a unique approach. Role playing in a classroom or workshop situation and viewing training videos are two other effective instructional methods.

Several Library/Information Technology student interns from the authors' college were recently based in academic library reference departments for fieldwork and spent their initial days shadowing seasoned staff interacting with students. Their comments on reference training bears out the effectiveness of this method:

> The concept of the reference interview is becoming more clear as the students come in with their questions. Even a simple directional question, such as "Where are the current periodicals?" may need some clarification.
>
> It's interesting to see the different approaches each librarian takes to a search and what their favorite databases and search engines are.
>
> While covering reference [with the college librarian], I found out how much I enjoy helping people narrow down their huge, expansive topics. They often start with something completely unmanageable.
>
> I am feeling more and more comfortable in assisting students with their search needs. I get started by conducting the Reference Interview, get them started on Polycat or appropriate databases and then seek further assistance, if necessary.
>
> These [business] questions are once again a reminder that it is vital and time-saving if you can query the student and qualify their exact needs. One student started out wanting to know information about "the restaurant business in California." As it turned out, he needed the numbers of wine and beer licenses issued in California and pursued this upstairs in Government Documents.

Reference Service Policies

Clear-cut policies for reference services are essential to good customer service. Among the policy issues to consider are the level of staff (professional or paraprofessional or both) that will answer reference requests; which format of inquiry has priority (e.g., walk in, e-mail, telephone, fax, and, when conducted by in-house reference staff, virtual); and what time limitations, if any, are imposed per individual question. As with all policies, these issues should be re-evaluated as reference tools, habits, and customer preferences change. Traditionally, in most publicly accessed libraries, walk-in customers receive first priority over telephone or other electronic requests. Perhaps in the future, e-mail requests will be of such volume that they take priority over walk-in traffic. In that case, staffing patterns and service policies would need to be adjusted accordingly for a new customer preference.

REFERENCE: ART OR SCIENCE?

Is good reference work an art or a science? Actually, it is a combination of both. Certain core elements are present in any successful reference transaction. Success is based on a skillful reference interview combined with an efficient and appropriate matching of the customer's needs with available or attainable information sources.

The *science* of reference is in the ability to understand and characterize an inquiry by subject category and amount and type of information sought. For example, does the patron's request regard sociology or social work, social policy, or religious teaching? Does the person want a definition, an overview, a list of sources, everything on the topic, or only one specific fact? The right referral might be to a dictionary of social work or a religious encyclopedia, a specialized bibliography, a general almanac, or a Web site.

The *art* of reference is in the conduct of the interview. Personal style that is comfortable for the interviewer is important. The other end of the process, recommendation of a source, is also an art based on the experience of the staff member. There really is not a single right way to do it. That is why even very experienced reference staff like to observe other staff members. Each person develops pet information sources that work well for them. They also specialize by subject areas and personal interests. It is not a sign of weakness to turn to another staff member for collaboration in the process of trying to answer a patron's query. In fact, it is a sign of confidence and maturity. No staff member can know everything about every subject.

REFERENCE REALITY CHECK AND THE FUTURE

Of course, quality reference service is always dependent on adequate staffing and funding. Expectations of service must be adjusted when these resource levels are not optimal. For example, with limited numbers of workers, reference staff may be too busy to return to patrons for follow-up assistance. In that case, staff should use common sense shortcuts: get patrons started on their searches and recommend that they check back if they need more help or find a staff member if they need further assistance. Another technique is batching reference requests. For example, a staff member shows two or three people at once how to use the library catalog. In understaffed libraries, strong emphasis needs to be placed on the goal of teaching patrons how to be more self-sufficient in their library skills. The use of trained library science or library technology interns, docents, or other seasoned volunteers should be considered to augment permanent staff where appropriate.

Especially in facilities that are open to the general public, problem patrons are a daily reality of life. Problem patrons require patience and special attention whether they are the homeless, lonely seniors, people with mental illness, latchkey children, or other populations. Here again, staff training is commonplace to prepare and educate library workers in techniques for diffusing difficult, awkward, or potentially violent situations. Information centers and libraries often develop policies specifically to deal with recurring problem-patron issues. Having security staff on site and cultivating a good rapport with the local police are also common approaches.

As for the future, reference service in libraries and information centers will continue to be very visible, and staff will continue to have high levels of interaction with customers, though more may be in a virtual setting rather than primarily face to face. The anticipated growth in distance education courses and training, with its anytime–anyplace philosophy and capability, is already impacting existing reference service traditions. And the concept of focusing reference service on users who live within a local political or geographical funding area may also be challenged with the growth in electronic communication and research where traditional physical boundaries are overlooked.

STUDY QUESTIONS

1. Do you use the reference department of your local public library? Why or why not?

   If yes, did you visit the reference librarian in person or use their virtual help desk? How would you characterize the service you received?

2. As a student, do you use the reference department of your college library? How does it compare to the local public library? What kind of a reputation does it have among students on campus? Do they have a 24/7 virtual help desk or e-mail reference service for students?

3. Is it important to offer reference services 24/7? Why or why not? How do libraries work cooperatively to make this happen?

4. To see firsthand how a typical reference department operates, visit the reference department of a large, local library, preferably a university, college, or central public library. Spend about 30 minutes to an hour observing the reference desk operation. Summarize your observations in a one- to two-page report. Some things to discuss in your summary include the following: the number of personnel staffing the desk, the physical layout, the amount and type of customer activity, print and electronic reference materials on hand at the desk, and the proximity

to larger reference collections in the library. Do staff offer virtual or e-mail reference services? If possible, note sample questions asked by patrons during your visit.

5. Nonverbal communication plays a subtle but important role in the reference interview. List five positive nonverbal cues that are helpful to exhibit when working the reference desk (in person).

6. What approach would you suggest for dealing with a patron who repeatedly poses reference queries that perplex the librarian?

7. Is there an archives or special collections department in your college library or hometown? If so, visit it and observe the level of reference service provided. How does it differ from the general information desk in your college library?

RESOURCES

Print Resources

"Active Listening." *Public Management* (US) 79: 25–27 (December 1997).

Carlson, Scott. "Are Reference Desks Dying Out?" *The Chronicle of Higher Education* 20: A37 (April 2007).

Cassell, Kay Ann and Uma Hiremath. *Reference and Information Services in the 21st Century: An Introduction.* New York: Neal-Schuman Publishers, 2006.

Cirasella, Jill. "You and Me and Google Makes Three: Welcoming Google into the Reference Interview." *Library Philosophy and Practice* (June 2007), http://libr.unl.edu:2000/LPP/cirasella.htm (accessed August 14, 2007).

Huwe, Terence. "Being Organic Gives Reference Librarians the Edge over Computers." *Computers in Libraries* May: 39–41 (2004).

Hysell, Shannon Graff, ed. *Recommended Reference Books for Small and Medium-Sized Libraries and Media Centers, 2006.* Westport, CT: Libraries Unlimited, 2006.

Jennerich, Edward and Elaine Jennerich. *The Reference Interview in the Digital Age.* Westport, CT: Libraries Unlimited, 2006.

Jennings, Anita. "Determining and meeting personnel training needs: after computer proficiency was tied to salaries and promotions, staff tech training took on a whole new urgency." *Computers in Libraries* September: (2005); *Infotrac.* The Gale Group. Shasta County Lib., Mt. Shasta, CA. October 25, 2005 <web2.infotrac.galegroup.com>.

Katz, Bill, ed. *Digital Reference Services.* Binghamton, NY: Haworth Information Press, 2003.

Lindbloom, Mary-Carol et al. "Virtual Reference: A Reference Question Is a Reference Question...Or Is Virtual Reference a New Reality? New Career Opportunities for Librarians." *Reference Librarian* 93: 3–22 (2006).

Lupien, Pascal. "Virtual Reference in the Age of Pop-Up Blockers, Firewalls, and Service Pack 2." *Online Magazine* 30 No. 4(July/August 2006).

Rauscher. Megan. "Internet searches: Librarians do it better." (May 22, 2006), http://news.yahoo.com/s/nm/20060522/wr_nm/internet_searches_dc_1

Ronan, Jana Smith. *Chat And The Reference Interview Online.* Westport, CT: Libraries Unlimited, 2007.

Ross, Catherine Sheldrick, Kirsti Nilsen, and Patricia Dewdney. *Conducting the Reference Interview: A How-To-Do-It Manual for Librarians.* New York: Neal-Schuman Publishers, 2002.

Schmidt, Aaron and Michael Stephens. "IM me." *Library Journal* (April): 34–5 (2005).

West, Jessamyn, ed. *Digital Versus Non-Digital Reference: Ask a Librarian Online and Offline.* Binghamton, NY: Haworth Information Press, 2004.

DVDs

Conducting the Reference Interview. (29 min.). Towson, MD: Library Video Network, 2004.

Depicts basic techniques for performing a successful face-to-face reference interview as well as communicating with a patron in a digital reference modality.

Web Sites

Francoeur, Stephen. "The Teaching Librarian." January 14, 2004.

http://www.teachinglibrarian.org/

(accessed December 14, 2006)

Produced by an academic librarian, this helpful site "explores the intersection of reference services, technology, and instruction" and provides good definitions and discussions of traditional and more innovative, digital reference services. Also sponsors a blog on the topic of digital reference.

Sullivan, Danny. Editor. "Search Engine Watch." 19 October 2006.

http://searchenginewatch.com/

(accessed December 14, 2006)

An industry leader in everything there is to know about Internet search engines. For all levels of search engines users and for those who are submitting their Web sites to the engines, this has a wealth of news, analysis, discussion, and tips. The Search Engine Listings and Web Searching Tips links are especially helpful to librarians and researchers. Constantly updated.

WebJunction.org. "WebJunction's Focus on Virtual Reference." May 1, 2006

(accessed December 14, 2006)

WebJunction, the online community for library staff sponsored by OCLC, private grants, and federal grants, has many valuable learning resources, including this clearinghouse page that focuses on virtual reference issues.

NOTES

1. American Library Association, "@ Your Library: Attitudes Toward Public Libraries Survey 2006," (Chicago: KRC Research & Consulting, 2006), http://www.ala.org/ala/ors/reports/2006KRCReport.pdf (accessed October 19, 2006)

2. Nicole Fawcett, "Patients need help finding medical information, U-M study finds: Librarians provided new information, resources for 95 percent of patients," University of Michigan Health System Press Release, May 22, 2006, http://www.med.umich.edu/opm/newspage/2006/healthinfo.htm (accessed September 7, 2007).

3. William A. Katz, *Introduction to Reference Work, Vol. II: Reference Services and Reference Processes,* 8th ed. (New York: McGraw-Hill, 2002), 125.

4. William A. Katz, *Introduction to Reference Work, Vol. I: Basic Information Services,* 8th ed. (New York: McGraw-Hill, 2002), 16–19.

Chapter 8

Ethics in the Information Age

Ethical ideas should apply to all aspects of our lives. "Almost all (92%) workers report that maintaining honesty and integrity at work is very important, and 90% report that taking individual responsibility and having a good work ethic is important"—a greater emphasis than they gave "specific skills such as computer skills (50%)".[1] There are a lot of different opinions as to what really constitutes ethics. This chapter addresses one very specific slice of applied ethics—the ethics of providing access to information in a library setting.

Many of us equate law with ethics. Law and ethics are not *un*related. If they were the same there would be no reason to study ethics. Ethics can demand a higher standard than the law. At other times ethical beliefs have caused individuals to break the law. Examples from the 20th century include the nonviolent civil disobedience campaigns led by Indian leader Mohandas Karamchang Ghandi (later to be known as Mahatma or Great Soul Ghandi); Martin Luther King, Jr., during the 1950s and 1960s U.S. civil rights movement; persons attempting to preserve the environment; and those on both sides of the abortion issue. In many cases, the law is merely society's attempt to codify elements of ethical beliefs.

If the law is not the only guiding principle in making ethical decisions, then what else is to be considered? Fair treatment of others? Religious teachings? How does one arrive at truth? One explanation is that each person determines truth in one or a combination of the following methods:

Six Ways of Knowing Truth

1. *Rational thought.* Truth comes from logically correct thinking. (Everything grows out of Rene Descartes' observation, "I think, therefore I am.")

2. *Common sense.* Truth comes from what we all know in common.

3. *Sensory observation.* Truth comes from what we can see, touch, smell, taste, and hear.

4. *Intuition.* Truth comes from within the individual—a sort of sixth sense, an inner voice or consciousness.

5. *Scientific method.* Truth comes from rigorously testing hypotheses.
6. *Authoritarian faith.* Truth comes from an authority in which we have faith (e.g., the Pope, *The Bible*, Rush Limbaugh, Dr. Laura, Dr. Martin Luther King, Jr., our parents, Osama bin Laden, the government, a professional body, a mentor, Confucius, etc.).[2]

Only if a person relies on authoritarian faith in the government as the way to know truth will truth as defined by law and that as defined by ethics be identical. If one relies on any other way of finding truth, ethics and the law, on occasion, will lead one to different, however not necessarily contradictory, conclusions. It is the application of these various "truths" in the practice of the information professions that are explored here.

The revolutionary environment of information flowing over the Internet has raised the question of whether new systems are needed to control activity in this brave new world. Larry Lessig, who heads the Stanford University Center for Internet and Society, has become one of the most influential thinkers on how behavior can be controlled in cyberspace. Even though he is a lawyer, he sees laws as only one, and not necessarily the most effective, way to control behavior in the digital world. His model includes the following four constraints:

- Law
- Code
- Norms
- Market forces[3]

Of these, *law* is probably self explanatory. *Code* refers to constraints that programmers embed that do not allow certain actions. Examples include establishing firewalls and setting other limits to block undesired activities. *Norms*, in the sense Lessig uses the term, refer to the common ways that most people behave. Finally, *market forces* include all the economic incentives and disincentives that stimulate or retard human activity. More will be said about Lessig's control elements later in this chapter. Each may be in part based on ethical values, but none are synonymous with ethics. What then are the governing principles that should guide library workers in the digital environment? Activities that enable or constrain the flow of information are the most important defining concerns of those in the library industry.

Most information workers would enthusiastically embrace each of these "rights" in the abstract. However, in many real-world situations, they are conflicted by what the preamble to the *Code of Ethics of the American Library Association* describes as "ethical dilemmas [that] occur when values are in conflict."[4]

Ethical values within the library community are discussed within the context of whether they increase or impede access to information. Some values, such as *intellectual freedom and the right to know* are generally values that increase access to information. Other values, such as the *right to privacy*, the *right to intellectual property*, and the *right to protect children* tend to restrict information.

For decades, libraries have been in the forefront on many of these issues. Recently, the advent of the World Wide Web has made it appear that many new ethical issues have been added. The Patriot Act and other post 9/11 responses to the terrorist threat, in the United States and elsewhere, have made it even more critical for library workers to understand the underlying issues. At the very least, these events have caused us to reassess and redefine our values in new terms. However, for the most part, the ethical issues library workers face today are a continuum of old ethical issues in new situations.

What is the relationship between ethics and behavior? In a macro sense, a somewhat simplistic but still instructive proverb is that our core ethics are most clearly acted out when no one is watching. Applying that insight to ethics within the library workplace requires that individuals overlay their personal ethics with the values and norms that have been adopted by the library profession.

Complicating the situation even further, each person considering ethical issues must decide whether there are *absolute ethical principles* that can be applied universally, or whether *situational ethics* cause the correct answer to vary from one setting to another. Are there some absolutes upon which we all can agree? Is it possible that two people both desperately trying to do the ethical thing will adopt very different courses of action? In applied ethics, often it is necessary to decide what RIGHT is and what WRONG is. However, the real tension comes in situations where two or more RIGHT concepts appear to be in conflict.

ETHICS IN CYBERSPACE

Ethics can be considered to be professional standards of conduct. When individuals take actions in cyberspace, certain common courtesies have come to be expected. One such list can be found in *The Core Rules Of Netiquette*.[5] While these rules form a good foundation for the appropriate behavior of all who perform actions in cyberspace, the issues are more complex for those of us who conduct our careers in this environment.

Within the context of this chapter, many of the situations we will be considering will place us in roles other than that of one private individual relating to another. These additional roles include those of:

- a professional relating to clients;
- an employee relating to fellow employees;
- a supervisor relating to subordinates; and/or
- an agent of the government.

Although we do not generally think of ourselves as such, most library employees are *agents of the government* because we work in public institutions. Many concepts, such as justice, truth, half-truth, honesty, morality, and so on, apply whether we are considering individual to individual interaction or workplace transactions. Within the workplace, additional concepts such as informed decisions and client confidentiality come into play.

INFORMATION IS POWER

Definitely, information is power. The question becomes, who has the power? Who controls the information? In a democracy, the citizens, individually and collectively, are assumed to be in control. In a totalitarian state, the government is able to maintain control, at least in large part, because it controls the flow of information. Many of the conflicts in this chapter are issues about whether the state or individual citizens will have control over the flow of information.

We tend to think of information as fixed in a specific location:

In a book

In a database

On a Web page

However, in the 21st century, it is often useful to remember that information can also be in liquid form. Think of it as being able to flow from one location to another, or from one person to another. Some factors encourage and enable this flow. Others impede it. Some factors impede the flow of some information some of the time and encourage the flow of other information at other times.

THE PLAYERS

Although this is an oversimplification of a complex process, assume that all the players in this drama can be lumped into three categories: individuals; corporations; or governments.[6]

What each of these players does to impede or encourage the flow of information has an impact on the other two groups of players. At times, each of the three groups of players will assert that they have certain rights. Any one of these three groups can enhance its rights, but only at the expense of one or both of the other groups of players, which must in turn give up some of their rights.

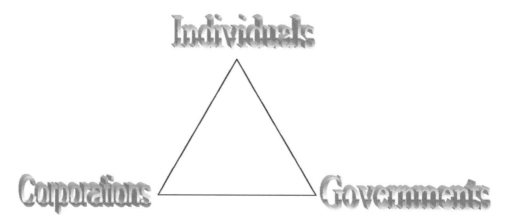

Figure 8.1. The players controlling information flow.

Try to visualize the location of a piece of information as being somewhere within the above triangle. The closer it is to one of the corners of the triangle, the more it is controlled by the player at that point of the triangle. If a player has total control of an item of information (items of information located totally in one of the three corners), that player alone can decide whether to keep it private, to share it, or to give it away. Other players can try to gain control. However, it is a *zero sum game.* As one player gains control, another loses privacy and ownership. Such a situation causes players to see their options in terms of *win-lose* propositions. That is, one player can win something of value only if another loses something.

If information is power, then power is freedom. The freedom or power to act in the self-interest of any of these three groups is constrained or counterbalanced by the freedom or power to act possessed by the other two entities. For example, as the power of government increases, the freedom of corporations and/or of individuals decreases. The U.S. government crackdown on corporate accounting practices, as the result of abuses at Enron, WorldCom, and other corporations, is an example where the government increased its power by restricting the freedom of corporations. The *USA Patriot Act* is an example of the government increasing its power by restricting some freedoms of individuals. On the other hand several recent court decisions have restricted the power of the government to regulate the Internet and have also found parts of the *Patriot Act* to be unconstitutional, therefore increasing the freedom of individuals and corporations. The balance is constantly shifting. However, there is a constant amount of freedom to be shared among the players. As one group gains power and freedom from accountability, one or more of the others lose by the same amount—the zero sum game.

Where should the balance point of freedom be located within the triangle above? Each of us may arrive at a different answer to this question. However, each of the groups represented by the corners of this diagram can make compelling arguments as to why their power needs to be increased. They usually rationalize it as being in the interest of all of us. However, that power can only be increased if the other groups give up some freedom.

THE CONFLICT OF "RIGHTS"

The conflict of ownership of information can best be understood by an examination of various "rights" that are often claimed by one or more of the players. The following "rights" will be featured in this chapter:

- The right to access information
- The right to keep information private
- The right to benefit from creativity by owning intellectual property
- The right to security by controlling information

As the following diagram illustrates, the more one of these rights is emphasized, the less importance other rights can receive. For example, the impact of the events of September 11, 2001 resulted in a greater push for protection/

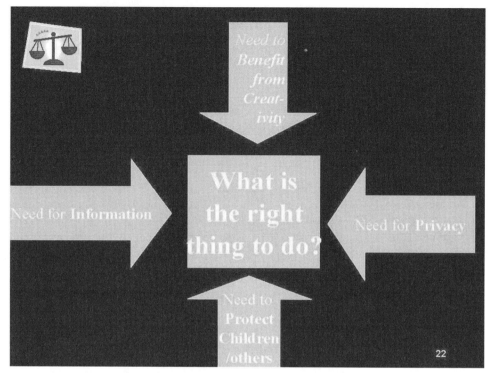

Figure 8.2. The conflict of needs.

security—the arrow at the bottom of the diagram. Greater emphasis on security changed the balance in the United States away from individual rights, at least temporarily, by emphasizing the need for increased security. In this example, the box representing "the right thing to do" would shift and force one or more of the other arrows to contract. Again, it is a zero sum game. One right must give way for another to gain.

"Nothing is more dangerous than an idea, when it is the only idea you have."[7] This is particularly true with decisions about ethical behavior in the Information Age. Those who try to define their own behavior and the behavior of others from the perspective of only one of the above rights are doing all of us a disservice. In so doing they often discredit their own point of view by pushing their single-theme agenda well beyond the point where it can be considered to be credible.

THE RUBIK'S CUBE OF ETHICAL DECISION MAKING

Actually, ethical decisions are often more complex than can be diagramed on a two-dimensional piece of paper such as the illustration above. Maybe you remember the Rubik's Cube craze that briefly swept the country two decades ago. The Cube, a puzzle with many permutations, seems to illustrate the complexity of making ethical decisions in the Information Age. This may be a bit

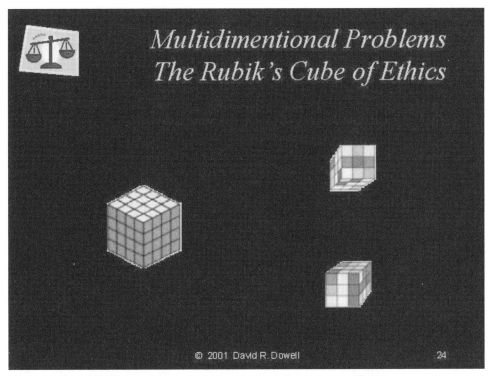

Figure 8.3. Multidimensional problems: The Rubik's cube of ethics.

of a stretch. However, try to visualize the following: while looking at the big Cube below on the left, try to imagine that the triangle of Individuals, Corporations, and Governments is transposed to the top surface of the cube. Now, try to imagine that the four competing rights represented by the arrows in the illustration immediately above are transposed on one of the vertical surfaces. While holding these images in your mind, assume that a new technology gives the Cube one twist clockwise. Mind boggling! But so is the effort to do right thing in many of the situations we face these days.

Arriving at the right answer is often very difficult. In many situations reasonable people can disagree over what the appropriate balance point of the various rights should be as we struggle to reconcile technological possibilities with human values.

Within an ethical context one would hope that all players would strive to achieve a balance to make a win-win scenario is possible. As discussed above, such a solution is not often possible. Therefore, when considering the ethical aspects of a course of action, not only are the motives of the decision maker important. Consequences, both long-term as well as short-term, that flow from that decision, are also very relevant. In the sections that follow, each of the four needs/rights in the illustration above will be discussed briefly in general terms relevant to society as a whole. The discussion will then narrow to specific applications important in the library workplace.

FREEDOM TO ACQUIRE INFORMATION

Government control of information is essential for the efficient functioning of totalitarian dictatorships, a fact that motivates the Chinese government to attempt to restrict what its citizens are able to access over the Internet. Corporate control of some information is essential for the efficient functioning of a capitalistic economy. Freedom of individuals to access information is essential to the effective functioning of democratic society. Libraries and the Internet are key institutions that provide individuals with access to the vast array of information they need to function as citizens. These institutions also have the potential to be powerful agents in a capitalist economy. Both have the potential to provide almost unlimited power to average citizens by providing them with the information they need to control their lives.

These rights should not be taken for granted. Everyone on our planet certainly does not enjoy them. And once we have achieved these rights, we must be vigilant to keep them. Some rights that we have long enjoyed have been called into question by the increased powers granted by the governments to themselves both in the United States and around the world.

Library workers have both the opportunity and the responsibility to protect our democratic way of life by insuring that all our citizens are able to make informed decisions in all aspects of their lives. Like those in the armed forces they may not have salaries that are as generous as those in the corporate world, but they can play a vital and patriotic role in preserving and extending freedom of opportunity for all. So far no one has suggested a universal oath of office for library workers; however, the oaths taken by all new citizens, members of the armed services, and holders of federal office include the words "I will support and defend the Constitution and laws of the United States of America against all enemies, foreign and domestic." Most of us are not called upon to defend the Constitution against foreign enemies; however, it is just as patriotic to stand up against domestic threats that would deny any citizens the opportunity to have the information they need to freely exercise their Constitutional rights.

First Amendment

The following section on our freedoms and the *First Amendment* to the U.S. Constitution contains several excerpts from a statement by the American Civil Liberties Union (ACLU), a much misunderstood and maligned national organization that opposes regulation of any form of speech. The ACLU is almost a "four letter word" in some circles. This has resulted because the organization will defend the rights of all citizens to express their views, even it the organization disagrees with the content of the expression and even finds that expression distasteful. A fuller statement of the ACLU's position can be found at the organization's Web site, which is cited in the footnote below.

> Freedom of speech, of the press, of association, of assembly and petition—this set of guarantees, protected by the *First Amendment,* comprises what we refer to as freedom of expression. The Supreme Court has written that this freedom is "the matrix, the indispensable condition of nearly every

other form of freedom." Without it, other fundamental rights, like the right to vote, would wither and die.[8]

The *First Amendment* is actually only one sentence long. The part most germane here consists of only 10 words—the two phrases in bold below:

Congress shall make no law respecting an establishment of religion, or prohibiting the free exercise thereof; or **abridging the freedom of speech,** or of the press; or the right of the people peaceably to assemble, and to petition the government for a redress of grievances.

However, from this brief statement has grown a set of laws, court decisions, and practices that have shaped the development of our country.

In spite of its preferred position in our constitutional hierarchy, the nation's commitment to freedom of expression has been tested over and over again. Especially during times of national stress, like war abroad or social upheaval at home, people exercising their *First Amendment* rights have been censored, fined, even jailed. Those with unpopular political ideas have always borne the brunt of government repression. During WWI, a person in the United States could be jailed just for giving out anti-war leaflets. Out of those early cases, modern *First Amendment* law evolved. Many struggles and many cases later, ours is the most speech-protective country in the world.

Free speech rights still need constant, vigilant protection. New questions arise and old ones return. Should flag burning be a crime? What about government or private censorship of works of art that touch on sensitive issues like religion or sexuality? Should the Internet be subject to any form of government control? What about punishing college students who espouse racist or sexist opinions? In answering these questions, the history and the core values of the *First Amendment* should be our guide.[9]

Libraries and the *First Amendment*

In the following sections, various policy statements of the American Library Association will be quoted or referred to. These policies have no legal standing. Libraries are not required to follow them. It is up to each governing entity that sets policy for individual libraries to decide which, if any, policies of the ALA they will adopt as their own.

The first premise in the ALA Code of Ethics (see Appendix C) states:

I. We provide the highest level of service to all library users through appropriate and usefully organized resources; equitable service policies; equitable access; and accurate, unbiased, and courteous responses to all requests.

If this ideal is to be achieved, some level of information must be available to all residents who are citizens or are striving to become citizens. Particularly in tax-supported libraries, all residents should be treated the same, and all should have access to the same information resources and services. No single customer should be treated as being more important than another. The defining ethic for librarians and other library workers should be the compulsion to provide information to clients. This driving force of library workers is only slightly different than the role of those who work in bookstores, publishing houses, the broadcast media, and other related occupations. However, that difference in role is significant. The library worker's focus is first on the consumer and then on the information needed by that customer. Also, neither the library worker nor the library directly profit monetarily from each successful transaction that benefits a customer. All clients have an equal right to receive the information they need.

Within the library context, concern for the *First Amendment* is usually expressed in terms of the intellectual freedom of citizens to inquire about any subject in which they are curious. *Intellectual freedom* is defined by the ALA as "the right of every individual to both seek and receive information from all points of view without restriction. It provides for free access to all expressions of ideas through which any and all sides of a question, cause or movement may be explored."[10]

> II. We uphold the principles of intellectual freedom and resist all efforts
>   to censor library resources.

The *Freedom to Read Statement* (see Appendix D) was originally drafted in 1953 by librarians and publishers and was last revised in 2004. This statement has been endorsed by numerous organizations interested in reading and in the freedom of access to information. Links to a number of policies related to censorship of various types of materials are listed at the end of this chapter. These include policies about videotapes, materials for children, electronic information, meeting room scheduling, information on sexual orientation, exhibits and bulletin boards, and the labeling of materials as to their age appropriateness.

Therefore, intellectual freedom is a right of library clients—not a right of library employees. Rather it is the ethical obligation of library employees to insure that library clients can exercise their intellectual freedom. The California Library Association gives a very eloquent rationale for the need for intellectual freedom:

> Libraries have always accepted the challenge to provide for the educational and recreational needs of the public. Inherent in this challenge is the seed of intellectual freedom.
>
> Intellectual freedom, guaranteed by the First, Fourth and Fourteenth Amendments to the U.S. Constitution, is one of the safeguards of a democratic society. To defend this freedom, we must fight any attempts to limit access to library materials, meeting rooms, exhibits and programs. When censorship hits the library, in whatever form, from whatever source, we believe that the public's right of access to information and the right to choose for themselves what to read, what to see, even what to know is denied. Intellectual freedom continues to stand for freedom to think, to speak and to receive information.[11]

Library educator Lester Asheim, in a classic statement for the kind of information that should be available in libraries, stated, "The best approach to any theory or idea advanced is to hold it up for examination, asking what evidence exists to persuade the examiner to prefer this theory over another. Tolerance for the free expression of any proposition advanced is essential for the advancement of man's knowledge of his universe."[12] Basically, it is not the role of library staff to ensure that their clients only get the politically correct truths.

Rather it is the role of library staff to enable citizens to secure the information they need to make an informed decision for themselves.

Free democratic societies are based on the premise that informed citizens are capable of governing themselves. Libraries, particularly American libraries in the 20th century, have been an embodiment of this belief. Public libraries have seen to it that their mission is to help create and maintain an informed citizenry. Other libraries have similarly tried to foster a culture of access to information for their specific clientele.

Access to information and the right to know are basic premises upon which democracy, libraries, and the Internet are based. However, are these concepts without limits? It is generally assumed that a person's right to swing his or her arms stops somewhere short of another person's nose. In a similar fashion, a person's right to know is limited by another person's right to privacy.

PRIVACY

The Right to Privacy

Author and computer scientist Dr. Joseph S. Fulda argues, "If no one knows what I do, when I do it, and with whom I do it, no one can possibly interfere with it...that a society cannot be free if citizens do not have a right to privacy. Privacy is essential because a government that is ignorant of an individual's thoughts and deeds cannot act to impinge on his or her rights."[13] Privacy, said Supreme Court Justice Brandeis, is "the right to be left alone—the most comprehensive of rights, and the right most valued by a free people."[14] To others, privacy means the right to protect ourselves and our loved ones. Closely related to this is the right to protect our physical property and our ideas.

Fourth Amendment

The legal basis for our privacy rights flows from the *Fourth Amendment*, although you will not find the word "privacy" in it. *"The right of the people to be secure in their persons, houses, papers, and effects, against unreasonable searches and seizures, shall not be violated, and no Warrants shall issue, but upon probable cause, supported by Oath or affirmation, and particularly describing the place to be searched, and the persons or things to be seized."*[15]

Threats to Privacy

Threats to our privacy can come from any or all of the following directions:

- From the government
- From private organizations
- From other individuals

These threats are real. We must be aware of them and prepared to protect ourselves from them; but we must not become consumed by our fears.

FTC Privacy Agenda

The Federal Trade Commission sees itself as the nation's consumer protection champion, and as such plays a vital role in protecting consumers' privacy. The agency's pro-privacy agenda emphasizes both enforcement and education. On the FTC Web site the agency addresses many of the new possibilities and the problems that new technologies have presented:

> [A]dvances in computer technology have made it possible for detailed information about people to be compiled and shared more easily and cheaply than ever. That's good for society as a whole and individual consumers. For example, it is easier for law enforcement to track down criminals, for banks to prevent fraud, and for consumers to learn about new products and services, allowing them to make better-informed purchasing decisions.[16]

But

> At the same time, as personal information becomes more accessible, each of us—companies, associations, government agencies, and consumers—must take precautions to protect against the misuse of that information.[17]

While the government can be the protector of individual citizens, it also has the potential to be the biggest threat to their privacy.

Threats from the government

Perhaps the most famous fictional threat of a government to individual privacy was written by George Orwell. In his 1949 book, *1984,* he described a nation in which the government, "Big Brother," exercised almost total thought control over the citizens. Orwell died in 1950 and did not live to see what life was really like in 1984. However, his book was such a profound wakeup call that his prediction became a self-defeating prophesy. Enough people heeded his warning so that his dire vision did not come to fruition. "We don't live in Orwell's world because of Orwell. 'Self preventing prophesies' help us think ahead and avoid the quicksand and potholes."[18]

Moving from fiction to real life, there has been a recurring struggle over the decades to protect the privacy of inquiry in libraries.

> The *Library Awareness Program* was an attempt at foreign counterintelligence aimed at Soviet spies. The FBI wanted to know what was interesting to people from Eastern Europe when they visited premier research libraries in the United States. In the late 1980's, the American Library Association publicly opposed the program, and it was dropped. The vast majority of states have since passed patron record confidentiality laws.[19]

The main thrust of this program was to try to get librarians to report any Middle Europeans (from the Soviet sphere of influence) who seemed to be interested in technical topics. At that time, one of the authors was director of a university library in Chicago that specialized in engineering and science. Given the ethnic breakdown of the population of Chicago, a large percentage of the users of that library would have fit the FBI profile.

After the tragic terrorist attack on New York City on September 11, 2001, Congress quickly passed The *USA Patriot Act.* "With this law we have given sweeping new powers to both domestic law enforcement and international intelligence agencies and have eliminated the checks and balances that pre-viously gave courts the opportunity to ensure that these powers were not abused."[20] A more detailed account of the Library Awareness Program and the Patriot Act can be found in Herb Foerstel's recent book, *Refuge of a Scoundrel: The Patriot Act in Libraries.*[21] In this book Foerstel recounts an engaging and sometimes inspiring description of the continuing melodrama in which library employees and others struggle against those who would impose police-state tactics to protect our freedom in the name of security. Or is it to protect our security in the name of freedom?

It apparently was the intent of the drafters of the *USA Patriot Act* that it would trump state laws on the confidentiality of library records discussed below. However, the Patriot Act has yet to be subjected to full-scale judicial review. Some legal scholars believe that the current U.S. Supreme Court in its recent decisions has given great deference to states' rights over federal rights. It remains to be seen if this law, passed in haste at the height of a very emotional time in our country, will survive intact as an important law that increases the power of the federal government at the expense of the rights of individual citizens.

More recently, the warrantless surveillance of the communications of U.S. citizens by the National Security Agency (NSA) has created controversy since it was brought to public attention by the *New York Times* in December, 2005. At this writing it appears that the Bush Administration has bowed to public and congressional pressure and decided not to pursue such surveillance in the future without court approval.[22] Eternal vigilance is still needed to maintain our liberties against any future erosion.

Threats from Corporations

While the government has long been called Big Brother when it is viewed as invading the privacy of individuals, some are starting to call corporations Little Brothers when they endanger the privacy of individuals. There are cur-rently many Web sites that give out a wide variety of information. Some of the information they offer is very similar to that available through their traditional (i.e., print) format. Some charge for this service and some allow access to at least a limited product if you "register to read." This is true of sites like the *Los Angeles Times.* Whether you have to pay or not, you have to identify yourself to log on. After you log on, your movements through the Web site can be traced. Therefore, someone could trace what pages you read or at least visit.

This in itself is not necessarily good or bad. However, it is very different than in the print world. Previously, someone could tell that you either subscribed to or did not subscribe to the newspaper. They really had no idea whether or not you opened it. With the online version, it is possible to trace the sections you visit, how long you have each page open, and in what order you visit the pages.

Sites like *Amazon* use this information to make recommendations to us. When one orders a book, the site will suggest that customers who bought that book also were interested in certain other titles. This can be a helpful customer service and/or it can be an invasion of our perceived privacy.

Americans give very mixed signals as to whether they really care about their online privacy. Poll results suggest that online privacy is a big concern, but actions contradict these findings. Only time will tell if government legislation will be an effective tool to make us more safe online.

Personally identifiable information is of commercial value. Mailing lists, particularly those of paying customers or of politically active citizens, are very marketable items worth a lot of money when large numbers of addresses are involved. For example, it could be worth a lot of money for a life insurance company or a medical insurance company to know who had been looking up a lot of information about breast cancer or AIDS. They might not want to offer insurance to these people, or to offer it only at a much higher rate than the norm.

Threats from Individuals

Identity theft is one of the biggest threats we face from other individuals. The Federal Trade Commission site has this warning about identity theft:

> And then there are unscrupulous individuals, like identity thieves, who want your information to commit fraud. Identity theft—the fastest-growing white-collar crime in America—occurs when someone steals your personal identifying information, like your SSN, birth date or mother's maiden name, to open new charge accounts, order merchandise or borrow money. Consumers targeted by identity thieves usually don't know they've been victimized. But when the fraudsters fail to pay the bills or repay the loans, collection agencies begin pursuing the consumers to cover debts they didn't even know they had.[23]

If protecting your personal information is important to you, you need to know what steps put you at risk and what you can do to protect yourself. The FTC has posted a variety of resources that help you protect your information from unscrupulous individuals as well as from corporations and the government. The Commission Web site, *Privacy Initiatives* http://www.ftc.gov/privacy/, offers a wide array of information that may help you both as an individual and as you consider these ideas.

Collision of Free Speech and Privacy

Free speech and the right to privacy often collide. A few areas of conflict between these two rights will be mentioned in this section. If you reflect a minute or two, you can think of other areas where these rights are in opposition. We are not free to express information we know to be false about individuals or other entities. There is a mass of legal precedent, let alone ethical principles, that make libel and defamation taboo. There is growing concern about the availability and use of true, but private information about individuals.

Privacy to Inquire: "The Freedom to Read"

III. We protect each library user's right to privacy and confidentiality with respect to information sought or received and resources consulted, borrowed, acquired or transmitted."

"The freedom to read is essential to our democracy. It is continuously under attack. Private groups and public authorities in various parts of the country are working to remove or limit access to reading materials, to censor content in schools, to label "controversial" views, to distribute lists of "objectionable" books or authors, and to purge libraries. These actions apparently rise from a view that our national tradition of free expression is no longer valid; that censorship and suppression are needed to avoid the subversion of politics and the corruption of morals. We, as citizens devoted to reading and as librarians and publishers responsible for disseminating ideas, wish to assert the public interest in the preservation of the freedom to read.[24]

Information seekers have the right to use library materials and services, including consultation with staff, without having the nature of their inquiry broadcast to anyone. With respect to reading materials, this policy has led to the confidentiality of circulation records that would disclose what any individual might have read. This right is not a constitutionally protected right such as that enjoyed by legal counsel or the clergy. However, the ALA has long been on record in recommending that all libraries develop a policy that states that

such records shall not be made available to any agency of state, federal, or local government except pursuant to such process, order, or subpoena as may be authorized under the authority of, and pursuant to, federal, state, or local law relating to civil, criminal, or administrative discovery procedures or legislative investigative power.[25]

The ALA policy goes further to state that the library should "resist the issuance or enforcement of any such process, order, or subpoena until such time as a proper showing of good cause has been made in a court of competent jurisdiction."[26]

Most libraries have adopted such policies. Staff members, particularly those at public service desks, need to be oriented so that they will not be taken unaware and be intimidated if someone carrying a badge or some other authority figure demands to see the circulation records of a given patron. The same would apply to requests for the names of anyone who has checked out books on a given subject (e.g., bomb making or computer hacking). Should classroom teachers have access to what books students check out? In a college setting the answer is clearly no. In a K-12 setting the answer may be more problematic.

Library staff also should view such patron information only on a "need-to-know" basis. Library staff members should not have access to such information unless that information is needed to perform a legitimate library function (e.g., processing of overdue notices). In addition, library staff members need to be vigilant about protecting other personal information about customers. They have no business giving out telephone numbers, addresses, or social security numbers to anyone and may be placing the library in jeopardy of legal liability of invasion of privacy by doing so.

Confidentiality of inquiry applies equally when customers consult staff about how to locate information. To the extent possible, reference inquiries should be conducted in an environment in which questions can be asked and answered in a confidential manner. The classic stereotype of inappropriate behavior is for a staff member to say in a loud voice to a teenager, "And why do you need to know about birth control?"

One other element of confidentiality is that researchers may be investigating a potentially marketable idea. If this is the case, then it is inappropriate to share with anyone else even the fact that another person is researching that topic.

A lot of information collected by publicly supported libraries may be considered to be public information and therefore subject to disclosure under freedom of information requests—a direct conflict between the right of access to information and the right of privacy. Sometimes it is better not to collect information that the library might not wish to disclose that links specific patrons to the information they access. We also need to consider carefully how long we should keep backups of the information we do need to collect.

State Laws

California is one of many states that have adopted laws to shield the privacy of library circulation records:

> In enacting this chapter, the Legislature, mindful of the right of individuals to privacy, finds and declares that access to information concerning the conduct of the people's business is a fundamental and necessary right of every person in this state.

All registration and circulation records of any library which is in whole or in part supported by public funds shall remain confidential and shall not be disclosed to any person, local agency, or state agency except as follows:

(a) By a person acting within the scope of his or her duties within the administration of the library.

(b) By a person authorized, in writing, by the individual to whom the records pertain, to inspect the records.

(c) By order of the appropriate superior court.[27]

Most states have similar laws; however, readers are advised to check the laws in their own states.

When two detectives or FBI agents flash their badges at you and demand to see patron records, like most law-abiding people, you would be inclined to do anything they request you to do. Individuals who are ordinarily very competent professionals get brain freeze in such a situation. However, this is exactly where you get your chance to protect the Constitution. Therefore, it is important that you have thought through, in advance, what your course of action should be in such a case. Your library should have a policy as to how staff should respond is such a situation. Make sure you know what it is.

Science fiction author and privacy advocate David Brin observes that whenever a conflict arises between privacy and accountability, people demand the former for themselves and the latter for everybody else.[28] He applies this to governments and corporations as well as to individuals. For example, governments want privacy for themselves, but insist on accountability for individuals and corporations. Individuals and corporations want privacy for themselves and accountability for everyone else.

In summary, most state laws protect the privacy of much of the information libraries keep on patrons. Of particular concern is personally identifiable information including social security numbers, phone numbers, addresses, birthdates, and any other information that might help an identity thief or a stalker. Also, any information about the intellectual interests of a person or of his or her academic progress is probably legally as well as ethically protected. Again, information is power, and such power needs to be used responsibly, legally, and ethically. Otherwise one is malpracticing a profession and violating a trust.

INTELLECTUAL PROPERTY

IV. We respect intellectual property rights and advocate balance between the interests of information users and rights holders. [The last half of this statement was just added in January, 2008 and was the only change in the 1995 version of the Code.]

Even though *intellectual property* law has existed for hundreds of years and has been the fastest growing area of law for some time, the phrase "intellectual property" did not appear for the first time in that venerable shaper of legal discourse *Black's Law Dictionary* until 1999:

> A category of intangible rights protecting commercially valuable products of the human intellect. The category comprises primarily trademark, copyright, and patent rights, but also includes trade-secret rights, publicity rights, moral rights, and rights against unfair competition.[29]

This definition has not evolved far from an 1845 court case, the date of the first recorded usage of the term: "Only in this way can we protect intellectual property, the labors of the mind, productions and interests as much a man's own...as the wheat he cultivates."[30]

In the 21st century, our economy is rapidly becoming one in which the value of corporations is based more on the value of their intellectual property than on their physical property. Some in the corporate very clearly understand this, but many are still struggling with the concept of whether, or how, intellectual property should be entered in a balance sheet or a profit and loss statement.

Legal Basis for Intellectual Property

Copyrights and patents have their basis in the U.S. Constitution:

"Congress shall have the power **to promote the progress of science and useful arts,** by securing **for limited times** to **authors** and **inventors** the exclusive right to their respective writings and discoveries;" (Article 1, Section 8, U.S. Constitution)

Within the library environment, the most common manifestation of intellectual property is copyrighted materials. It is not the purpose of this book to make readers conversant in the vagaries of this topic. However, a level of awareness as to where some of the associated legal minefields may be planted can be useful. Library staff members are often expected to be resources within their organizations for advising others as to what is permitted under copyright law. It is useful to be able to direct colleagues to information about the subject.[31] On the other hand, it is dangerous to make pronouncements in an area in which even intellectual property lawyers are hesitant to make definitive statements.

Simply stated, copyright is "legal protection provided to authors and/or publishers which protects them against unauthorized copying of their work."[32] Attorney Rebeca Delgado-Martinez Valette defines it in a little more detail:

Copyright is a protection that covers published and unpublished works of literary, dramatic, musical, artistic, pictorial and certain other intellectual creations, provided such works are fixed in a tangible medium. This means that if you can see it, hear it and/or touch it—it may be protected. If it is an essay, if it is a play, if it is a song, if it is a funky original dance move, if it is a photograph, HTML coding or a computer graphic that can be set on paper, recorded on tape or saved to a hard drive, it may be protected. Copyright laws grant the creator the exclusive right to reproduce, prepare derivative works, distribute, perform and display the work publicly. Exclusive means only the creator of such work has these privileges; not just anybody who has access to it and decides to grab it.[33]

Copyright is balanced by the right of fair use. Any users of a copyrighted work are allowed to make fair use of that work. Fair use is a widely discussed but much misunderstood concept. Fair use means that the work is being used in a legally acceptable manner that does not require the specific permission of the copyright holder or payment of royalties to the author or publisher. For it to apply, the use generally must be personal or educational and not for profit.

The most common example of legitimate fair use is to make a single copy of a work for one's own personal use. Personal use means that the copy will not be shared with others in any way. Any shared use or further dissemination of information in the copy is restricted in the same manner because use of the original document is restricted by the copyright law. This provision is the basis for the common library practice of having self-service copiers for patron use. Although the patron has the right to make a copy for personal use, the library does not have the right to systematically make multiple copies for patrons.

Basically, the liability of complying with the copyright law is shifted from the library to the patron by the omnipresent warning sign posted near public copy machines in libraries.[34]

Additional factors that determine whether a use is fair use include the nature of the work, the amount and percentage of the original to be used, and the effect of the use on potential sales of the original.[35] The most important issue is whether the proposed use of the work will diminish the commercial value of the copyright for its holder. If it would replace sales that otherwise might take place, then the owner of the copyright deserves compensation. If the use is so inconsequential that no sales could be reasonably expected to be affected, then this would suggest a fair use of the item. Other specific guidelines apply if the item is for classroom use or for library reserve desk use. Copyright holders are often very generous in granting permission for clearly specified and limited educational use of their materials. However, one should never presume that this will be the case. Authors deserve recognition that their works are being used, even if they are willing to forego compensation.

Technology is now adding a layer of complexity. Electronic publishing is making it possible to sell works on a per-use basis. Journal articles or individual issues of journals can now be downloaded on demand. The publishers do not have to guess in advance what the demand for a particular item will be. Royalties can be collected and the text and graphics downloaded as demand occurs. Not only is this changing the landscape of copyright and licensing, it has the potential for changing the role of the library as a warehouse. In the 20th century, libraries had to try to anticipate future need and acquire items just in case someone wanted access to them at some future time. Now it is increasingly possible through electronic downloading to acquire the information needed at the time it is requested.

Traditionally, we have thought of this in terms of buying containers of information (e.g., a book, a video, or a periodical). Although we often thought of what we were doing in terms of acquiring the physical item, what we were in fact doing was acquiring the information embedded within that item. This distinction may seem abstract. However, in understanding our role in the Information Age, it is a very important distinction. We have always bought information and not just the container.

Perhaps that distinction can be more clearly understood by considering what a book really is and how its value is determined. A book is, at the most basic level, pages of paper with some ink on them fastened together with glue. One way of determining the economic value of a book would be to weigh the ounces of paper and the amount of glue and ink contained in the book. Next, one would determine the unit values for paper, ink, and glue. With this information in hand, one should be able to establish the market value of that book. Were it only that simple.

Of course, there is value added in the cutting of the paper and in applying the ink to the pages. And, what about the fancy cardboard or leather that is used for the outside protector or cover of the book? Still, establishing a fair price for a book is a fairly objective process. What really gives a book value in the marketplace is the pattern of the ink on the pages and not the amount of ink on the pages. It is the ideas behind the words, pictures, and other graphical presentations that give a book value. Unfortunately, establishing a fair price for these ideas is far more complicated. On the other hand, this process of setting a price for books is one to which we have become accustomed throughout our lifetimes and now take for granted.

In the electronic age, this process of setting a fair price is quickly developing an entirely different dimension. Technological innovation has significantly tipped the balance in the marketplace, at least temporarily, in favor of the producers. Social forces have not yet reacted sufficiently to force a new equilibrium, where all interests are in a rational, if delicate, balance. In this stage of technological advance, the publishers have seized the initiative and are attempting to define the price of access to their advantage. At the same time, consumers are reluctant to pay the legitimate cost of production and distribution of something as intangible as information.

Copyright expert Mary Minnow defines intellectual property in the following manner:

> Intellectual property is the intangible personal property that results from mental processes. There are four types of intellectual property that have legal protection in the U.S.: copyright, trademark, patents and trade secrets. What matters most to libraries? Copyright![36]

Copyright in Libraries

Publishers and librarians agree on most things and are partners in many causes (e.g., *The Freedom to Read Statement* and efforts to promote basic literacy). However, when it comes to copyright, sometimes they could not be farther apart. On the surface, publishers are not mentioned in the Constitution when it authorizes Congress to give authors the exclusive right to control the use of their respective writings.

In the mind of the average citizen, copyright is intended to balance the rights of authors and those of the general public. In real life, the battles are generally between the perceived rights of the public and the alleged rights of *aggregators* (e.g., publishers and producers) who get the original authors, artists, or composers to sign over their copyrights in exchange for publishing the creation. Sometimes the battles are between the original creators and the aggregators.

All parties in this drama have a vested interest in interpreting the copyright law to their own advantage. A former colleague once said, "Copyright means what the party with the loudest mouthpiece who gets to court first says it means." Although not literally correct, there is a lot of truth in his statement. Publishers of paper, plastic, and software will claim copyright extends farther than it really does. On the other hand, users will claim it doesn't extend as far as it does.

Below is a model that illustrates what is covered by copyright (figure 8.4). It is often difficult for a citizen, even with the best of intentions, to know what is appropriate to use and what is not. In this graphic, you will note that there are some things that all reasonable people will agree on as being appropriate use of information by anyone. In this illustration, that would be anything

Figure 8.4. Appropriate use of copyrighted materials?

that falls into the black circle in the center. There are also things that all reasonable people will agree are subject to copyright protection. In this illustration, this would be represented by anything outside the larger of the two circles. The fun part is the area between the two circles. Reasonable people may disagree as to whether materials within this area are protected by copyright. Equally relevant, judges might disagree if a dispute were taken to court.

For materials in this area, there is no sure guideline as to whether one is required to seek permission from the copyright holder and perhaps pay a royalty if requested, or whether one should assert that either the material is in the *public domain* or subject to *fair use* for some other reason. The course of action you should take, if you find yourself in this situation, depends on how risk adverse you are or how risk adverse your employer is.

Within this area represented by the donut above, risk varies. The closer one stays to the smaller black circle, the less likely one is to be sued for inappropriate use of copyright materials. In addition, if one is sued, it is less likely that the suit would be successful for the plaintiff. Also, if a court case is lost, it is more likely that a good faith defense would minimize damages that might be imposed by the judge. That is, you violated copyright in good faith because it was a situation that was not clear-cut as to who had the right to use the expression. In other words reasonable people could conclude that the use might have been fair use.

Public Domain

Once upon a time almost everything was considered *in the public domain,* which refers to things that anyone was free to use as they wished. Some of those things included:

- Air
- Water
- Land
- Game
- Timber
- Minerals
- Fruit, etc.

Gradually, the concept of individual (or corporate) property rights has been extended to remove more and more of these "goods" from the *public domain.* As the planet has become more densely populated, less and less is still considered in the public domain. Of the items listed above, only air is still in the public domain. And even air cannot be freely used to ventilate toxins and other hazardous fumes.

Within the realm of intellectual property, a similar doctrine applies. Any creation for which no one owns copyright is considered to be in the public domain. These public domain items can be used freely by anyone in any way.

Fair Use

Even for copyrighted materials there are fair uses that can be made. Under the *fair use* doctrine of the U.S. copyright statute, it is permissible to use limited portions of a work including quotes, for purposes such as commentary, criticism, news reporting, and scholarly reports. How big the quotations can be is a highly technical issue that is beyond the scope of our discussion here.

This doctrine has been codified in *section 107* of the copyright law.

Section 107 contains a list of the various purposes for which the reproduction of a particular work may be considered "fair," such as criticism, comment, news reporting, teaching, scholarship, and research. Section 107 also sets out four factors to be considered in determining whether or not a particular use is fair:

1. the purpose and character of the use, including whether such use is of commercial nature or is for nonprofit educational purposes;
2. the nature of the copyrighted work;
3. amount and substantiality of the portion used in relation to the copyrighted work as a whole; and
4. the effect of the use upon the potential market for or value of the copyrighted work.

The distinction between "fair use" and infringement may be unclear and not easily defined. There is no specific number of words, lines, or notes that may safely be taken without permission. Acknowledging the source of the copyrighted material does not substitute for obtaining permission.[37]

Much more latitude is given to fair use in not-for-profit educational settings in which most libraries are found. Even more latitude is allowed within the classroom setting. Some of this latitude has been extended by the *Teach Act* to closed, online classes offered over the Internet.[38]

For those of you working in or planning to work in libraries there are several areas of copyright about which you should be alert. Again, this chapter will not make you a copyright expert. Rather is it hoped that you will have your awareness raised so that you will seek guidance if and when you find yourself faced with some of the following situations. At such a time, you should consult your institution's policies and *Circular 21* from the Copyright Office, *Reproduction of Copyrighted Works by Educators and Librarians.*[39] Among the topics covered in this document are the photocopying of books and articles, the copying of audiovisual materials, and the photocopying of materials for classroom use.

Sometimes the distinctions are rather subtle to the uninitiated. For example, in general individuals are authorized to make a single copy of copyrighted materials for their own use as long as they do not share it with others. If the library staff makes the copy and then sells it to the patron for a dime, this could be considered a violation of the law. (Debatable, but stranger things have happened.) However, if the patron makes the photocopy at a coin-operated machine, this is generally considered to be within the fair use provision of the law. The same 10¢ changes hands, but the library is not legally considered to be involved in the transaction. However, the library does have an obligation under the law to post the following notice near the coin-operated copiers:

(c) *Form and Manner of Use.* (1) A Display Warning of Copyright shall be printed on heavy paper or other durable material in type at least 18 points in size, and shall be displayed prominently, in such manner and location as to be clearly visible, legible, and comprehensible to a casual observer within the immediate vicinity of the place where orders are accepted.[40]

This circular also describes under what conditions libraries can copy music and can furnish copies of periodical articles to other libraries as interlibrary loans. It is not permissible for a library to copy

such aggregate quantities as to substitute for a subscription to or purchase of such work" shall mean: (a)with respect to any given periodical (as opposed to any given issue of a periodical), filled requests of a library or archives (a "requesting entity") within any calendar year for a total of six or more copies of an article or articles published in such periodical within five years prior to the date of the request. These guidelines specifically shall not apply, directly or indirectly, to any request of a requesting entity for a copy or copies of an article or articles published in any issue of a periodical, the publication date of which is more than five years prior to the date when the request is made.[41]

Those of you who may work in school libraries may wish to examine *Circular 21* in order to get a basic understanding of what uses of copyrighted materials are permissible for classroom use. If you work in a library you are often considered to be the site expert on copyright. Be careful about falling into the trap of trying to interpret law that is very complex—especially in the area of multimedia and electronic information. You do not have the expertise, nor are you being paid the big bucks to make these kinds of fine legal distinctions. Mistakes can be costly. When in doubt refer questions to a district expert or legal counsel.

What Works Are Protected?

Copyright protects "original works of authorship" that are fixed in a tangible form of expression. The fixation need not be directly perceptible so long as it may be communicated with the aid of a machine or device. Copyright protection subsists from the time the work is created in fixed form. The copyright in the work of authorship immediately becomes the property of the author who created the work. Only the author or those deriving their rights through the author can rightfully claim copyright. Mere ownership of a book, manuscript, painting, or any other copy or phonorecord does not give the possessor the copyright. The law provides that transfer of ownership of any material object that embodies a protected work does not of itself convey any rights in the copyright.

What Is Not Protected by Copyright?

The following can not be copyrighted:

- Works that have not been fixed in a tangible form of expression
- Titles, names, short phrases, and slogans; familiar symbols or designs; mere variations of typographic ornamentation, lettering, or coloring; mere listings of ingredients or contents
- Ideas, procedures, methods, systems, processes, concepts, principles, discoveries, or devices, as distinguished from a description, explanation, or illustration.
- Works consisting entirely of information that is common property and containing no original authorship (for example: standard calendars, height and weight charts, tape measures and rulers, and lists or tables taken from public documents or other common sources)

Works by the U.S. Government are not eligible for U.S. copyright protection. Works of state and local governments are less clearly defined. The federal government felt it could give its own rights away; and state and local governments tend to think that the federal government has taken care of copyright so many do not address this issue at all.

Notice of Copyright

The use of a copyright notice is no longer required under U.S. law, although it is often beneficial. Because prior law did contain such a requirement, however (prior to when the United States signed the international Berne Agreement March 1, 1989), the use of notice is still relevant to the copyright status of older works.

Use of the notice may be important because:

- it informs the public that the work is protected by copyright,
- it identifies the copyright owner,
- and it shows the year of first publication. Example: © 2001 David R. Dowell

The use of the copyright notice is the responsibility of the copyright owner and does not require advance permission from, or registration with, the Copyright Office. Although not legally required, registration makes it easier to collect damages should that become necessary.

How Long Does Copyright Endure?

A work that is created (fixed in tangible form for the first time) on or after January 1, 1978, is automatically protected from the moment of its creation and is ordinarily given a term enduring for the author's life plus an additional 70 years after the author's death. Under the law in effect before 1978, terms of copyright were somewhat shorter.

It is hard to see that the extensions of copyright are encouraging the progress of science and useful arts. It is easy to accept the arguments that such extensions enrich Disney and other corporate aggregators of copyrights. There is a direct parallel between the last series of copyright extensions and when the copyright on Mickey Mouse would have expired and rights to the rodent would have fallen into the public domain.

Intellectual Property in the Digital Age

All of our old problems still exist in the digital age. They are compounded by the new and more fluid formats for recording expression. Who owns what information on the Internet? How can these rights of ownership be protected in cyberspace? As usage of the Net intensifies and more is at stake, these questions are becoming increasingly important and increasingly controversial.

Lawyers, legal scholars, judges, lawmakers, and Internet users disagree about how the existing set of legal rules should be applied to this new medium—and disagree even more about whether and how those rules should be modified to manage the medium better. The *Digital Millennium Copyright Act (DMCA)* was the first comprehensive attempt to codify new rules. Fair use took a beating in the passage of that law. Some provisions have already been re-versed in legislation like the *Teach Act,* a recent law that allows, under certain conditions, distance education classes to exercise essentially the same lati-tude that was already in place in a physical classroom. But this is just the first skirmish. The ultimate decision is years if not decades away. Stay tuned.

Creative Commons

The latest attempt to swing the pendulum back toward a balance aimed at promoting progress in science and the useful arts is Creative Commons. This is very new, but it seems to be gaining some momentum. If you think for a minute you will recall hearing the phrase "all rights reserved." The thrust of Creative Commons is "some rights preserved." To understand how this concept works, please visit the comic strip that illustrates it at the following URL:

Figure 8.5. Creative Commons.

http://creativecommons.org/about/licenses/com ics1. The authors saw, for the first time, a book using this form of copyright in June, 2004. The logo for Cre-ative Commons is a take off on the original © symbol for copyright.

As both creators and consumers of intellectual prop-erty, we hope to see this symbol more and more.

U.S. Supreme Court Justice Sandra Day O'Connor summed up the purpose of copyright:

> The primary objective of copyright is not to reward the labour of authors, but [t]o promote the Progress of Science and useful Arts. To this end, copyright assures authors the right to their original expression, but en-courages others to build freely upon the ideas and information conveyed by a work. This result is neither unfair nor unfortunate. It is the means by which copyright advances the progress of science and art.

Ethics in the Workplace

> V. We treat co-workers and other colleagues with respect, fairness and good faith, and advocate conditions of employment that safeguard the rights and welfare of all employees of our institutions.

This article of the code is not specific to libraries or to information profes-sionals. However, it is important that all library workers know that they are expected to treat colleagues with respect. The second part of this article re-flects the do-gooder nature of library workers—one of the refreshing qualities of most people in this occupational group. Library work seems to attract em-ployees who have an active concern for the welfare of others.

> VI. We do not advance private interests at the expense of library users, colleagues, or our employing institutions.

As with Article V, there is nothing particularly unique in libraries that raise this particular ethical admonition. All employees need to monitor their behavior to make sure they are not taking advantage of their customers or employers for personal gain. This whole area will probably expand as more attention is paid to use of employer e-mail for personal use. Liability concerns are causing employers to pay attention to how e-mail is being used. Courts have held that any e-mail, however frivolously intended or by what level of staff it was authored, has the potential to subject employers to harassment and other claims. Again, though, libraries do not have special concerns beyond those held by organizations in general.

VII. We distinguish between our personal convictions and professional duties and do not allow our personal beliefs to interfere with fair representation of the aims of our institutions or the provision of access to their information resources.

Herein lies one of the greatest professional dilemmas for many library workers. Although most are able to hold to the fairness suggested in this article, it is often personally traumatic to offer unbiased information on topics on which they have very strong personal views. It is difficult to keep personal feelings from slipping out, even with the best of intentions. Continual self-monitoring is needed to ensure that personal beliefs do not color fair and balanced advice that allows the customers to find the information they need to allow them to make decisions and to further their ends.

In our country libraries offer individuals access to a vast array of information on almost any side of any conceivable topic of potential inquiry.

- All views can be presented.
- Readers must weigh different points of view and evaluate the credibility of the authors.
- The readers, not the library, decide what they wish to believe.
- Relevant questions for those who aspire to work in the information industry include:
- How much information should flow?
- Who wants more information to flow?
- Who wants less information to flow?
- Do individuals change their positions on these questions depending on what information is being considered?
- What is really in the public interest?
- Who gets to decide?

Individuals and organizations can concentrate or deflect information. Those who work in the information industry should constantly examine their own actions to ask themselves in what ways they are increasing or impeding the flow of information to their clients, their coworkers, and their organization. Those of you who do not work in the information industry may find it useful to examine the various players in the drama of your lives to decide which actors enable you to find information and which actors attempt to withhold information from you.

These rights are espoused not just in the United States. *The Universal Declaration of Human Rights* was adopted by the United Nations General Assembly in 1948. The Preamble of this document states that:

> recognition of the inherent dignity and of the equal and inalienable rights of all members of the human family is the foundation of freedom, justice, and peace in the world...[and]...the advent of a world in which human beings shall enjoy freedom of speech and belief and freedom from fear and want has been proclaimed as the highest aspiration of the common people.

And, Article 19 states: "Everyone has the right to freedom of opinion and expression; this right includes freedom to hold opinions without interference and to seek, receive and impart information and ideas through any media regardless of frontiers."

The Freedom to Reads Statement, Appendix C, further elaborates on these ideas:

1. It is in the public interest for publishers and librarians to make available the widest diversity of views and expressions, including those which are unorthodox or unpopular with the majority.

2. Publishers, librarians, and booksellers do not need to endorse every idea or presentation contained in the books they make available. It would conflict with the public interest for them to establish their own political, moral, or aesthetic views as a standard for determining what books should be published or circulated.

3. It is contrary to the public interest for publishers or librarians to determine the acceptability of a book on the basis of the personal history or political affiliations of the author.

4. There is no place in our society for efforts to coerce the taste of others, to confine adults to the reading matter deemed suitable for adolescents, or to inhibit the efforts of writers to achieve artistic expression.

5. It is not in the public interest to force a reader to accept with any book the prejudgment of a label characterizing the book or author as subversive or dangerous.

6. It is the responsibility of publishers and librarians, as guardians of the people's freedom to read, to contest encroachments upon that freedom by individuals or groups seeking to impose their own standards or tastes upon the community at large.

7. It is the responsibility of publishers and librarians to give full meaning to the freedom to read by providing books that enrich the quality and diversity of thought and expression. By the exercise of this affirmative responsibility, they can demonstrate that the answer to a bad book is a good one, the answer to a bad idea is a good one.

Links to a number of policies related to censorship of various types of materials are listed at the end of this chapter. These include policies about videotapes, materials for children, electronic information, meeting room scheduling, information on sexual orientation, exhibits and bulletin boards, and the labeling of materials as to their suitability.

Librarians have the greatest personal difficulty when it comes to issues that relate to what information sources are suitable for children. In this regard they mirror the society in which we live. In our communities there are very vocal citizens who demand that young people (and often all people) be protected from ideas and expression with which they do not personally agree. On the other hand, ALA policy is stated in absolute terms in Article V of the Library Bill of Rights:

> Article V of the *Library Bill of Rights* states, "A person's right to use a library should not be denied or abridged because of origin, age, background, or views." The "right to use a library" includes free access to, and unrestricted use of, all the services, materials, and facilities the library has to offer. Every restriction on access to, and use of, library resources, based solely on the chronological age, educational level, literacy skills, or legal emancipation of users violates Article V.

> VIII. We strive for excellence in the profession by maintaining and enhancing our own knowledge and skills, by encouraging the professional development of co-workers, and by fostering the aspirations of potential members of the profession.

Most libraries support staff education in some form—either formal or informal. It is only natural that libraries and library workers have a special commitment to encouraging lifelong learning. Building on the foundation of commitment to education, library workers and libraries have a mutual responsibility to ensure that staff develop the new knowledge and skills that are needed now and those that will be needed in the future. Without a major commitment to staff development, library customers will not receive the continuing high level of service they have come to expect. In addition, we constantly need to attract the best possible employees at every level of library employment. All of us need to be ambassadors for librarianship.

AND WHAT TO DO ABOUT THE CHILDREN?

Advocates of restricting access to library materials frequently do so with the best of intentions. Most often, they justify their actions on the basis of the need to protect children. Sometimes the justification is to protect everyone. Other times, the rationale is to prevent the misuse of public funds.

In these arguments there is a parallel with another contentious public policy issue of our generation—abortion. Protection of the unborn, protection of the mother, and protection of tax dollars from inappropriate uses are the most commonly voiced reasons for not allowing access to abortions.

For most people, it is easier to discuss these issues in the abstract than it is to deal with their application in public policy. Those on the two extremes of these sensitive socio–political issues do not feel ambiguity between theory and practice. However, for those less doctrinaire, such issues are not so clear cut.

Protecting children is a legitimate goal of civilized society. However, is it the responsibility of the state, through its schools and libraries, to determine what each child should have access to? ALA's position is that a library should not restrict access for all children, strictly because of their chronological age, from information that some might find offensive or inappropriate:

> Libraries are charged with the mission of developing resources to meet the diverse information needs and interests of the communities they serve. Services, materials, and facilities that fulfill the needs and interests of library users at different stages in their personal development are a necessary part of library resources. The needs and interests of each library user, and resources appropriate to meet those needs and interests, must be determined on an individual basis. Librarians cannot predict what resources will best fulfill the needs and interests of any individual user based on a single criterion such as chronological age, level of education, or legal emancipation.
>
> Librarians and governing bodies should not resort to age restrictions on access to library resources in an effort to avoid actual or anticipated objections from parents or anyone else. The mission, goals, and objectives of libraries do not authorize librarians or governing bodies to assume, abrogate, or overrule the rights and responsibilities of parents or legal guardians. Librarians and governing bodies should maintain that parents—and only parents—have the right and the responsibility to restrict the access of their children—and only their children—to library resources. Parents or legal guardians who do not want their children to have access to certain library services, materials or facilities, should so advise their children. Librarians and governing bodies cannot assume the role of parents or the functions of parental authority in the private relationship between parent and child. Librarians and governing bodies have a public and professional obligation to provide equal access to all library resources for all library users.[42]

What Type of Books are Challenged These Days?

Ninety-seven percent of the books challenged are material in schools, school libraries, or public libraries. Of these, almost three-fourths were in schools or school libraries.[43]

The 10 most challenged books of 2006 reflect a range of themes and include the following titles:

- *And Tango Makes Three* by Justin Richardson and Peter Parnell. Challenged for homosexuality and for being anti-family, and considered unsuited to age group;

- *Gossip Girls* series by Cecily Von Ziegesar. Challenged for homosexuality, sexual content, drugs, and offensive language and considered unsuited to age group;

- *Alice* series by Phyllis Reynolds Naylor. Challenged for sexual content and offensive language;

- *The Earth, My Butt, and Other Big Round Things* by Carolyn Mackler. Challenged for sexual content, for being anti-family, and for offensive language, and considered unsuited to age group;

- *The Bluest Eye* by Toni Morrison. Challenged for sexual content, offensive language, and considered unsuited to age group;
- *Scary Stories* series by Alvin Schwartz. Challenged for occult/Satanism, violence, and insensitivity and considered unsuited to age group;
- *Athletic Shorts* by Chris Crutcher. Challenged for homosexuality and offensive language;
- *The Perks of Being a Wallflower* by Stephen Chbosky. Challenged for homosexuality, sexually explicit, offensive language, and considered unsuited to age group;
- *Beloved* by Toni Morrison. Challenged for offensive language, sexual content, and considered unsuited to age group; and
- *The Chocolate War* by Robert Cormier. Challenged for sexual content, offensive language, and violence.

Off the list this year, but on for several years past, are the *Catcher in the Rye* by J. D. Salinger, *Of Mice and Men* by John Steinbeck, and *The Adventures of Huckleberry Finn* by Mark Twain.[44] While some long time classics are perennially at or near the top of this list, some trends may be seen. J. K. Rowling's Harry Potter books propelled her to the top of this list on multiple occasions a few years ago. However, she has not cracked the top 10 since 2002. At this writing it is interesting to speculate whether the final, and somewhat darker, *Harry Potter and the Deathly Hallows* will once again return her to this dubious distinction.

CURRENT ISSUES

Ethical issues on the front burner in the early 21st century continue to involve the protection of children. The new element is Internet access. Access to the Internet is also the basis for an even more far-reaching social and political issue that is being called the "digital divide." At their core, these are not totally new issues. Instead, they are extensions of old ones.

For libraries, the Internet opens up a world of information. Much of it is good, but some is bad and some is downright ugly. As the World Wide Web continues to mature and increasingly delivers on its promise to transform our economy, its rough edges become more widely known. "Life in the gutter of the Information Superhighway" is the way one report described this area of cyberspace.[45] According to this report of children who have gone into an online chat room, one in four has been solicited for sex, and one in five has been sent provocative pictures through a Web contact.[46] Without knowing more about how this survey was conducted, the actual numbers may be suspect. However, no matter what the exact numbers are, it is clear that the Internet can be a dangerous place—especially for unsuspecting children.

Concerns about such perils have led concerned citizens to pursue solutions on two separate fronts. One attempted remedy has been through the development of filtering software that attempts to ensure that offending sites or messages are blocked. The second effort has been through the enactment of laws that restrict what can be communicated over the World Wide Web.

Internet Filtering

Filtering software has been highly touted as a way to protect children from the perils of cyberspace. So far it has met with only limited success, both legally and functionally. As an aid to parents in managing home computers, filtering software has matured significantly in the past few years. Even so, it may give parents a false sense of security if they rely on software alone to protect their children from exposure to unwanted sites. As a device to protect the users of public access Internet workstations, it is far from successful.

Filtering software uses a variety of methods to identify potentially objectionable sites. Some ask information specialists, parents, and teachers to classify and rate sites. Others identify harmful material by searching online content and Web site addresses for keywords such as *sex* or *breast.* Others use a combination of the above methods. Some provide updates as often as daily, as they try to keep in touch with dynamically evolving Internet content.

Other approaches taken by authors of filtering software are to provide

a time management function that allows parents to control the time of day that children are able to access the Internet; control the total number of hours per day or week spent online; [and tracking of] the sites that their children have visited.[47]

Parents can subsequently decide whether any of these sites should be blocked.

Parents clearly have the right and the responsibility to protect their children. However, the issues change significantly when the state attempts to mandate a solution that will apply to all. Public libraries have become battlefields for the resolution of the issue of state-mandated limits to inquiry. Public libraries often serve very diverse communities, different segments of which have very different views of what information is acceptable and what is unacceptable.

Internet use policies are necessary in all types of libraries before a challenge is received. They are absolutely critical in public libraries. Special and academic libraries for the most part serve only clients who are chronologically adults. The primary focus of school libraries is to serve the needs of children. Policies can be crafted for one age group or the other much more easily than can policies that attempt to meet the needs of both groups.

Excerpts from a recent press release from the ALA suggest that most public libraries are now prepared. Results of a survey conducted by the Library Research Center, University of Illinois state that

95 percent of public libraries have a formal policy in place to regulate public use of the Internet and that most others are developing such policies.

To ensure that people are using the Internet responsibly, 80 percent of respondents say they purposely locate computer terminals in open spaces and often near a staff person's desk.

The survey's results on children's access to the Internet showed that nearly 64 percent of respondents require permission from parents before children can use the Internet.

Almost 50 percent have received informal complaints about Internet access, but only 7 percent were about content. Most were about faulty equipment or a slow response time.[48]

Legislative Remedies

On the political front, two major legislative initiatives were enacted into law during the last years of the 20th century. Both the Communications Decency Act and the Child Online Protection Act, as their names imply, were crafted and marketed as measures to protect children. However, key provisions of the first were overturned in a landmark Supreme Court decision that went a long way toward defining permissible free speech on the Internet. The second, at this writing, is currently under judicial review with key portions of it at least temporarily stayed until this process is completed.

Communications Decency Act (CDA), 1996

The Communications Decency Act was Congress's first attempt to regulate online speech. "The CDA prohibited posting 'indecent' or 'patently offensive' materials in a public forum on the Internet—including web pages, newsgroups, chat rooms, or online discussion lists."[49] The act attempted to extend to the Internet controls similar to those common to broadcast television. Key parts of the act were struck down by a unanimous three-judge federal panel, which was subsequently upheld by the Supreme Court. In his opinion Federal Judge Stewart R. Dalzell wrote, "The Internet may fairly be regarded as a never-ending worldwide conversation. The Government may not, through the *CDA*, interrupt that conversation. As the most participatory form of mass speech yet developed, the Internet deserves the highest protection from governmental intrusion."[50] "In fact, while that decision was indeed momentous, all that it really held was that government regulation of the Internet must be consistent with *First Amendment* principles, and that the *CDA* was not, because it restricted far more speech than was necessary or appropriate to deal with the problem of minors' access to 'indecency.'"[51]

Child Online Protection Act (COPA), 1998

After portions of the CDA were declared unconstitutional, Congress attempted to craft a somewhat narrower version with the same intent. It was sometimes called CDA II or Son of CDA. Its title, like that of its predecessor, suggests the intent to promote decency and to protect children. "The Child Online Protection Act makes it a crime for anyone, by means of the World Wide Web, to make any communication for commercial purposes that is 'harmful to minors,' unless the person has restricted access by minors by requiring a credit card number."[52] Possession of a credit card is thus presumed to be an indicator that the holder of that card is an adult—a questionable assumption in today's society.

Free speech advocates find this law flawed in many of the same ways the courts found CDA to be deficient. According to these groups, COPA creates problems in the following areas:

> Imposes serious burdens on constitutionally-protected speech, including materials such as the Starr report, movies, and television programs, when disseminated through popular commercial Web sites such as *CNN*,

Yahoo!, or *MS-NBC*. Medical sites such as *OBGYN.net* and sexual awareness sites such as *PlanetOut* also risk restriction under *COPA*.

Fails to effectively serve the government's interest in protecting children, since it will not effectively prevent children from seeing inappropriate material originating from outside of the U.S. available through other
Internet resources besides the World Wide Web, such as chat rooms or
email.

Does not represent the least restrictive means of regulating speech,
according to the Supreme Court's own findings that blocking and filtering software might give parents the ability to more effectively screen out
undesirable content without burdening speech.[53]

Early in 1999 in federal court in Philadelphia, Judge Lowell Reed temporarily blocked the implementation of COPA until a full trial could be held to
determine its constitutionality. Unlike the CDA judicial process, which was
given fast track status, this review may take years to work its way through the
almost inevitable appeals process. In his ruling, Judge Reed wrote, "[I]t is not
apparent to this Court that the defendant can meet its burden to prove that
COPA is the least restrictive means available to achieve the goal of restricting
the access of minors to this material."[54]

While this judicial review is underway, many in Congress attempt to mandate Internet filtering for children by attempting to attach such provisions to
other bills to achieve this end. One of the more recent examples was the effort
of Senator John McCain to require that any school to which E-rate funds were
allocated must filter its Internet workstations to which children would have
access.

The final word has yet to be spoken on how best to protect children from
the hazards of the online world. Improvements in filtering software continue
to evolve. On the legal front, legislation continues to be proposed, adopted,
and subjected to judicial review. In these processes we get closer to the goal
of our society: to protect children while preserving the rights of adults to exercise their rights to engage in free expression of constitutionally protected discourse. Libraries remain on the front line of the battle as they have for decades
in the skirmishes over free expression through print works.

How Do We Protect the Children and the Rest of Us?

Congress has made three attempts to protect children, and perhaps the
rest of us, before they crafted legislation that could be upheld by the Supreme
Court. Each law was more narrowly drawn than the last until the Court finally
upheld the *Children's Internet Protection Act* (*CIPA*) in a 2003 ruling that allows
the government, in certain situations, to restrict Internet surfing at public and
school libraries that receive certain kinds of federal funding. This effort pitted
those with free-speech concerns against efforts to shield children from online pornography. The case resolved, at least for the moment, whether federal
funding could be stripped from libraries that don't install filters on computers
to block sexually explicit Web sites. The decision affected the more than 14 million people a year who use public library computers to do research, send and
receive e-mail, and, in some cases, log on to adult Web sites.[55]

Do Individuals in our Society Need Protection in Cyberspace?

Who needs protection in cyberspace?

- None of us?
- All of us?
- Older people?
- Adults who never finished high school?
- People with IQs under 100?
- Women?
- College students?
- Christians?
- Children?

Who Gets to Decide?

Should some people in our society be restricted in their ability to exercise rights and responsibilities generally given to adults? Should citizens in training, also known as children, have a protected environment in which to thrive? If so, who should provide it?

- The community?
- The state?
- Parents?

Many of you have heard the old African proverb, "It takes a village to raise a child." Hillary Clinton used it as the title of a book. Certainly the community has an interest in seeing that children grow into responsible adults.

The federal government is clearly the state, but so are publicly funded libraries. The federal government has made a series of attempts to regulate behavior in cyberspace. Three major pieces of legislation have been passed since the advent of the WWW. These laws all have uplifting-sounding titles. At first look one might wonder how anyone could be opposed. The first is called the Communications Decency Act (CDA), and the second effort the Child Online Protection Act (COPA). However, the courts have found that these laws were too broad and violated the free speech rights of adults when less restrictive remedies were available.

The third law, Children's Internet Protection Act (CIPA), which requires libraries that accept federal funding to filter Internet access, was finally upheld by the Supreme Court in 2003:

The *CIPA* requires the filtering or blocking of certain visual depictions and requires libraries to adopt and implement an Internet safety policy and operate "technology protection measures" (blocking and filtering) if they receive—

E-rate discounts for Internet access, Internet service, or internal connections;

Funds under title III of ESEA to purchase computers used to access the Internet or to pay the direct costs associated with accessing the Internet; or

Funds under the state grant programs of LSTA to purchase computers used to access the Internet or to pay the direct costs associated with accessing the Internet.[56]

This has caused some public libraries to refuse to accept such funding and therefore avoid the restrictions of CIPA.

DOPA

The latest congressional attempt to protect children on the "Wild Wild Web" is the Deleting Online Predators Act (DOPA) of 2006. DOPA bans children from getting access to many of the extremely popular social networking sites that have been the latest online growth fad. It passed the House by a vote of 410–15, but has yet to be acted upon by the Senate. Sponsors are attempting to keep *MySpace* and similar sites out of libraries and schools under the pretext that these sites are fertile ground for online predators to prey on children. "Opponents of the bill point out that the language of the *DOPA* bill would extend such filtering [*CIPA*] to include websites based on specific technologies rather than specific content, including websites based on those technologies which are used for educational purposes."[57] For example, it is unclear whether the bill as written could be considered to outlaw some distance education course sites if there were minors in the class. Actually, home schooled minor students often enroll in such classes. The discussion board and chat functions possibly could be construed to be in violation of this bill as it is currently worded.

Here again a new, cutting edge technology seems to have great potential to meet a need for reaching out and connecting. This might appear to be the antidote for those who seem to become addicted to and isolated as the result of the amount of time they spend online. On the other hand, anywhere that people congregate, can predators be far behind?

Libraries and schools are beginning to develop strategies that tap the popularity and power of this medium. Examples can be found of such applications at the following link: http://www.leonline.com/yalsa/positive_uses.pdf. It is unclear at this time whether the positive possibilities of this phenomenon will have a chance to be applied in schools and libraries before the perceived dangers close this venue for young adults—at least from publicly funded locations.

Unsafe Libraries

While the first two laws above targeted the Internet providers, the third was directed at libraries. This is because libraries are sometimes depicted as harmful to minors, if not to all of us.

Listeners who tuned in Dr. Laura Schlessinger's radio talk show on April 15 [2002] got a real earful: "The ALA"—American Library Association—"is boldly, brashly contributing to sexualizing our children," Schlessinger told her audience of 20 million. "And now the pedophiles know where to go." What a way to commemorate National Library Week.[58]

Dr Laura followed up this radio comment on her short-lived television show. As a part of an hour-long episode entitled "Unsafe Libraries," she equipped a 15-year-old girl with a hidden camera for a visit to the Denver Public Library. For a while Dr. Laura maintained information about libraries on her Web site. But she has since moved on to other things. For information on how libraries threaten the youth of America one must now visit sites like AFA Online: http://www.afa.net/lif/lif_template.asp.

Pornography

What is pornography? To some it is in the eye of the beholder. It is pictures, writings, or other material that are sexual explicit. Most of it is protected free speech. Pornography that is not protected free speech includes

- Obscenity
- Child pornography
- Material that is "Harmful to Minors."

States may regulate pornography that is not protected free speech.

Someone must like pornography, because porn sites were some of the earliest Web sites to actually be profitable. Current estimates range as high as $11 billion a year for revenue from pornography—much of it from the WWW.

Obscenity

Miller v. California was the U.S. Supreme Court decision in 1973 that remains the basis for defining what is obscene. Obscenity is not protected free speech. *Obscenity* depicts or describes sexual conduct. In addition, it must meet each of the following three criteria:

- The average person, applying contemporary community standards, finds that the work taken as a whole appeals to the prurient interest.
- Depicts or describes, in a patiently offensive way, sexual conduct specifically described by the applicable state law.
- The work taken as a whole lacks serious literary, artistic, political, or scientific value.

Child Pornography

Child pornography is also not protected free speech. *Child pornography* is the visual depiction children engaged in sexually explicit or lascivious conduct, or the visual depiction of what appears to be a minor involved in sexual conduct.

Harmful to Minors

Although children do have *First Amendment* Rights, states may enact laws regulating sexually explicit materials as not legal for minors, even though the items are not obscene. Not all states have harmful-to-minors laws. However, if states do have such laws they must meet these standards:

- They must use least restrictive means to limit expression;
- they must state a compelling need:
- they must offer a clear definition of what is restricted;
- they must not block an adult from access; and
- they must be harmful to a 17-year year-old minor.

As you may guess by now, harmful-to-minors laws have proved difficult to craft and more often than not have been overturned by the courts.

Majority Rule versus Individual Rights

In reviewing whether expression is protected free speech, courts generally have ruled that, in most instances, the rights of the individual take precedence over the preferences of the majority. Often this concept is not popular among the general public. Supreme Court Justice Anthony M. Kennedy described this difficult concept of the rights of the individual when he wrote:

When a student first encounters our free speech jurisprudence, he or she might think it is influenced by the philosophy that one idea is as good as any other, and that in art and literature objective standards of style, taste, decorum, beauty, and esthetics are deemed by the Constitution to be inappropriate, indeed unattainable. Quite the opposite is true. The Constitution no more enforces a relativistic philosophy or moral nihilism than it does any other point of view." "The Constitution exists precisely so that opinions and judgments, including esthetic and moral judgments about art and literature, can be formed, tested, and expressed. What the Constitution says is that these judgments are for the individual to make, not for the Government to decree, even with the mandate or approval of a majority. Technology expands the capacity to choose; and it denies the potential of this revolution if we assume the Government is best positioned to make these choices for us.

It is rare that a regulation restricting speech because of its content will ever be permissible. Indeed, were we to give the Government the benefit of the doubt when it attempted to restrict speech, we would risk leaving regulations in place that sought to shape our unique personalities or to silence dissenting ideas. When *First Amendment* compliance is the point to be proved, the risk of non-persuasion—operative in all trials—must rest with the Government, not with the citizen.[59]

Unsafe for Children?

Is the Internet really unsafe for children? At the very least, some parts of it are for some children. So who decides? Do we throw the baby out with the bathwater? As a first step, parents, library workers, and others must become aware of the resources that are available to them to make informed decisions. Sites like GetNetWise http://www.getnetwise.org are good starting points. This site opens with the statement:

> The Internet offers kids many opportunities for learning, constructive entertainment, and personal growth. At the same time, parents are concerned about the risks kids face online. The challenge for parents is to educate themselves and their children about how to use the Internet safely.

While ALA is one of the many official sponsors of GetNetWise, the Association advocates that parents, and not the state (of which publicly funded libraries are one arm), must be the ones to make decisions about what their own children experience in libraries. In the last analysis each library must decide what policies it will follow. As you see in the readings this week, these decisions are often contentious and sometimes litigious.

ALA Policy

The question of what children should have access to in libraries is one of the most difficult to deal with for library workers. There are no universal answers that meet the development needs of every child at all stages of his or her development. ALA's policy is often difficult to apply and challenges library workers to carefully consider their own ethical values and the policies of their employers. ALA's policy is stated as follows:

> Library policies and procedures which effectively deny minors equal access to all library resources available to other users violate the Library Bill of Rights. The American Library Association opposes all attempts to restrict access to library services, materials, and facilities based on the age of library users.
>
> Article V of the Library Bill of Rights states, "A person's right to use a library should not be denied or abridged because of origin, age, background, or views." The "right to use a library" includes free access to, and unrestricted use of, all the services, materials, and facilities the library has to offer. Every restriction on access to, and use of, library resources, based solely on the chronological age, educational level, or legal emancipation of users violates Article V.
>
> Libraries are charged with the mission of developing resources to meet the diverse information needs and interests of the communities they serve. Services, materials, and facilities which fulfill the needs and interests of library users at different stages in their personal development are a necessary part of library resources. The needs and interests of each library user, and resources appropriate to meet those needs and interests, must be determined on an individual basis. Librarians cannot predict what resources will best fulfill the needs and interests of any individual user based on a single criterion such as chronological age, level of education, or legal emancipation.
>
> The selection and development of library resources should not be diluted because of minors having the same access to library resources as adult users. Institutional self-censorship diminishes the credibility of the library in the community, and restricts access for all library users.

Librarians and governing bodies should not resort to age restrictions on access to library resources in an effort to avoid actual or anticipated objections from parents or anyone else. The mission, goals, and objectives of libraries do not authorize librarians or governing bodies to assume, abrogate, or overrule the rights and responsibilities of parents or legal guardians. Librarians and governing bodies should maintain that **parents—and only parents—have the right and the responsibility to restrict the access of their children**—and only their children—to library resources. Parents or legal guardians who do not want their children to have access to certain library services, materials or facilities, should so advise their children. Librarians and governing bodies cannot assume the role of parents or the functions of parental authority in the private relationship between parent and child. Librarians and governing bodies have a public and professional obligation to provide equal access to all library resources for all library users.

Librarians have a professional commitment to ensure that all members of the community they serve have free and equal access to the entire range of library resources regardless of content, approach, format, or amount of detail. This principle of library service applies equally to all users, minors as well as adults. Librarians and governing bodies must uphold this principle in order to provide adequate and effective service to minors.[60]

Filters Chosen by Parents versus State Approved Filters

Filters in and of themselves are not good or bad. Like other technologies, they are either effective or ineffective in meeting the objectives of those who install them. Parents may want to choose them for their home computers if they are convinced the filters will screen out what they want and let through what they need. It is much more problematic for agencies of the state to start selecting filters for publicly funded computers. When one of the authors ran a program, one file that got flagged was labeled "SEX,SEX,SEX,SEX..." It turned out to be a census record in which the gender of those enumerated had columns headed by the term "Sex."

The particular program mentioned above also screens for categories other than pornography. It also flags other terms that give you clues as to the values of its creators. This is something important to know if you ever need to choose a filter.

Pornography seems to get all the attention on the Internet as the corrupter of children and the rest of us. Certainly there is pornography on the WWW. It is there because there is a market for it. For the most part it is not illegal, even if it is in poor taste and inappropriate. If there was not a market for it, it would gradually disappear. One wonders why pornography gets so much attention when other inducements to the corruption of children such as violence, gambling, and drugs seem to have much more potential to destroy lives. Possibly the graphic nature of the WWW may have, at least until now, proved to be a more effective platform for pornography than for the other vices mentioned above. The others seem to do better in other venues. Gambling, and particularly poker, seems to be catching on fast on TV cable channels.

NATIONAL SECURITY

Until now most of our discussion in this chapter has assumed that adult citizens are able to satisfy their basic needs for survival. This section will explore some more basic rights or needs that may, at least at times, take precedence over concepts like the right to information, the right to privacy, or the right to own property.

The prior edition of this book was in the final production process on September 11th, 2001. National security was not considered to be a big issue when talking about the ethics of information flow. At least for the short term, 9/11 changed our world view. Now we have to re-evaluate some of the rights we have been discussing in this chapter as to whether they are really as essential to us as we might have thought. Are there other things that are even more important to us? Is our national survival being threatened to the extent that we should be willing to forego some of our hard earned and cherished freedoms?

In a sense, the terrorists seem to be winning. The goal of terrorists is to create terror. Using that definition, they have been incredibly successful—at least temporarily. They have caused us to change the way we lead our lives and invest our resources.

Two recent books provoke thoughts that may give some perspective to recent events—one by Herb Foerstel and one by Richard Clark.

> Foerstel's new book seems to address two needs. One is to recount an engaging and sometimes inspiring description of the continuing struggle in which library employees and others join forces against those who would impose police-state tactics to "protect our freedom" in the name of security. (Or is it to protect our security in the name of freedom?)
>
> The second purpose would to be to document some of the legal issues involved. These include a listing of the components of the Patriot Act, Homeland Security Act, and similar acts and policies that the Justice Department has initiated under the cover of fighting terrorism. This portion of the book is a reference source for those wishing to conduct further research, those writing library policies on how to respond to investigative inquiries, or those actually facing the need to respond to such a request for information.[61]

Richard Clark, who served as terrorism advisor to several presidents, Democratic and Republican, including both Presidents Bush, had a best selling book entitled *Against All Enemies: Inside America's War on Terror.*[62] At the ALA Annual Conference in Orlando in 2004, Clark challenged library workers and others to rededicate ourselves to follow the oath taken by all federal officials "to protect the United States Constitution against all enemies FOREIGN AND DOMESTIC." What a profound marching order for library workers and all other citizens. Now we just have to figure how to balance these needs.

DIGITAL DIVIDE

The *digital divide* is a much discussed topic in any comprehensive public policy consideration of the social consequences of the digital technology revolution. It refers to the polarization of our society into two extremes: (1) the "information haves," and (2) the "information have nots." This kind of division in our society is not new. However, in some ways, the digital divide seems to have the potential to widen the traditional gap between the rich and the poor and to make it more difficult for the poor to have an opportunity to take part in the new digital economy. Not only have women and some ethnic minorities been slow to become consumers of the Net digital opportunities, they have also been greatly under-represented in the new jobs created in the past decade. Since the publication of the first edition of this text, it has become obvious that we need to look at the international aspects of this phenomenon as well. Related emerging issues for future consideration appear to be the exportation of high tech jobs and the emergence of Internet scams as a major source of revenue for some third-world countries. For example, recently many technology related jobs have been moving to India, and Internet fraud is said to be the third highest grossing industry in Nigeria.

What is the Digital Divide?

- Is it a "racial ravine"?
- Is it gender based?
- Is it rural versus urban?
- Is it poor versus affluent?
- Is it old versus young?
- Is it educated versus undereducated?

Is the Digital Divide important?

- Politically?
- Economically?
- Morally?

This "racial ravine," as it was called in a recent federal report,[63] has profound implications for those of us committed to providing access to information as a means to empower all persons to participate as productive members of our society. Although recent evidence continues to show these different patterns of Internet use, the root causes do not appear to be racial. Rather,

> income is the main driver of Internet adoption...
>> younger people are more likely to be online...
>> educated people are more likely to be online...[and]
>> technology optimists are more likely to be online.[64]

Once these variables are taken into account, the effect of race on Internet use all but disappears. In addition, there is little difference in behavior between the ethnic groups once they do get online.[65]

It is clear that African Americans, Latinos, residents of city ghettos and isolated rural areas, and those from low income families have thus far not had the same level of access to the opportunities of cyberspace as have other

Americans. This disparity attracted much rhetoric from political leaders in the opening days of the 21st century. But, so far, no solutions have emerged to significantly equalize access to education, vocational information, and opportunities that are increasingly available on the World Wide Web.

Middle Class and Democracy

A stable democracy functions best when there is a large middle class and relatively small upper classes and lower classes. Middle class citizens have a stake in the system and have something to lose if the system fails. Middle class members tend to own homes and other material things. As a result, strong middle classes like stability so they can protect what they have and legitimately aspire to improve their status.

As a general rule, the smaller the middle class is in a society, the less efficient and stable a democracy can be and the riper that society is for instability, revolution, and a dictatorial government. In societies where there are small upper and middle classes and large lower classes (e.g., many of the Third World developing countries), it is hard to maintain any political, social, or economic stability without a strong dictator. Civil disorder breeds best when there are large gaps between the haves and the have-nots. The have-nots are left with little to lose. Therefore they are easily persuaded to follow anyone who seems to promise them a change that will improve their wretched position in society.

Is the Digital Divide important economically? Can the rest of us afford to pay the cost of bringing along those who don't have the resources or the interest in going digital? Can the rest of us afford not to pay the cost of staying connected economically and socially with the digitally unconnected of our society or of other societies of planet Earth?

Is the Digital Divide important morally? Are we our sister's keepers? What about individuals' having a responsibility for taking care of themselves? What about the children on the wrong side of the divide? Do they get left behind?

Is the Digital Divide narrowing? It depends on what you are measuring. The once huge gender gap has all but disappeared. Personal computers are in more and more homes. Internet connectivity at home has changed dramatically in just the last couple of years. But is bandwidth adequate to span the gap so that all have access to the digital economy? And what will be the next barrier?

Will the Digital Divide always be a moving target? First it was a home computer. Next it was an Internet connection. Now it's a broadband connection. Will there always be something else?

What can be done to narrow or bridge the Digital Divide?

- Education in schools
- Work force training
- Public access terminals in libraries and in other public places
- The government tax deductions for purchasing home computers and Internet connectivity

- Corporations subsidizing employees to purchase home technology
- Individuals volunteering to teach skills to those who otherwise might be left behind

Which of these are worth the economic cost to society? Which are worth the political risk to ignore?

Libraries and the Digital Divide

According to ALA's, Office for Information Technology Policy,

Libraries are central to Digital Divide solutions because the Digital Divide is not just about access to a computer. Libraries have worked to bridged the divide between the information 'haves' and 'have nots' for more than 100 years. In the digital age, libraries are addressing and will continue to address the challenges of information and technology literacy.[66]

Now, as much as ever, libraries have a role to play in helping extend the political and economic benefits of our free society and economic prosperity to all residents of our country. Libraries, particularly public libraries, are one of the few avenues of access to the World Wide Web for many who have yet to be able to afford a computer or online connections. Clearly, the ostrich approach of burying our heads in the sand is not a viable option for libraries. As larger amounts of government and private information are distributed online, libraries need to make sure that their policies of acquiring and disseminating information help shrink rather than widen this gap. Free and unfettered access to this information for all is critical to the strengthening of our democracy. More outreach is needed if the racial ravine is to be bridged. It appears that those who have computers at home are the ones most likely to use computers at work, at school, and at libraries.[67]

WRAPPING IT ALL UP

Right now we live in a period during which our society is viewed as being under attack from a terrorist threat. What happens when a group faces an external threat? Whether that threat is to a country, a company, a family, or a library the following things happen:

- We circle the wagons.
- We sacrifice individual goals for the common good—particularly lower level needs for security or survival.
- Leaders say "Trust me."
- We trade freedom for security.
- We value internal bonding and group unity more than individual differences.
- We detain suspicious individual.
- We give more powers to law enforcement.

While some of these actions may be necessary—at least for the short term—they run counter to the freedoms that we claim to be the primary distinguishing characteristics that make our country great. As citizens, each of us has the obligation to search our ethical values and hold ourselves and the mighty accountable for doing the right thing. Former Supreme Court nominee Robert Bork reminds us that separating the rhetoric from the real issues is often difficult:

> The issue of the balance between security and civil liberties will be with us, in various guises, for a long time to come. The reality we face means that no resolution of such issues will be wholly satisfactory.[68]

Within the context of working in the information industry, ethical issues are not easy either. However, as you try to sort all this out over the course of your career, perhaps it will be useful to go back to where this chapter begins. The basic players remain the same. Remember that we have a finite amount of freedom and a finite amount of accountability. You can move it around, but you can't make more or less of either.

STUDY QUESTIONS

1. Which of the six ways of knowing truth listed in this chapter do you use in determining what is the right thing for you to do?
2. Why is access to information particularly valuable in a society like ours?
3. Why is privacy valuable in a society like ours?
4. Why should individuals be able to profit from their ideas?
5. Under what conditions should details about the information sought by library patrons be made available to others?
6. What does "fair use" have to do with copyrighted materials?
7. Do parents or the state know better how to protect children from harmful influences?
8. Why were the Harry Potter titles challenged as to whether they should be in schools and libraries?
9. Is filtering appropriate and effective to protect children using the Internet?
10. Is resolution of the "digital divide" important to our society?

Resources Section

ALA, "Core Values Task Force II Report" http://www.ala.org/ala/oif/statement spols/corevaluesstatement/corevalues.htm

Intellectual Freedom

ACLU. Freedom Network. http://www.aclu.org/FreeSpeech/FreeSpeechMain.cfm
ALA. Office for Intellectual Freedom. http://www.ala.org/template.cfm?Section=oif

American Library Association. "Intellectual Freedom." *Policy Manual 53.* http://www.ala.org/alaorg/policymanual/intellect.html

Asheim In Cyberspace. http://www.ala.org/Template.cfm?Section=IntellectualFreedombasics&Template=/ContentManagement/ContentDisplay.cfm&ContentID=49363

California Library Association. *Intellectual Freedom Manual* (1992, revised), http://online.sfsu.edu/~chrism/toc.html

Privacy

ACLU. Freedom Network. http://www.aclu.org/

ALA. Office for Intellectual Freedom. http://www.ala.org/alaorg/oif/

American Library Association. *Policy on Confidentiality of Library Records.* http://www.ala.org/alaorg/oif/pol_conf.html

Brin, David. "A Dangerous World: Transparency, Security and Privacy." http://www.davidbrin.com/privacyarticles.html#ts

cookiecentral.com. *Cookies and Privacy FAQ.* http://www.cookiecentral.com/content.phtml?area=4&id=10

Electronic Privacy Information Center. http://www.epic.org/

Foerstel, Herbert N. *Refuge of a Scoundrel: The Patriot Act in Libraries.* Westport, CT: Libraries Unlimited, 2004.

FTC. http://www.ftc.gov/

Regulating Internet Privacy. http://www.jbpub.com/cyberethics/five.cfm

Intellectual Property

Creative Commons. http://creativecommons.org/about/licenses/comics1.

Intellectual Property Issues. http://www.jbpub.com/cyberethics/four.cfm

U.S. Copyright Office. http://www.loc.gov/copyright/

U.S. Copyright Office. "Reproduction of Copyrighted Works by Educators and Librarians." *Circular 21,* http://www.copyright.gov/circs/circ21.pdf

Intellectual Property

Crews, Kenneth D. *Copyright Essentials for Librarians and Educators.* Chicago: American Library Association, 2000.

Delgado-Martinez Valette, Rebecca. *What Is Copyright Protection.* http://www.whatiscopyright.org

Stanford University Libraries. *Copyright & Fair Use.* http://fairuse.stanford.edu/

United States Copyright Office. http://www.loc.gov/copyright/

University of Texas System Administration Office of the General Counsel. *Copyright Management Center.* http://www.utsystem.edu/OGC/IntellectualProperty/cprtindx.htm

Digital Divide

Nauer, Kim. "The Information Revolution could create information haves and information have-nots." in Paul A. Winters, *The Information Revolution: Opposing Viewpoints.* San Diego, CA: Greenhaven Press, 1998, 131–39.

Steve Gibson. "The Information Revolution will not create information haves and information have-nots," in Paul A. Winters, *The Information Revolution: Opposing Viewpoints.* San Diego, CA: Greenhaven Press, 1998, 140–46.

"How Safe Is Your Public Library?" *http://www.afa.net/lif/howsafe.pdf*

AFA Online. http://www.afa.net

AFA Online. *Library Internet Filtering Resources* http://www.afa.net/lif/resources.asp

Young Adult Library Services Association (YALSA). "Social Networking and DOPA." http://www.leonline.com/yalsa/positive_uses.pdf

ALA. *Library Bill of Rights* and Its *Interpretations, http://www.ala.org/freedom/lbr.html*

AFA Online. http://www.ala.org/alaorg/oif/children.html

AFA Online. http://www.ala.org/washoff/patriot.html

ALA, "Digital Divide: Scope." http://www.ala.org/ala/ourassociation/governingdocs/aheadto2010/digitaldivide.htm

NOTES

1. John J. Heldrich Center for Workforce Development and Center for Survey Research and Analysis, *Work Trends: Americans' Attitudes About Work, Employers and Government: Making the Grade? What American Workers Think Should Be Done to Improve Education* (Rutgers University, June 14, 2000), 2.

2. Roughly paraphrased from a class lecture by Gregory D. Pritchard, Philosophy 101, Oklahoma Baptist University, 1962.

3. Richard A. Spinello. *Cyberethics: Morality and Law in Cyberspace. Third Edition* (Sudbury, MA: Jones and Bartlett, 2006), 2–7.

4. *Code of Ethics of the American Library Association,* adopted by the ALA Council, June 28, 1995; amended January 22, 2008.

5. "The Core Rules Of Netiquette," excerpted from *Netiquette* by Virginia Shea, http://www.albion.com/netiquette/corerules.html.

6. For a more complex model of stakeholders, consult Richard Spinello's *Cyberethics: Morality and Law in Cyberspace*, p. 33.

7. Emile Chartier, alias Alain.

8. "Freedom of Expression," excerpted from the American Civil Liberties Union (2005), http://www.aclu.org/freespeech/gen/21179pub20051031.html.

9. Ibid.

10. "Intellectual Freedom and Censorship Q & A," (American Library Association, 2000), http://www.ala.org/ala/aboutala/offices/oif/basics/ifcensorshipqanda.pdf (accessed July 4, 2009)

11. California Library Association, "Why Intellectual Freedom?" *Intellectual Freedom Manual,* http://online.sfsu.edu/~chrism/ifm1.html.

12. Lester Asheim, "Not Censorship but Selection," *Wilson Library Bulletin* 28 (September 1953): 63–67.

13. Joseph S. Fulda, "A Loss of Privacy Harms Society," *Opposing Viewpoints: Civil Liberties,* Tamara L. Roleff, Ed. Opposing Viewpoints Series (Greenhaven Press: 1999).

14. Justice Louis Brandeis, *Olmstead v. U.S.* (1928).

15. *U.S. Constitution,* Amendment IV, The Bill of Rights (1791).

16. FTC Web site, www.FTC.gov/privacy/ (accessed 6/30/2009).

17. Ibid.

18. David Brin, *The Transparent Society: Will Technology Force Us to Choose Between Privacy and Freedom?* (New York: Perseus, 1998).

19. *Snoops in the Stacks,* http://www.drewhendricks.freeservers.com/library.htm

20. *EFF Analysis Of The Provisions Of The USA PATRIOT Act That Relate To Online Activities* (Oct 31, 2001), http://www.eff.org/Censorship/Terrorism_militias/20011031_eff_usa_patriot_analysis.htm

21. Herbert N. Foerstel, *Refuge of a Scoundrel: The Patriot Act in Libraries* (Westport, CT: Libraries Unlimited, 2004).

22. "Bush won't reauthorize eavesdropping," http://news.yahoo.com/s/nm/20070117/ts_nm/surveillance_bush_dc_3 (accessed June 9, 2009).

23. U.S. Federal Trade Commission, *FTC Consumer Alert: Tips for Protecting Your Personal Information,* http://www.ftc.gov/bcp/conline/pubs/alerts/privtipsalrt.pdf

24. ALA, *The Freedom to Read Statement* (2000), http://www.ala.org/alaorg/oif/freeread.html

25. ALA, *Policy on Confidentiality of Library Records* (1986). http://www.ala.org/alaorg/oif/pol_conf.html

26. Ibid.

27. *California Code,* Section 6267.

28. David Brin, *The Transparent Society: Will Technology Force Us to Choose Between Privacy and Freedom?* (Perseus, 1998).

29. Bryan A. Garner, ed., *Black's Law Dictionary,* 7th ed. (St. Paul, MN: West Group, 1999), 813.

30. J. A. Simpson and E.S.C. Weiner, *The Oxford English Dictionary* Vol. VIII, 2d ed. (Oxford: Clarendon, 1989), 1068.

31. Two very useful sites for finding out more about copyright basics are http://fairuse.stanford.edu/ and http://www.utsystem.edu/OGC/IntellectualProperty/cprtindx.htm

32. Stella Keenan, *Concise Dictionary of Library and Information Science* (London: Saur, 1996), 173.

33. Rebecca Delgado-Martinez Valette, *What Is Copyright Protection,* http://www.whatiscopyright.org

34. Federal law describes what these signs must say and even that they must say it in font that is at least 18 points: "NOTICE WARNING CONCERNING COPYRIGHT RESTRICTIONS The copyright law of the United States (Title 17, United States Code) governs the making of photocopies or other reproductions of copyrighted material. Under certain conditions specified in the law, libraries and archives are authorized to furnish a photocopy or other reproduction. One of these specified conditions is that the photocopy or reproduction is not to be "used for any purpose other than private study, scholarship, or research." If a user makes a request for, or later uses, a photocopy or reproduction for purposes in excess of "fair use," that user may be liable for copyright infringement. This institution reserves the right to refuse to accept a copying order if, in its judgment, fulfillment of the order would involve violation of copyright law."

35. The University of Texas maintains a very helpful tutorial on copyright and fair use for those who want to understand how to apply these concepts in more detail: http://www.utsystem.edu/OGC/IntellectualProperty/cprtindx.htm

36. Mary Minnow, Info People Workshop Handout, April, 2002.

37. U.S. Copyright Office, "Fair Use" (November 8, 2002), http://www.copyright.gov/fls/fairuse.html

38. "Congress Eases Copyright Restrictions on Distance Education," *Chronicle of Higher Education,* October 18, 2002.

39. U.S. Copyright Office, *Reproduction of Copyrighted Works by Educators and Librarians,* Circular 21.

40. Ibid.

41. Ibid.

42. ALA, *Free Access to Libraries for Minors: An Interpretation of the Library Bill of Rights*, adopted June 30, 1972, amended July 1, 1981; July 3, 1991, by the ALA Council. http://www.ala.org/Template.cfm?Section=interpretations&Template=/ContentManagement/ContentDisplay.cfm&ContentID=8639 (accessed July 10, 2007).

43. Ibid.

44. http://www.ala.org/ala/oif/bannedbooksweek/challengedbanned/challengedbanned.htm#mfcb (accessed July 25, 2007).

45. CBS News, *Children, Sex & The Web*, June 10, 2000.

46. Ibid.

47. Center for Democracy & Technology, Amicus Brief Child Online Protection Act (COPA), January 11, 1999, http://www.cdt.org/speech/copa/990111amicus.html (accessed August 3, 2000).

48. ALA News Release, "New survey shows 95 percent of public libraries have policies to manage the Internet," July 2000, http://www.ala.org/news/v5n25/internetsurvey.html (accessed August 5, 2000).

49. Center for Democracy and Technology, http://www.cdt.org/speech/cda/ (accessed August 4, 2000).

50. Thomas J. DeLoughry and Jeffrey R. Young, "Federal Judges Rule Internet Restrictions Unconstitutional: In striking down law that many said violated academic freedom, the jurists call for "the highest protection" for the Internet," *The Chronicle of Higher Education*, June 21, 1996, http://chronicle.com (accessed August 4, 2000).

51. Steven McDonald, "Point of View: The Laws of Cyberspace: What Colleges Need to Know," *The Chronicle of Higher Education*, October 31, 1997, http://chronicle.com/ (accessed August 4, 2000).

52. Center for Democracy and Technology, http://www.cdt.org/speech/cda/ (accessed June 30, 2009).

53. Ibid.

54. Ibid.

55. Thomas E. Cavanagh and Christy Eidson,"The Digital Divide in PC Use." *Across the Board*, 37, no.4 (2000), p. 55.

56. Ekaterina O. Walsh, "The Truth About the Digital Divide, *The Forrester Brief*, (April 11, 2000).

57. Ibid.

58. ALA, Office for Information Technology Policy, "Digital Divide," http://www.ala.org/oitp/digitaldivide/index.html

59. Walsh.

60. Gina Holland, "Supreme Court to tackle Internet-library surfing," Associated Press wire service, November, 13, 2002.

61. "*CIPA* Questions and Answers," July 16, 2003, http://www.ala.org/ala/washoff/WOissues/civilliberties/cipaweb/adviceresources/CIPAQA.pdf

62. Wikipedia, "Deleting Online Predators Act of 2006," http://en.wikipedia.org/wiki/Deleting_Online_Predators_Act_of_2006 (accessed July 23, 2009).

63. Patrizia Dilucchio, "Dr. Laura targets the new Sodom: Libraries," http://www.salon.com/tech/feature/1999/05/27/dr_laura/

64. *United States et al. v. Playboy Entertainment Group.*

65. ALA, "Free Access to Libraries for Minors: An Interpretation of the Library Bill of Rights," http://www.ala.org/alaorg/oif/free_min.html (accessed July 3, 1991).

66. David R. Dowell, review of Foerstel, Herbert N. *Refuge of a Scoundrel: The Patriot Act in Libraries* (Westport, Conn.: Libraries Unlimited, 2004) in *College and*

Research Libraries Vol. 65, No. 5 (September 2004), http://www.ala.org/ala/acrl/acrlpubs/crljournal/crl2004/crlseptember/foerstelreview.htm.

67. Richard A. Clark, *Against All Enemies: Inside America's War on Terror* (Free Press, 2004).

68. Robert Bork, "Having Their Day in (a Military) Court," *National Review,* December 17, 2001.

Chapter 9

Job Search: Basics

The array of professional knowledge and skills you possess are of no value to you or anyone else unless you can find an appropriate setting in which to put them to use. Generally, this will be within an organization. Finding the appropriate setting requires a well-planned and carefully executed job search strategy.

GETTING READY FOR THE JOB SEARCH

According to news reports and personnel experts, current American workplace trends include fundamental change, outsourcing of staff, increased dependence on technology, and changing demographics as the workforce ages and results in shrinking supplies of qualified workers in many fields.

As a backdrop to these identified trends, workers can expect multiple job changes throughout their careers and a resulting need for the continual updating of their skills. The days of working solely for one employer until retirement are as *passé* as chunky computer screens.

These general workplace trends are true in the library and information center sector as well. Whether you are a new graduate or a seasoned professional, you should keep your job-hunting skills honed; you will most likely put them to use several times during the course of your working life.

Early 21st-Century Library and Information Center Job Markets

The field has entered a very dynamic period, such that the librarian or library technician of today can only speculate on how the profession will continue to change with future technological innovations. For those uncomfortable with continual change, this pattern may cause dissatisfaction or a departure from the field.

According to the U.S. Department of Labor's *Occupational Outlook Handbook for 2006/07* (see figure 9.1), the job outlook for the field overall is mixed,

Figure 9.1. Both in print format and on the Web, the annual *Occupational Outlook Handbook* is a useful tool for those seeking an overview of the job outlook in libraries and information centers, as well as other related fields.

with slower-than-average job growth predicted for librarian-level positions in traditional environments, but with employment growth in related occupations with a strong emphasis on computer and organizational skills, such as private corporations, consulting firms, and information brokers. However, another dynamic in the field is that a large number of librarians are expected to retire in the next 10 years, while the number entering the profession has been declining; the end result is that job opportunities overall should be quite good for librarians.[1]

For library technicians, according to the *Occupational Outlook Handbook*, jobs are expected to grow as fast as the average for all occupations through the year 2014. The increasing use of library automation may be one of the factors to spur job growth among library technicians. Here again, special libraries present the largest potential employment growth for library technician-level openings.[2]

Regardless of the level of employment, technological competency is mandatory for entering the library and information field, and, once employed, workers can expect the demand for ongoing learning and upgrading of skills in this
area to continue.

Who Am I, Professionally Speaking?

Before embarking on a job search or compiling a resume, serious job hunters need to spend time thoughtfully taking stock of their own skill sets and
considering what an ideal job situation would be. This self-assessment may
well be the hardest part of the job search process, even though filling out
multiple-page application forms with tiny lines and too-small spaces is always
onerous.

Before beginning your search, consider the following logistical issues:

Do you have a preference for working in a particular type or size of library
or information center?

Are you willing to relocate? If not, what are your geographical limitations?

Are you seeking part-time or full-time employment?

Are you able and willing to work out of your home or to telecommute? Do
you have the discipline needed to work independently?

Do you prefer traditional office hours? Are you willing to work evenings,
weekends, or variable hours?

Are you an entrepreneur? Would you enjoy starting your own business?

Are several steps needed to reach your ultimate career goal?

Your Skill Set

Try to enumerate your unique set of skills. For what are they best suited?
Designing and maintaining Web pages? Teaching? Instructing and working
with elementary school children? Some of each? Is a lot of public interaction
appealing to you or a turnoff? For guidance in taking stock of your skills and interests, browse the current print edition of the perennial favorite, Richard
Bolles's *What Color Is Your Parachute: A Practical Manual for Job-Hunters and
Career-Changers.*

Recommended sources for stretching your mind as to the varieties of employment within the library and information business are *Straight from the
Stacks: A First-Hand Guide to Careers in Library and Information Science,* by
Laura Townsend Kane, and *A Day in the Life: Career Options in Library and
Information Science,* edited by Priscilla K. Shontz and Richard A. Murray. Traditional and non-traditional careers paths are featured here in short chapters written by real people who are employed in public, school, academic,
and special libraries and in careers outside of the familiar such as working
for outsourcing companies, vendors, or publishers, serving as independent

consultants, and technical writing and teaching. (See the resources section below for complete citations).

The Other Side of the Job Market

Filling a vacant or newly created position is very costly both in time and money. Employers do not take this lightly. Too often job seekers focus almost exclusively on their own needs and give short shrift to the point of view of the employer. Making an effort to understand and respond to the reasons employers seek to fill positions may provide the job seeker with some competitive insight.

Even though most library employers are caring individuals, they do not make hiring decisions based on whether you are behind on your rent, your daughter needs $3,500 worth of orthodontic work next year, or you need just six more quarters to qualify for full Social Security benefits. Although these may be powerful motivators for you, these are not convincing reasons, in and of themselves, for an employer to hire you. In fact, sharing these needs too early in the employment process may prove to be counterproductive.

A more productive job-seeking strategy is to look at the situation from the perspective of potential employers. Why are they looking for new employees? Do they need to add new knowledge and skills not currently present in their organization? Do they need additional people with the same skills as existing staff? How much of the needed knowledge and skills can the employer afford for you to learn on the job? Which must be present in the new staff member on day one? Is the employer attempting to maintain current operations or to go in new directions?

Some investigation will help you be realistic about how you match up with the needs of the employer. This is an opportunity to demonstrate your research skills and to involve your network of friends in assisting you to achieve your goal. In addition, most employers will appreciate the thoughtful initiative and analytical ability that you demonstrate by exploring their situation in advance.

First, collect all the public data, such as the position posting or advertisement, information about the library agency, and data about employment conditions and benefits with the organization of which the library is a part. Next, contact your network of friends and colleagues who might know something about the position and the library. After you have absorbed this information, you may want to contact the immediate supervisor directly, either by telephone or e-mail. Do this with care. Some supervisors may be reluctant to have contact with applicants outside the formal selection process. Others will welcome the opportunity to do some recruiting. Remember that the impression you make will carry over to the formal selection process. Nothing is off the record. Therefore, call with a specific purpose—ask some questions that, when answered, will affect whether you apply or how you target your formal application. Do not call just to chat or to shoot the breeze. The underlying purpose is to establish the foundation of a business relationship.

Once you have a good idea of what expectations the employer has for the prospective employee, you will have a more realistic view of your suitability for the position. If it appears that you match up well with the expectations for the position, you will have a good starting point for how best to present yourself as the candidate who can solve the problem that led to the current recruitment.

Carefully analyze the posting. Is it specific to an individual position, or is it for a class of jobs? Stated another way, is this an application process to fill a specific opening or is it merely to establish eligibility to be placed on a list (possibly in order of priority) for any hiring decisions made during the next six months or the next year? Or is it a recruitment to identify a candidate pool for possible future assignments as they become available; this last scenario is most common in academic teaching settings.

The Competition

As you start to enter the next step in your marketing plan, you need to focus on another element in the employment process—the competition. Your competitors are not potential employers. Rather, they are other potential employees who look, walk, and talk a lot like you. When you write your cover letter to introduce yourself as the solution to an employer's problem, you need to think about who your competition is likely to be for this specific job. It's not good enough to simply be qualified for the job. You must appear better qualified than the other qualified candidates. Of all the people who may apply for the job and meet the minimum qualifications, why should employers think that you are a better solution to their problem than any of the other candidates? Is your education more relevant? Have you demonstrated better skills? If so, which ones? Do you have more applicable experience? Find at least one area where you should have an advantage over most other applicants for the job and start building a convincing application package to sell to potential employers.

Internships and Volunteer Experience

If related work experience is not one of your most competitive job assets, you may want to consider the benefits of an internship or volunteer stint before completing your formal educational program or as you prepare to embark on a job search. An internship can offer a valuable sneak preview into the world of work. As an intern in a library or information center, you can sample various working environments, network with library personnel in your geographical region, and gain valuable hands-on experience. Interning in the field can be quite eye-opening and can provide a very different learning experience than the traditional classroom venue. A successful internship can also serve as an important source for job referrals and letters of recommendation in the future. Remember that each experience should be a building block to your ultimate career objective. It should be taken seriously so that you not only learn all you can, but also leave behind an advocate who will want to help you succeed in future steps down your chosen career path.

Internships typically come in two forms: (1) paid internships, and (2) practicums. Paid internships are when a business or government agency has set aside funds to hire students for summer or other short-term periods as a learning experience. Often, these are not widely advertised, and the hiring agencies may rely on word of mouth to recruit candidates. Professors, counselors, and job placement personnel are good sources to contact about potential paid internships. Querying library-related listservs can also be productive.

Unpaid internships or practicums are set up as academic courses with enrolled students earning college credit for their field hours. Practicums are frequent and valuable components in both community college level library/ media technician programs and in graduate library and information school curricula. Many programs require them. Others will be willing to try to set up such opportunities.

In the event that no formal internship opportunities are available, serving as a volunteer staffer in a library or information center can provide some beneficial work experience for the novice, student, or re-entry worker. Many public library agencies and academic facilities have ongoing placement of volunteers. Begin by discussing your career goals and educational background with the department head or branch librarian where you would like to volunteer to explore what opportunities might best serve their needs and yours. As with an employer filling a paid staff position, the internship site will be looking for a volunteer who can dig in and provide help where needed within their organization; don't make the mistake of thinking that an internship opportunity exists solely to fit your interests or needs. Flexibility and being open to learning new things are very attractive qualities in an intern. Successfully completed internships and volunteer situations can provide relevant experience to place on resumes when entering a field or changing careers.

THE JOB HUNT

Job openings are advertised in a variety of media: newspapers, Web sites, hotlines, and industry newsletters, as well as informally through word of mouth. Subscribing via e-mail to listservs that focus on your special area of employment interest—for example, law libraries, business information centers, or school media centers—is one way to find out about openings nationwide and beyond. Traditional job classified ads are published in local and regional newspapers, both online and in print.

Agencies such as city and county public libraries, universities, colleges, museums, and private companies often post their openings on their organization's Web site, as well as recruit through flyers, newspapers, listservs, mailing lists, and so on. Resume submission via e-mail is becoming commonplace in high-tech private industries and may be an option for public sector agencies.

Trade publications such as *Library Journal, School Library Journal, American Libraries, Chronicle of Higher Education,* and many others carry regular job announcements in their print editions as well as posting them on their Web sites.

Librarian positions tend to be advertised over a wider area than do library technician positions. It is generally assumed that paraprofessionals must be recruited from within the local commuting area, but that librarians may be willing to relocate for the right job. Whether or not these presumptions are correct, most employers will formulate their recruiting efforts on this basis. Therefore, paraprofessionals who are willing to relocate may have to exercise greater initiative to locate job listings than do librarians.

For example, library technicians may need to subscribe to a local newspaper in an area they want to relocate to, or have a friend there carefully watch the job ads to become aware of appropriate openings. The advent of the Internet has created another avenue for locating jobs that are not advertised beyond the local area—that of browsing through the classified ads of newspaper Web sites in targeted cities.

Proactive Job Searching

Scanning the classified ads in any medium is one approach, but creative and energetic job searchers will also want to target and directly approach agencies for whom they are interested in working. Tools such as the annual *American Library Directory* are indispensable for locating major library agencies in a given geographical area and gleaning some very basic information about their collections, budgets, staffing, and so forth. Most state libraries also produce a directory of library agencies within their borders. However, neither of these tools will include all of the smaller, private companies or agencies with internal information centers or libraries.

Visiting the Web sites of library agencies is a fresh means of learning about the organizations and how they present themselves to their clientele and the world at large. For agencies open to the public, there is still nothing like an in-person visit to observe, explore, and get a feel for services, staffing, and facilities. In addition, many part-time or temporary positions are not formally advertised and may be discovered only through an onsite visit or inquiry.

Any prospective library or information industry employee should be well equipped with the research skills needed to locate background information on a potential employer. This situation provides a test case for putting your reference skills to work by searching company or agency profiles, statistics, news coverage, press releases, floor plans, or mission statements to help yourself in your job search.

Outsourcing

Although many first-time employees tend to seek full-time, traditional positions as staff in library agencies, private industry, government information centers, and schools, jobs with outsourcing firms are also an area of growth in the field.

What is outsourcing? Basically, it is supplementing an in-house workforce by hiring outside contractors from the private sector. Outsourcing may mean hiring a freelance consultant, turning to a temporary employment agency for staffing needs, or going out to bid to contract with a private company that will perform certain specified services. Historically, libraries have used automation, architecture, public relations, and management consultants, and have contracted out services such as book approval plans and cataloging.

Contracting out library services has gone on quietly since at least the 1960s, especially in military and government libraries. In the last decade, several small city library systems or public library agencies, especially those with fiscal shortages, have contracted with private firms to staff, manage, and operate their entire library systems. On a much smaller scale, libraries of all types regularly turn to outside sources for short-term employee needs, consulting, or special skills. Some commonplace examples of outsourcing include operating special libraries, such as those on military bases, providing manpower to relocate a collection to a new facility, or hiring a consultant to prepare a specialized report.

In terms of employment options, outsourcing translates into diverse opportunities for entrepreneurs. Freelance librarians and library technicians, information brokers, consultants, Web masters, Web page designers, and others may serve as independent contractors to library agencies, private industry, or consumers. Typically, they work independently, supply their own work space and equipment, and are paid per hour or per project. The U.S. Bureau of Labor estimates that in total there were 10.3 million freelance workers in the United States as of 2005.[3]

Although there are no definite figures available for the library and information field, outsourcing trends and the growing reliance on telecommuting indicate continued opportunities here. Temporary employees, on the other hand, may be hired by the library through a personnel agency that specializes in supplying trained staff for short-term or temporary needs—such as the startup of a new branch library, a move to new quarters, a collection inventory, or weekend staffing.

The Appeal of Outsourcing

Outsourcing appeals to a library because it means a cost savings on fringe benefits for personnel; it allows a company or library to meet a sudden or unusual demand; it provides flexibility in staffing; and it allows permanent staff to focus on interactions with patrons or other customized services that do not lend themselves well to outsourcing.

What does outsourcing offer to the employee? For those who prefer flexible or part-time hours, a variety of changing work venues, or a steady stream of new challenges, outsourcing may be the answer. It can also be an effective way to sample or preview the field when considering a career change or shifting to a different focus within the profession. For those with lifestyle needs such as retirement or parenthood, outsourcing can be an attractive option.

Conferences

Whether searching for outsourcing opportunities or for a permanent job with a library or information center, attending conferences is another key means of networking and data gathering in your job search.

State and national library industry trade associations (e.g., Council of Library Media Technicians, Medical Library Association, Special Library Association, American Society for Information Science, American Library Association) typically have free job information centers or placement services as part of their annual conventions, where employers may conduct on site interviews or staff a recruitment booth

While job-hunting, consider attending such a conference in your state or region to tap this service as well as to sit in on presentations and hear the current issues under discussion by practitioners. One of the biggest reasons for attending trade conferences for workers at all levels is the networking value in making new professional contacts.

Most of these same associations maintain Web sites with information on current job openings. See the resources section below for some examples.

JOB SEARCH TOOLS

There are three standard documents that typically comprise the job application packet: (1) the resume, (2) a cover letter, and (3) the application form. Each is different in format and in the data they convey about an applicant; effectively done, each one should complement the other.

Resume

The resume is a canvas upon which you paint a portrait of those demonstrated skills and knowledge you are offering to employers. Each brush stroke (i.e., word) should be added for a purpose—to convey to employers a particular message about how you will be able to solve their problems after you are employed. Keep it focused on what they want to know, not what you want to brag about.

In general, your resume should not be changed every time you apply for a job. It should represent you. However, if you are applying for very different positions (e.g., a job in a public library or a position in a university archives), you may want to consider tailoring various versions of your resume.

Data Sheet, Curriculum Vitae, or Resume?

In this chapter, the term *resume* is used in its broadest connotation. As Goldilocks had a choice of three sizes of bear, there are actually three different resumes that vary in length: (1) the data sheet, (2) the curriculum vitae, and (3) the resume. The data sheet is a bare bones outline with no embellishments. It usually comprises less than a page and gives little flavor for you and your style. An example of information on a data sheet would be "A.S., Library / Information Technology, Cuesta College, 2007." Because your purpose in creating a resume is to communicate your attributes in a way that makes you stand out from your competitors in the job market, the data sheet, as Goldilocks would say, is not nearly long enough to accomplish your purpose.

At the other extreme, the curriculum vitae is too much information for most library positions. On the other hand, if you are applying for a librarian position in a university, many colleges, and some private research organizations, this is exactly what is expected to be competitive. You should list professional papers you have presented, articles you have published, committees you have served on, and funded or in-progress research you have conducted. The vitae cannot be too lengthy if each item is legitimately professional and verifiable. However, if the job does not fall into the above categories, such activities—no matter how relevant in your mind—should be summarized or limited to only the most recent. An overly lengthy resume outside of the academic or research environment could actually work against you. You may be viewed as not genuinely committed to libraries outside the academic or research sector or too "nerdy" to relate to the clientele at hand.

For most positions, the true resume or summary is the appropriate model to follow. In using the resume, unless you have considerable professional experience—generally, more than 5 or 10 years—you should keep this summary to one page. As mentioned previously, this is the place to describe yourself in terms that will encourage employers to see you as a solution to their vacancy.

To Include or Not to Include Information

When crafting your resume, the real question you should address is what knowledge and skills you are trying to market at this point in your career. You may possess knowledge and skills that you do not want to pursue at this stage in your life. Focus your attention on where you want to go, rather than where you have been. For example, if you are going through a career change, too much emphasis on the field you are leaving may give the impression that you are not truly committed to your new chosen field. However, many skills are transferable.

Several years ago, one of the authors was asked by a mutual friend to counsel a neophyte to the library field who was having a crisis of confidence as she tried to launch her new career. As she told the story, a family emergency had forced her out of the employment market just as she had completed her library degree. A year and a half later, she was sure employers would doubt her level of commitment and wonder whether she had been in jail or homeless during the gap in her resume.

Further conversation revealed that her father-in-law died just before she graduated. He had been running a large dairy farm in Wisconsin. She and her husband had put their careers on hold and moved to the farm so they could manage a liquidation of the property and its assets. It took 18 months to sell the farm, its equipment, and its herd at a time when the market was advantageous and also to resettle her mother-in-law into a new home. During this period, her husband ran the dairy side of the operation and she handled the business side, including keeping all of the records. Hundreds of thousands of dollars were involved. Can you think of any knowledge and skills this applicant demonstrated that would be useful in a library setting? After thinking the situation through, she decided that she had demonstrated many useful and marketable skills during her stint as the business manager of a family enterprise during its orderly liquidation.

As you progress through your vocational self-analysis, you will be ready to start drafting a resume. The purpose of the resume is to sketch an honest picture of the person you are trying to market. Every phrase in the resume should be another brush stroke portraying the professional knowledge and skills you want to apply in your new job. Facts about you that do not add to this persona—however proud of them you are—have no place in the resume; many resume writers forget this important rule of thumb and, as a result, end up with a muddled, unfocused resume. At the same time, some of the images you paint can be subtle. For example, one of the qualities employers need on the job is the ability to work as a member of a team. If possible, you should list something on your resume that indicates that you have demonstrated teamwork in the workplace. However, if you have not yet had an opportunity to document this in a job setting, perhaps success in community organizations, sports teams, or student clubs will suffice. This is but one example of the myriad of small impressions that can be conveyed with a well-constructed resume.

Common attributes that employers look for are listed at the end of this chapter. The checklist can serve as a tool to evaluate whether you have included something in your resume to spark the interest of a potential boss about the kinds of skills you are prepared to bring to their organization.

Resume Formatting

Books on resume preparation provide differing advice about the sequence of the sections of your resume. Sometimes it makes sense to decide on the particular area in which you are likely to have an advantage over your competitors for the position. Again, the point is not to prove that you are qualified for the position. Several others may also be qualified. Your goal is to show that you are the *most* qualified person for the job. Ask yourself, are you likely to have more work experience than your fellow job applicants? If so, then your job history should be the lead item in your resume. If your advantage is education, that section should come first. If your expertise is computer skills or a foreign language, make sure these are prominently displayed. Arrange your resume so that employers can look it over and quickly zero in on whatever item interests them most.

A good resume should showcase your skills, education, and relevant work experience and echo the qualifications spelled out in the job advertisement. Regardless of the method you choose for compiling a resume or the finished format, experts recommend starting the process by compiling a personal data list. You will need to gather the pertinent facts and dates about your prior job history, education, and training before you can start organizing these data into a selling tool.

Computer screening of resumes is becoming more popular, especially in the high-tech industry. A resume is electronically submitted by the candidate, then searched for the number and occurrence of key vocabulary and phrases relevant to the employer's job description. Based on the ranking from this keyword analysis, a candidate may or may not warrant an interview.

Many Web sites, software, and books exist to help you format or lay out your resume. Some of the best have hundreds of samples to illustrate good and bad resumes. Your college career center or local public library is likely to stock many titles. We have provided addresses of several helpful Web sites and recommended titles in the resources section at the end of this chapter. In addition, here are some basic tips that apply to all resumes:

- Check spelling in the document and show it to at least one other person before sending it out. Neatness and spelling should be impeccable.
- Never submit a typed or handwritten resume; use a word processor.

- Choose a standard business font, not an artsy or hard-to-read typeface.
- Clearly present contact information (i.e., home, work, cellular, or fax telephone numbers; e-mail address).
- Leave out personal information about hobbies, age, marital status, health, and religion.
- Use action words and phrases throughout the resume.
- Ask a professional in the field to review it and make comments on your draft.

Cover Letter

A cover letter with your resume provides an opportunity to highlight in narrative form the most important items from your application and resume. It also serves as a sample of your written communication skills and lets you demonstrate that you know something about the agency or company. The purpose is to make a connection between the job opening and the person described in the resume. The letter should be brief—normally less than one page. Your intent should be to guide a reader through the cover letter as quickly as possible and urge him or her to be eager to read your resume to learn more about you.

The opening sentence should indicate very clearly for which job you are applying. Remember that the first person to read it will most likely be a human resources clerk. That person may not care about your wonderful qualifications, but you do want the clerk to place your application packet into the correct file. Organizations often recruit simultaneously for many positions. In addition, such offices receive a high volume of mail every day.

Your next task is to demonstrate to the personnel who screen applications that you have thoughtfully and thoroughly read their job posting. Veteran library personnel officers often get cover letters that appear to have been sent to them by mistake or to have been recycled from a very different job search without modification. Be enthusiastic, but remain professional. One of the authors received, over the course of a year and a half, two separate applications from the same person for two very different jobs. Each letter claimed that the advertised vacancy was exactly the one for which the applicant had patterned all of his education and years of experience. If you are inclined to such hyperbole, be careful not to send it to the same employer twice.

Next, show that you have carefully analyzed your skills. Use a few key phrases from the actual posting as you highlight a couple of the most important areas in which you meet or exceed the requirements. Suggest that, as employers read the enclosed resume, they will see additional areas in which your knowledge and skills are appropriate to meet their needs.

Close by stating your eagerness (within reason) to discuss further with them how you are prepared to solve the problem that led them to post the opening, and, as a result, support their efforts to provide quality services to their customers. Keep the entire letter to a single page.

Application Form

These are tools used to screen applicants and to narrow the pool to those who merit an interview. Especially for civil service-type jobs, such as public libraries, schools districts, and public colleges and universities, be sure to follow application instructions *precisely.* If you omit some information or a required part of the packet, this alone can disqualify you, regardless of how wonderful your skills are.

Often, application forms are generic, gathering the most basic employment history and background information from applicants at all levels within an organization. This is where the importance of a resume as a personalized statement comes into play.

In summary, the purpose of the cover letter is to stimulate the reader to carefully examine your resume. The purpose of the resume is to procure an interview. It is the primary tool of the job search, and you should expect to work through several drafts before arriving at a finished product.

Electronic submission of completed application forms or application packets has become fairly commonplace as an option for many public sector agencies (city or county libraries; colleges and universities, etc.) Here again, follow specific formatting and submission instructions very carefully.

References and Letters of Recommendation

Most application forms request a list of employment-related references. That is, names and contact information of people who can vouch for your work experience, job performance, education, or all three. As a courtesy to your reference person and as a safeguard for yourself, always ask first before listing someone as a job reference. Be sure that your reference person is comfortable about giving you a positive endorsement. If asking for a letter of recommendation, allow adequate lead time for its preparation. (Contacting a potential reference for a letter the night before the application deadline is not a smart idea.) Although not always required, an appropriate, well-written letter of recommendation from a former employer, an intern supervisor, or an instructor can be another asset in your application packet. Refrain from listing reference contacts on your resume—a resume is not the appropriate place for such information.

INTERVIEWING SKILLS

Once selected for an interview, the wise candidate takes time to prepare. Be aware that you are likely to be involved in a group interview where several staff members will ask you questions in turn. The crux of the interview is to persuade the panel or group that you are the best person for the job in question. You can affect this persuasion in several ways: using your appearance, demeanor, presentation, and interpersonal skills, and crafting thoughtful responses to the questions posed. From the panel's perspective, there is much more going on than just hearing a right or wrong answer. This is a chance for them to evaluate how you think on your feet, your personality, your job philosophy, and your technical knowledge. This holds true whether you are interviewing for a civil service list, with a private sector employer, or with an outsourcing agency.

There are many books, videos, and Web sites available on interviewing skills. A few resources are listed in the resources section; public libraries, college career centers, local bookstores, and online booksellers should carry many titles on this topic. Although every job interview is different, there are some standard questions that a candidate can expect, and, thus can prepare thoughtful, appropriate answers. Some typical interview questions include the following:

- Describe your qualifications for this job.
- Why are you interested in this position?
- Why do you want to work for our company/organization?
- Describe your strengths.
- Describe your weaknesses.
- What are your career goals; where do you see yourself in five years?
- How would you deal with the following situation? (Usually a scenario where you need to solve a problem, assist customers, enforce a policy, demonstrate sensitivity to patrons or staff, and so on.)
- What accomplishment in your work life are you the most proud of and why?
- Describe a difficult situation and how you handled it.
- You may be asked questions to test your knowledge of library technology, information science, Internet skills, recognition of key author names, and so on.
- You may also be expected to perform computer skills demonstrations and answer questions to determine your proficiency with various software programs, library-specific systems and products, and Internet use, among others.

Although many interviews will be structured in such a way as to make this impossible, the book *The Five Minute Interview* outlines a method for beginning an interview in a positive way. The strategy is for the candidate to ask the first significant question. That question would be worded something like: "It would help me to focus my responses to your questions if you could take just a minute and share with me your key expectations for the successful candidate." Don't try to force this question if the opening is not there. It can be asked at the end of the interview. However, the earlier it is asked and answered, the more advantageous the information will be.[4]

Do take advantage of any final opportunity to pose questions to your interviewers. Come prepared with a list of questions about the job, the library, and the parent organization. Also, be prepared to sum up your key qualifications, reaffirming your enthusiasm for and interest in the position. This is your last chance to make an impression on the interviewers and is all too often overlooked by applicants in their eagerness to conclude the session.

If you think you need practice with interviews, consider applying for a job opening or two that you may be only slightly interested in, just to experience the application process and the interview session. Such practice will provide you exposure to the process and can serve as a dry run for future interview situations.

Questions about a candidate's personal life, sexual orientation, ethnicity, age, health, religion, and so on, are all examples of illegal interview questions. Be tactful in your responses; try to steer the conversation to another topic. If you are asked inappropriate or suspect questions, report them to the personnel analyst or board after your interview.

If you are not the chosen candidate, you may want to call the human services or personnel department and ask for feedback on your interview performance. Constructive comments noted by the panel may help you improve in your next interview. At the same time, be understanding if local policy does not allow them to provide this information to you.

The following lists include interview tips that can help you accomplish a successful interview:

Interview dos:

Dress professionally. This may vary from organization to organization. As a rule of thumb, you should dress a half step more conservatively than you would if you were already working in the job.

Be on time (or early) for the interview. Aside from the rudeness of being late, the interview committee may be on a tight schedule and may not have the opportunity to make up the time. Also, arrive early enough to allow a visit to the restroom for any last minute grooming needs.

Answer questions concisely, using specific illustrations or examples to make your point.

If asked a complex or multipart question, attempt to answer it. Do not hesitate to look straight at the person who posed the question and inquire as to whether you covered all parts of it.

Be attentive and polite.

Be confident.

Interview don'ts

Don't drink too much caffeine prior to the interview. Your natural adrenaline flow will be sufficient stimulation.

Don't ramble on. Answer each question efficiently and move on.

Don't make negative comments about yourself or any former employers.

Don't focus on any health or personal problems you may have.

Don't chew gum.

Don't wear overly strong cologne or aftershave.

Don't initiate a conversation about salary at this point.

For further consideration, realize that potential employers have a problem finding staff members who:

can learn quickly;

can organize work and time;

can set priorities and focus on what is important;

can analyze complicated problems;

can generate several potential solutions;

can concentrate on complex details;

can interact well with all kinds of people and meet the public well;

can perform their jobs in a manner that makes it easier for co-workers, superiors, and subordinates to do their own jobs well;

can follow through on long, complex procedures;

can think linearly;

can write well;

can work independently;

can see the big picture;

can balance many activities simultaneously;

can teach others, train others, or both;

can think well on their feet;

can listen well with both their ears and their eyes;

can speak well;

can understand the environment in which they work;

can keep focused on the customer;

are goal oriented;

are responsible;

are looking for better ways to do things;

are computer literate;

are intellectually curious;

are service oriented;

are emotionally secure;

are intelligent;

are creative;

are team players;

are not "binary brained";

are dependable;

are self-starters;

are flexible;

are fast workers;

are accurate;

are honest;

actively seek opportunities to grow both personally and professionally;

have a thorough knowledge of their profession in general and their specialty in particular;

have high professional standards; and

enjoy learning new things.

STUDY QUESTIONS

1. Why is it important to keep your job hunting skills updated?

2. What are some of the trends predicted for the library and information center workforce? What trends do you see in your geographic region?

3. What is outsourcing? Can you find examples of outsourcing companies in your state? Do contract jobs appeal to you?

4. How do the resume, cover letter, and application form differ in the information they present about a candidate?

5. Divide your class into small groups of four. Choose one person to be the interview candidate and have the other three role-play as the interview panel. Have the panel devise several typical questions and pose them to the candidate in a mock interview situation. Afterwards, give feedback to the interviewee on his or her performance.

6. Why is networking important to a job hunter? Describe some opportunities for networking in the library and information science field. Have you developed a network of contacts yet?

RESOURCES

Print Resources

Aho, Melissa, Marcia Franklin, Susan Wakefield, and Sara Wakefield. "Internships are the Appetizers of the Library World So Nibble, Nibble, Nibble..." *Library Journal* (June 2006).

Bolles, Richard Nelson. *What Color Is Your Parachute: 2007; A Practical Manual for Job Hunters and Career-Changers.* Berkeley, CA: Ten Speed Press, 2006.

Gordon, Rachel Singer. "Finding a Library Job." *Library Journal* (June 2005). http://www.libraryjournal.com/article/CA6250888.html.

Ireland, Susan. *The Complete Idiot's Guide to the Perfect Resume.* 4th ed. Indianapolis, IN: Alpha Books, 2006.

Jackson, Tom. *The Perfect Resume: Today's Ultimate Job Search Tool.* New York: Broadway Books, 2004.

Kane, Laura Townsend. *Straight from the Stacks: A First-Hand Guide to Careers in Library and Information Science.* Chicago: American Library Association, 2003.

Kuntz, Tom. "Next Time, Eat the Pizza After the Interview." *New York Times* January 24, 1999: sec 4, p. 2.

Newlen, Robert R. *Resume Writing and Interviewing Techniques that Work: A How-To-Do-It Manual for Librarians.* New York: Neal-Schuman Publishers, 2006.

Shontz, Priscilla K. and Richard A. Murray, eds. *A Day in the Life: Career Options in Library and Information Science.* Westport, CT: Libraries Unlimited, 2007.

Web Sites

American Library Association

http://www.ala.org/

(accessed July 2, 2007)

ALA maintains an extensive, up-to-date Web site that features news releases, conference dates, legislation updates, job-hunting resources, and current job listings on their ALAjobLIST.

Archeus's WorkSearch

http://www.garywill.com/worksearch/

(accessed July 2, 2007)

This site is sponsored by Gary Will, a consultant and speaker who works with clients on job search and recruitment. It includes many links to tips and articles on resume preparation and job interviewing.

Chronicle of Higher Education

http://chronicle.com/search/jobs/

(accessed July 2, 2007)

The leading weekly paper (available in print and on the Web) for news and trends in academia also features a jobs listing that includes professional librarian openings. Search their job database by state, institution, or job title.

Council on Library/Media Technicians

http://colt.ucr.edu/

(accessed July 2, 2007)

Council on Library/Media Technicians (COLT) is an organization specifically devoted to library technicians and library support staff. The Web site lists upcoming conferences, COLT publications, and posts regional job openings from selected chapters, and has links to many national and international job lines.

JobWeb

http://www.jobweb.com/

(accessed July 2, 2007)

JobWeb site is full of career postings as well as how-to information on resumes, interviews, and so forth. Produced by the National Association of Colleges and Employers, "America's bridge between higher education and the world of work." The site is well organized and frequently updated.

Library Job Postings on the Internet

http://www.libraryjobpostings.org/

(accessed July 2, 2007))

Writer, librarian, and blogger Sarah L. Johnson's Library Job Postings on the Internet debuted in 1995 and has been going strong since then. One of the Web's most comprehensive guides to library-related jobs. A faculty librarian at Booth Library, Eastern Illinois University, Johnson maintains this service for free. Organized by job type (e.g., archives and records management, academic) or by geographic region.

Monster

http://www.monster.com/

(accessed July 2, 2007))

One of the most well-known general job search sites on the Web. Besides its job search function, there are many excellent articles on all facets of the job search—interviews, cover letters, job references, dressing for success, ethics, and so on.

Special Libraries Association

   http://www.sla.org/

(accessed July 2, 2007)

The SLA Website features job listings and many other career resources; some portions of the site are available to members only.

NOTES

1. Bureau of Labor Statistics, "Librarians," in *Occupational Outlook Handbook, 2006/07,* http://www.bls.gov/oco/ocos068.htm#outlook (accessed June 25, 2007).

2. Bureau of Labor Statistics, "Library Technicians," in *Occupational Outlook Handbook, 2006/07,* http://stats.bls.gov/oco/ocos113.htm#outlook (accessed June 25, 2007).

3. "Independent contractors in 2005," *Monthly Labor Review* [TED: The Editor's Desk], July 29, 2005, http://stats.bls.gov/opub/ted/2005/jul/wk4/art05.htm (accessed June 25, 2007).

4. Richard H. Beatty, *The Five Minute Interview: A Jobhunter's Guide to a Successful Interview,* 3rd ed. (New York: John Wiley & Sons, 2002).

Evolving Library Services

While today's high school and college students have grown up with online access as an integral part of their lives, playing a major role in their daily learning, working, and social networking, an historical view reminds us that life did exist before the advent of the Internet. However, as with many institutions, libraries were changed irreversibly by the flourishing of this remarkable tool. Although early Internet protocols, such as the endless menus of Gopher and the UNIX commands of Telnet, were clunky and limited primarily to academics and technical professionals, by the mid-1990s the masses began to discover the Internet.

Using hypertext transfer protocol (HTTP), the Web combines intuitive point-and-click technology to access visually appealing multimedia and hyperlinked documents. Its ease of use, graphical nature, and accessibility are an incredible improvement over past utilitarian protocols. Users choose which hyperlinks to follow as they pursue research, shop, make travel arrangements, or just surf to browse what is available. Hypertext mark-up language (HTML) and its more powerful brother extensible mark-up language (xml) are the coding that allows this document linkage to take place and are relatively simple languages to learn. With the added help of numerous mark-up editing software and multimedia programs, the ability to create a multimedia Web document is readily available to anyone with a little know-how, patience, computer access, and space with a Web hosting service for storing the files.

WEB 2.0 AND LIBRARY 2.0

And with the maturing of the Web in the decade following its début, the variety of applications it offers and the plethora of information sources available continue to grow exponentially. Authors of recent articles in the main stream news media (*New York Times, Chronicle of Higher Education*), as well as in the blogosphere, have pondered on just how much the library profession has changed, and what that means to librarians and technicians now entering the field as well as to those up-and-coming leaders and managers.[1]

265

Setting the stage for current change in the library profession is the phrase "*Web 2.0*," which is commonly used to indicate a kind of second generation of Internet usage featuring the hugely popular social-networking sites; tools such as blogs and wikis; and other means of encouraging, sharing, and promoting user-generated content.

Parallel to this concept is the term "*Library 2.0*," which has gained popularity in the library and information industry. It refers to a new approach to doing business that incorporates the trademarks of Web 2.0 into daily library operations: OPAC systems, collection development suggestions, and so on. To date, its hallmarks are encouraging patron input on operations, promoting borrowers' opinions about library collections and individual book titles, and promoting more of a perceived customer-library dialog than in the past.

Industry leaders stress that to be relevant, the modern library needs to be, in the words of Joe Janes, University of Washington, "somewhere and everywhere."[2] So, yes, maintain valued core services that are offered inside the brick and mortar libraries that draw patrons inside. But at the same time develop a strong virtual presence for those patrons who have information needs but do not care to physically come to the library. Core onsite services include story hour; traditional onsite, walk-in reference assistance; a hard copy book collection; public access computers; author and other cultural programs. Simultaneous to these core onsite services, offer e-reference and vibrant electronic resources and integrate MySpace, Bebo, Flickr, and other social networking tools into your institutional homepage. Be prepared to meet patrons where they spend much of their study, research, and discretionary time: online.

Today's Web has something for everyone. Colorful, interactive, kid-friendly sites attract children from an early age; seniors eagerly follow their investments online and search for important medical data to assist with health decisions; students conduct research for academic papers from the comfort of their homes; and business professionals market, buy, and sell products online. Average citizens can locate information about their local city government, including information about how to contact elected officials, the building permit process, job openings, and more. It is almost impossible today to make travel plans without using airline, train, and lodging Web sites for pricing, availability, ticket purchase, and real-time scheduling updates.

Online shopping—both retail and business-to-business—has overcome earlier jitters about secure servers for handling credit card purchases, reasonable return policies, adequate inventory, and prompt filling of orders to be accepted and highly popular. For many individuals, shopping online has become the preferred medium over an in-store shopping experience—especially during the high volume Christmas holiday season. According to ComScore Networks, a company that tracks online spending, consumer online retail spending at U.S. Web sites for the 2006 holiday season reached $23.11 billion, marking a 26 percent increase versus the same end-of-year period in 2005.[3]

WEB USAGE

Tracking Internet statistics is a rather slippery pursuit because of the medium's ever-changing nature, but some usage milestones and trends can be ascertained. According to the *Computer Industry Almanac*, 9th edition, there were 147 million adults worldwide using the Internet by the end of 1998, as compared to 61 million in 1996. In 1998, more than half of these users—defined as those accessing it at least once a week—resided in the United States.[4] By the summer of 2001, worldwide use numbers increased to 513.4 million, with 180.7 million or 35 percent residing in North America.[5] In the intervening years, a major shift has taken place, especially as Internet use and acceptance has taken hold in Asia. By late 2007, Internetworldstats.com reported 1,244 million total users worldwide, with only 19 percent residing in North America.[6]

Meanwhile, resource-poor third world countries with limited access to technology are decidedly behind in Internet usage. In addition to the lack of computers and aging or nonexistent infrastructures in many poorer nations, freedom of information is not a universally embraced concept. Repressive government regimes such as China and Iran actively monitor and censor Internet access for their citizens.

In terms of usage by gender, by mid-1999, various studies began to indicate that women had made great strides [7] and constituted half of American adult users of the Web at that time, just as they continue to do today.[8] This contrasts sharply with early Internet use surveys in 1996 that showed a substantial gender gap, with males dominating Web usage by about a four-to-one ratio.

EFFECT ON LIBRARIES AND RESEARCHERS

Not since the introduction of moveable typeface has the library field been enveloped in such dramatic change as that brought by the Internet revolution that began in the 1990s. Many of the long-touted promises of the information technology age that were heralded in earlier decades came true with the development of the World Wide Web, and even more continue to unfold. All aspects of library operations have been impacted greatly, from daily staffing needs, to the publishing industry, to patron services. A librarian's job description is dramatically different from a decade ago, with computer proficiency and teaching skills both critical requirements. Duties of other library staff members have also been changed unalterably. Even the physical plant and the design of library and information center facilities have undergone major modification to reflect the reliance on online use. And the expectations by patrons of a library's offerings have adjusted accordingly. One of the most asked questions in a modern library today is: "Do you have wireless Internet access?" If the answer is no, that library may just have lost a patron.

Information Access and Publishing Trends

The world of publishing has been turned upside down as the old method of distributing information solely in paper format has been revolutionized by the Web delivery system. As a result, instant and often free access to all types of journals, magazines, newspapers, book reviews, government documents, legal codes, and images is now a reality for researchers. More hard copy materials are being transferred to Web format every day, reaching wider audiences, and gaining greater exposure for the publisher. For periodicals, simultaneous publication in hard copy and on the Web is commonplace for both scholarly journals and popular magazines, although the two versions may differ. The Web has also given birth to e-zines and e-journals, publications found exclusively on the Web with no corresponding hard copy editions.

For Free and For Fee

In the idealistic culture of the Web, the myth of free access to all information thrives. And from many users—especially those outside of a business or corporate environment—a commonly heard cry is, "You mean they are gonna charge me to get into their Web site?" Information is a sought-after commodity, and, no, it never has all been free; there is no reason to think the Web will alter that. Although numerous publishers do offer all or some of their online publications free of charge, many have access or subscriber fees, just as they do in hard copy format. For researchers accustomed to libraries paying the subscription costs, direct access fees may come as a surprise. For example, searching the *Los Angeles Times* newspaper Web site is free, but retrieving an article from the online archives costs a few dollars per article or requires a paid subscription. Customers are also often unaware of the true cost to libraries of commercial databases, such as *Ebscohost, ProQuest, Infotrac, Avery Index to Architectural Periodicals,* or others that they are able to access while on a school campus, in a corporate library, or remotely with a special password. Libraries need to do more to promote these services and help those customers understand what a bargain they can get via their library card. Expect pricing for Web products—especially services targeted toward libraries—to vary widely as publishers and their customers continue to test the waters on pricing patterns.

From Breaking News to the Classics

Although the English language currently remains the dominant language on the Web, there is a wide diversity of foreign language materials available online, from daily newspapers, to museum exhibits, to scholarly papers, to political manifestos. This virtual language lab opens up a whole new world of information for immigrants, business travelers, foreign language students, and tourists, as well as native speakers.

The Web provides an exciting and highly competitive forum for current events reporting. Virtually all the major U.S. dailies and television news stations continually update their Web sites, offering breaking news as it happens along with audio and video clips. The dynamic news environment is no longer only the realm of journalists with newspaper wire service access. Blogs are also standard features of news Web sites, here again giving visibility to and a forum for the opinions and comments of the average person. The demand for and resulting explosion of user-generated content has transformed news publishing.

Another boon to researchers is the proliferation of full-text classics online. Commercial e-book services such as Netlibrary.com offer collections of electronic book titles to libraries and their patrons for an annual subscription price. Many titles in the public domain, such as those by Jane Austen, William

Shakespeare, Herman Melville, and others, can be downloaded or browsed for free on the Web thanks to the efforts of Project Gutenberg and others who work to make these titles digitally available.

Patron Services

The Web has opened up an enticing, multicolored smorgasbord of information to consumers. Although many sources now online, such as the *Occupational Outlook Handbook, The TomCat,* and various newspaper and proprietary databases, have long been familiar resources to librarians and serious researchers, their accessibility on the Web makes them seem to be brand new to the novice student or casual searcher. And it certainly makes it easier to keep these sources up-to-date.

The information search itself has become much easier for patrons. Ferreting out information from mysterious, bound books and indexes or clunky computer programs has been exchanged for the point-and-click ease, visual appeal, and 24-hour access of the Web. Published information—whether back issues of newspapers, today's stock quotes, current job listings, or esoteric government reports—receives much greater exposure to consumers when mounted on the World Wide Web and is no longer a trade secret of librarians.

Emphasis on Convenience

In addition, many library-specific services are new, improved, and more convenient for the computer savvy patron. Remote searching of Web-based public access catalogs lets patrons browse for items and initiate holds on desired titles from the comfort of their homes or offices. The majority of libraries place interlibrary loan requests using e-mail, which allows for improved fill rates and speedier patron service,

Students and researchers with access to commercial databases locate journal articles online, then conveniently send them to their e-mail accounts. Many academic institutions and larger libraries offer e-mail-based alert services or updates via RSS (Really Simple Syndication) feeds, which allow library users to receive notice of new publications in their interest areas or research specialties.

Electronic reserve reading is becoming a reality for college students. Instructors' lecture notes, sample quizzes, and articles and texts that are copyright compliant can be viewed on the Web or as part of a Blackboard course shell rather than only in the reserve reading room of the campus library.

Disabled Patrons

The mature Internet has made great inroads into changing the lives of those with disabilities. With the help of software to read text aloud, people with visual impairments share in the benefits of the Internet and are no longer dependent solely on Braille editions or books on tape. Those with motor/mobility difficulty or loss are able to navigate the Web with voice recognition software. Web accessibility—that is designing and editing Web sites so as to be equally accessible to all users, disabled or otherwise—is no longer just an optional concern, but may be legally required and is certainly an issue in terms of marketing a Web site so as to reach the widest audience possible.

Homebound individuals formerly reliant on library shut-in services can now have access in their homes to an enormous global resource with an Internet-ready computer and broadband access.

Family Historians

Samplings of the largest, richest library and archival collections of American historical records are increasingly showing up on the Web. With major funding often from private industry, digitization projects have been underway at repositories such as the Library of Congress and the National Archives. Portions of George Washington's and Thomas Jefferson's letters and diaries are online, both in facsimile images and as transcriptions. The digitization of historical photographs and images from major archives opens up unpublished, historical treasures to schoolchildren, genealogists, and scholars.

The world's largest repository for family history records, The Church of Jesus Christ of Latter-day Saints' Family History Library in Salt Lake City, Utah, is currently conducting pilot tests for the transfer of some of their voluminous holdings to the Web. Now stored in a specially outfitted underground vault, the Mormon collection contains more than two million rolls of microfilm, 700,000 microfiche, and 280,000 books.[9] Their popular Web site serves as a powerful index to the microform and print collection and to genealogical data submitted by family historians.[10] See chapter 5 for more discussion on this.

From the smallest to the largest library, and for all categories of researchers, the Internet revolution has resulted in a tremendous increase of available resources. Gone are the days of strolling through a library's book stacks and thinking, "I guess that's all they have." Collections now extend well beyond the physical shelves to the virtual warehouse.

IMPACT ON STAFF

For library staffers at all levels, the Internet has brought fundamental change to business as usual. Acquisitions operations have been streamlined with online ordering from vendors' and publishers' Web sites. Staff training possibilities have been made richer and more relevant with the growth in teleconferencing. And the burgeoning of continuing education offerings (often called "*Webinars*") emphasizes distance-friendly delivery of courses. The ever-popular *YouTube* site has proved highly practical for delivering staff training in addition to its recreational value.

Electronic discussion groups, listservs, and group channels provide convenient venues for making contacts for problem solving and information sharing among colleagues. These tools provide fresh avenues for discussion among library and information center employees on a global basis. Because e-mail and the Web are not geographically bound, responses to a query are just as likely to come from an online colleague in Australia or Europe as from a local librarian. In addition, opportunities are extended to staff who previously would not have had access to them because of limited travel funds to attend faraway conferences.

Staff can also go online for the latest industry news and reporting. Many library trade periodicals have sprouted Web versions, and there are numerous specialty e-journals that cater to areas of the field, such as the pioneering *Associates* newsletter, which is dedicated to library support staff issues (see http://associates.ucr.edu/index.html).

The rise of the Internet and reliance on digital information has created new job classifications within library and information center environments. The need for digital librarians—those who create and manage digital library services, collections, and repositories—is on the rise. Knowledge of imaging technologies, markup languages, Web technology, and more go hand-in-hand with an understanding of how a library operates and a customer service orientation. In all but the biggest organizations, employers want both knowledge of key information sources and collection development theory, plus Web technology skills.

In schools and colleges, librarians and technicians work closely with instructors to identify and create multimedia resources for classroom presentations or distance education; the Web is increasingly being used as the mechanism for delivering instruction to students.

This leads again to the critical need for constant retraining and skills updating for all library personnel—from seasoned staffers now on the job to new recruits just entering the library and information science field. The new developments and creative energy brought to the field by the Internet and technological change require staff who are committed to growth and a parallel commitment of libraries to provide opportunities for staff development.

Modern Services Demand New Floor Plans

For many libraries, existing floor plans are incompatible with a 21st-century concept of service delivery. Information centers and libraries are rapidly evolving from the more static role of book depository to dynamic high-tech information centers and group learning spaces. This is a major cause for librarians to rethink their facilities' layouts. Today there is a need for greater numbers of computer workstations; in many cases, open access labs of 30–100 computers are typical in schools, colleges, and public libraries. If separate from existing reference service points, these areas require additional staffed service counters.

Older audiovisual centers, which once focused on the now obsolete 16-mm films and other older media, are being converted to teleconference areas or multimedia labs. New uses for old spaces may require remodeling, expansion, or at least a reworked floor plan. Heavy-duty cabling for electricity and data connections can be difficult and costly to provide in older buildings. This may lead to incorporation of wireless networks and appliances to serve the needs of customers and staff. Wireless networks are getting faster, but wired networks will continue to be faster for the foreseeable future—generally by a factor of 5 to 1. So wireless has the advantages of portability and ease and economy of deployment—particularly in older facilities, which are lacking modern broadband cabling. However, wired networks have a real advantage where speed of data movement is important.

Study carrels and cozy chairs need to be interspersed with suitable furniture and outlets for patrons' laptop computers and accessible terminals with appropriate adaptive features for disabled patrons. All service desks must be Internet-ready and proximate to patron computer banks, whereas large stack areas need OPACs interspersed at convenient locations throughout. Some of the physical plant issues range from the critical upgrading of high-speed cabling to partitioning off quiet reading or study areas from heavily trafficked, noise-intensive computer areas. Learning commons are also very popular in academic libraries: typically, a *learning common* is a flexible open space where students can gather in groups at tables or comfortable chairs to study together, and where presentations, lectures, or art exhibits might also be held. And, of course, the traditional strict library rule "no food, no drink" has been relaxed in many venues due to patron preference to be able to enjoy coffee or snacks as they study or read. Independent and chain bookstores have long embraced this *café* atmosphere in their retail space. Public and academic libraries nationwide are implementing creative solutions to change their thinking and to adapt some sections of their space for eating.

Santa Monica Public Library, in its beautiful headquarters library remodel, has come up with an attractive compromise: the rehabbed library building wraps around an outdoor patio with a detached café. Patrons sip coffee, eat breakfast, and read outside in the patio as they wait for the library to open. Staff benefits from having an onsite restaurant for quick lunches, impromptu meetings, or work breaks.

Librarians Are Teachers

Information managers, librarians, and library technicians have always drawn from their teaching skills as they walk individual patrons through the mysteries of the card catalog, call numbers, periodical indexes, shelf locations, and other tools essential to locating information. In the Internet era, add to that basic skill set the need to train users in keyboarding, computer basics, Web use, e-mail access, and specific programs, along with the ability to differentiate between reliable and spurious information sources.

The greatest challenge of the 21st century will be attempting to provide our customers with critical thinking skills in how to sort out the proverbial wheat from the chaff. Often, electronic information available through libraries has not passed through the filtering process to which information published on paper is subjected. What is a welcome gain in timely distribution is often more than offset by loss in quality control. Accuracy is not checked to the same degree. Authority and reliability of the author is not pre-verified for the consumer. We will continue to be challenged as to how to best help our patrons learn to locate reliable information on the Web.

Instructional presentations to small groups, entire classrooms, or computer labs are a daily duty that require competency in public speaking and teaching, along with knowledge of diverse learning styles. In addition, strong computer skills, patience, and an ability to problem solve are musts. Those contemplating a career in the field need to carefully ponder these requirements and consider their comfort level with public speaking, instructing, and computer usage, in addition to a love for books.

FUTURE HAPPENINGS

A little history of the development of the Internet is instructive, because that history is now being repeated, almost step-by-step, with the emergence of Internet2. Begun in late 1996 by a consortium of U.S. universities, Internet2 is an effort by the research and academic communities to build upon and improve the technology of the highly popular original Internet. Internet2 combines the financial support and advanced research efforts of some 200 leading universities and the private sector, along with North American, Asian, and European government partners to develop and deploy advanced network applications and technologies, accelerating the creation of tomorrow's Internet.

The ever-increasing traffic on the Web, the need for improved connectivity, and the growth in e-commerce with its multimedia advertisements and banners have led these high-level users of the Internet to look for an alternate route for their data. Feeling that the current network is too clogged by commercial and personal users, Internet2 members are committed to paying for the research, upgrading of technologies, and organizational structure needed to provide a more reliable, faster network for sophisticated, serious research use. They also expect that the newer network applications they pioneer will eventually benefit all levels of Internet users.

Internet2 is recreating the partnership among academia, industry, and government that fostered today's Internet in its infancy. The primary goals of Internet2 are to:

- create a leading edge network capability for the national research community;
- enable revolutionary Internet applications; and
- ensure the rapid transfer of new network services and applications to the broader Internet community.[11]

Basically, Internet2 is a newer and faster Internet. Much of the difference is that now that some of us have lived through the first wave, we may have a clearer picture of where Internet2 is heading.

To long-term Internet veterans, it may seem as if, to paraphrase the inimitable Yogi Berra, "It's beginning to look like déjà vu all over again." The original Internet started in a very similar manner. Much of the impetus for the original Internet came from the need of faculty and graduate students at major research universities to have access to one of the handful of super computers that had been funded by the National Science Foundation (NSF). NSF couldn't afford to fund super computers on every campus, so they facilitated researchers, whose projects they sponsored, to have what were at that time considered high-speed connections to the nearest NSF-supported super computer.

However, the transmission speeds achieved then would be considered intolerable even for home modem connections today.

At that time the Internet was only a dedicated wire from the super computer center to the next major research university, which was then connected to the next major research university, and so on. Other universities, colleges, and entities were not connected, nor were they considered in the planning. So far, this sounds very similar to the evolution of Internet2.

What happened next with the original Internet will also probably happen with Internet2. But even our current Internet system is a tangled maze of information providers that is often impenetrable to the novice user.

In terms of library-specific developments, leading institutions are making serious attempts at taming the Web by applying familiar principles of information organization to cyberspace. By creating and maintaining sophisticated portals or indexes to recommended Web and electronic resources, these digital projects facilitate Internet research by librarians, students, and serious researchers. The Librarian's Internet Index (http://www.lii.org/) has become a standard tool for reference librarians across the nation.

Just as libraries have banded together in networks and consortia to share physical collections and resources, the trend now is in developing cooperative interfaces to their collective Web resources. Good examples of cooperative digital asset management and delivery are the California Digital Library (http://www.cdlib.org), touted as the 11th campus of the University of California state system, and the Colorado Virtual Libraries site (http://www.aclin.org/). Under the umbrella of the Arizona Memory Project, a wide variety of cultural institutions in that state are participating in a major effort to build a model statewide digital library. "Despite the differences in holdings and professional practices (including archival, museum and library disciplines), a digital consortium such as the Arizona Memory Project made it possible to tie together a myriad of unique collections and make them accessible to new audiences," observed former project start-up director Marisa Ramirez.[12] See their Web site (http://azmemory.lib.az.us) for updates on this project, which draws from a diverse array of agencies including state government, large and small museums, historical societies, churches, colleges, and others.

As was alluded to previously, no one owns the Internet; it just grew up. After the major research universities were connected, other institutions arranged to pay for dedicated communications lines to connect to the nearest organization that was already connected, and so it went. Likewise, no one organization maintains the Internet. If there is a problem, it's often unclear to the user who should be responsible for fixing it. Similarly, no one entity, either nationally or internationally, makes rules that apply to all things in all places. What a tangled Web we weave! Although this lack of definition is often frustrating, it is one of the features that has allowed the Internet to develop and permeate our lives so quickly.

GETTING COMFORTABLE WITH ADVANCING TECHNOLOGY

So is there a downside to this remarkable global network, the Internet that has so transformed our lives? Any new technology is invariably accompanied by new issues and unforeseen problems as it evolves and as diverse users continue to interact with it. In the meantime, the many controversial aspects of the Internet provide plenty of fodder for public discussion among the media, educators, scientists, futurists, and users themselves.

The Haves Versus the Have Nots

A familiar societal concern about the proliferation of the Internet is how the phenomenon affects those with no access to or understanding of computers. Commonly referred to as the "have nots," the disadvantaged, disabled, low-income, poorly educated, immigrant, and elderly groups fall into this category. In addition, there are those who, due to lifestyle preferences or religious beliefs, choose not to use computers, electronic communication tools, and so on. The Pew Internet & American Life Project recently conducted a very interesting survey to investigate patterns of participation and categories of users entitled *A Typology of Information and Communication Technology Users* [13] In addition to frequency of use for the Internet and other tools, they measured participant attitudes, whether participants were generating and publishing Web content, and user demographics.

Visit their Web site to take the typology test yourself and see how you compare with other users in the nation: http://www.pewinternet.org/quiz/quiz.asp.

Non-users and have nots are being bypassed as information publishers assume that the Web is the standard tool and that every office and home is equipped with a contemporary, broadband, multimedia personal computer. Is the burgeoning reliance on online information and entertainment catering to the wealthier, better-educated population and leaving the poor, elderly, and others even farther behind? If so, how can equitable access be ensured, and what is the role for libraries and information centers in this regard?

Information Credibility and Research Habits

In the fervor to publish around the clock, editorial and reporting standards can fall by the wayside as each media outlet rushes to scoop its competitors. The old editorial consideration of "Should we go to press with this?" can be lost in the rush to be first, leaving the Web fertile ground for gossip, innuendo, and inaccuracies. As with any information source, Internet data requires novice and experienced researchers alike to apply scrutiny to what they find. And because of its self-publishing nature, Web-based information bears a need for an extra measure of evaluation. Spurious descriptions of whales in the Minnesota River (there aren't any) and "world history" accounts that no Nazi concentration camps existed, can be found on legitimate-looking sites.[14]

Researchers—especially younger students—have a tendency to think exclusively in terms of the Internet as a source. In many cases, they are unaware of reference books, subscription databases, or other sources and are forsaking tools that may be better suited to their task for a general Google search. A corollary of this sole reliance on Web resources is that novice researchers have less tolerance for using text-based resources and are more in need of a photo fix or a sound bite to summarize complex ideas. Numerous studies also show that for Americans (and likely others worldwide), less time is spent on sustained, in-depth reading, with browsing and scanning on the rise. Additionally, a much discussed survey showed that the average number of books read per year by Americans has dropped to four.[15] This decline typically and understandably causes great lament to librarians. A more productive response might be to look deeper at strategies both to continue to appeal to those who do read frequently and, at the same time, aggressively promote newer resources such as downloadable MP3 files, e-books, and other alternative modalities with nonreaders in mind.

The technology of the Web also encourages plagiarism. Just cut and paste, and, *voila*, you have a term paper. Some professors claim to see a rise in highly fragmented, choppy term papers, and amalgams of paragraphs with multiple font sizes cobbled together from the many Web sites critiquing popular study topics, such as Shakespeare's plays or current political issues. Although plagiarism is as old as the hills and will always be a temptation, the Web makes it much easier to substitute original thought with snippets of someone else's comments (no matter what their credentials may or may not be).[16] This has led to the rapid growth of plagiarism detection systems such as Turnitin.com and others to help educate students about the necessity of respecting the intellectual property of others.

The Internet as a Reliable Archive

The Internet is still young, but its original emphasis on current and contemporary information remains. Owners of Web publishing ventures may reach different conclusions as they answer questions like the following: Is it a profitable venture to convert older magazines, newspapers, journals, and public domain works to the Web? Will people pay for access to archival files, as they will for the latest issues? Publishers are still determining pricing and packaging of access to their holdings. Some of the larger publishing firms such as Proquest have led the way with products like their *Los Angeles Times* and *New York Times Historical Newspaper* databases. For those larger libraries with a need for historical data from the 19th and 20th centuries and that can afford such products, the databases are a boom; but for many libraries these are out of reach budget-wise.

A library-specific corollary issue is that of perpetual access to periodicals. Will an online commercial database always maintain access to archival issues? Or will they suddenly drop or omit the older files, leaving a huge gap of back issues within the library collection. Or will there be a separate fee for access to archival files? This issue is critical for all research institutions as they decide whether to become heavily dependent on the many Web-based periodical indexes and databases. Professors, students, scholars, and researchers expect libraries to be repositories for non-current periodicals, books, government documents, and the like. As library networks or consortia negotiate contracts with commercial publishers of online products, perpetual access is a major point of negotiation. A related problem that is just starting to receive attention is to what extent organizations, through their libraries or other archival sources, have a responsibility to preserve information that may have only been published on their institution's Web site. One emerging piece of a solution is the digital or institutional repository mentioned earlier.

Health Effects

Science has yet to thoroughly document the mental and physical health effects from the increasing amount of time humans now spend in front of computer screens, some days logging more hours in cyberspace than in the real world. But certain trends are apparent. Carpal tunnel syndrome and repetitive-use injuries have long been commonplace among data entry operators, and are on the rise among youth who have grown up from a very early age with substantial keyboarding use—both on full keyboards and with the more compact key pads found on the ubiquitous personal digital tools such on Blackberrys, cell phones, and so on.

In addition to physiological effects, there are psychological effects as well. As use of the Internet has become so all pervasive in Americans' daily lives, so has the rise of various Web-based addictions. Some professionals suggest that "6 percent to 10 percent of the Internet users in the U.S. have a dependency that can be as destructive as alcoholism and drug addiction, and they [the doctors] are rushing to treat it."[17]

Online bullying—especially among pre-teens and teenagers—is another trend that has arisen due to the safe harbor of anonymity offered by online communication; many K-12 school districts now have formulated policies with disciplinary actions for offenders in an attempt to dissuade this new, uglier version of playground taunting.

Other research has focused on whether use of the Internet presents an increased risk of isolation or depression. For example, Carnegie Mellon University conducted an early study in 1998 suggesting that using the Internet can cause isolation, loneliness, and depression. In a two-year survey of 169 Pittsburgh residents, researchers found that using the Internet for as little as one hour per week resulted in an average increase of 1 percent on a depression scale; 0.04 percent on a loneliness scale; and a loss of 2.7 members of the user's social group.[18] This seems logical to some, but counterintuitive to others, who feel that computers help them connect with others. Clearly, more time and more study are needed.

As the Internet strongly encourages us to replace traditional interpersonal transactions, such as in-person banking and shopping, with virtual commerce, it remains to be seen whether there will be an increased sense of isolation or frustration. Will virtual commerce dead-ends frustrate like the endless voicemail loop, leaving us longing to speak to a live person? Of course, this issue did not first appear with the Internet. All forms of automation, including telephone answering machines, have contributed to this phenomenon.

Current health trends indicate that obesity levels among Americans remain high with 34 percent of U.S. adults aged 20 and over termed obese, according to a study by the Centers for Disease Control and Prevention in 2007.[19] Obesity, a major risk factor for heart disease, certain cancers, and type 2 diabetes, is often linked to a sedentary lifestyle.

Increased reliance on computers—whether for work or for pleasure—can't help but further compete for our discretionary time and make it that much harder to engage in exercise or physical fitness activities. Children are especially at risk as they may develop early behavior patterns with less time spent in daily physical activity and more time spent in inactive forms of play, such as watching TV, playing video games, text messaging, and using computers.

And there is the issue of technology overload. The proliferation of newer, faster, cheaper, more convenient electronic tools is an amazing convenience from which we all benefit, but it can also be a mixed blessing. In a business environment that assumes that one is always available by e-mail, pager, cellular telephone, fax, or other invention, where are the boundaries between privacy and access in our personal lives? Is the virtual reference librarian available to answer a patron query 24 hours a day, seven days a week (24/7)? Managing the use of modern communication tools and technology to prevent psychological stress from the constant pressure to be on duty is an important contemporary issue. Do we skillfully use our iPhones and Blackberrys to manage our lives, or are they controlling us?

As the phenomenon of the Internet continues to mature, future inventions will help resolve some of these current pressing issues while simultaneously ushering in a host of new challenges. Count on the Internet to spark discussion among the old and the young, the technological gurus, Luddites, and novices as to its virtues and vices. But the changes ushered in by the Internet, and particularly by the World Wide Web, will not go away. Nor will the pace of change abate. In fact, it is likely to continue to accelerate.

SUMMARY

If the dynamic environment described in the preceding chapters seems attractive to you, you may have a future in library science. If you are over 30 and contemplating a career change, you will not be alone. In the 20th century, librarians and library technicians alike typically chose their careers after spending some time in other endeavors.

Students in graduate library schools had an average age of 30. The men were likely to be between 27–33. Women, on the other hand, were 22–55 years of age.[20] Students in library technology programs historically have been primarily female and fortyish. This latter demographic was encouraged because most library/information technology course work predominantly had been scheduled at night. With the rise of distance education in the field and the strong integration of Web development skills with more traditional library knowledge, it remains to be seen if the increasing need will result in younger, "geekier" males being attracted to the career pathways within librarianship.

Whatever the gender and age demographics of those employed in the library business turn out to be, their mission will be to solve information problems for their clients. In this quest, the only predictable constant appears to be change. The cascading development of technology and the resulting explosion of both formats and quantity of information will make problem-solving skills in this field more necessary than ever. In the early 21st century, the retirement of the baby boomers is bringing a great need to recruit large numbers of both librarians and library technicians for the coming decade. This larger-than-normal turnover of staff will create both challenges and opportunities for all of those employed in libraries.

STUDY QUESTIONS

1. Describe how you use the Web in your personal life and in your course work. What are your favorite Web portal pages?

2. Do you pay for access to any Web-based subscription databases, social networking sites, or online services? Why or why not?

3. What attributes of e-mail have made it so accepted and popular? What are the negative aspects of e-mail? How many different e-mail accounts do you have and why?

4. How does your public library differ now from when you were a high school student? Does the building have WiFi access? A computer lab area?

5. What are your favorite social networking sites? Why do you favor these?

6. Take the Pew Internet & American Life Project typology test and see which user sector you fit into. Do you feel this is an accurate characterization of your habits? (http://www.pewinternet.org/quiz/quiz.asp)

7. Has the burgeoning of the Internet left libraries obsolete? Why or why not? Are libraries doing a good job of repositioning themselves as the average patron becomes more technologically savvy?

Print Resources

Burke, John J. *Neal-Schuman Library Technology Companion: A Basic Guide for Library Staff.* 2nd ed. New York: Neal-Schuman, 2006.

Gordon, Rachel Singer. *The Nextgen Librarian's Survival Guide.* Medford NJ: Information Today, 2006.

Herring, Mark Y. "10 Reasons Why the Internet is No Substitute for a Library." *American Libraries* (April 2001): 76–78.

Jost, Kenneth. "Libraries and the Internet." *CQ Researcher* 9 (June 1, 2001): 467–87.

Kennedy, James R., Lisa Vardaman, and Gerard B. McCabe, eds. *Our New Public, A Changing Clientele: Bewildering Issues or New Challenges for Managing Libraries?* Westport, CT: Libraries Unlimited, 2008.

Lathrop, Ann and Kathleen Foss. *Guiding Students from Cheating and Plagiarism to Honesty and Integrity: Strategies for Change.* Westport, CT: Libraries Unlimited, 2005.

Stebelman, Scott. "Cybercheating: Dishonesty Goes Digital." *American Libraries* (September 1998): 48–50.

Tapscott, Don and Anthony D. Williams. *Wikinomics: How Mass Collaboration Changes Everything.* New York: Portfolio, 2008.

Web Sites

Associates: The Electronic Library Support Staff Journal

http://associates.ucr.edu/

(accessed January 29, 2008)

Founded in 1994 and published three times a year, this well-written electronic journal deals with all issues concerning library support staff. The journal's Web site also maintains an easily accessed archive of back issues.

Falling Through the Net: Defining the Digital Divide

http://www.ntia.doc.gov/ntiahome/digitaldivide

(accessed December 2, 2007)

An early report released by the Department of Commerce's National Telecommunications Administration in their ongoing efforts to study American telephone, computer, and Internet usage. Specifically, the report documents the increasing gap along ethnic lines between those with access to computers and those without.

Internet2

http://www.internet2.edu/

(accessed January 29, 2008)

For background and updates on the progress of this project, visit the home page of the Internet2 consortium.

Librarians' Internet Index

http://www.lii.org

(accessed January 29, 2008)

Highly regarded and popular among reference librarians throughout the United States, this selective Internet ready-reference tool is extensive and regularly maintained.

Pew Internet & American Life Project.

http://www.pewinternet.org/PPF/r/67/report_display.asp

"The Digital Disconnect: The Widening Gap Between Internet-Savvy Students and their Schools."

(accessed March 15, 2008)

Liz Castro on HTML, XHTML, and CSS

http://lizcastrohtml.blogspot.com/

(accessed January 29, 2008)

Liz Castro is the author of many bestselling, very practical books on Web page design, style, and XXX, including the 6th edition of *HTML, XHTML, and CSS: Visual Quickstart Guide.* Follow her blog on key Web building issues and design tools including HTML, XHTML, Cascading Style Sheets, Blogger, and most recently, iPhoto.

NOTES

1. Scott Carlson, "Young Librarians, Talkin' 'Bout Their Generation," [Information Technology column], *The Chronicle of Higher Education*, October 19, 2007.

2. Joe Janes, "Reference 2.0: Ain't What It Used to Be...And It Never Will Again," (Keynote Speech at Internet Librarian Conference, October 30, 2007).

3. "Holiday E-Commerce Spending Up 26 Percent with Surge Continuing the Week Before Christmas," *ComScore*, December 28, 2006, http://www.comscore.com/press/release.asp?press = 1162 (accessed November 25, 2007).

4. David Plotnikoff, "Honoring Internet's Best and Worst," *Telegram-Tribune* (San Luis Obispo, CA), March 22, 1999.

5. Scope Communications Group, "NUA: Internet, How Many Online?" http://www.nua.net/surveys/how_many_online/index.html (accessed November 26, 2001).

6. Miniwatts Marketing Group, "Internet Usage Statistics: The Internet Big Picture; World Internet Users and Population Stats," November 2007, http://www.internetworldstats.com/stats.htm (accessed November 25, 2007)

7. "Women Equal Number of Men Online," *eMarketer* April 4, 1999, http://www.emarketer.com/estats/040599_women.html (accessed April 8, 1999).

8. Deborah Fallows, *How Women and Men Use the Internet* (Washington, DC: Pew Internet & American Life Project, 2005), http://www.pewinternet.org/PPF/r/171/report_display.asp (accessed March 15, 2008).

9. Kristen Moulton, "Mormons Offer Online Family Tree: New Mormon Web Site Lists and Charts More than 400 Million Names," *AOL News*, May 24, 1999.

10. The Church of Jesus Christ of Latter-day Saints, "Family Search Internet Genealogy Service," http://www.familysearch.org/ (accessed January 29, 2008).

11. Internet 2, "About Internet2," September 10, 2002, http://www.internet2.edu/html/about.html (accessed March 15, 2008)

12. Marisa Ramirez, former Digital Repository Coordinator, Arizona Memory Project, e-mail message to authors, February 26, 2008.

13. John B. Horrigan, *A Typology of Information and Communication Technology Users* (Washington, DC: Pew Internet & American Life Project, 2007), http://www.pewtrusts.org/news_room_ektid21192.aspx (accessed February 1, 2008).

14. Tina Kelley, "Whales in the Minnesota River? Only on the Web, Where Skepticism Is a Required Navigational Aid," *New York Times*, March 4, 1999.

15. Alan Fram, "One in Four Read No Books Last Year," *Washington Post*, August 21, 2007, http://www.washingtonpost.com/wp-dyn/content/article/2007/08/21/AR2007082101045.html (accessed March 15, 2008).

16. David Rothenberg, "How the Web Destroys the Quality of Students' Research Papers," *Chronicle of Higher Education* (August 14, 1997), A44.

17. Sarah Kershaw, "Hooked on the Web: Help is on the Way," *New York Times*, December 1, 2005.

18. Joshua Quittner, "Bummed Like Me," *Time*, September 14, 1998, 84.

19. CDC National Center for Health Statistics Office of Communication, "New CDC Study Finds No Increase in Obesity Among Adults; But Levels Still High," November 28, 2007, http://www.cdc.gov/nchs/pressroom/07newsreleases/obesity.htm (accessed March 15, 2008).

20. David R. Dowell, *The Relation of Salary to Sex in a Female Dominated Profession: Librarians Employed at Research Universities in the South Atlantic Census Region*. Dissertation, University of North Carolina at Chapel Hill, 1986, pp. 38-44.

Appendix A

Library and Information Studies Education and Human Resource Utilization a Statement of Policy

EXECUTIVE SUMMARY

In 1999 the 1st Congress on Professional Education created four task forces. Task Force #4, Personnel Stratification, now Library Career Pathways, was charged with the review of the means, methods, and expectations for entry into the library professions.

Initially, the Task Force reviewed a policy statement entitled, "Library Education and Personnel Utilization" which the Council of the American Library Association had adopted on June 30, 1970. This ALA policy document appeared in need of some (but remarkably little) revision, given its age. The Library Career Pathways Task Force updated the statement, incorporating a more current view of librarianship and its partner professions. Feedback is encouraged on the draft document that is below. You may send comments to the Task Force Chair, *Julie G. Huiskamp* or any member of *the Library Career Pathways Task Force.*

Major revisions to the document include:

- The substitution of library and information studies and the inclusion of the title Specialist where the terms library education, library science, librarianship, and Library Assistant/Technical Assistant have previously appeared;

283

- The recognition that the library and information studies realm of practice includes several professions at various levels of entry;
- The acknowledgment of support staff as integral contributors to and participants in the library professions;
- A statement encouraging professional preparation which would include a broad educational background for study in the humanities, the sciences, and the social sciences, over preference to a narrowly defined, specialized field of study.

The document continues to demonstrate several points of career entry at levels from high school graduation through the Masters level, considered the terminal degree for professional practice. Qualifications and expectations at all levels are described in narrative form, and through the means of a graphic *"Career Lattice"*.

The statement on career development and continuous learning draws a distinct difference between the individual responsibility for professional development expected of librarians and specialists, and the library managers' responsibility for providing access to continuous learning for support staff contributors.

DRAFT

Library and Information Studies and Human Resource Utilization*
Proposed Revision to A Statement of Policy Adopted by the Council of the American Library Association, June 30, 1970**

1. The purpose of the policy statement is to recommend categories of library personnel, and levels of training and education appropriate to the preparation of personnel for these categories, which will support the highest standards of library service for all kinds of libraries and the most effective use of the variety of skills and qualifications needed to provide it.

2. The phrase "library and information studies" is understood to be concerned with recordable information and knowledge and the services

---

* Throughout this statement, wherever the term "librarianship" is used, it is meant to be read in its broadest sense as encompassing the relevant concepts of information science and documentation; wherever the term "libraries" is used, the term refers to public, academic, corporate, medical and other special libraries; current models of media centers, learning centers, educational resources centers, information, documentation, and referral centers are also assumed. To avoid the necessity of repeating the entire gamut of variations and expansions, the traditional library terminology is employed in its most inclusive meaning.

** The policy statement adopted by ALA with the title Library Education and Manpower. In the spring of 1976, the Office for Library Personnel Resources Advisory Committee edited this statement to remove sexist terminology. This version of the statement includes changes recommended by the Library Career Pathways Taskforce in January of 2001 and is provided for comment to the library community.

and technologies to facilitate their management and use. Library and information studies encompasses information and knowledge creation, communication, identification, selection, acquisition, organization and description, storage and retrieval, preservation, analysis, interpretation, evaluation, synthesis, dissemination, and management.

3. To meet the goals of library service, both professional and supportive staff are needed in libraries. Thus, the library occupation is much broader than that segment of it which is the library profession, but the library profession has responsibility for defining the training and education required for the preparation of personnel who work in libraries at any level, supportive or professional.

4. Skills other than those of librarianship also have an important contribution to make to the achievement of superior library service. There should be equal recognition in both the professional and supportive ranks for those individuals whose expertise contributes to the effective performance of the library.

5. A constant effort must be made to promote the most effective utilization of personnel at all levels, both professional and supportive. The tables in Figure 1 suggest a set of categories which illustrate a means for achieving this end.

6. The titles recommended here represent categories or broad classifications, within which it is assumed that there will be several levels of promotional steps. Specific job titles may be used within any category: for example, catalogers, reference librarians, children's librarians would be included in either the "Librarian" or (depending upon the level of their responsibilities and qualifications) "Senior Librarian" categories; department heads, the director of the library, and certain specialists would presumably have the additional qualifications and responsibilities which place them in the "Senior Librarian" category.

7. Where specific job titles dictated by local usage and tradition do not make clear the level of the staff member's qualification and responsibility, it is recommended that reference to the ALA category title be used parenthetically to provide the clarification desirable for communication and reciprocity. For example:

REFERENCE ASSISTANT (LIS Associate)
HEAD CATALOGER (Senior Librarian)
LIBRARY AIDE (LIS Assistant)

8. The title "Librarian" carries with it the connotation of "professional" in the sense that professional tasks are those which require a special background and education on the basis of which library needs are identified, problems are analyzed, goals are set, and original and creative solutions are formulated for them, integrating theory into practice, and planning, organizing, communicating, and administering successful programs of service to users of the library's materials and services. In defining services to users, the professional person recognizes potential users as well as current ones, and designs services which will reach all who could benefit from them.

FIGURE 1

CATEGORIES OF LIBRARY PERSONNEL—PROFESSIONAL

Library-Related Qualifications	Non-Library Related Qualifications	Basic Requirements	Nature of Responsibilities
Senior Librarian	Senior Specialist	In addition to the requirements for Librarian/Specialist— relevant experience and continued professional development	Top-level responsibilities including but not limited to administration; superior knowledge of some aspect of librarianship; or of other subject fields of value to the library.
Librarian	Specialist	For Librarian: Master's degree For Specialist: Appropriate professional degree for the specialty.	Professional responsibilities which may include those of management and supervision requiring independent judgment; interpretation of rules and procedures; analysis of library problems; and formulation of original and creative solutions for them. (Normally utilizing knowledge of the subject field represented by the academic degree.)

CATEGORIES OF LIBRARY PERSONNEL—SUPPORTIVE

Library-Related Qualifications	Non-Library Related Qualifications	Basic Requirements	Nature of Responsibilities
LIS Associate	Associate Specialist	Bachelors degree (with preferred coursework in library and/or information science); OR bachelors degree, plus additional applicable academic work.	Manager is hired or promoted into the job based on previous library work experience; the library specialist has extensive experience, perhaps supplemented by job-sponsored training in a specialized area— e.g. interlibrary borrowing/ lending; preservation; book searching and replacement; second-tier reference; copy cataloging; etc.
LIS Assistant	Assistant Specialist	At least two years of college-level study; or AA degree, (with or without library technical assistant training) preferred; OR post-secondary school training and relevant skills; OR certificate program.	Tasks performed as supportive staff following established policies and procedures and may include supervision of such tasks.
Clerk (Exact titles vary depending on type of library circumstance.)	Clerk (Exact titles vary depending on type of library circumstance.)	High school diploma or equivalent.	Assignments as required by the individual library.

9. The title "Librarian" therefore should be used only to designate positions in libraries which utilize the qualifications and impose the responsibilities suggested above. Positions which are primarily devoted to the routine application of established rules and techniques, however useful and essential to the effective operation of a library's ongoing services, should not carry the word "Librarian" in the job title.

10. It is recognized that every type and size of library may not need staff appointments in each of these categories. It is urged, however, that this basic scheme be introduced wherever possible to permit, where needed, the necessary flexibility in staffing.

11. The salaries for each category should offer a range of promotional steps sufficient to permit a career-in-rank. The top salary in any

category should overlap the beginning salary in the next higher category, in order to give recognition to the value of experience and knowledge gained on the job.

12. Libraries should pay particular attention that stratification of personnel not occur along lines of race, ethnicity, or gender. If these patterns of stratification occur, steps should be taken to investigate and ameliorate possible discrimination. Libraries should promote the full education, utilization, and promotion of all employees regardless of race, ethnic background, or gender. Libraries and programs of library and information studies should be particularly sensitive to discrimination patterns that reflect the prejudices of society and should take proactive measures to combat the effects of these influences.

13. Inadequately supported libraries or libraries too small to be able to afford professional staff should nevertheless have access to the services and supervision of a librarian. To obtain the professional guidance that they themselves cannot supply, such libraries should promote cooperative arrangements or join larger systems of cooperating libraries through which supervisory personnel can be supported. Smaller libraries which are part of such a system can often maintain the local service with building staff at the Associate level.

LIBRARY CAREER LATTICE

If one thinks of Career Lattices rather than Career Ladders, the flexibility intended by the Policy Statement may be better visualized. The movement among staff responsibilities, for example, is not necessarily directly up, but often may be lateral to increased responsibilities of equal importance. Each category embodies a number of promotional steps within it, as indicated by the gradation markings on each bar. The top of any category overlaps in responsibility and salary the higher category.

Comments on the Categories

14. The Clerk classifications do not require formal academic training in library subjects. The assignments in these categories are based upon general clerical and secretarial proficiencies. Familiarity with basic library terminology and routines necessary to adapt clerical skills to the library's needs is best learned on the job.

15. The Assistant categories assume certain kinds of specific "technical" skills; they are not meant simply to accommodate advanced clerks. While clerical skills might well be part of a Assistant's equipment, the emphasis in an assignment should be on the special technical skill. For example, someone who is skilled in handling multimedia equipment, or at introductory data processing, or display art might well be hired in the Assistant Specialist category for these skills, related to

FIGURE 2

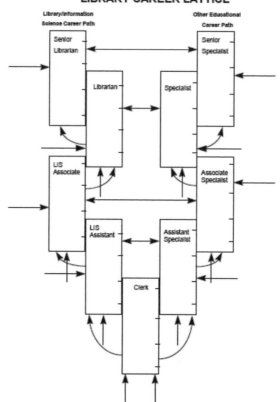

librarianship only to the extent that they are employed in a library. An LIS Assistant is a person with certain specifically library-related skills-in preliminary bibliographic searching for example, or utilization of certain equipment or technology-the performance of whose duties seldom requires a background in general education.

16. The Associate categories assume a need for an educational background like that represented by a bachelor's degree from an accredited four-year institution of higher education (or foreign equivalent). Assignments may be such that library knowledge is less important than general education, and whether the title is LIS Associate or Associate Specialist depends upon the nature of the tasks and responsibilities assigned. Persons holding the B.A. degree, with or without a library science minor or practical experience in libraries, are eligible for employment in this category. Titles within the Associate category that are assigned to individuals will depend upon the relevance of their training and background to their specific assignments.

17. The Associate category also provides the opportunity for persons of promise and exceptional talent to begin library employment below the level of professional (as defined in this statement) and thus to combine employment in a library with course work at the graduate level. Where this kind of work/study arrangement is made, the combination of work and formal study should provide 1) increasing responsibility within the Associate ranks as the individual moves through the academic program, and 2) eligibility for promotion, upon completion of the master's degree (or appropriate professional degree for the specialty), to positions of professional responsibility and attendant reclassification to the professional category.

18. The first professional category-Librarian, or Specialist-assumes responsibilities that are professional in the sense described in paragraph #8 above. A well-rounded liberal education plus graduate-level study in the field of specialization (either in librarianship or in a relevant field) are seen as the minimum preparation for the kinds of assignments implied. The title, however, is given for a position entailing professional responsibilities and not automatically upon achievement of the academic degree.

19. The Senior categories assume relevant professional experience as well as qualifications beyond those required for admission to the first professional ranks. Normally, it is assumed that such advanced qualification shall be held in some specialty, either in a particular aspect of librarianship or some relevant subject field. Subject specializations are as applicable in the Senior Librarian category as they are in the Senior Specialist category.

20. Administrative responsibilities entail high-level specialty, and appointment to positions in top administration should normally require the qualifications of Senior Librarian with a specialization in administration. This category, however, is not limited to administrators, whose specialty is only one of several specializations of value to the library

service. There are many areas of specialized knowledge within librarianship which are equally important and to which equal recognition in prestige and salary should be given. Highly qualified persons with specialist responsibilities in some aspects of librarianship-archives, bibliography, reference, for example-should be eligible for advanced status and financial rewards without being forced to abandon their areas of major competence for administrative responsibilities.

Implications for Formal Education

21. The academic degree (or evidence of years of academic work completed) is recommended as the single best means for determining that the applicant has the background required for the position. If an ALA-recognized Master's degree or state or provincial certification is unavailable, examinations may be valid and reliable tests of equivalent qualification.

22. In the selection of applicants for positions at any level, and for admission to library and information studies, attention should be paid to personal aptitudes and qualifications in addition to academic ones. The nature of the position or specialty, and particularly the degree to which it entails working with others, with the public, or with special audiences or materials should be taken into account in the evaluation of a prospective student or employee. Importance should be placed on the education and employment of individuals with diverse ethnic backgrounds who are multilingual and, additionally, on those who possess a multicultural perspective.

23. As library services and technologies change and expand, as new audiences are reached, as new media and technology take on greater importance in the communication process, and as new approaches to the handling of materials continue to be introduced, the kinds of preparation required of those who will be employed in libraries will become more varied. Degrees in fields other than librarianship will be needed in the Specialist categories. For many Senior Librarian positions, an advanced degree in another subject field rather than an additional degree in librarianship, may be desirable. Previous experience need not always have been in libraries to have pertinence for appointment in a library.

24. Because the principles of librarianship are applied to the materials of information and knowledge broader than any single field, and because they are related to subject matter outside of librarianship itself, responsible education in these principles should be built upon a broad background in education which includes the humanities, the sciences, and the social sciences, rather than a narrowly specialized background.

25. Training courses for Library Technical Assistants at the junior or community college level should be recognized as designed for the preparation of supportive rather than professional staff. Graduates of the two-year programs may take the additional work leading to the

bachelor's and master's degrees, but it is an indirect way to prepare for a professional career, and the student should be so informed.

26. Emphasis in the two-year Technical Assistant programs should be more on skills training than on general library concepts and procedures. In many cases it would be better from the standpoint of the student to pursue more broadly-based vocational courses which will teach technical skills applicable in a variety of job situations rather than those limited solely to the library setting.

27. Undergraduate instruction in library science other than training courses for Library Technical Assistants should be primarily a contribution to liberal education rather than an opportunity to provide technological and methodological training. This does not preclude the inclusion of course work related to the basic skills of library practice, but it does affect teaching method and approach, and implies an emphasis on the principles that underlie practice rather than how-to-do-it, vocational training.

28. Certain practical skills and procedures at all levels are best learned on the job rather than in the academic classroom. These relate typically to details of operation which may vary from institution to institution, or to routines which require repetition and practice for their mastery. The responsibility for such in-service parts of the total preparation of both librarians and supportive staff rests with libraries and library systems rather than with the programs of library and information studies.

29. The objective of the master's programs in library and information studies should be to prepare librarians capable of anticipating and engineering the change and improvement required to move the profession constantly forward. The curriculum and teaching methods should be designed to serve this kind of education for the future rather than to train for the practice of the present.

30. Certain interdisciplinary concepts are so intimately related to the basic concepts underlying library service that they properly become a part of the library and information studies curriculum rather than simply an outside specialty. Where such content is introduced into library and information studies it should be incorporated into the entire curriculum, enriching every course where it is pertinent. The stop-gap addition of individual courses in such a specialty, not integrated into the program as a whole, is an inadequate assimilation of the intellectual contribution of the new concept to library and information studies and thinking.

31. In recognition of the many areas of related subject matter of importance to library service, library and information studies should make knowledge in other fields readily available to students, either through the appointment of staff members from other disciplines or through permitting students to cross departmental, divisional, and institutional lines in reasoned programs in related fields. Intensive specializations at the graduate level, building upon strengths in the parent

institution or the community, are a logical development in library and information studies.

32. Programs of library and information studies should be encouraged to experiment with new teaching methods, new learning devices, different patterns of scheduling and sequence, and other means, both traditional and nontraditional, that may increase the effectiveness of the students' educational experience.

33. Research has an important role to play in the educational process as a source of new knowledge both for the field of librarianship in general and for library and information studies in particular. In its planning, budgeting, and organizational design, programs of library and information studies should recognize research, both theoretical and applied, as an imperative responsibility.

Career Development and Continuous Learning

34. Career development and continuous learning is the shared responsibility of the individual, the employer, formal education providers, and professional associations. Continuous learning is essential for all library and information studies personnel, supportive and professional, whether or not they seek advancement.

35. Employers are responsible for providing training that supports the work of their organization. This can take the form of planned staff development activities or less formal activities such as committee assignments and special projects.

36. Employers are responsible for providing support for individual career development and continuous learning. Examples of support include release time, sabbaticals, tuition reimbursement, and mentoring programs. Such support is essential in hiring and retaining an excellent workforce.

37. Education providers are responsible for developing and making available learning opportunities that reflect the needs of the library and information studies profession. To address individual learning needs and styles, these must be available in multiple formats and in a variety of locations.

38. Professional associations are responsible for providing learning opportunities that meet the needs of their membership. These may take the form of workshops, conference programs and articles in professional journals. Workshops and conference programs should be planned to ensure adherence to the best practices of adult learning theory.

39. For the individual, career development and continuous learning includes both formal and informal learning situations and need not be limited to library and information studies. In some cases, post-masters and doctoral programs may be appropriate as formal activities. Informal activities may include joining electronic lists, reading relevant literature, and practicing new skills.

Library Career Pathways Taskforce Members
Gail W. Avery, Jonathan Franklin
Judy Card, Suzi Hayes
Janice H. Dost, Julie G. Huiskamp, Chair
David R. Dowell, Jiun-Huei C. Kuo
Isabel R. Espinal, Madison Mosley, Jr.
Paulette A. Feld, Jane Robbins
Bernard Fradkin, Christine Robinson

Appendix B
Library Bill of Rights

The American Library Association affirms that all libraries are forums for information and ideas, and that the following basic policies should guide their services.

I. Books and other library resources should be provided for the interest, information, and enlightenment of all people of the community the library serves. Materials should not be excluded because of the origin, background, or views of those contributing to their creation.

II. Libraries should provide materials and information presenting all points of view on current and historical issues. Materials should not be proscribed or removed because of partisan or doctrinal disapproval.

III. Libraries should challenge censorship in the fulfillment of their responsibility to provide information and enlightenment.

IV. Libraries should cooperate with all persons and groups concerned with resisting abridgment of free expression and free access to ideas.

V. A person's right to use a library should not be denied or abridged because of origin, age, background, or views.

VI. Libraries which make exhibit spaces and meeting rooms available to the public they serve should make such facilities available on an equitable basis, regardless of the beliefs or affiliations of individuals or groups requesting their use.

Reprinted with permission of the American Library Association.

Adopted June 18, 1948, by the ALA Council; amended February 2, 1961; amended June 28, 1967; amended January 23, 1980; inclusion of "age" reaffirmed January 24, 1996.

Appendix C
Code of Ethics of the American Library Association

As members of the American Library Association, we recognize the importance of codifying and making known to the profession and to the general public the ethical principles that guide the work of librarians, other professionals providing information services, library trustees and library staffs.

Ethical dilemmas occur when values are in conflict. The American Library Association Code of Ethics states the values to which we are committed, and embodies the ethical responsibilities of the profession in this changing information environment.

We significantly influence or control the selection, organization, preservation, and dissemination of information. In a political system grounded in an informed citizenry, we are members of a profession explicitly committed to intellectual freedom and the freedom of access to information. We have a special obligation to ensure the free flow of information and ideas to present and future generations.

The principles of this Code are expressed in broad statements to guide ethical decision making. These statements provide a framework; they cannot and do not dictate conduct to cover particular situations.

    I. We provide the highest level of service to all library users through appropriate and usefully organized resources; equitable service policies; equitable access; and accurate, unbiased, and courteous responses to all requests.

Adopted June 28, 1997, by the ALA Council; Amended January 22, 2008.

II. We uphold the principles of intellectual freedom and resist all efforts to censor library resources.

III. We protect each library user's right to privacy and confidentiality with respect to information sought or received and resources consulted, borrowed, acquired or transmitted.

IV. We respect intellectual property rights and advocate balance between the interests of information users and rights holders.

V. We treat co-workers and other colleagues with respect, fairness, and good faith, and advocate conditions of employment that safeguard the rights and welfare of all employees of our institutions.

VI. We do not advance private interests at the expense of library users, colleagues, or our employing institutions.

VII. We distinguish between our personal convictions and professional duties and do not allow our personal beliefs to interfere with fair representation of the aims of our institutions or the provision of access to their information resources.

VIII. We strive for excellence in the profession by maintaining and enhancing our own knowledge and skills, by encouraging the professional development of co-workers, and by fostering the aspirations of potential members of the profession.

Reprinted with permission of the American Library Association.

Appendix D
The Freedom to Read Statement

The freedom to read is essential to our democracy. It is continuously under attack. Private groups and public authorities in various parts of the country are working to remove or limit access to reading materials, to censor content in schools, to label "controversial" views, to distribute lists of "objectionable" books or authors, and to purge libraries. These actions apparently rise from a view that our national tradition of free expression is no longer valid; that censorship and suppression are needed to counter threats to safety or national security, as well as to avoid the subversion of politics and the corruption of morals. We, as individuals devoted to reading and as librarians and publishers responsible for disseminating ideas, wish to assert the public interest in the preservation of the freedom to read.

Most attempts at suppression rest on a denial of the fundamental premise of democracy: that the ordinary individual, by exercising critical judgment, will select the good and reject the bad. We trust Americans to recognize propaganda and misinformation, and to make their own decisions about what they read and believe. We do not believe they are prepared to sacrifice their heritage of a free press in order to be "protected" against what others think may be bad for them. We believe they still favor free enterprise in ideas and expression.

These efforts at suppression are related to a larger pattern of pressures being brought against education, the press, art and images, films, broadcast media, and the Internet. The problem is not only one of actual censorship. The shadow of fear cast by these pressures leads, we suspect, to an even larger voluntary curtailment of expression by those who seek to avoid controversy or unwelcome scrutiny by government officials.

Such pressure toward conformity is perhaps natural to a time of accelerated change. And yet suppression is never more dangerous than in such a time of social tension. Freedom has given the United States the elasticity to endure strain. Freedom keeps open the path of novel and creative solutions, and enables change to come by choice. Every silencing of a heresy, every enforcement of an orthodoxy, diminishes the toughness and resilience of our society and leaves it the less able to deal with controversy and difference.

Now as always in our history, reading is among our greatest freedoms. The freedom to read and write is almost the only means for making generally available ideas or manners of expression that can initially command only a small audience. The written word is the natural medium for the new idea and the untried voice from which come the original contributions to social growth. It is essential to the extended discussion that serious thought requires, and to the accumulation of knowledge and ideas into organized collections.

We believe that free communication is essential to the preservation of a free society and a creative culture. We believe that these pressures toward conformity present the danger of limiting the range and variety of inquiry and expression on which our democracy and our culture depend. We believe that every American community must jealously guard the freedom to publish and to circulate, in order to preserve its own freedom to read. We believe that publishers and librarians have a profound responsibility to give validity to that freedom to read by making it possible for the readers to choose freely from a variety of offerings.

The freedom to read is guaranteed by the Constitution. Those with faith in free people will stand firm on these constitutional guarantees of essential rights and will exercise the responsibilities that accompany these rights.

We therefore affirm these propositions:

1. It is in the public interest for publishers and librarians to make available the widest diversity of views and expressions, including those that are unorthodox, unpopular, or considered dangerous by the majority.

Creative thought is by definition new, and what is new is different. The bearer of every new thought is a rebel until that idea is refined and tested. Totalitarian systems attempt to maintain themselves in power by the ruthless suppression of any concept that challenges the established orthodoxy. The power of a democratic system to adapt to change is vastly strengthened by the freedom of its citizens to choose widely from among conflicting opinions offered freely to them. To stifle every nonconformist idea at birth would mark the end of the democratic process. Furthermore, only through the constant activity of weighing and selecting can the democratic mind attain the strength demanded by times like these. We need to know not only what we believe but why we believe it.

2. Publishers, librarians, and booksellers do not need to endorse every idea or presentation they make available. It would conflict with the public interest for them to establish their own political, moral, or aesthetic views as a standard for determining what should be published or circulated.

Publishers and librarians serve the educational process by helping to make available knowledge and ideas required for the growth of the mind and the increase of learning. They do not foster education by imposing as mentors the patterns of their own thought. The people should have the freedom to read and consider a broader range of ideas than those that may be held by any single librarian or publisher or government or church. It is wrong that what one can read should be confined to what another thinks proper.

3. It is contrary to the public interest for publishers or librarians to bar access to writings on the basis of the personal history or political affiliations of the author.

No art or literature can flourish if it is to be measured by the political views or private lives of its creators. No society of free people can flourish that draws up lists of writers to whom it will not listen, whatever they may have to say.

4. There is no place in our society for efforts to coerce the taste of others, to confine adults to the reading matter deemed suitable for adolescents, or to inhibit the efforts of writers to achieve artistic expression.

To some, much of modern expression is shocking. But is not much of life itself shocking? We cut off literature at the source if we prevent writers from dealing with the stuff of life. Parents and teachers have a responsibility to prepare the young to meet the diversity of experiences in life to which they will be exposed, as they have a responsibility to help them learn to think critically for themselves. These are affirmative responsibilities, not to be discharged simply by preventing them from reading works for which they are not yet prepared. In these matters values differ, and values cannot be legislated; nor can machinery be devised that will suit the demands of one group without limiting the freedom of others.

5. It is not in the public interest to force a reader to accept the prejudgment of a label characterizing any expression or its author as subversive or dangerous.

The ideal of labeling presupposes the existence of individuals or groups with wisdom to determine by authority what is good or bad for others. It presupposes that individuals must be directed in making up their minds about the ideas they examine. But Americans do not need others to do their thinking for them.

6. It is the responsibility of publishers and librarians, as guardians of the people's freedom to read, to contest encroachments upon that freedom by individuals or groups seeking to impose their own standards or tastes upon the community at large; and by the government whenever it seeks to reduce or deny public access to public information.

It is inevitable in the give and take of the democratic process that the political, the moral, or the aesthetic concepts of an individual or group will occasionally collide with those of another individual or group. In a free society individuals are free to determine for themselves what they wish to read, and each group is free to determine what it will recommend to its freely associated members. But no group has the right to take the law into its own hands, and to impose its own concept of politics or morality upon other members of a democratic society. Freedom is no freedom if it is accorded only to the accepted and the inoffensive. Further, democratic societies are more safe, free, and creative when the free flow of public information is not restricted by governmental prerogative or self-censorship.

7. It is the responsibility of publishers and librarians to give full meaning to the freedom to read by providing books that enrich the quality and diversity of thought and expression. By the exercise of this affirmative responsibility, they can demonstrate that the answer to a "bad" book is a good one, the answer to a "bad" idea is a good one.

The freedom to read is of little consequence when the reader cannot obtain matter fit for that reader's purpose. What is needed is not only the absence of restraint, but the positive provision of opportunity for the people to read the best that has been thought and said. Books are the major channel by which the intellectual inheritance is handed down, and the principal means of its testing and growth. The defense of the freedom to read requires of all publishers and librarians the utmost of their faculties, and deserves of all Americans the fullest of their support.

We state these propositions neither lightly nor as easy generalizations. We here stake out a lofty claim for the value of the written word. We do so because we believe that it is possessed of enormous variety and usefulness, worthy of cherishing and keeping free. We realize that the application of these propositions may mean the dissemination of ideas and manners of expression that are repugnant to many persons. We do not state these propositions in the comfortable belief that what people read is unimportant. We believe rather that what people read is deeply important; that ideas can be dangerous; but that the suppression of ideas is fatal to a democratic society. Freedom itself is a dangerous way of life, but it is ours.

This statement was originally issued in May of 1953 by the Westchester Conference of the American Library Association and the American Book Publishers Council, which in 1970 consolidated with the American Educational Publishers Institute to become the Association of American Publishers.

Adopted June 25, 1953, by the ALA Council and the AAP Freedom to Read Committee; amended January 28, 1972; January 16, 1991; July 12, 2000; June 30, 2004.

A Joint Statement by:

American Library Association
Association of American Publishers

Subsequently endorsed by:

American Booksellers Foundation for Free Expression
The Association of American University Presses, Inc.
The Children's Book Council
Freedom to Read Foundation
National Association of College Stores
National Coalition Against Censorship
National Council of Teachers of English
The Thomas Jefferson Center for the Protection of Free Expression

Reprinted with permission of the American Library Association.

Index

About the Authors

DENISE K. FOURIE is the lead instructor of Library/Information Technology at Cuesta College, San Luis Obispo, California. She has over 25 years of varied experience in the library field, including serving as a reference librarian in public and academic libraries, a consultant, and an instructor. She received her B. A. from the University of California, Berkeley, and her Masters in Library Science (M.L.S.) from the University of Southern California. Ms. Fourie also manages Library Concepts, a consulting firm working with government, school, university, and business clients on library, archival, and information-related projects.

DAVID R. DOWELL, recently retired as Director of Library/Learning Resources and Distance Education at Cuesta College, previously held library management posts at Pasadena City College, Illinois Institute of Technology, Duke University, and Iowa State University. Active in management, personnel and education issues within ALA, he holds graduate degrees from the University of Illinois and the University of North Carolina. His most recent book, edited with Gerard B. McCabe, was *It's All About Student Learning: Management Community and Other College Libraries in the 21st Century* (2006). In 2007 he was the recipient of the EBSCO Community College Learning Resources and Library Leadership Award.